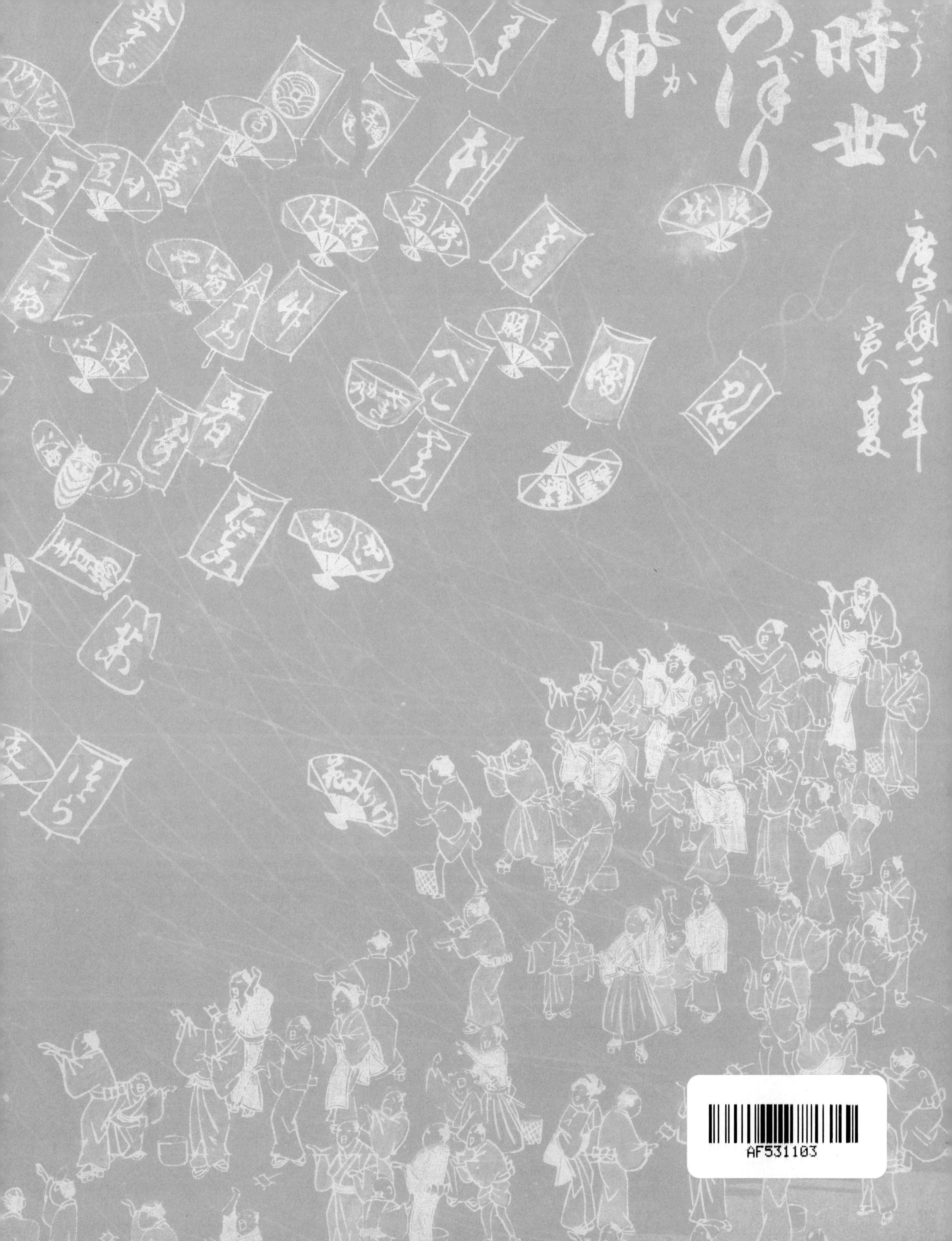
時世のぼり凧
慶應二年
寅夏
AF531103

JAPANESE KITE PRINTS

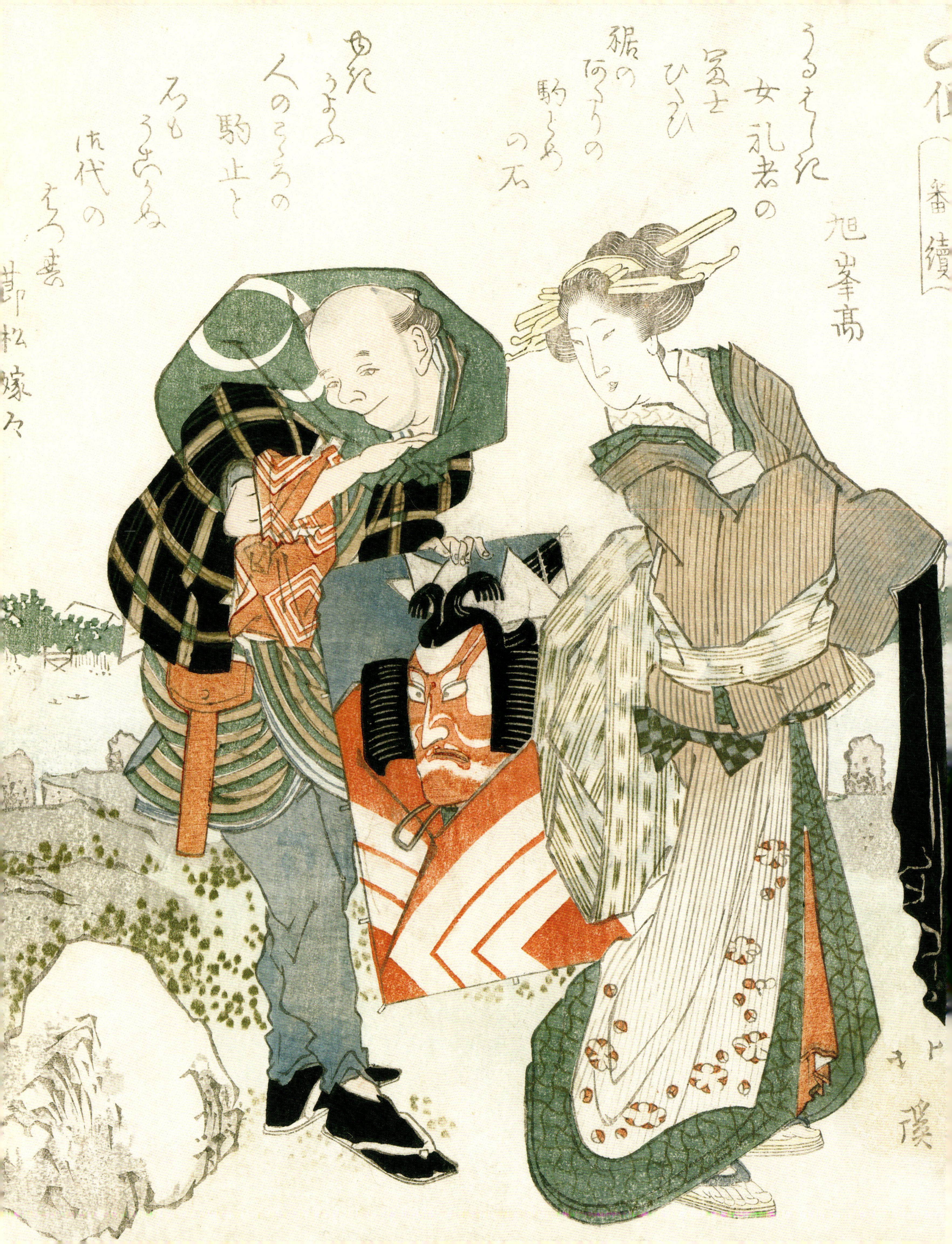

番續
旭峯高

Japanese Kite Prints

Selections from the Skinner Collection

John Stevenson

The Drachen Foundation

Seattle

for C

Warmest thanks to Cynthea Bogel, Yuriko Courtney, and Megumi Inoue for their erudite assistance. Thanks also to Scott Skinner and Ali Fujino, followers of bliss and perfect exemplars of the power of positive thinking. And to Ed Marquand and his team at Marquand Books and iocolor, who make the production of beautiful books seem easy.

Library of Congress Cataloging-in-Publication Data
Stevenson, John
Japanese kite prints : selections from the Skinner collection / John Stevenson.
p. cm.
Includes bibliographical references and index.
ISBN 0-295-98454-6 (hardcover : alk. paper)
1. Kites in art—Catalogs. 2. Wood-engraving, Japanese—Catalogs. 3. Color prints, Japanese—Catalogs. 4. Prints—Private collections—Washington—Seattle—Catalogs. 5. Skinner, Scott—Art collections—Catalogs. I. Title.
NE1326.5.K58S74 2004
769'.49796158'0952—dc22 2004008121

Designed by Jeff Wincapaw
Typeset by Jennifer Sugden
Produced by Marquand Books, Inc., Seattle
www.marquand.com
Printed and bound by CS Graphics Pte., Ltd., Singapore

Unless otherwise indicated, prints are from the Skinner Collection.

All Skinner Collection prints in this book were scanned directly on a Heidelberg flatbed scanner by iocolor, Seattle.

Measurements include margins and are from the edge of the paper (not the design), height first.

Diacritics are not used for Japanese words and place names that have entered the English language, such as Tokyo, shogun, and Shinto.

Page 2: Toyota Hokkei, *Woman with Servant and Danjūrō Kite,* c. 1820 (detail, see plate 14)
Page 5: Toyota Hokkei, *The Hero Raikō with Shutendōji Kite,* c. 1830 (detail, see plate 13)
Pages 6–7: Toyohara Kunichika, *Competition between Youthful Radiant Willows,* 1870 (detail, see plate 73)

Distributed by
University of Washington Press
P.O. Box 50096
Seattle, WA 98145-5096
www.washington.edu/uwpress

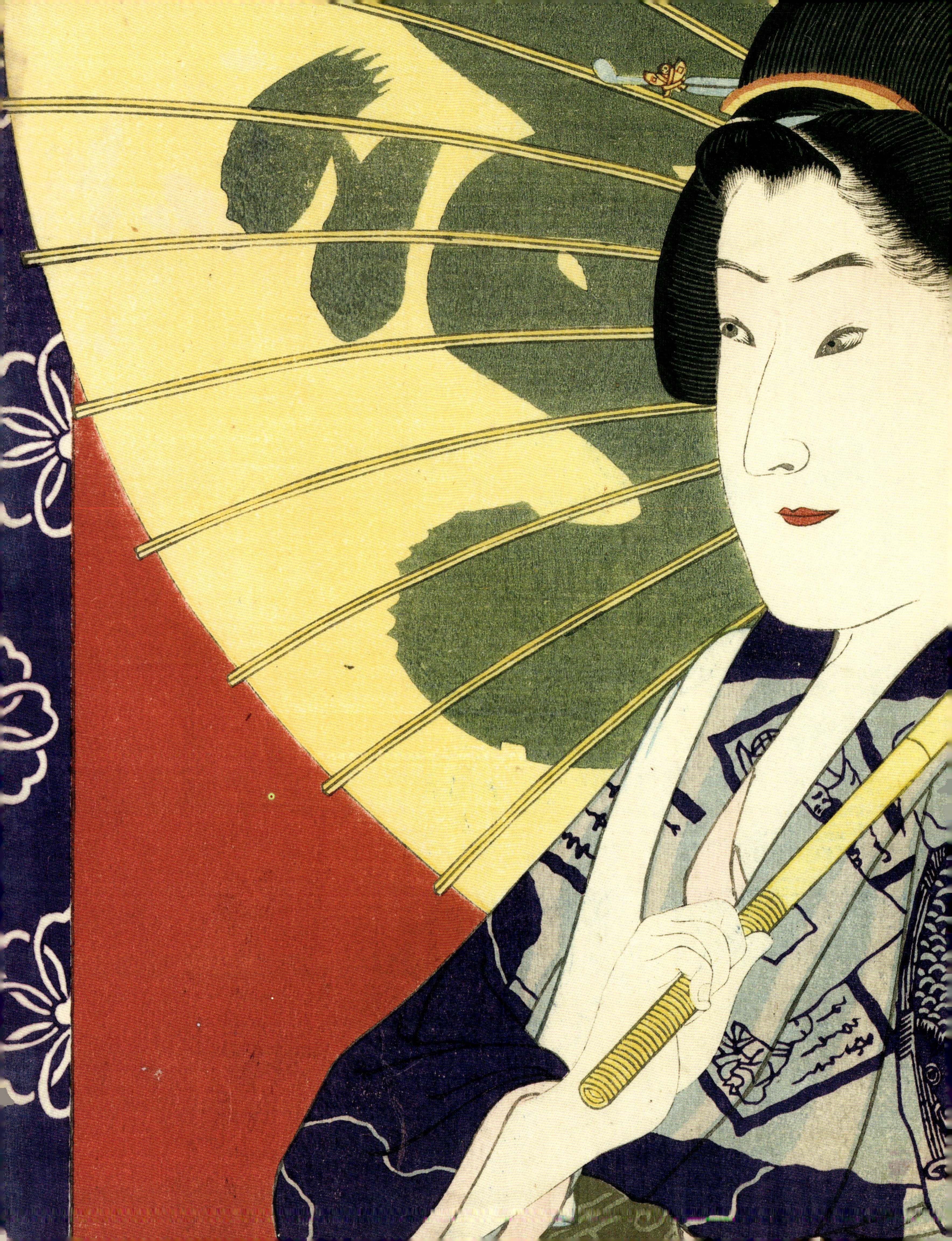

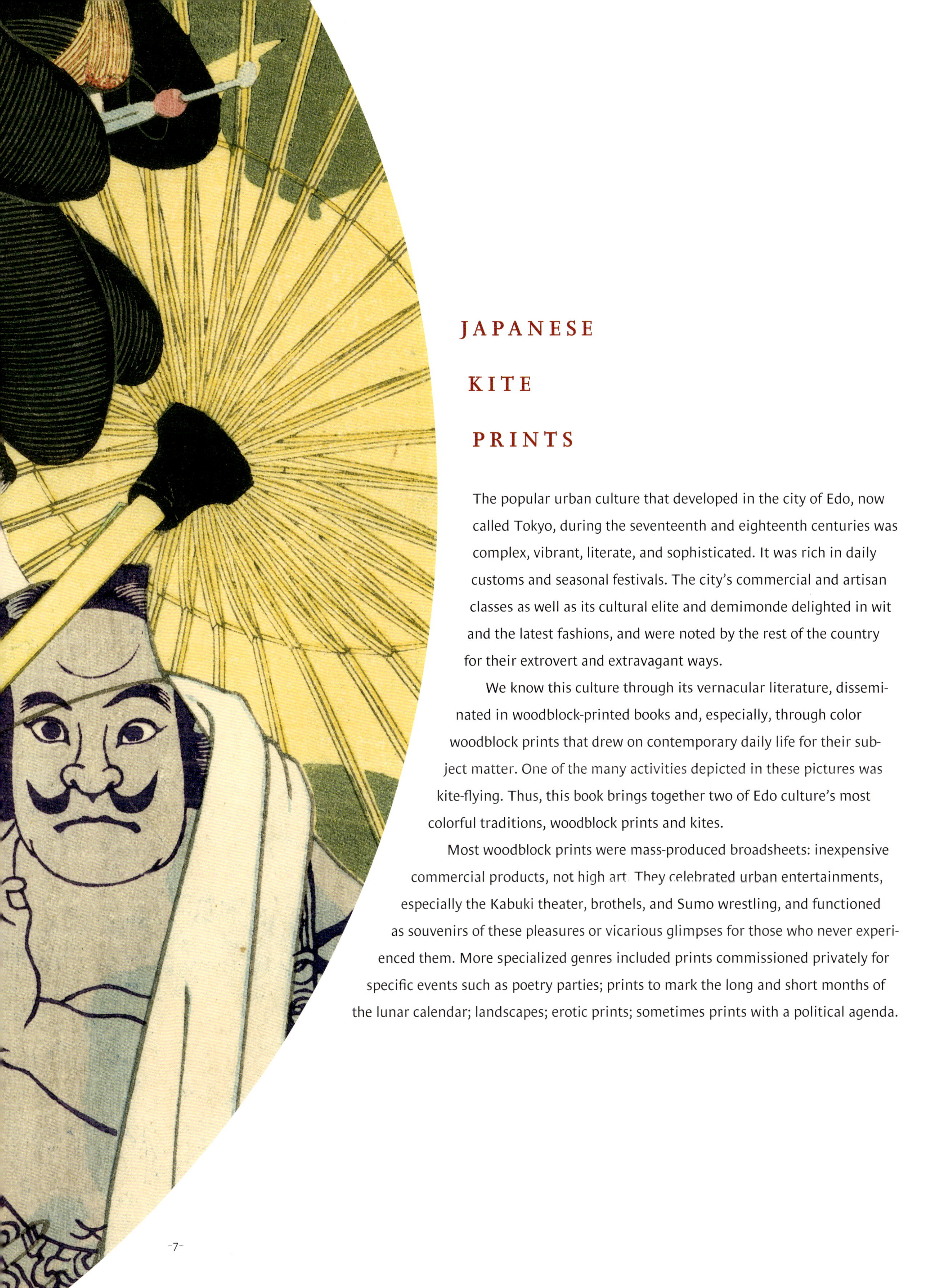

JAPANESE KITE PRINTS

The popular urban culture that developed in the city of Edo, now called Tokyo, during the seventeenth and eighteenth centuries was complex, vibrant, literate, and sophisticated. It was rich in daily customs and seasonal festivals. The city's commercial and artisan classes as well as its cultural elite and demimonde delighted in wit and the latest fashions, and were noted by the rest of the country for their extrovert and extravagant ways.

We know this culture through its vernacular literature, disseminated in woodblock-printed books and, especially, through color woodblock prints that drew on contemporary daily life for their subject matter. One of the many activities depicted in these pictures was kite-flying. Thus, this book brings together two of Edo culture's most colorful traditions, woodblock prints and kites.

Most woodblock prints were mass-produced broadsheets: inexpensive commercial products, not high art. They celebrated urban entertainments, especially the Kabuki theater, brothels, and Sumo wrestling, and functioned as souvenirs of these pleasures or vicarious glimpses for those who never experienced them. More specialized genres included prints commissioned privately for specific events such as poetry parties; prints to mark the long and short months of the lunar calendar; landscapes; erotic prints; sometimes prints with a political agenda.

Their subjects are as rich and vigorous as the culture of old Edo; these prints live and breathe today as they enthusiastically present star actors and celebrity courtesans or informal vignettes of everyday life.

Kites capture the imagination as they capture the breeze. Kites were flown throughout Japan, at religious and secular festivals and for the sheer thrill of holding the wind in one's hands that we can share today with those energetic Edoites. At the same time as artists were experimenting with woodblock-printing techniques during the eighteenth century, kite-flying became an increasingly popular pastime. As a beloved and ubiquitous sport, kite-flying found its way into all the forms of prints mentioned above, whenever print artists made kites the subject of a design or chose them as unselfconscious details of an urban scene. The influence went two ways, with kite-makers copying woodblock-print designs to decorate their creations of bamboo, cloth, and paper.

Japanese woodblock prints are known collectively as *ukiyo-e,* pictures of the floating world, a pun on a Buddhist concept of the fleeting world of desires, also pronounced *ukiyo.* (*E* means picture, and besides prints the term *ukiyo-e* may also refer to paintings with "floating-world" themes.) A novel of the mid-1660s first defined the irresponsible but delicious floating world as follows:

> In this world everything is a source of interest. And yet just one step ahead lies darkness. So we should cast off all gloomy thoughts about our earthly lot and enjoy the pleasures of snow, moon, flowers, and autumn leaves, singing songs and drinking wine, living our lives like a gourd bobbing buoyantly downstream. This is the floating world.[1]

In their enjoyment of the details of daily existence, woodblock prints exemplify the exuberant love of life expressed in this definition. They are a wonderful window onto the customs of the time and are a measure of the preoccupations of contemporary society. To an extent, print images are idealized and the people they depict are caricatures. The Kabuki stars with their dramatic poses are larger than life; indentured women are dressed in supremely luxurious robes; even the hills in landscapes are made to appear steeper and more imposing than they were in reality. But many prints are nevertheless close to being snapshots of daily life—at least, as close as we will get. From before the camera was invented, woodblock prints provide charming records of everyday life in the old capital of Edo.

The prints in this book are with a few exceptions the products of Tokugawa Edo (1603–1867) and Meiji Tokyo (1868–1912). When it was made the seat of government by the Tokugawa shogunate in the first years of the seventeenth century, Edo was little more than a provincial castle town. Kyoto remained the center of culture and Osaka the economic hub of the country. In the early eighteenth century, the fiction of Ihara Saikaku, an Osaka writer, defined floating-world literature, and Edo's Kabuki theaters still relied heavily for plots on the Osaka *bunraku* puppet theater. As late as the mid-eighteenth century, the Shinmachi pleasure district in Osaka and the Shimabara in Kyoto were regarded at least as highly as Edo's Yoshiwara, which came to dominate public consciousness as the height of elegant delights.

But woodblock prints of the *ukiyo-e* school were very much a creation of the new capital. Though other print schools existed, including those of Osaka and Kyoto, the *nishiki-e,* brocade prints, of Edo were much more numerous and varied. The term *nishiki-e* deliberately compared multicolored prints—as typical products of Edo—with the famous brocade textiles of Kyoto; visitors to the "eastern capital" of Edo would buy prints as local souvenirs to take back to their hometowns. A self-confidence and an awareness of a special Edo identity flourished.[2] The word *edokko,* meaning someone born and bred in Edo and indicating a proud identification with the city (an equivalent of the term Cockney in London), was first used in a comic poem of 1771. During the second half of the eighteenth century the term *meisho,* meaning famous place (we will see this word used often in the titles of landscapes in this book), began to be used in Edo prints for Edo locations, drawing the word away from reflexive historical or literary associations with Heian-period Kyoto. The range of ways in which Edo prints explored noteworthy or commonplace facets of daily life far exceeded those of prints and illustrated books produced in Osaka or Kyoto. Kites were one of these facets of daily life; this book follows the history of woodblock prints through designs depicting kites and shows how kites were used and enjoyed in old Japan.

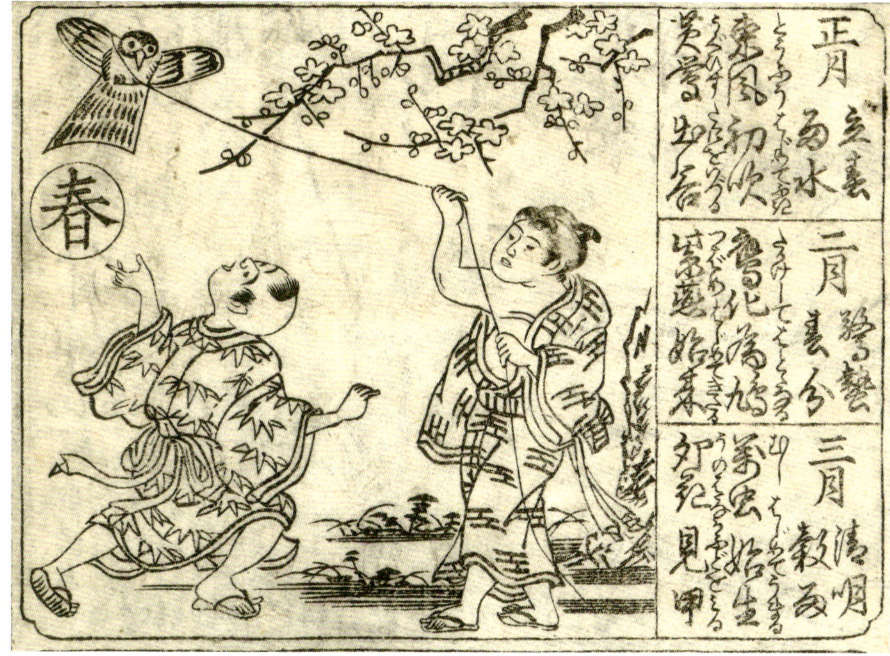

Fig. 1. Illustration defining the seasons—this is spring—from a woodblock-printed book titled *Fūgetsu ōrai* (Scenes of Nature), an almanac of 1821, 7.8 × 11.1 cm.

Kites are first mentioned in Japan in the *Hizen no kuni fudoki,* a compilation of local records begun in the year 713, and the *Nihongi,* a chronicle dating from about 720. Two words for kite are given in the *Wamyō ruiju sho,* a Japanese dictionary compiled in the 930s, which was written in Chinese characters but based on a Japanese pronunciation of the words. The words are *shiroshi* and *shien,* both meaning paper hawk. The first kites in Japan may have been bamboo and paper constructions in the form of a hawk, shaped like the letter T with long wings and small body (similar, for example, to the hawk kites depicted in plates 11, 20, and 34). This shape is both aerodynamically viable and lends itself to representations of birds and insects, creatures associated with flight. From this shape developed *tobi* or hawk kites (figure 1); *sode* or sleeve kites, in the form of a kimono; and eventually *yakko* kites, based on the outstretched figure of the lowest-ranking retainer of a feudal lord. Both *tobi* and *yakko* kites are very well represented in this book.

The *Wamyō ruiju sho* was compiled by a Nara bureaucrat named Minamoto Shitago, who worked in the Department of Shinto and the Bureau of Divination. This suggests the religious and ritual connotations of Japanese kites, as they came alive in the wind and energetically carried prayers up to heaven. The two priestly families of the Shinto Grand Shrine of Izumo flew kites in the shape of the character for crane, *tsuru;* cranes were believed to live for a thousand years and therefore symbolized longevity. Huge kites were built and flown at festivals. Kites were flown in the countryside during springtime as prayers for good harvests, and it was believed that the harvest could be predicted by a kite's flight and the direction from which it fell out of the sky. In Hoshubana, now the site of a festival where perhaps the largest kites in Japan are flown,[3] a kite's flight was believed to forecast the year's silkworm production. Kites were sometimes flown in the autumn with stalks of rice tied to them to give thanks for a plentiful harvest. Kites could be bought at both Buddhist and Shinto temples and shrines as charms against sickness and misfortune. There is a record of kites being flown in 1558 for the birthday celebration of Prince Yoshihiro, first son of the Lord of Hikuma Castle, by a retainer called Sabashi Jingorō. Kites were flown for good luck on many occasions but came to be particularly associated with the lunar New Year—two weeks of festivities held in late January or February by the western calendar—and, to a lesser extent, with Boy's Day, the fifth day of the fifth month.[4]

Without entirely losing its quasi-religious connotations, kite-flying became a more secular pastime during the eighteenth century. Early representations of kites being flown by young boys for fun appear on two genre paintings from the beginning of the eighteenth century: *Scenes Around the Capital* (Kyoto) of about 1700, a folding screen attributed to Tosa Daijō Genyō;[5] and *The Way to the Yoshiwara* by Okumura Masanobu (figure 2).[6] Among the many lively figure-groupings in each painting, two boys

Fig. 2. Detail of a hanging scroll depicting the approach to the Yoshiwara. Okumura Masanobu, first half of the Kyōhō era (1716–36), ink and colors on paper, size of whole painting 62.1 × 78.2 cm. Courtesy of Sebastian Izzard.

Two boys fly a rectangular kite with three tails in the fields outside the Yoshiwara pleasure quarters. To the right a *yakko* in his customary uniform and heavy side-whiskers accompanies a group of three samurai.

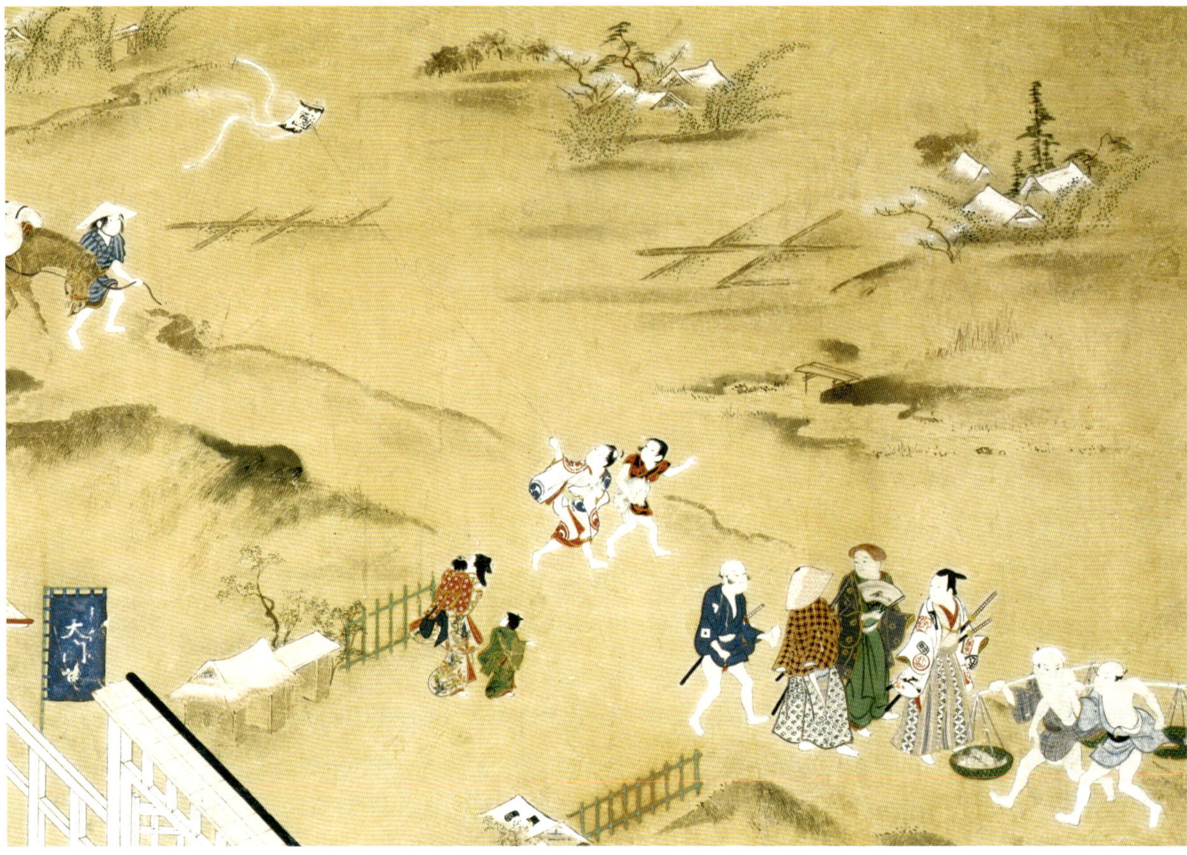

fly a kite—somewhat octopus-shaped, with four tails, in Genyō's painting; a rectangular kite with three tails in Masanobu's (figure 2). An illustrated encyclopedia titled *Wakan sansai zu-e* of 1712 shows a kite with five writhing tails, a line, and a reel; the accompanying characters read *ikanobori,* literally squid flag or banner, using a dialect word for kite. In the same year a man called Kakinoki Kinsuke attached himself to a large kite and tried to steal a gilded fish finial (see plate 76) from the top of Nagoya Castle; he failed and was executed.

During the course of the eighteenth century, kites were mentioned increasingly in literature and illustrated in the developing art of woodblock prints. One of the finest early depictions of kites in a print is an extra-large hand-colored *uki-e,* perspective picture, by Masanobu, from a series of 1745 depicting famous places in Edo; it shows a long-tailed kite flying merrily over the Sakai-chō theater district at New Year (figure 3). Another early depiction is the page from a woodblock-printed book of about 1752 in plate 1, showing a man crazily running to keep his small kite aloft. In these examples, kites are being flown for pleasure rather than for religious reasons.

Nevertheless, the ritual significance and symbolism of kites persisted. For example, flying a kite successfully was used as a metaphor for ruling the nation. In 1782 Matsudaira Sadanobu, chief councilor to the shogun, based a famous treatise on government, titled approximately "The Words of a Parrot,"[7] on the concept. The New Year celebrations of 1784 required that the shogun, Tokugawa Ieharu, fly a twelve-foot-wide kite, painted by the head of the official Kano studio with auspicious designs of cranes and pine trees. As Ieharu was flying the kite, a gust of wind tore the guide-rope out of his hands. (Figure 4 shows how massive festival kites could be.) Four retainers who tried to hang on to the rope were lifted into the air and dashed to the ground; three died.[8] Out of control, the kite narrowly

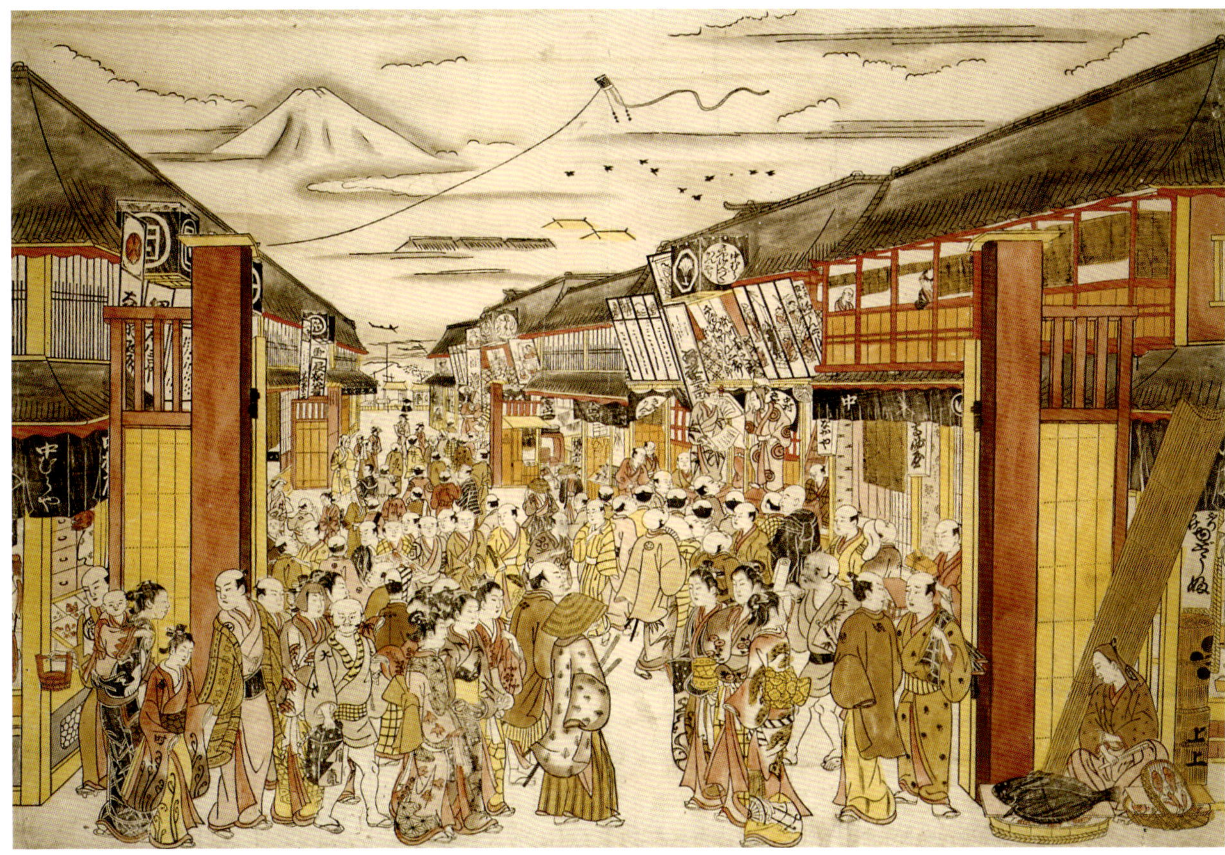

Fig. 3. "Large Perspective View of the Theater District in Sakai-chō and Fukiya-chō" *(Sakai-chō Fukiya-chō shibaimachi ō-uki-e).* Okumura Masanobu, 1745, hand-colored, large-format *uki-e* (perspective picture), 43.8 × 64.5 cm. Courtesy of the Museum of Fine Arts, Boston, William Sturgis Bigelow Collection, 1911; 11.19687.

The rectangular shape of the kite flying over the theater district, with its two stabilizing tails and a long streamer, was typical of Edo kites. Besides the Soga Brothers play *Hagoromo kotobuki Soga,* the signs outside the Nakamura Theater on the right of the street are advertising their annual performance of a play based on the story of Shutendōji (see plate 13).

missed striking the shrine of the shogunate's founder, which would have been inauspicious indeed. After this experience, the State Council decided that the ritual should be abandoned. Ieharu, who obviously lacked heaven's blessing, died two years later. A samurai at his successor's court wrote a parody of Sadanobu's treatise and Ieharu's incompetence at flying kites that was illustrated by the *ukiyo-e* artist Kitao Masayoshi; a rectangular kite with two large tails and a *tobi* kite were shown flying alongside an auspicious phoenix.[9] With a title meaning "That Parrot Keeps on Squawking," the parody was very popular and sold a record-breaking 15,000 copies, to the indignation of shogunate officials.

Kites and woodblock prints shared a common fate as targets of a moralistic government. Legitimacy and proper rule were sensitive preoccupations of the Tokugawa shogunate, which seized power at the beginning of the seventeenth century after decades of civil war and owed its supremacy to naked force; the Tokugawas ruled from Edo while a largely figurehead emperor remained in Kyoto. The government attempted to control the morals of the people with an intermittent flow of sumptuary laws: what different classes were required to wear, what size their houses could be, and myriad other details. Enthusiastic kite-flying sometimes led to scuffles and brawls, and in 1655 the government restricted kite-flying within the capital; that the edict was not effective is suggested by a similar one issued the following year.

Both woodblock prints and kites were affected by sumptuary laws of the 1780s that, among other prohibitions, outlawed extravagant decoration of kites (for example, with gold and silver) and prohibited privately published calendar prints. Calendar prints, called *egoyomi,* indicated the long and short months of the coming year and were considered a monopoly of the government—the production of the delicate design of plate 7 could have sent its creators to prison. In 1796, the Morozakiya establishment in Funamatsu-chō began selling large kites that were made of more than two sheets of paper brightly painted by professional artists. Prices were very high, but spoiled children were said to want only the products of Morozakiya.[10] This sort of wasteful spending was frowned on by the neo-Confucian government, whose mercantilist theories assumed a zero-sum economy where consumption in one field meant an overall loss to the whole, with little concept of investment or a dynamic expanding pie. Local *daimyo,* feudal lords, similarly tried to encourage thriftiness; for example, in 1807 the lord of Hamamatsu Castle decreed that kites should not be ostentatiously decorated or more than four feet square. Edoites were traditionally contemptuous of authority, and kite-flying itself could be a mild form of rebellion against a strictly stratified hierarchy. Commoners loved to fly kites over the compounds of noble families in Edo: though not specifically forbidden, this was considered a way of thumbing the nose at social superiors.

The wide-ranging Tempō reforms of the early 1840s included restrictions on both the sale of large painted kites and the number of colors used in woodblock prints. Actor prints, *yakusha-e,* were specifically banned, temporarily putting the figure painter and print-artist Kunisada (plates 19, 24, 27) out of a job. Kuniyoshi (plates 28, 29, 32), his rival, found imaginative ways to continue to illustrate actors, including putting their faces on kites (figure 5). High-profile artists, publishers, and actors were vulnerable to vindictive officials; Utamaro (plate 2) and Kuniyoshi were both arrested at different times for ignoring the government's inconsistently applied restrictions on the subject material of woodblock prints. Successful actors, sometimes rich and vastly popular but of low social status, were also at risk. In 1842 the governor of Edo, seeking to blame economic problems on high-living commoners who turned the social order upside down, confiscated the house of the most successful actor of all, Ichikawa Danjūrō VII (plates 12, 14, 28), and exiled him from the capital. The humiliation may have been a residual cause of his son's suicide (see plate 49). Offending the authorities continued to be an occupational hazard for artists under the new Meiji government. In 1870 Kyōsai (plates 79–81) was thrown in jail for painting satirical works at a *shogakai,* painting party; he received fifty lashes and needed several months to recover.

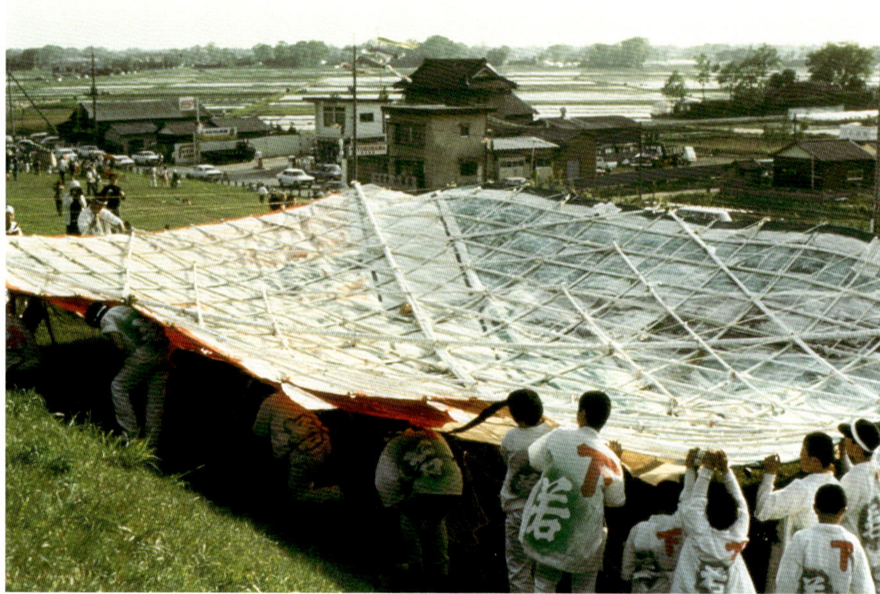

Fig. 4. Raising a giant kite at the Hoshubana kite festival. Skinner and Fujino 1997, 15.

JUST AS WOODBLOCK PRINTS were regarded as typical products of the city of Edo, most of the kites depicted in woodblock prints were also specifically associated with the capital. In the middle of the eighteenth century there were about a hundred kite-makers in Edo; as late as World War II there were about thirty-five. Some landscape prints produced

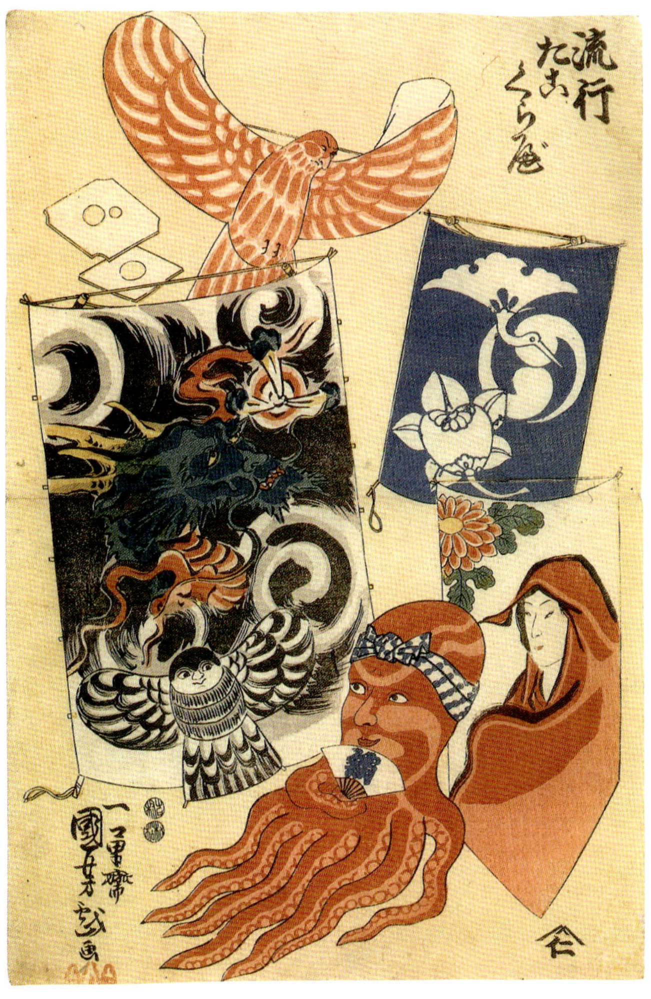

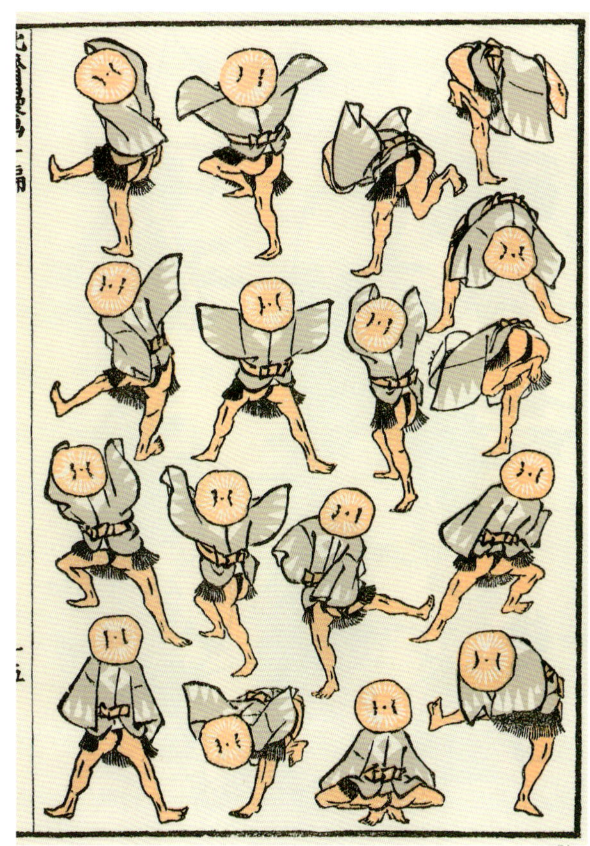

in Edo show kites being flown in the countryside, especially along the great trunk road from Edo to Kyoto known as the Tōkaidō (plates 6, 23, 51), but kite festivals that took place in the provinces were not natural subjects of *ukiyo-e,* as most print-buying consumers were located in the capital and were primarily interested in records of scenes familiar to them.

The typical Edo kite was a bamboo-and-paper rectangle, large or small, with a brightly painted design from a Kabuki play. The large rectangular kite painted with a Soga Brothers design that boys are preparing to fly in plate 47 is a good example. During the An'ei era (1772–80), kites appeared that were modeled on *yakko* retainers, known for their swagger and high-handed treatment of commoners. Their pretensions were satirized in the *yakko-odori* (*yakko* dance), a comic dance first improvised during the Genroku era (1688–1703) and still sometimes performed in geisha houses. Perhaps it was vicarious satisfaction at seeing a bully bob up and down at the end of a string that prompted the invention of this form of kite. Kites were considered a specialty of the Yotsuya district of Edo; a *yakko* and a *tobi* kite appear together in a design titled *Yotsuya* from a *surimono* series called *Tōto meibutsu awase* (Famous Products of the Eastern Capital) of the late 1810s.[11]

With kites particularly popular in Edo, the Edo term for kite, *tako,* eventually came into general use throughout the country. The pronunciation is the same as the word for octopus (though written with a different character), perhaps because an early kite with multiple tails looked like an octopus (see figure 2). The sound *ika,* which can mean squid, was also used to mean kite, perhaps for the same

Fig. 5. Kites with human faces. Utagawa Kuniyoshi, 1847–48, *ōban* woodblock print, 35.9 × 24.9 cm. Private collection.

Kuniyoshi has sought to evade the prohibition against portraying actors in prints by depicting them as kite decorations. Several of the shapes and themes here are shown in the kite shop of plate 69; see also the inset to plate 48.

Fig. 6. The *yakko* dance. Katsushika Hokusai, 1815, adaptation of a page from volume 3 of the *Manga* sketchbooks, 18.1 × 12.6 cm.

reason. Both *tako* and *ika* are often used with the word *nobori,* meaning banner. The word *ika* is used several times on the prints in this book, for example, in plates 13, 26, 46, and 67, which all show Edo prints, and in plate 70, an Osaka print. This suggests that the Edo-dialect word *tako* did not yet predominate in the mid-nineteenth century. In the Osaka print, the word is used to make a pun on *ka,* meaning price. When the word *ika* is used today it often indicates a kite that can be rolled up (like a rolled-up dried-squid snack?). For example, the hexagonal *rokkaku* kite of Sanjō, whose central spar can be removed, enabling it to be rolled up for portability, is called *ika.* In Nagasaki, where the basic shape of a kite was a fish rather than a hawk or octopus, an early term for kite was *ago,* from *agobata,* flying fish. Another Nagasaki term was *komoribata,* flying bat.

The range of kite shapes that had developed by late Edo is remarkable. Perhaps the most impressive selection shown together in a print here appears in the skies above the actors in plate 28—the shapes include a catfish, crane, spider's web, and the king of Hell. In the book *Kyōbun azumanamari* (Crazy Description of Eastern Dialects) of 1813, four popular types of kites were categorized: square kites painted with large characters; kites painted with a picture; kites in the shape of an object, like a *yakko, tobi,* or kimono; and specialty kites, such as kites with lights for night-flying.[12]

Plates 44 and 45 show a range of shapes that were popular three decades later. Besides the *yakko* and *tobi's* basic T shape, these include all sorts of unlikely items, such as a fan, a gourd, the lantern outside a shop, and a samurai's helmet. These were auspicious if not aerodynamically friendly shapes. Many characters from folklore appear, such as a tofu-loving goblin with a long tongue, a big-bellied badger with a detachable tail, and a one-legged umbrella ghost. Kite shapes were based only partially on geometry; often the creative impetus appears to have been supplied by the significance of an auspicious object rather than whether a shape would fly well.

Similarly, the decoration of most kites had symbolic cultural overtones—the choices of Japanese kite-makers were thoughtful. One may contrast the arbitrary decoration choices for kites made in modern societies, even kites made in Asian countries with vast cultural heritages. Plates 40 to 43 provide examples of many designs painted on the rectangular kites of Edo in the mid-nineteenth century, especially the faces of legendary heroes and single, boldly brushed characters that had a power all their own. The richness of Japan's literature and folktales was reflected in the visual arts and crafts to an extent as great as in any other culture of the world. The closest equivalent in contemporary Europe was Christian iconography derived from Biblical stories, mixed with such medieval characters as the Green Man and other nature spirits, that appear in illustrated books and the sculpture of rural churches.

Outside Edo, other regions of Japan had specialized kite-shapes, such as the seven-sided Suruga kite (first flown early in the sixteenth century to mark a victorious battle) and the *hata* of Nagasaki, a slightly off-square fighting kite noted for its deceptively simple design and great maneuver-

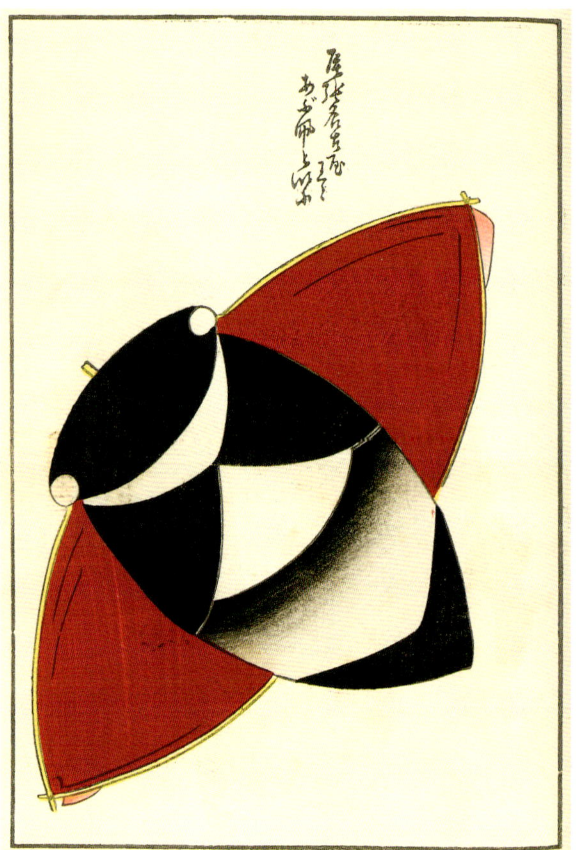

Fig. 7. A Nagoya *abutako,* literally gadfly kite, from the woodblock-printed book *Unai no tomo* (Collection of Folk Toys), 1911. 25.1 × 15.7 cm. See also plate 92.

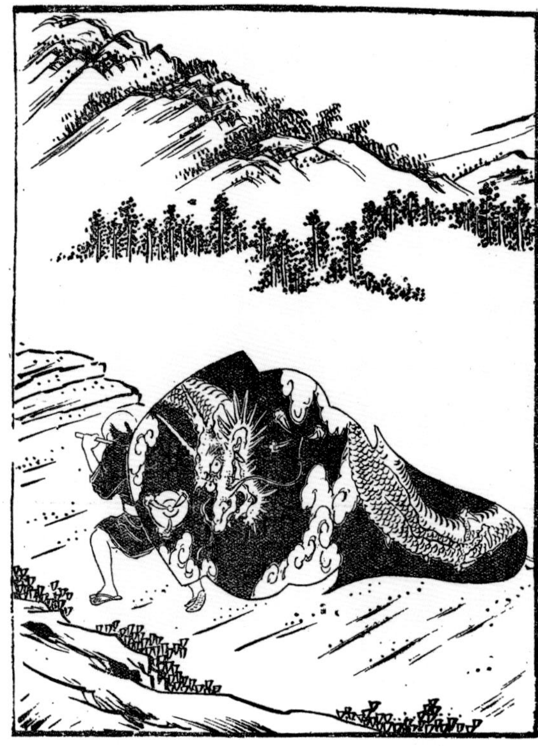

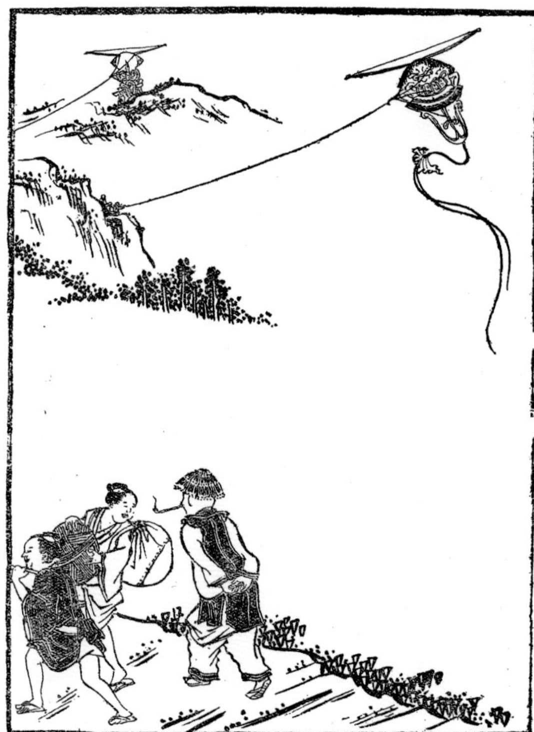

Fig. 8. Large kite with dragon design. Pages from the woodblock-printed book *Nagasaki meishō zue* (Pictures of Scenic Spots of Nagasaki), c. 1820; each page approximately 17.5 × 13.2 cm.

A man in Chinese clothing smokes a pipe as he follows a large kite being carried into the mountains near Nagasaki; two similarly shaped kites already flying have huge hummers, many feet across.

ability. Nagoya was known for kites shaped like insects, such as cicadas and butterflies (figure 7); Sanjō, near Niigata, was famous for hexagonal kites.

Rare illustrations of non-Edo kites are included in an early nineteenth-century woodblock-printed book, *Nagasaki meishō zue* (Pictures of Scenic Spots of Nagasaki).[13] Through most of the Edo period, Nagasaki was the only port in Japan allowed to trade with the outside world. A relatively large number of Chinese vessels visited Nagasaki each year and a substantial Chinese trading community became established there. In figure 8 we see a Chinese man walking behind a huge dragon-kite being carried up a mountain by two men; dragons are associated with China in Japanese traditions. This kite-shape is known as *baramon.*[14] The only other foreign nationals allowed entry to Nagasaki were the Dutch. They were severely restricted in their movements; in figure 9, Dutch merchants fly kites from the roofs of their company buildings. The kites are flat rather than bowed, and therefore more skittish and difficult to fly. The commentary explains how glass brought in by foreigners was ground down and used with paste on the lines of *hata* fighting kites to cut the lines of opposing kites. Also mentioned is the big kite-fighting festival that was held on the tenth day of the third month at the Konpira Temple in Nagasaki. Fighting kites never became more than a local passion in Japan, and the sport did not become widespread as it did in, for example, India and Thailand. The closest we come in this book is plate 38, where a boy tries to bring down his friend's kite with a weighted line.

A characteristic of woodblock prints is the loving detail with which everyday items are depicted. Many of the kites in this book are very carefully drawn, and we can tell exactly how they were constructed. Large kites had complex frames of bamboo, others were very simple. Plate 75 shows part of a large rectangular kite from the back, the frame clearly visible. The main bridle-lines and tail-ropes made of natural materials were much thicker than kite lines are today; they were kept coiled in baskets and fed out as the kite ascended. Such baskets can be seen in plates 53 and 75. The typical rectangular Edo kite had two thick

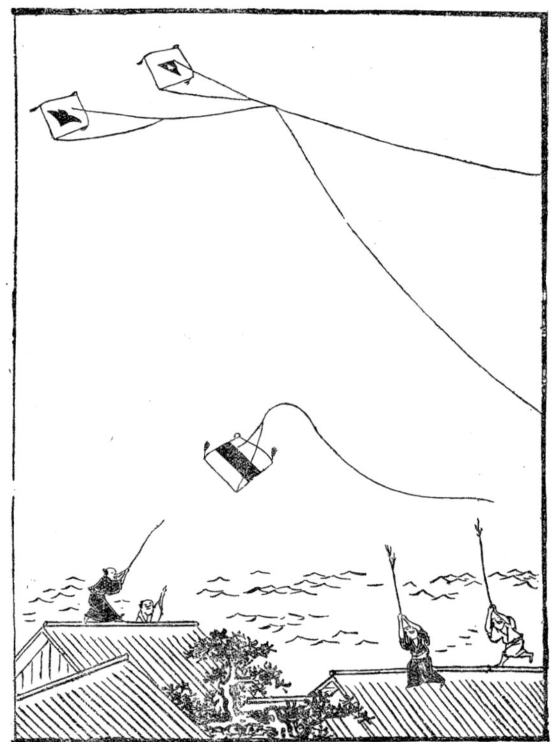

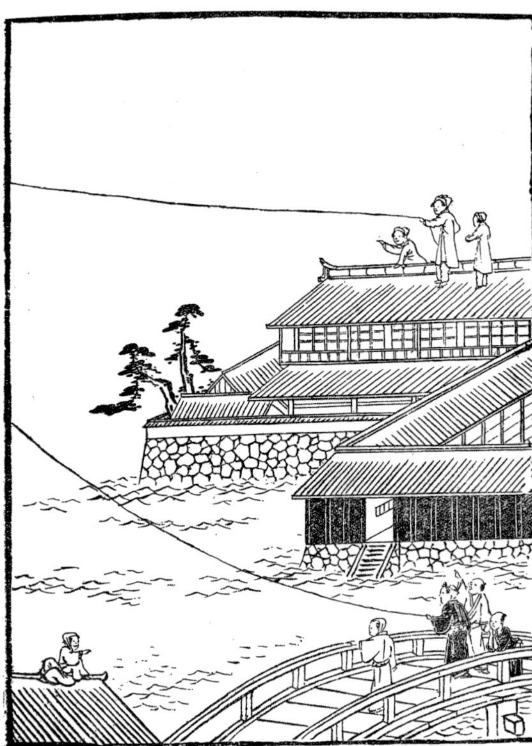

Fig. 9. *Hata* fighting kites. Pages from the woodblock-printed book *Nagasaki meishō zue* (Pictures of Scenic Spots of Nagasaki), c. 1820; each page approximately 17.5 × 13.2 cm.

Dutch merchants fly a *hata* fighting kite from the rooftop of their factory building in Nagasaki. Townsmen attempt to cut its line with another kite, as children run to retrieve a third falling kite with branched sticks.

trailing tail-lines for stability, one from each lower corner—as in plate 47, where three little boys are preparing to fly a kite so big that it will carry them away if they succeed. The lines and knots are drawn with the accurate detail that seems to have been a preoccupation of print artists. In Kuniyoshi's glorious triptych of plate 32, five tail-lines lead from the two lower corners of the Daruma kite being readied for flight; each knot and twist is carefully drawn. In plate 69 we are presented with an actual kite store, complete with hanks of line and a wide range of kite shapes. The shopkeeper shows how to hold the many lines that were attached to the front of the kite to maintain an even tension over its face. The way the lines were looped when a kite was not in use can be seen in the kite held by a servant.

Kuniyoshi's Daruma is the largest kite in the book. Japanese festival kites could be much bigger, but any kite larger than a man was enough to provide plenty of excitement on a windy day. Daruma (the Japanese transliteration of Bodhidharma) was the Indian monk who brought Chan (Zen) Buddhism to China in the sixth century (and, the Japanese say, traveled on to Japan in the seventh); he was a beloved figure, and his fierce expression as he struggled to gain enlightenment was used to decorate several kites in this book. He meditated for nine years in front of a wall, till the wall crumbled and his legs fell off; this gave rise to an irreverent comparison to the sanctity and suffering of courtesans, who owed their brothels ten years of service (see plate 69).[15] The smallest kites in the book are probably the designs in plates 40 to 45, which may have been cut out and used as tiny toys (a tradition continued today by the kite-maker Nobuhiko Yoshizumi, who makes kites less than an inch high that catch the slightest breeze and can be flown indoors). The most difficult kite to fly illustrated here would have been the multiple branch-train kite made up of six separate cranes, seen in plate 7. The ways of harnessing the aerodynamics of branch-train kites are extremely sophisticated, and show the lengths to which kite aficionados will go in pursuit of their sport. A simple train kite like the one in plate 47, where the birds follow each other in a line, is much easier to control. Examples of train kites are the much-acclaimed, and sometimes huge, centipede kites of China, which can reach several hundred feet in length.

A distinctive feature of several of the kites illustrated is a hummer: a bowed, taut string or piece of bamboo that would vibrate violently in the wind, making sound. Sometimes they were made of baleen or whalebone, and one name for a hummer was *kujira unari,* roaring whale (see plate 11). The noise produced is often much more than a hum—there are Chinese stories in which hummers on kites were used to frighten an opposing army, just as Mongolian arrows were constructed with holes in the metal head that positively screamed. Japanese municipalities sometimes outlawed hummers because of their weird sounds; during World War II they were banned because their sound could be mistaken for a falling bomb. The noise of a hummer, however, can be pleasant. The author remembers being charmed in Indonesia, talking with a man who habitually flew his kite in the evening until it could no longer be seen in the darkness; he would then tie it outside his window so that the first thing he heard when he woke was the sound of the hummer. Tropical winds can be very dependable, blowing steadily in the same direction for hours, even days. In Hong Kong the author remembers letting a kite go when it got dark rather than reel it in; next morning he saw it still fluttering high in the sky half a mile away, tension maintained in its line that had become tangled in undergrowth.

The choice of subjects and the details of a print were not arbitrary; each detail had a purpose, reinforcing the associations and mood of a print. Artists tended to follow established genres and themes, including seasonal signifiers, famous places, and local festivals. There was a great deal of visual punning and wordplay; sometimes a title specifically uses the word *mitate-e* (a disputed term meaning approximately parody picture; see plates 28 and 69) to indicate this. It had been common practice since at least the Heian period, a thousand years before, to link certain places with specific poetic sentiments and emotions. Subjects ran the danger of becoming captive to their associations—cherry blossoms symbolized transient female beauty, maple leaves or the full moon evoked the nostalgia of the dying year, whether the viewer liked it or not. Responses could become automatic and an image hackneyed; it required the genius of a good artist to keep a subject fresh. Two locations on the Tōkaidō, for example, Kakegawa and Fukuroi, became associated with kite-flying; if an artist depicted them, he was almost expected to include kites. Although kites were enjoyed throughout the year and throughout the country, they were strongly associated with New Year celebrations. Again and again we see kites shown in New Year contexts. The most common theme of this book is kites flying over the city of Edo at New Year, and several prints, especially some impressive triptychs, commemorate Kabuki performances associated with New Year. The tightly knit richness and interwoven complexity of traditional Edo culture is suggested by the motifs and details that constantly recur in this book. Many traditions, such as the Seven Lucky Gods (see plates 79–81), and including kites themselves, did not have their origins in Japan but were thoroughly and naturally absorbed into Japanese popular culture.

As signifiers of the New Year, kites enjoyed pleasant associations. For most people in a society that did not take vacations, New Year was their only leisure time. It was also a time when debts were expected to be cleared and slates wiped clean. New Year was considered the first day of spring, and the symbolism of starting anew was very strong. Many *hatsu,* firsts, were celebrated (see plate 11): the first calligraphy of the year, the first poem composed, the first dream, the first water drawn from the well to make tea. As we see in the game board of plate 39, the first sale of the year was significant for superstitious merchants. There were many traditional foods to be eaten at New Year (sea bream, *mochi* riceballs, and lobsters are all shown here) and games to be played. Boys flew kites, girls played shuttlecock—that is what boys and girls did at New Year. New Year prints depicted kites, treasures, young women dressed in their fashionable best, and lots of male children, all subjects with positive associations. The responses that kite prints inspired in viewers would have been happy ones, similar to Christmas themes in the West; indeed, traditional Japanese New Year decorations include pine branches, like the traditional Christmas tree of northern Europe. Several types of *kadozuke,* gate visitors, illustrated in the prints in this book (such as plates 54, 78, and 87), entertained Japanese households at New Year, just as children in Victorian England moved from house to house along a street singing Christmas carols for pocket money and "figgy pudding."

THE PRINTS IN THIS BOOK are selected from the Skinner Collection, which has been put together in a decade with great energy and enthusiasm. Kite specialists know Scott Skinner through the Drachen Foundation in Seattle, an institution he established that is dedicated to the study of kites and the archiving of kite-related material from around the world. The collection mirrors the development of woodblock prints, and the ninety-three designs selected from it encapsulate the styles and formats that developed in the years between the middle of the eighteenth and the end of the nineteenth century. Japanese society experienced profound changes during these years; the collection documents those changes and gives a short but surprisingly complete overview of the history of woodblock prints.

The single criterion in the collection's accumulation has been that a print contain a representation of a kite, either as a main theme or a detail; artist, format, condition, and cost have been irrelevant. The earliest print in the collection dates from the middle of the eighteenth century and the latest from the beginning of the twentieth. All the major print formats are represented, from a beautiful Utamaro *ōban* (large-format print) to book prints and a *surimono* by Hokusai; from landscapes by Hiroshige and his students and high-quality Kabuki and genre triptychs to nostalgic evocations of dying Edo traditions at the end of the nineteenth century. At over three hundred sheets and growing, the collection is statistically large enough for conclusions to be drawn from it. A very approximate ratio of Daruma, *yakko, tobi,* and other kite shapes and decorations emerges, perhaps indicating their relative popularity. When well over half of the prints in the collection relate to New Year kite-flying, we may infer that a similar proportion of all prints that depict kites relate to New Year themes. Other interesting relationships are the numbers of Kabuki prints, *bijin-e* (pictures of beautiful women), genre scenes of urban life, and landscapes.

With the exception of a handful of groupings, the designs in this book are presented chronologically. The first illustration in the book is from a small woodblock-printed volume of about 1752, before multicolor *nishiki-e* prints were fully developed. Two fine designs of Kintarō, the archetypal Golden Boy, follow; these date from the last years of the eighteenth century, usually considered the elegant apogee of woodblock prints. Plate 18, a charming design by Eizan with delicate and unusually fresh colors, continues this tradition.

There follows a group of exquisite *surimono,* a word that literally means rubbed (that is, printed) thing. *Surimono* were privately issued woodblock prints, usually commissioned by individuals or groups to commemorate particular events, often a poetry-composing party or a celebration of a favorite Kabuki actor's performance.[16] Plate 8 is a particularly significant example for its relationship to the history of Kabuki. *Surimono* were extremely popular in the last years of the eighteenth century and the first decades of the nineteenth. Actor fan clubs and poetry groups would mark their gatherings by issuing *surimono,* combining delightfully complex visual puns with erudite wordplay. A form of poetry called *kyōka,* literally mad verse, comic poems of thirty-one syllables, was used to complement the images, often with no obvious relevance to them. The meanings of the poems were often extremely abstruse, and working out their allusions was part of the contemporary pleasure of viewing *surimono.* The designs were usually small-format, printed on high-quality paper to very high printing standards. *Surimono* might be made either before an event as gifts for the participants, or after the event as souvenirs. As they were privately published, they were not subject to government censorship. They were usually commissioned from a well-known print artist, though sometimes the person giving the event designed or even carved the blocks for the print himself. The multitalented actor Danjūrō VII drew an unorthodox portrait of himself for a *surimono* announcing a name change.[17] As mentioned, the subgenre of *surimono* calendar prints that showed the long and short months of the coming year were technically illegal, and artists therefore hid the calendrical information in ingenious ways (see plate 7). Many, perhaps most, *surimono* celebrated New Year events, and kites, as New Year markers, were a common *surimono* subject.

The first of several triptychs of Kabuki performances with themes from the Soga Brothers story follows the group of *surimono.* It had become an Edo tradition to produce a play at New Year featuring the Soga Brothers, two orphans who devoted their young lives to killing their father's murderer. They succeeded and were killed themselves, quickly becoming folk heroes. Based on a real vendetta that resulted in the assassination of a high-ranking lord, the story inspired a number of Kabuki plays. New Year performances often consisted of a single scene related only loosely to the story, with the role of the villain turned into a hero played by a troupe's lead actor and kites often incorporated because of the season. Two very unusual L-shaped triptychs of 1857 show a Kabuki actor as a *yakko* kite being flown by a rowdy friend of the Soga Brothers (plates 58 and 59). In a fan-shaped diptych of 1871 by Kunichika (plate 74), the actor Onoe Kikugorō V, dressed as the younger of the Soga Brothers, presents his fans with a new interpretation of the story in which he takes the role of a *yakko* kite.

Other Kabuki prints include Kuniyoshi's triptych of plate 28 and an *onnagata* (a male actor in a female role) as a young man-about-town (plate 29). Kunisada parodies the famous story of a strong woman who stopped a runaway horse by stepping on its loose reins, showing an *onnagata* in high *geta* stepping firmly on the line of a kite painted with a horse design (plate 27).

Several prints of beautiful women, *bijin-e,* dressed in their best as they celebrate New Year, use kites as signifiers of the season. In many *bijin-e* the young ladies are almost mannequins, the focus being on their clothes; the finest example here is plate 33, with its effective palette of a few compatible colors. The colors of Kunisada's design of young girls playing the New Year game of shuttlecock, plate 30, are also delightfully fresh. Unwittingly or not, Eisen injects social commentary into his *bijin-e* of plate 31. The tradition of girls playing shuttlecock at New Year is continued in Shuntei's 1898 triptych of plate 90, where again the girls' beautiful robes were intended to be as important to the viewer as the print's narrative.

A number of landscapes and cityscapes in the collection show kites. The earliest is plate 6, in which Hokusai depicts kites at Kakegawa, the twenty-seventh station on the Tōkaidō highway from Edo to Kyoto. Hiroshige and then Kunisada followed his example with designs of Kakegawa (plates 23 and 24). In plates 51 and 52 the wind has blown on to the next station, Fukuroi, portrayed in two landscapes by Hiroshige. This is followed in plate 53 by a reinterpretation of their elements by one of Hiroshige's students. In these three prints kites are being flown in the countryside, where the purpose may include prayers for a good harvest. Both Hiroshige and Hokusai also show kites being flown for fun in lively, detailed scenes of the capital in their most important series: Hokusai's "Thirty-Six Views of Mount Fuji" and Hiroshige's "One Hundred Famous Views of Edo."

An insight into daily commercial life can be seen in the woodblock-printed game board of plate 39, given to patrons by a thread-merchant as a New Year gift and advertisement. In plate 46 a customer, probably a Kabuki actor, chooses a couple of kites for sale at a small stall; in plate 69 we see the interior of a much larger kite store. Painful economic realities are apparent in a diptych of 1866 titled *Tōsei nobori ika* (Today's Rising Kites, plate 70). A myriad kites fly high, each bearing the character for an everyday necessity or service, satirizing the inflation of the last years of the Tokugawa shogunate. For decades the economy had been unstable—the playfulness and high spirits of woodblock prints hid great hardships for many layers of society. Edo lost half its population of at least a million during the 1860s, with more than 300,000 people leaving the capital in 1867, the tumultuous year when the feudal shogunate was replaced by the reformist government of Meiji.[18] The dislocation of this period was extreme, and resulted in a lowering of production standards of woodblock prints. Rather crudely carved triptychs of 1873 and 1878 reflect this (plates 68 and 77). The downward trend in

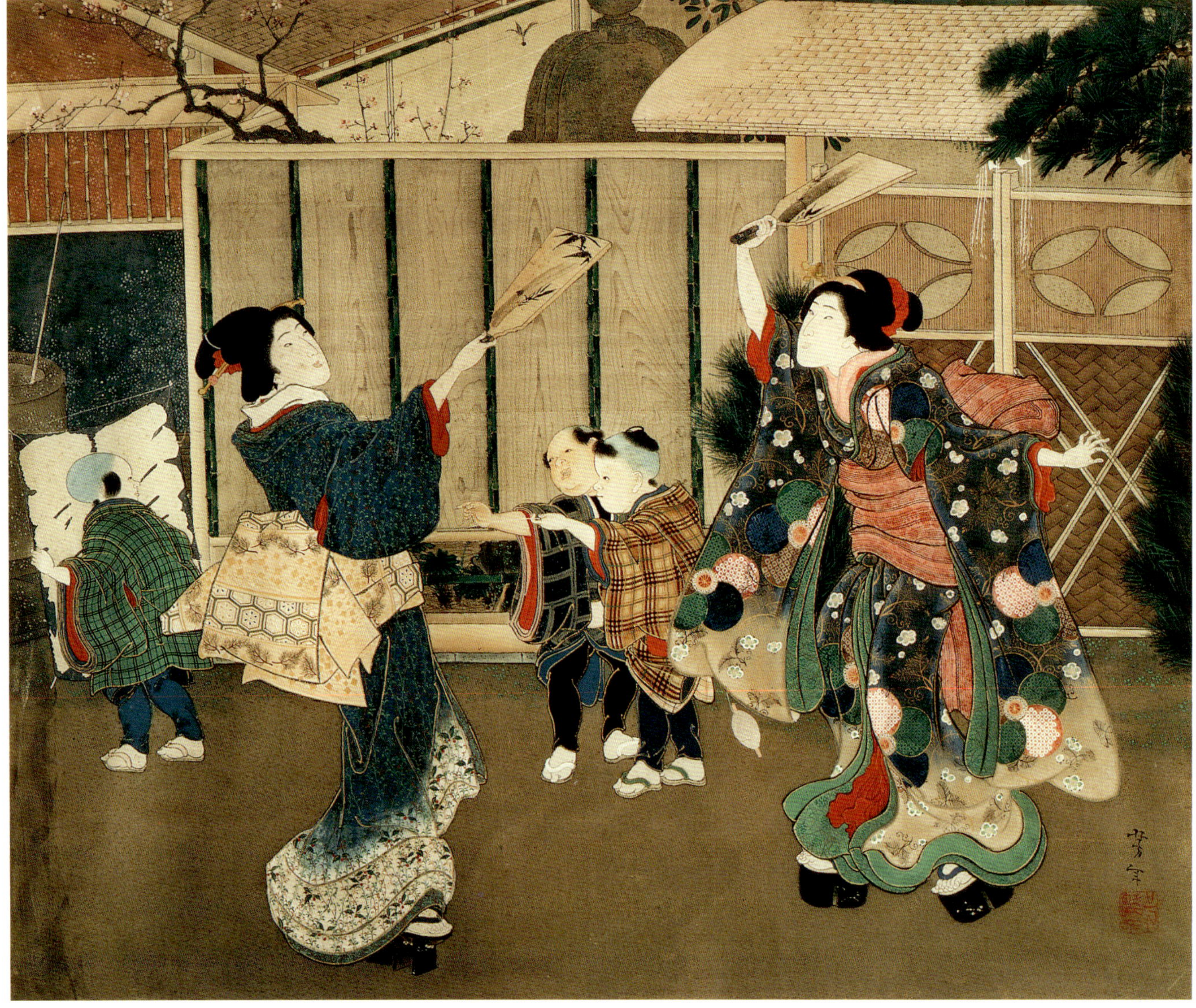

quality can also be seen in early Meiji landscapes—compare Hiroshige III's landscape of plate 72 with Hiroshige's plates 54 and 56, or even Hiroshige II's plate 65. The market was finding it difficult to maintain past standards.

The diptych satirizing inflation was made in Osaka, the economic center of Japan, and Osaka's economic troubles were typical of the whole country. Osaka had its own woodblock-print tradition, focused largely on the Kabuki theater. Later Osaka prints were typically produced in the smaller *chūban* format; the quality of their printing and materials was often extremely high, and many expensive

Fig. 10. *January: Celebrating the New Year.* Tsukioka Yoshitoshi, mid-1860s, ink and colors on silk, 37.5 × 55.2 cm. Courtesy of Los Angeles County Museum of Art, Herbert R. Cole Bequest, M.84.31.540.

Three little boys with shaven heads prepare to fly a kite as two *bijin* play shuttlecock. A New Year pine-and-bamboo decoration can be seen at the right; a budding plum tree and mature pine hang over the wooden fence. Kite-flying, a largely proletarian occupation, was a fairly common theme of woodblock prints but a rare subject for paintings. This painting may be the first of a series commissioned to celebrate the five major festivals of the Edo year; see plates 32 and 33, also Keyes and Kuwayama 1980, 22–23. Its colors are unusually brilliant and fresh.

techniques, such as complex embossing and metallic pigments, were utilized. Only one Osaka Kabuki print is included here (plate 62); there is also an Osaka comic print (plate 60). Three Osaka prints out of a total of ninety may be an accurate reflection of the ratio of Edo and Osaka prints.

Edo woodblock-print artists and their consumers prided themselves on being on the cutting edge of fashion in the theater, clothes, hairstyles, literature, the general art of living. This continued during Meiji: in plate 75 young men flying kites wear new western fashions; plate 76 features the brand-new Mitsui Bank building; and plate 77 presents a range of westernized novelties in a compressed view of downtown Tokyo. The game board of plate 82 enthusiastically contrasts traditional pastimes with new inventions such as tricycles, rickshaws, street lamps, and horse-drawn streetcars against a backdrop of newly popular rising-sun flags.

Ten years later, a mild nostalgia for the old traditions seems to have set in. Chikanobu's Picture of the New Year (plate 78) is taken from his series *Edo sunago nenju gyōji* (Annual Celebrations in Edo). Kites fill the skies above an idealized street scene near Edo Castle, including a shogunal procession and many street performers. This looking backward was something new in woodblock prints; ancient events had often been parodied before, but they were given contemporary settings. Gekkō's diptych titled *Torimazete,* Mixture or Variety, deliberately contrasts traditional and modern elements in a New Year collage, including a Japanese kite flying beside a western-style flagpole.

As part of its emulation of the West, Meiji Japan became increasingly nationalistic. The army and navy were modernized; the Japanese Empire even began to covet overseas colonies. Two kite prints shown here reflect Japan's new aggressiveness toward its neighbors. In plate 83, triumphalist children in military uniforms play with kites, one of which bears characters meaning Great Victory. In plate 89, two boys with western haircuts prepare a kite with a design of a smart mustachioed Japanese officer attacking a Chinese mandarin.

By the end of the century, woodblock prints were losing their identity as inexpensive pictures of the floating world or vignettes of daily life. New methods of mass production of images, such as lithography and photography, were making woodblock prints obsolete. Prints became the conscious expression of an artist rather than a commercial response to a mass market that demanded to be entertained. The specificity of Hiroshige's views of Edo, for example, which were easily identified by their audience, provided them with a validity that the untitled generic landscape of plate 89 does not have.[19] *Bijin-e* became distanced and bland. The direct relationship between the viewer and a seasonal celebration, or a Kabuki performance, or a holiday outing to a particular place, which gave meaning to most of the designs in this book, disappeared. Woodblock prints had lost their popular roots.

Kites also declined in popularity, and many skills were lost—for example, how to make a *beka* kite using a single sheet of paper and a hundred bamboo "bones," which would fly without a tail. By the early 1970s there was only one traditional kite-maker and his shop left in Tokyo.[20] Recent decades, however, have seen a resurgence of interest in kites. The combination of traditional craft with modern materials and construction techniques has produced kites with capacities far beyond a young Edo boy's dreams. Traditional festivals have been revived and new international festivals established. Passionate kite aficionados meet in Japan and around the world to swap knowledge and gossip, on the Internet and in person. Japanese kite associations are flourishing and each year more kites come alive in the wind, delighting those who fly them and those who watch. It is a primal pleasure to see a kite shake itself and rise into the sky, to hold a kite-line and play it like a fish. We see from the images in this book how universal these pleasures are.

Notes

1. The much-quoted opening of Asai Ryoi's *Ukiyo monogatari* (Tales of the Floating World), translated by Timothy Clark, in Nakane 1991, 179.

2. Hockley 2003, 70–74, analyzes the growth of what he calls Edocentrism during the eighteenth century.

3. Streeter 1974, 117. Since the late 1880s, the Hoshubana festival kites have measured about 48 by 36 feet, about the size of a 100-*tatami* house; before Meiji they were about half this size.

4. New Year festivals have declined over the last century, though they are still widely celebrated, and kites are now more usually associated with Boy's Day.

5. Rotondo-McCord 2002, 167 and 277.

6. Izzard 2003, 35.

7. Matsudaira Sadanobu, *Ōmu no kotoba* (The Words of a Parrot), referenced Screech 2000, 267, n. 3.

8. Stories of people being killed by large kites are not apocryphal. Tal Streeter tells of a more recent accident, at a festival in Hoshubana, north of Tokyo, in 1971, when a sudden gust swept a man holding the tail of a giant kite sixty feet into the air and killed him; Streeter 1974, 119.

9. Screech 2000, 20–21.

10. Rogers 1999, 178.

11. Illustrated Keyes 1985, 130.

12. Rogers 1999, 178.

13. *Nagasaki meishō zue* c. 1820, 486–89 (the *meishō* of the title is written in different characters from the more usual *meisho*). I am indebted to Timon Screech for this fascinating reference.

14. The island of Gotō, off the west coast of Kyushu toward China, still has a tradition of large monster-faced kites with the same general shape as the ones shown here, which is believed to have originated in China.

15. The popular legless Daruma dolls, which bounce back up when laid on their backs, inspired further salacious comparisons.

16. This is the traditional definition of *surimono*. The existence of multiple editions of *surimono* designs such as those illustrated in plates 13 and 16, with different seals or other details, suggests that their popularity and market extended beyond single private events.

17. Illustrated in Bowie 1979, 21; see also plate 8 in this book.

18. Jansen and Rozman 1986, 347.

19. Kawase Hasui, the leading *shin-hanga* landscape artist of the Taishō era (1912–26), specifically rejected *meisho*, famous places, as print subjects, preferring an abstracted mood to a realistic representation.

20. Streeter 1974, 41.

THE PRINTS

1

Toba Picture with Rectangular and Ōkame Kites
anonymous
publisher: Terada Ioemon, Osaka
c. 1752
two book pages (together 25.1 × 29.4 cm)

Three men fly kites on a gusty day. One clasps a rectangular kite with a long tail that revolves in the wind; another threads an Ōkame kite through a ring on a long bamboo pole; a third rushes by madly to keep his kite aloft. The pole may be a device to get more height or reach for the kite or to avoid obstacles; it appears to be a flying technique that has not survived. The blustery weather is suggested by the sweep of the men's tonsured hair, the waving tails of the Ōkame kite, and the acute angle of the third man's kite-line.

These pages come from an uncolored woodblock-printed book titled *Toba-e ōgi no mato.* Besides hand-coloring, artists and publishers were already experimenting with color woodblock-printing by the mid-eighteenth century, though the first full-color single-sheet *nishiki-e,* brocade pictures, did not become commercially popular until the mid-1760s.

Kyōga, crazy pictures, like these were not captioned and did not tell a sequenced story like today's *manga* comic books; each image was appreciated separately for its energetic humor. Another illustration from a copy of the *Toba-e ōgi no mato* in the British Museum also shows figures blown about in a high wind: a male dancer with long sleeves and a pot-bellied workman with skinny limbs contending with an open parasol.[1] The British Museum prints have no writing in the corners and the two characters to the top right here, meaning second month (a windy time in Japan but not New Year, traditionally the most popular period for flying kites), appear to have been added by hand.

The original *Toba-e,* Toba pictures, of the book's title were the satirical *Chōjū giga,* frolicking animal, handscrolls of the twelfth or early thirteenth century, purportedly by the artist-abbot Toba Shōjō. In these handscrolls, frogs battle rabbits, monkeys dress as priests, and very fat and very thin peasants wrestle with each other. They bear little resemblance to the figures here except that all are caricatures. Pictures inspired by *Toba-e* are first mentioned in a book of 1710; these thin, grimacing, long-limbed figures in loincloths became popular, inspiring several later print artists, including Hokusai, Hiroshige, and Kuniyoshi.

Already by the mid-eighteenth century kites took myriad different forms. One depicted the pudgy face of Ōkame, a popular figure of fun—sometimes described as the goddess of mirth or folly—who features in the mythological creation of the Japanese islands. Amaterasu, the sun goddess, was offended by her irreverent brother (he threw a flayed horse at her) and retired to a cave that she sealed with a large rock, leaving the universe in darkness. The worried gods begged her to return, but she refused. They lit fires in front of the cave and began feasting; Ōkame danced on an upturned tub until all her clothes fell off, to the gods' great amusement. Intrigued by their laughter, Amaterasu peeped out and was immediately pulled back into the world, which rejoiced again in her light.

1. Illustrated Hillier 1987, 602.

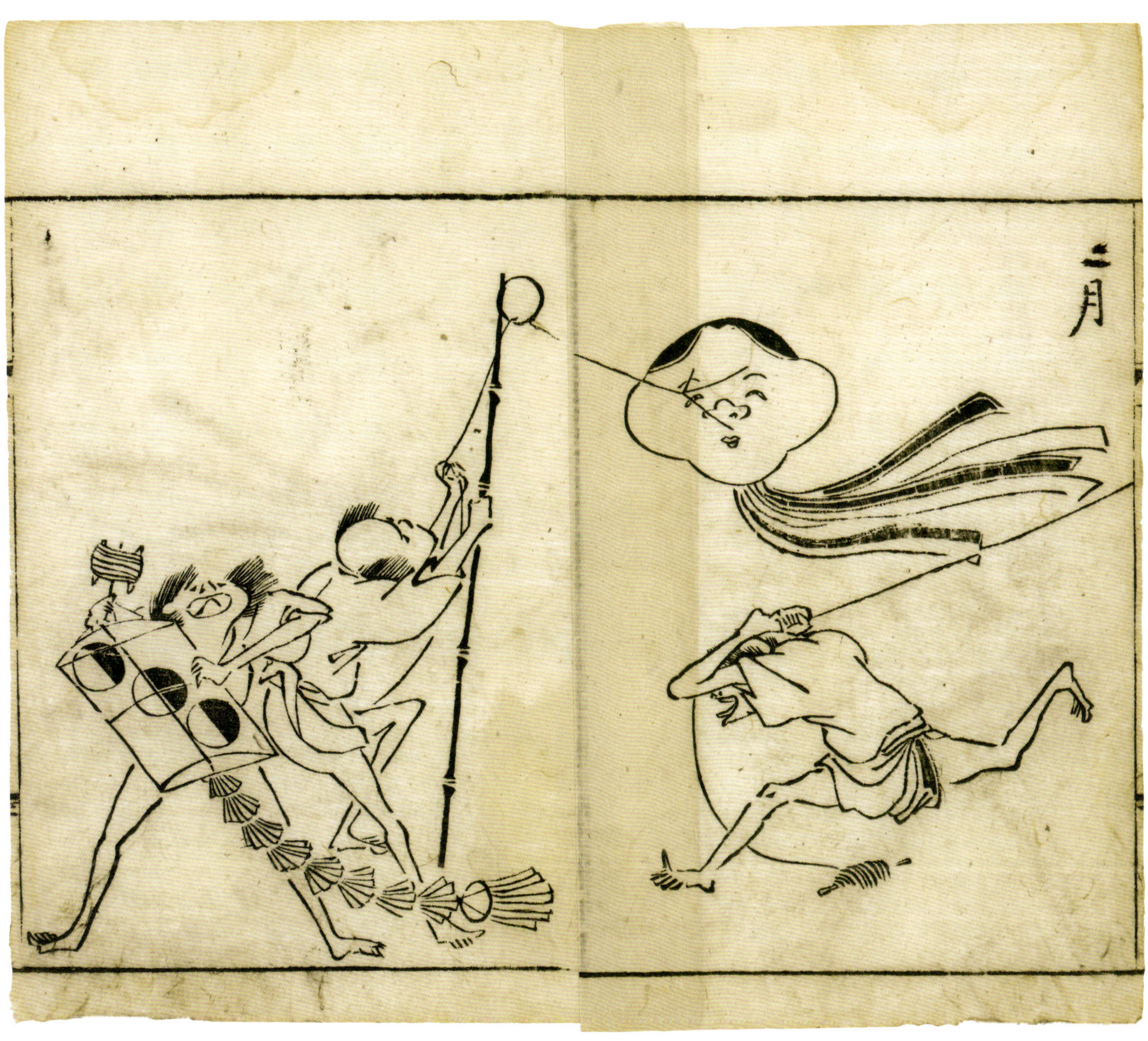
二月

2

Yamauba and Kintarō with Dragon Kite
Kitagawa Utamaro (1750–1806)
signed: *Utamaro hitsu*
publisher: Tsuruya Kinsuke
1796–99
ōban (36.2 × 23.4 cm)

3

Yamauba, Kintarō, and *Yakko* Kite
Ichirakusai Eisui (fl. c. 1790–1823)
signed: *Eisui ga*
publisher: Iwatoya Kisaburō
c. 1797–99
ōban (37 × 24.5 cm)

Each of these two prints is a different treatment of Yamauba (Mountain Woman) with her son Kintarō (Golden Boy), an archetypal child with supernatural strength who holds one of a boy's favorite playthings, a kite. Kintarō is always depicted as plump and healthy, with red skin and a full head of hair, sometimes shaved on the crown as young Japanese male infants were until they reached the age of four or five. Kintarō is a model of strength for young boys. The kites and the motifs on his robe in Utamaro's design, treasures of the Seven Lucky Gods (see plates 79–81), suggest New Year, but Kintarō is especially associated with Boy's Day, celebrated on the fifth day of the fifth month, and these may not be New Year prints.

On the death of her husband, an officer in the bodyguard of the tenth-century emperor Shujaku, Yamauba retired to the mountains to raise her son. The boy was already extremely strong: Yorimitsu, the Minamoto hero, came across him one day in the forest, pulling up a huge tree to bridge a river he wanted to cross. Yorimitsu gave him the name Kintoki, and he eventually became one of Yorimitsu's principal retainers. Utamaro was fascinated by the relationship between the wild but aristocratic woman and the lusty, mischievous boy, a relationship that he explored in a marvelous group of prints in the final years of the eighteenth century.

As a beautiful court lady living alone in the mountains, owing nothing to any man, Yamauba was a disturbing, elemental figure of patent sexuality. Her very long hair, the ultimate mark of feminine beauty in Heian times, is sometimes depicted as beautifully combed, sometimes unkempt. Sometimes she wears the finest robes but often she is half naked, wearing only a cloak made of leaves. Her son, while aware of his strength, was not in control of his situation, and displays all the impotent frustration of a young boy being teased and loved and nursed by his mother—yet in some prints he forgets his male belligerence and shows a passionate tenderness toward her.

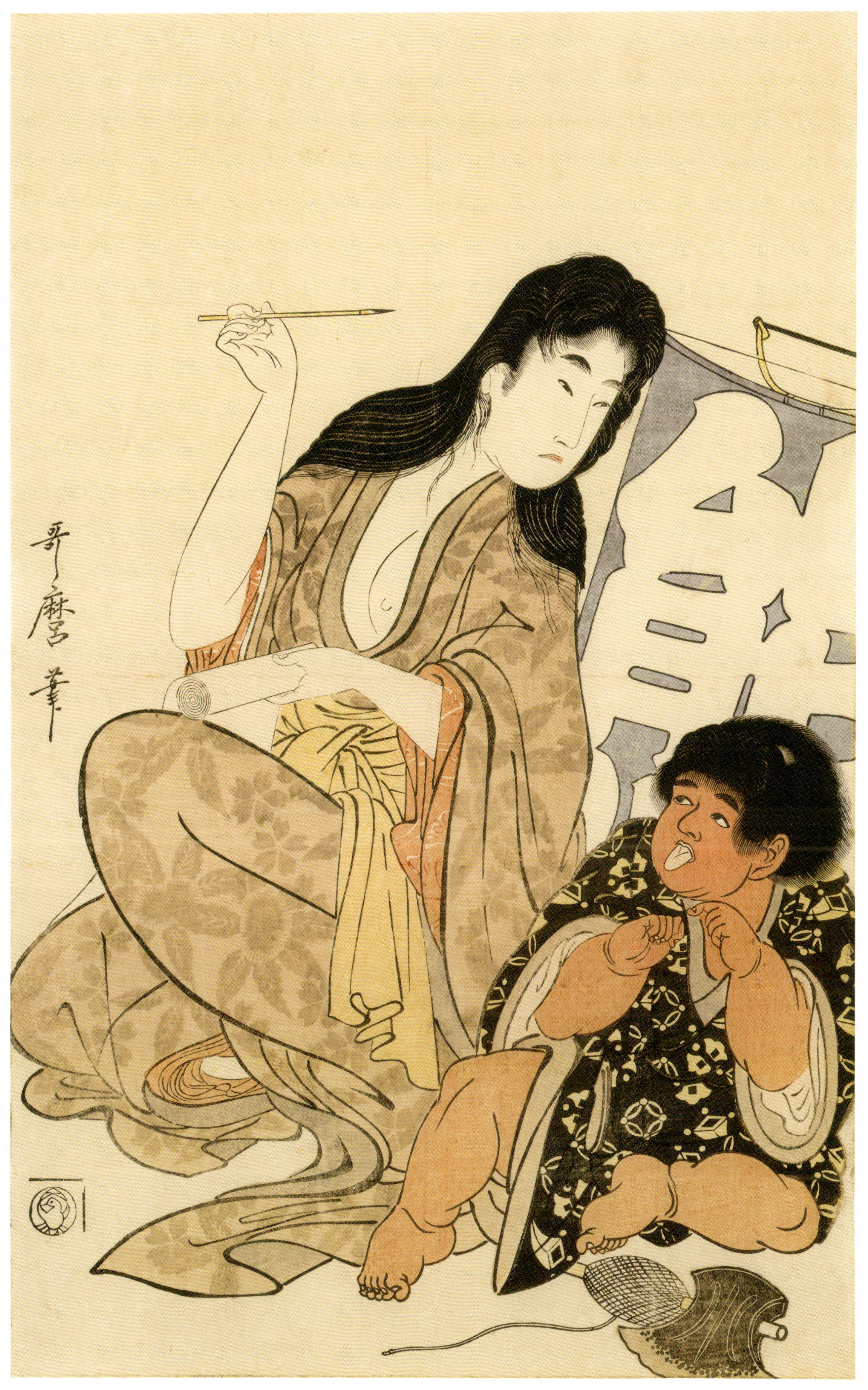
哥麿筆

The two play together spontaneously; in one of Utamaro's designs Yamauba holds Kintarō high in her arms as he reaches down joyfully for the whistle she holds in her lips; in another she ties his hands with a kite string and mercilessly makes fun of him.

Here Kintarō puts out his tongue at Yamauba as she prepares to give him a calligraphy lesson; she appears about to dab him on the nose for his impertinence (see plate 90). The character for dragon, associated with masculinity and the sky, decorates Kintarō's kite, which has a hummer. Kintarō has used the handle of his axe, his iconic attribute and symbol of his courage and strength, as the winding bar for his kite-line. In Eisui's print, Kintarō dangles a *yakko* kite, appropriate for its boisterous, playful associations.

Kitagawa Utamaro was the most successful print artist of his day, prolific and especially famous for his prints of women of the pleasure quarters. Ichirakusai Eisui was a follower of Eishi and specialized in *ōkubi-e,* large-head portraits; his output is so scarce that he may have been an amateur painter and print designer. Utamaro's many designs of Yamauba and Kintarō fall into two groups, one in which the figures are shown full length, the other where only Yamauba's head and shoulders are shown; the close-up treatments are notable for the intensity of their emotions. Utamaro's design here falls into the first group; the composition of Eisui's is conveniently and coincidentally similar to the other group. After two hundred years, Utamaro's print is in very good condition, a fine impression with unusually bright colors. It has seen little light, though the purple-blue of Yamauba's robe fades to brown over time even in darkness. The pattern on her robe is an unusual combination of cherry blossoms and chestnuts; the chestnuts signify her mountain home. Eisui's print is damaged and discolored but the beauty of this rare design lives on in the strength and harmony of its lines.

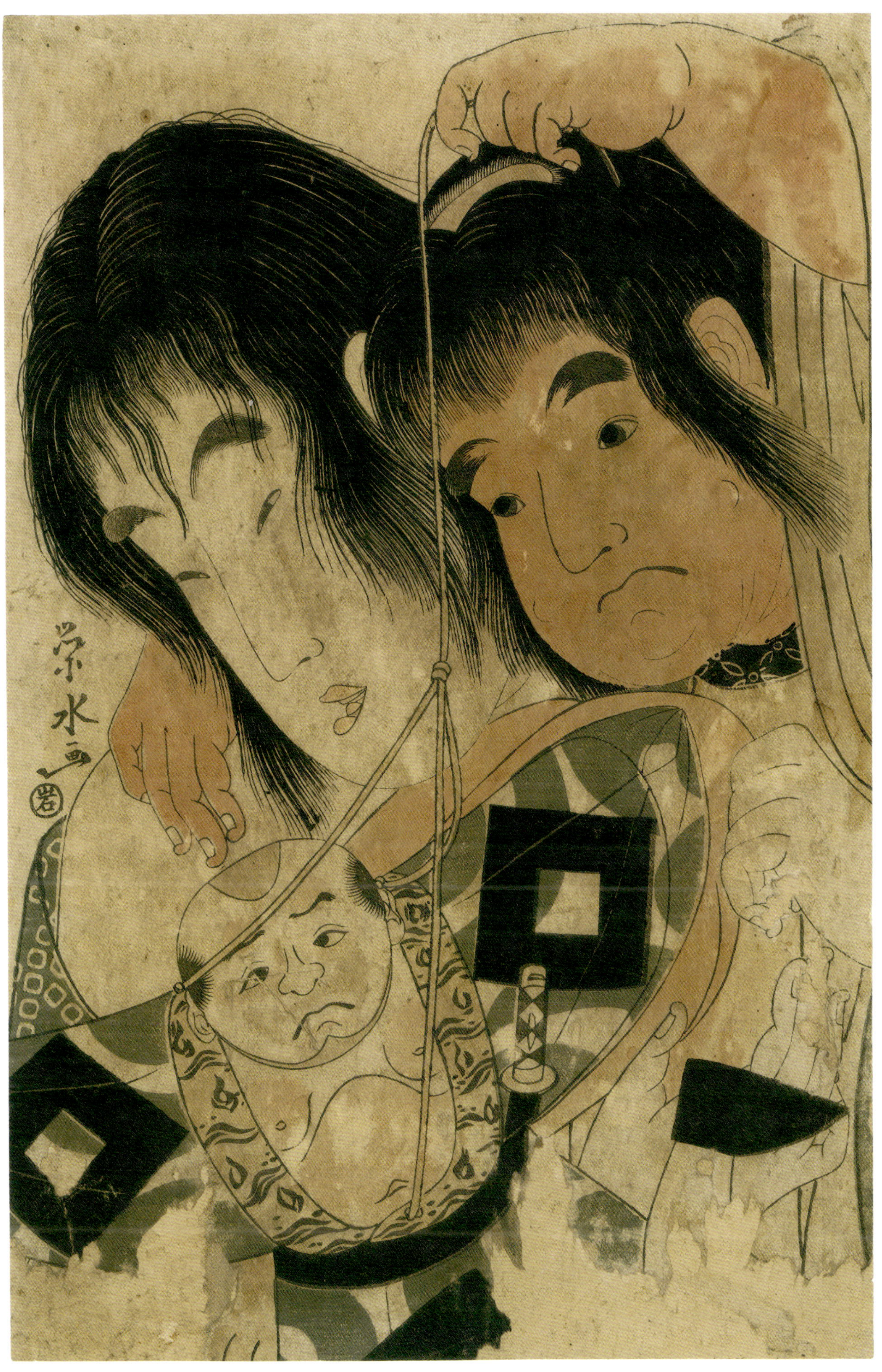
栄水画

4

Teahouse at Shinagawa Bay
Katsushika Hokusai (1760–1849)
unsigned
1800
two book pages (together 22.1 × 30.1 cm)

This scene opens volume one of an illustrated book by Hokusai titled *Tōto shōkei ichiran* (Fine Views of the Eastern Capital at a Glance); the eastern capital is Edo, distinguished from the western capital, Kyoto. A handsome young samurai and his attendant have arrived at a tea pavilion called the Sumi-no-e, a flimsy affair made of reed matting. The samurai has laid down his sword by a tray with smoking paraphernalia and is being relieved of his formal *hakama,* trousers, by the elegant fingers of the teahouse girl, as his attendant prepares a pipe for smoking.

The proprietor/serving girl is well dressed and coiffed. A pretty teahouse girl could gain many admirers. Some became famous, the subjects of popular poems and immortalized in woodblock prints. The black lines of this design are enhanced by four delicate woodblock colors, gray, gray-green, gray-blue, and pink, with a purple achieved by overprinting. The rather phallic shapes by the riverbank are mooring posts for boats.

Hokusai's lively eye delighted in the details of everyday life; note the spiral metal handle of the portable stove to dissipate heat. A portion of his *Manga* sketchbooks are devoted to technical problems that interested him, from complex roof structures to the workings of a water mill. He took care here to draw accurately the strings of the kite that the boy holds, with its long stabilizing tails. The boy, perhaps the teahouse girl's young son, prepares to launch the kite as a friend outside the picture to the left takes up the slack in the line. The characters on the kite, *senshu,* mean literally a thousand seeds, an auspicious phrase implying many offspring and prosperity; it was also the name of a well-known poetry group.

As the opening image of the book, the scene represents New Year, confirmed by a reference in the third poem to the Kabuki character Sukeroku, archetypal hero of the townspeople. In the play *Yukari no Edo zakura,* Sukeroku is the younger of the Soga Brothers in disguise. He spends his time in the Yoshiwara pleasure district searching for an heirloom sword: he provokes quarrels causing opponents to draw their swords so he can look at them. Kabuki performances based on Soga Brothers themes were a New Year tradition in Edo (see plate 19).

There are several sexual overtones in the poems, especially the last, which reads:

asobu hi wa	on a day of leisure
nori toru fune mo	a boat collecting seaweed
Shinagawa no	in Shinagawa
sue agete hosu	rests on a sandbank
ura no hatsuharu	at New Year

One of the most popular unlicensed pleasure districts in Edo was located in Shinagawa, and seaweed was slang for a girl's pubic hair. A boat collecting seaweed in Shinagawa was definitely a man looking for sex.

Hokusai is probably the most beloved of all Japanese artists, at least by foreigners. His designs of daily life bring alive the city of Edo, where the floating world with its myriad forms of entertainment was at its most intense and sophisticated.

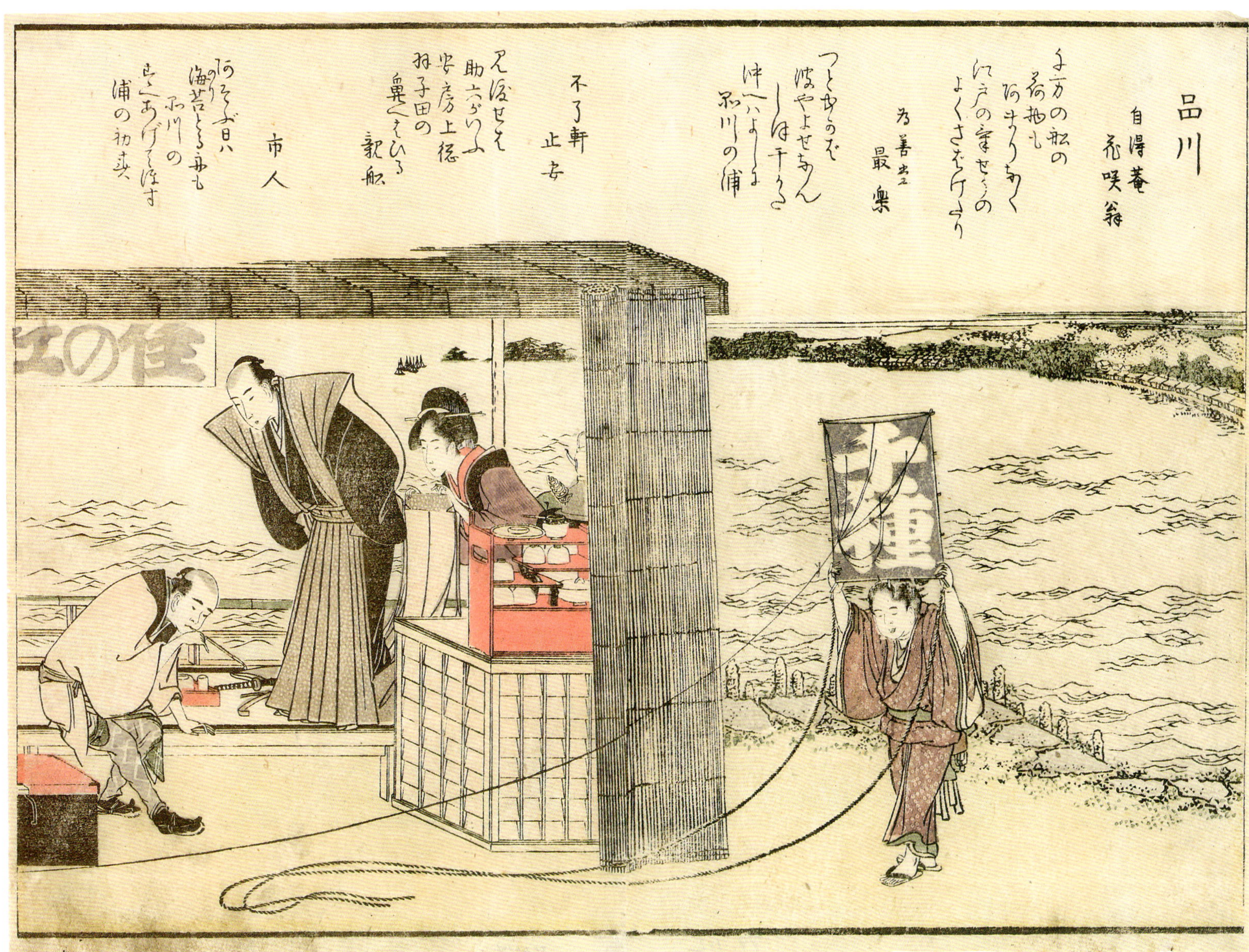

品川
自得菴
花咲翁
最楽
不了軒
止安
市人

5

New Year at the Hachiman Shrine, Ichigaya
Katsushika Hokusai (1760–1849)
unsigned
1804
two book pages (together 24.7 × 34.6 cm)

It is New Year, and two women are visiting the Shrine of Hachiman, Shinto god of war, at Ichigaya in the north of Edo, to pray for good fortune in the coming year. The word for their pilgrimage used in the poem on the left is *ehōmairi, ehō* meaning the auspicious direction of approach, which changed according to the zodiacal calendar.

The women, perhaps a mother and maid, have brought along two little boys. One has the topknot of a young boy and is beginning to struggle. He reaches out for his mother, who prepares to receive him; Hokusai has caught the interplay of their gestures beautifully. The older boy, his head shaved completely, walks proudly ahead with his New Year kite hanging on his back. He also celebrates the holiday with a bamboo branch from which dangle a model fish and a fruit, which may be made of sugar (see plate 38).

The Ichigaya Hachiman Shrine was a famous pilgrimage destination, as much for the entertainment it provided as for religious reasons. A theater was located within its walls, along with tea shops and food stalls, and the shrine was known—not only in Edo, according to one eighteenth-century observer, but throughout Japan—for its many prostitutes.[1]

A man approaches with a kerchief over his head, climbing the steep stone steps to the shrine. The shaved head of another follows him. They will pass under the wooden *torii* gate of the Shinto shrine, which is adorned with a sacred protecting rope and Shinto paper prayer slips. The men's bodies are cut off by the line of the steps, giving an exaggerated impression of the steepness of the hill on which the shrine is built. The view continues over the roofs of buildings, pilgrims entering the shrine, and a large stone wall, then disappears in cloud bands, which are a common convention in Japanese pictorial art.

We can see the shrine from another viewpoint in a print designed fifty years later by Hiroshige, which also has stylized clouds extending across it (see inset). Hiroshige's print similarly exaggerates the steepness of the hill. To the left of Hiroshige's design can be seen the outer barrack walls of the Owari clan, the site of the Military Academy during the Meiji period. The area still has a military barracks today; it was here that the novelist Mishima Yukio publicly disemboweled himself in 1970.

These pages are from the woodblock-printed book by Hokusai titled *Yama mata yama* (Mountain after Mountain). They are less delicately printed than the view of the Shinagawa Bay teahouse in plate 4, and their colors are coarser and a little out of register. As an Edo cityscape the image is idealized but as close to a photograph as we will get.

1. Smith 1986, plate 41 and extended caption.

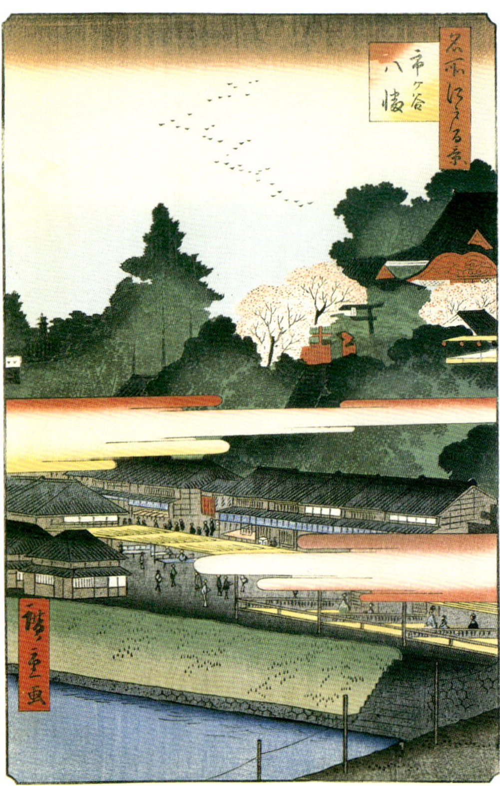

Ichigaya Hachiman Shrine, from Hiroshige's *Meisho Edo hyakkei* (One Hundred Famous Views of Edo), 1858.

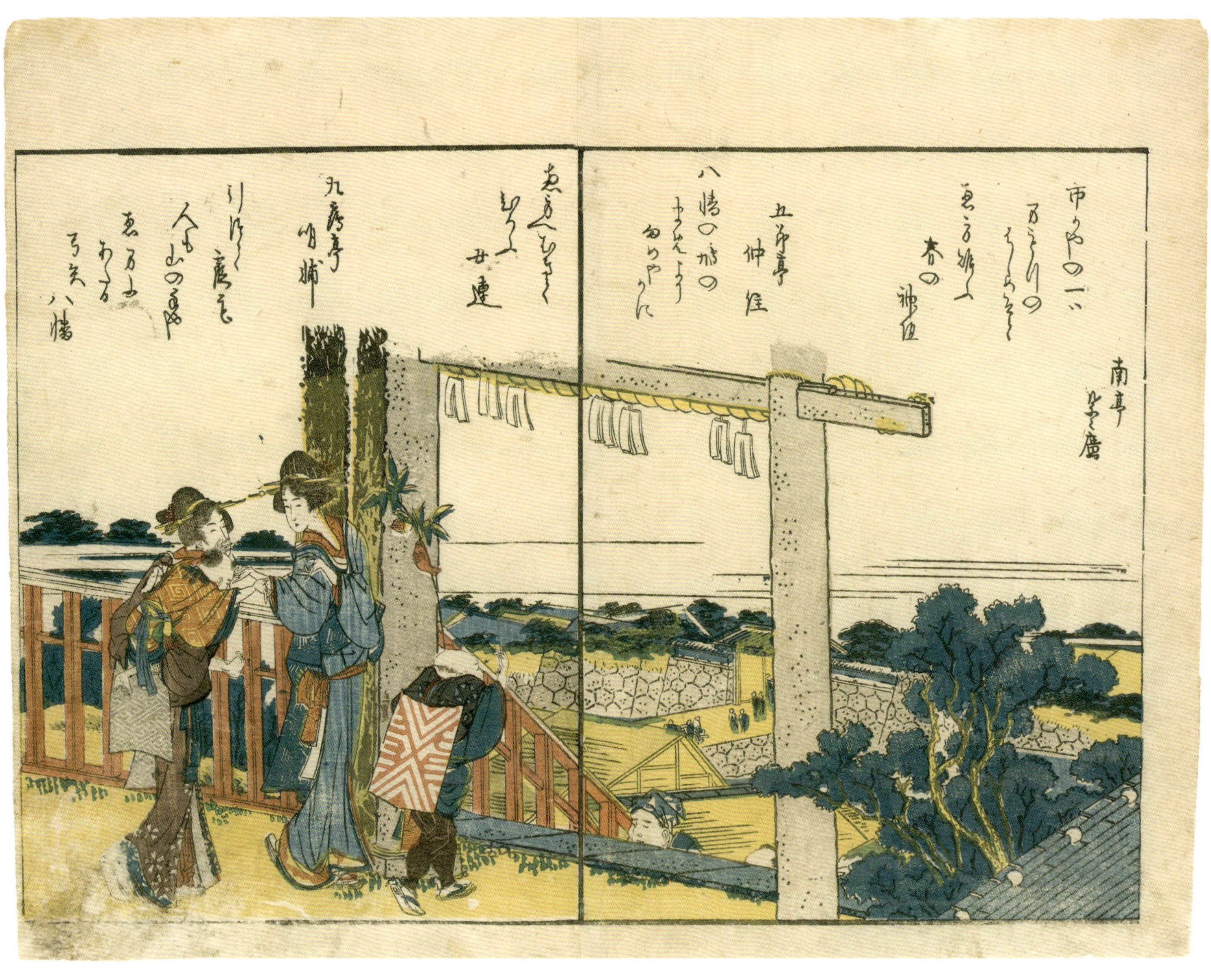

6

Kakegawa, from Fifty-three Stations of the Tōkaidō
Katsushika Hokusai (1760–1849)
unsigned
publisher: Iseya Rihei
1806
chūban (23.2 × 17.5 cm)

This print is from a series by Hokusai titled *Tōkaidō gōjusan tsugi* (Fifty-Three Stations of the Tōkaidō). A samurai riding nonchalantly on a horse and his servant smoke long-stemmed pipes as they travel along the great trunk road between Edo and Kyoto; the samurai wears a T-shaped tobacco-and-pipe pouch at his waist. The two overtake another traveler with a sword and bowl-like straw hat. The servant carries a long ceremonial pole; the master's traveling hat is slung over the pole, adding to the sense of relaxed ease that this print conveys.

It took about fourteen days to walk from Edo to Kyoto along the Tōkaidō, literally East Sea Road, which was over three hundred miles long and Japan's most important highway during the Edo period. There was little wheeled traffic, the forms of transport being foot and horse. The distance was traditionally divided into fifty-three relay stations, established about seven *ri* (twenty-eight kilometers) apart, to accommodate government couriers. Here travelers could find food and lodging. Each station came to be known for a particular characteristic: a ford over a river, a sweeping view, or a particular product that could be bought as a souvenir. Here at Kakegawa—station number 27 from Nihonbashi in Edo, the traditional center of the capital from which all distances were counted—three kites flutter merrily above the travelers. Famous places in Japan tended to become stereotyped and we will see kites flying at Kakegawa again, in Hiroshige's and Kunisada's landscapes of thirty years later (plates 23 and 24).

The most impressive kite here is a rather spectacular phoenix kite with ornate trailing tails. The symbols beside the large characters for Kakegawa are phonetic annotations in *furigana* script, added to aid reading.

Details in Hokusai's prints—here, for example, the bells on the horse's saddlecloth and the plaiting of its mane—are as delightful as his masterly depiction of demeanor, such as the servant's drawing on his pipe as he half-turns to look at the kites.

This small but elegant image has been achieved with economic use of line and color, a palette of yellow, green, and gray. The scene is limited to a pine tree, rocks, and a river, the distant view hidden behind conventional cloud bands. Swirls of very light embossing indicate the waters of the river. Landscapes were not yet the popular genre they were to become after the phenomenal success of Hokusai's Thirty-six Views of Mount Fuji and Hiroshige's Fifty-three Stations of the Tōkaidō thirty years later.[1] Many of the designs in Hokusai's *Tōkaidō gōjusan tsugi* series depict lively human activity and are not landscapes at all.

1. The first purely landscape *ukiyo-e* appears to be a print of Mount Fuji at sunrise by Koryūsai dating from the mid-1770s; see Hockley 2002, 52–53, regarding the human presence in *ukiyo-e* landscapes, which is to a lesser degree also a phenomenon of Chinese landscape paintings.

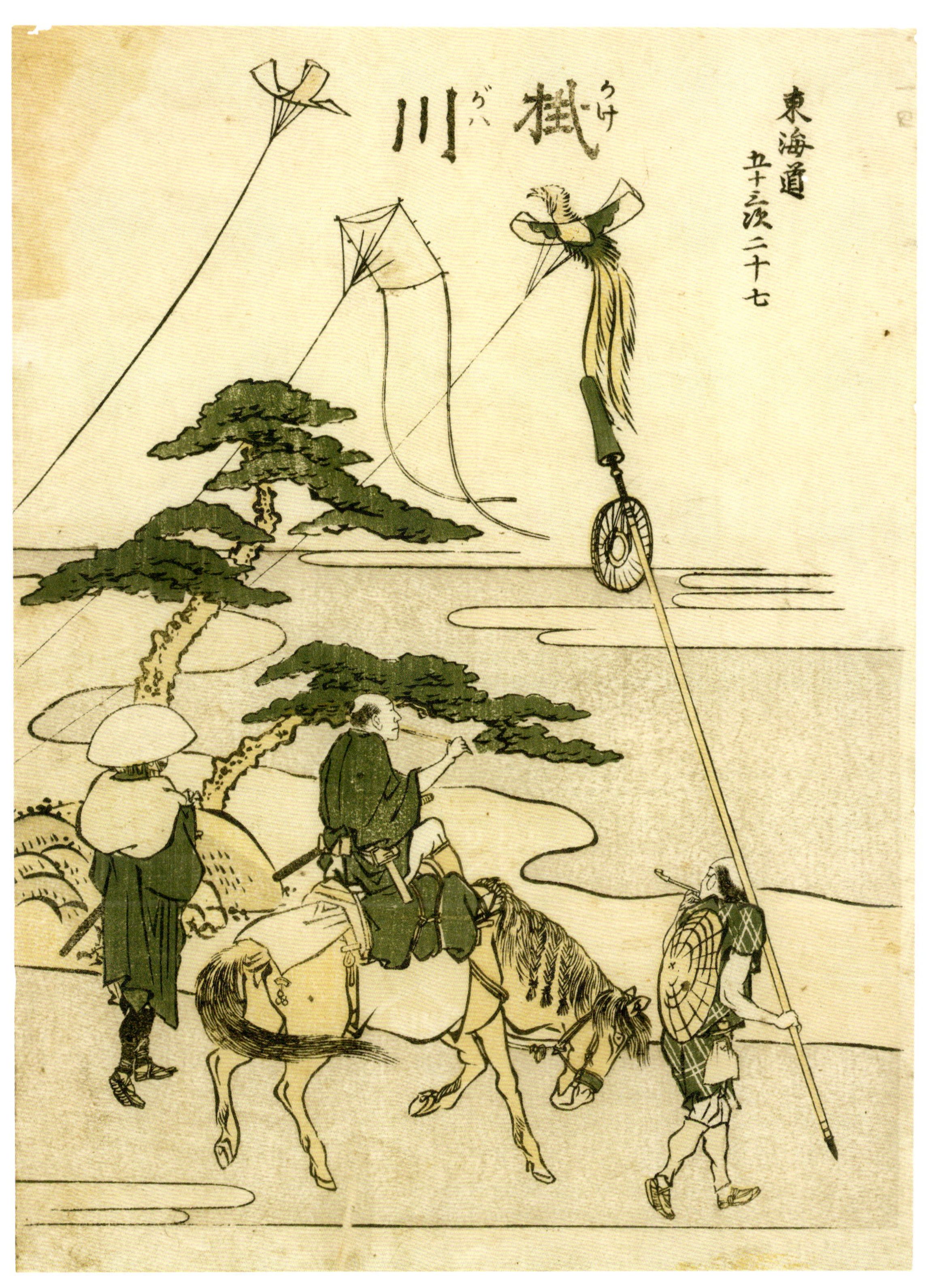
東海道
五十三次二十七
掛川

7

Crane Calendar Print
Hishikawa Sōri (fl. 1790–1810)
signed: *Sōri ga*
1803
surimono (13.3 × 18.5 cm)

Hokusai used the artist name Sōri on *surimono* and album leaves during the years 1796 to 1798; he then gave the name to one of his early students, Rinsai Sōji, who produced this delicate print in the style of his master. Sōri may have taken the name Hokusai when Hokusai changed his name again, to Taito, around 1810, and may have designed *surimono* that are now attributed to Hokusai.[1] Artists often changed their names as their life situations changed (see, for example, plate 33), though Hokusai changed his more often than most.

This is the earliest of a large group of *surimono* in the Skinner Collection. *Surimono* were privately issued woodblock prints commissioned to commemorate particular events, a poetry-composing party, for example, or the performance of a favorite Kabuki actor. *Surimono* often celebrated New Year events, and kites were therefore a common *surimono* subject. Motifs that indicated the long and short months of the coming year were also favorite *surimono* subjects. These pictorial calendars, known as *egoyomi,* were useful, as the long (thirty days) or short (twenty-nine days) months chosen to accommodate the vagaries of the lunar calendar were different each year. The decision regarding which months were long or short belonged to the government, who licensed the sale of calendars; privately issued calendar prints such as this were technically illegal. Artists therefore subtly concealed the different months within their designs, their ingenuity being one measure of the success of the print.

Here the short months are indicated by numbers on the auspicious paper slips dangling from the six cranes that make up a multiple branch-train kite being flown by a handsome young man. Symbols of immortality, cranes are said to bring good fortune and are associated with New Year; they are related to Mount Hōrai, Island of the Immortals, and pine trees, also New Year symbols of longevity. Branch-train kites are aerodynamically challenging, and much more difficult to fly than single-train kites, such as the traditional centipede kite of China, made up of an arrangement of separate disks, one after the other (a related Japanese example is shown in plate 47). Another Japanese branch-train kite is shown in the background of plate 33.

One of the young men's attendants, who has the shaved topknot of a young boy, holds a kite bearing the characters *mizunoto inoshishi,* tenth calendar-sign boar, indicating that this is the last year of a sixty-year cycle, the year of the Boar, equivalent to 1803. The sign on the *torii* temple gateway to the left reads Tomita, perhaps the name of the man who commissioned the print. The figure seated by the gateway is probably Fukusuke, a legendary large-headed dwarf who tells stories and is a symbol of good luck.

Surimono are normally small-format and finely printed on soft, high-quality paper. They were made to high printing standards and, because they were usually issued in small numbers, the blocks rarely became worn down. The lines of this print are extremely delicate, with expensive additions such as touches of metallic pigment, color grading on the riverbank, and subtle embossing indicating the waves of the river and the line on the spool. The vigorous young pine shoots on the ridge (rather than the twisted pine to the right of the design) suggest New Year, as does the battledore design on the robe of the young man flying the kite. The whole adds up to a thoughtful visual game that would have pleased the cultivated recipients of the prints.

1. Keyes 1985, 217, 376.

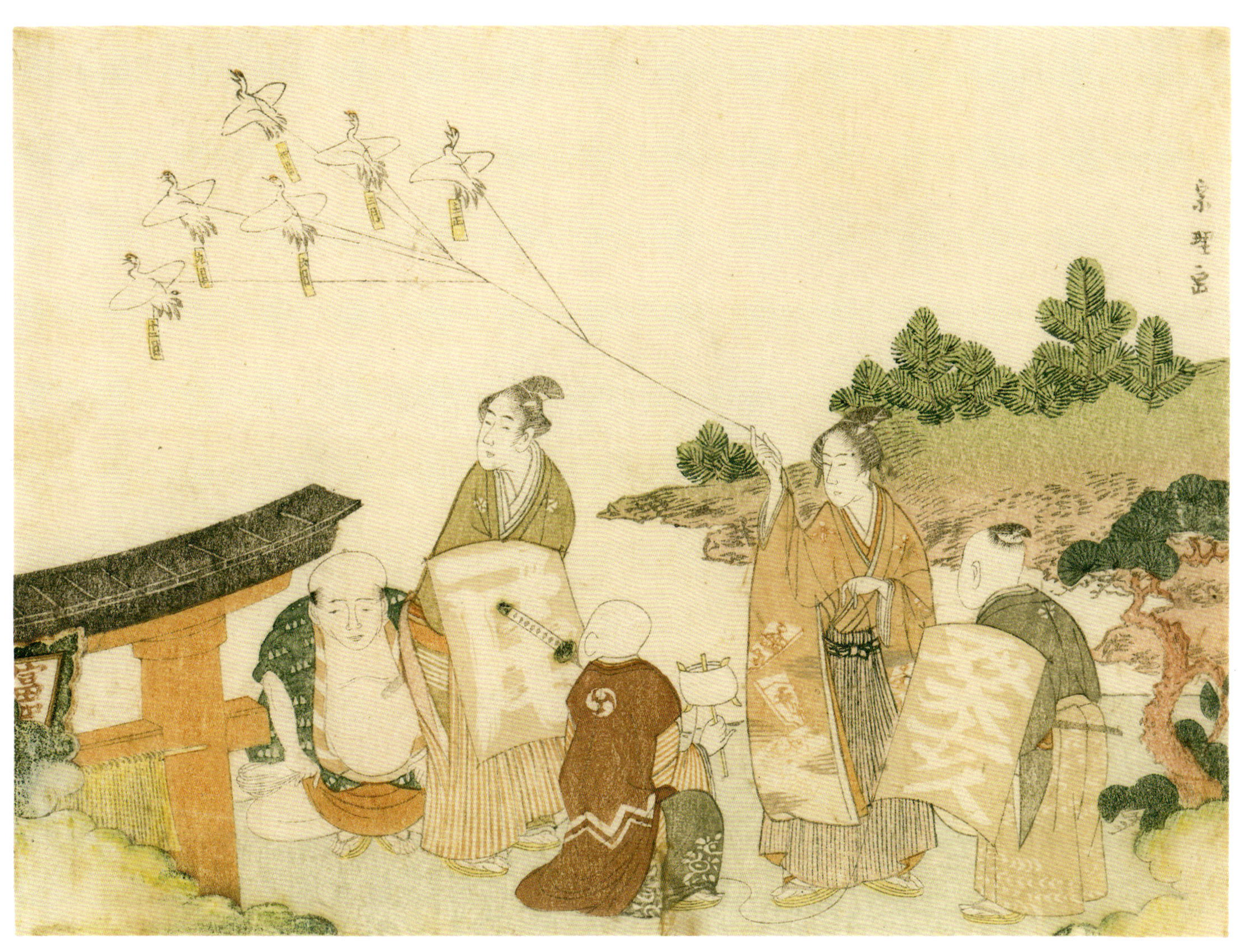

8

Kites and Cherry Blossom
Teisai Hokuba (1771–1844)
signed: *Hokuba ga*
c. 1802
surimono chūban yoko-e (20.3 × 26.7 cm)

Two rectangular kites are presented on a flowering cherry branch. Above them are three poems written in the cursive script favored on *surimono.* The first is a *kyōka,* a form of irreverent verse associated with poetry parties; the major characteristic of *kyōka,* which means crazy poem, was punning or allusion. The other two are *senryū,* comic equivalents of *haikai* or *haiku.* Composing such verses was more than simply a form of amusement: an extensive knowledge of classical literature was required, and it was considered a proof of education and elegant accomplishment by the samurai and educated merchants who practiced it.

This impression is very faded but beautifully printed, with delicately carved lines of verse. Cherry blossoms have been blind-embossed into the thick paper; the small dark marks are the stalks of the unpigmented blossoms. The design immortalizes the taking of a new name by a man who will from henceforth be known as Kimba (Golden Horse) to his friends, and is filled with the visual and verbal play that delighted the literate elite of the capital.

The first poem is signed Danshūrō Emba (1743–1822), who was a close friend of the preeminent actor of his day, Ichikawa Danjūrō V (1741–1806). It is introduced by a phrase that can mean, "On the occasion of the taking of the name Kimba by the young man who studies ridiculous jokes." The poem reads,

ikanobori	like a kite
nodokeki haruno	on this peaceful spring day
ito omouni	I'm thinking that—
soragoto nagara	although it's altogether an empty business—
na o ageyo kashi	your name will rise high in the sky

There are puns on the sounds *ito,* which can mean both "string" and "very much," and *sora,* meaning both "sky" and "empty."

The second poem, signed by Danshirō Kimba of the new name, is also introduced by a *kotobagaki,* explanation:

shokunshi no	to the assembled illustrious people
otoritake ni	I am thankful for my good fortune
adzukaru koto o	in receiving such patronage

The poem reads,

arigataki	blessed by
megumiya kaze no	a gracious wind
ikanobori	my kite flies high

The third poem is introduced by a phrase meaning, "Offering congratulations on a name change." It reads,

senkin no . . .	taking a young horse
. . . kane no koma o	worth a thousand pieces of gold
zakuragari	to a cherry-viewing party

The poem is signed Ichikawa Hakuen, the name used by Danjūrō V after 1796. The reference to a thousand gold pieces echoes a wish for a prosperous New Year in the words *senkin no haru,* a spring worth a thousand gold pieces, taken from a Song-dynasty Chinese poem (see plate 46; the first day of the New Year was considered the first day of spring).

Danjūrō V's face appears on the kite to the right; contemporaries would have recognized him especially by his long, sharp nose. His little *yamabushi* hat and bird-feather fan identify his role as the king of the *tengu* (mythological birdlike creatures) of Mount Kurama; he wears bold *kumadori* makeup. He had technically retired in 1796, so this depiction of him does not represent a current role.

His companion in the design is young Kimba, identified by the character for gold, *kin,* on his sleeve inside the three concentric squares that formed the crest of the Danjūrō line of actors. The young man may be Danjūrō's grandson, who went on to become the greatest actor of late Edo, Ichikawa Danjūrō VII (1791–1859). In Japanese folklore, the old *tengu* king taught martial-arts secrets to the young hero Yoshitsune on Mount Kurama, enabling him to jump and move like a bird and outwit his opponents. Presumably the scroll that Kimba

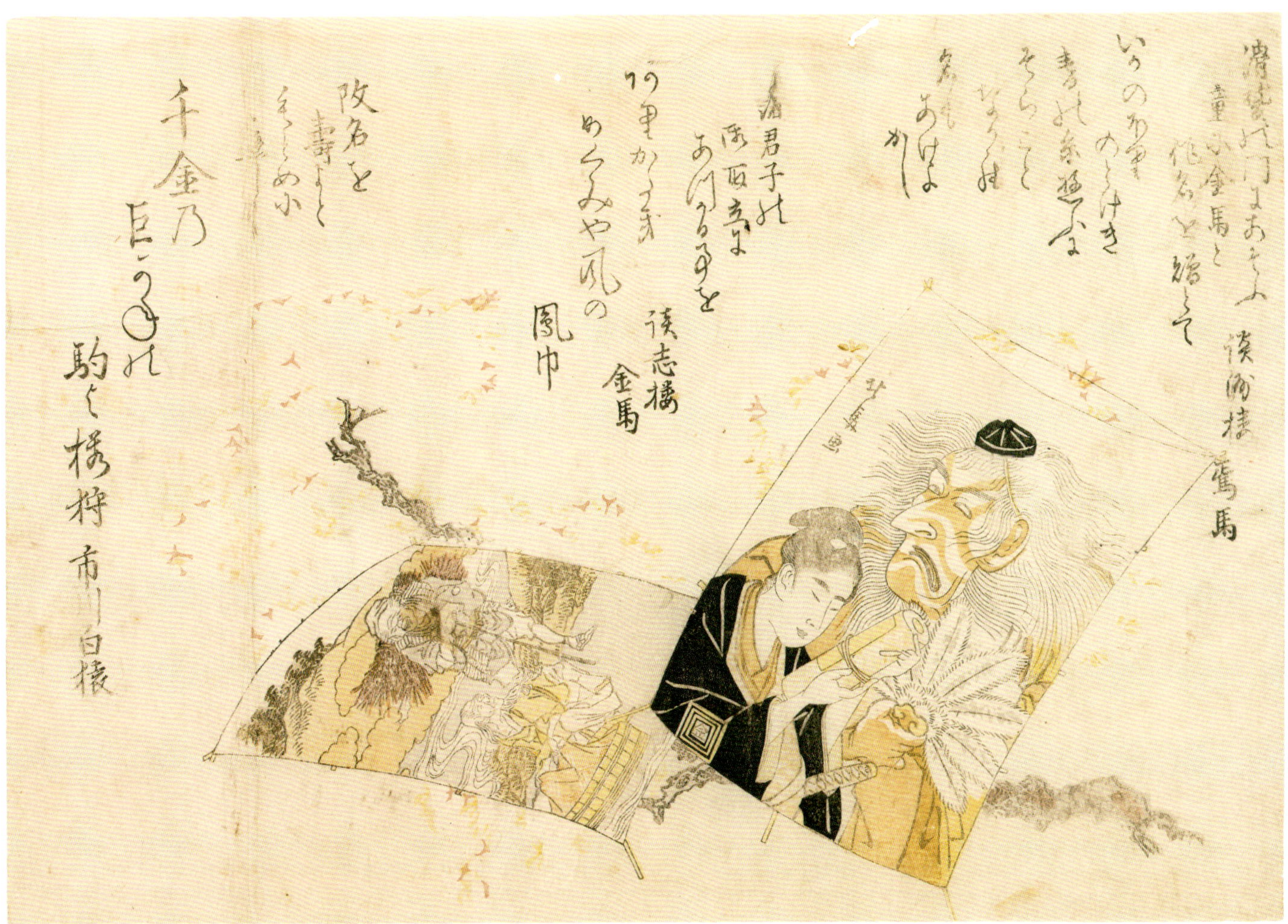

is receiving contains secrets of similar import. The older actor is taking the youth under his birdlike wing.

The allusions continue with the second kite, which shows an episode from the story of Momotarō, a magical child found by an old couple inside a peach. This is probably an allusion to a second name for Kimba's patron, Danshūrō Emba, who wrote the first poem and was known as Momokuri Sanju, meaning resident of the mountain of chestnuts and peaches; the print doubtless also contains more complex wordplay. Danshūrō Emba enjoyed a great reputation as an author, *kyōka* poet, and professional storyteller. He was adopted by the Ichikawa clan as Danjūrō V's half-brother and greatly assisted the young Danjūrō VII's career.

The artist Hokuba has signed his name on the kite with the design of the *tengu* king. Hokuba was an inactive retainer of the shogun and was an early student of Hokusai. Later in life he took religious orders. Hokuba has either anticipated the cherry blossoms, creating the design before the event to be presented to the guests, or made it afterward, as a souvenir of a great party. We can imagine the scene: on a fresh, sunny, early-spring day, a group of talented friends drink wine under the cherry blossoms, inspired by the breezes to write of kites rising into the sky. The presence of Danjūrō V, the leading actor of the day, indicates a group at the apex of cultured Edo society. Besides being a beautiful design, this small print is an important piece of Kabuki as well as print and kite history.

9

Ōhara Girl with Fallen Kite
Katsushika Hokusai (1760–1849)
signed: *Hokusai ga*
c. 1810
surimono shikishiban (21.4 × 17.6 cm)

A young woman carrying firewood on her head raises her hand to her mouth in surprise as a small *yakko* kite falls on her load. There is a hint, perhaps, at a popular song that compared the line of a fallen kite entwined around a beautiful girl with the entanglements of love (see plate 17). Several other prints here have the same theme; in plates 32, 33, and 35, for example, the motif has romantic overtones, though plates 66 and 87 are less kind.

The girl's clothing, especially her armbands, *tekkō,* indicate that she is an *Ōharame,* woman of Ōhara, a village north of Kyoto. Country women from the villages of Ōhara and Yase would bring firewood to sell in the city. Often their load was adorned with wildflowers and carried on their heads, and they became a picturesque subject for Shijō-school painters in the eighteenth and nineteenth centuries.[1] This girl's clothes are far too fine for the countryside, but the conceit was perfectly acceptable and typical of the optimistic, idealized world depicted in *ukiyo-e* prints and paintings. The right leg of the *yakko* is doubled behind him, showing how the legs on these kites had no bamboo framing to make them rigid but dangled loosely, functioning as tails.

The poem reads,

hatsugasumi	in the early morning haze
tateba surarito	she stands tall
yanagigoshi	with willow hips
shinayoki huri no	this slender good-looking
Ōharame	Ōhara girl

From about 1796 to 1810 Hokusai produced many *surimono* in long horizontal formats. These include a horizontal-format *egoyomi* of several Ōhara women loading charcoal onto oxen that dates from 1805, an Ox Year.[2] The combination of Hokusai's signature here with the print's squarish format suggests a date of about 1810.

1. Clark 1992, 162.
2. Illustrated in Keyes 1985, 214.

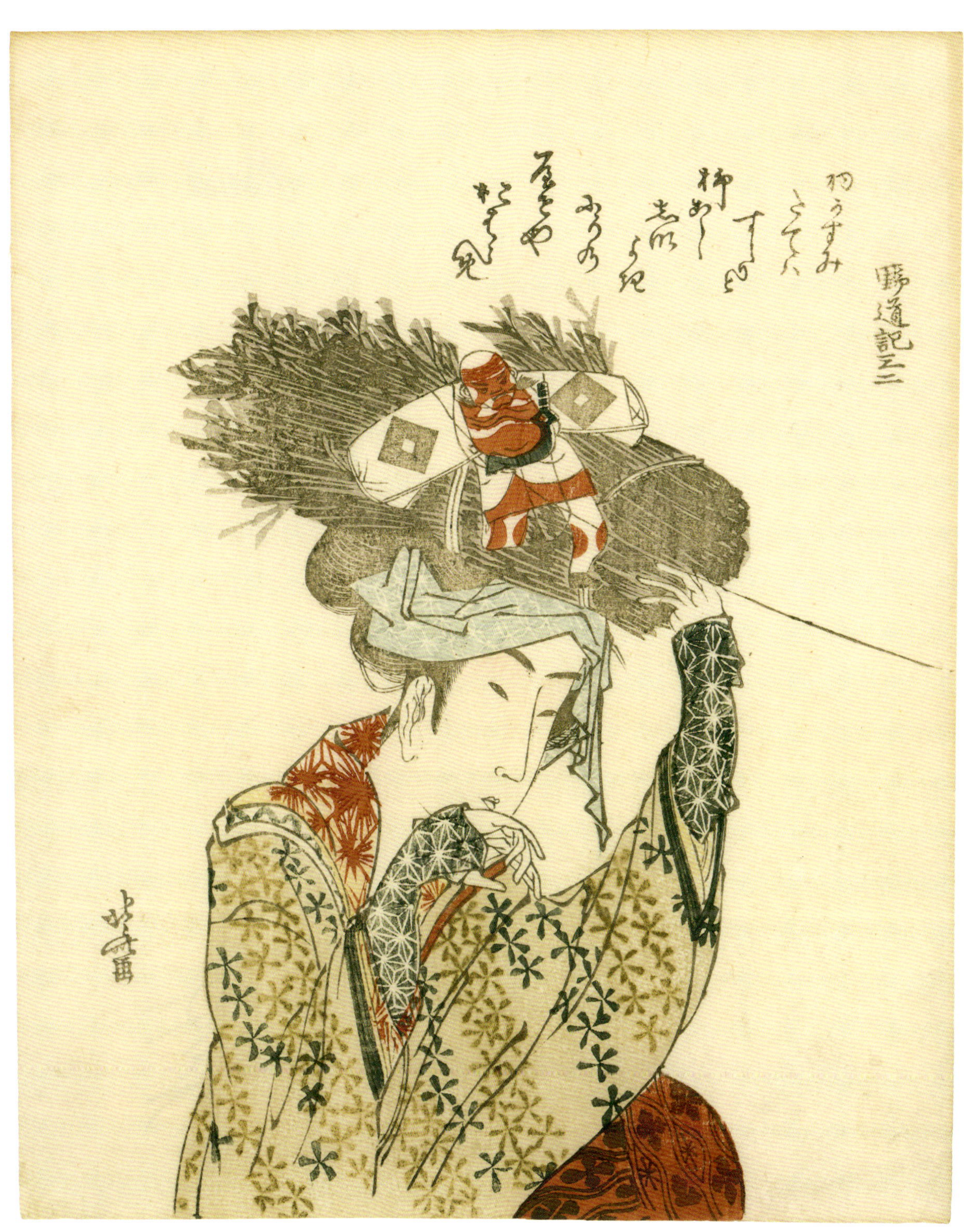

10

Boy Stringing New Year Kite
Ryūryūkyo Shinsai (active 1799–1823)
signed: *Ryūryūkyo Shinsai ga*
1808
surimono (13.3 × 18.5 cm)

A young boy happily strings his New Year kite. It bears the characters *kotobuki,* auspicious, and *fuku,* good luck. Behind him is a screen with a double-dragon surround, lightly embossed and printed with a metallic pigment. The characters on the screen talk of calming the five great dragons. The year just starting is clearly a Dragon Year. Shinsai's artist name, apparently derived from one of Hokusai's auxiliary names, means Dragon Studio.[1] It is possible that the patron of this print was a Buddhist dignitary: dragons were regarded as protectors of Buddhism, the boy's robe bears Buddhist swastikas, and the screen would be appropriate for a Buddhist temple. But the characters on the screen, *chin dai go ryū en* (if the last partially hidden character is *en*), also formed the name of a medicine, and this print may be a kind of advertisement.

To the left is a New Year construction, the approximate equivalent of a decorated Christmas tree; it includes young pine branches, bracken, and a round *mochi* ball made of pounded rice, arranged on a small lacquer table. The arrangement symbolized good fortune and was called *hōraidai,* Hōrai table, after Hōraizan, the Island of the Immortals.

The *kyōka,* crazy verses, read as follows:

odamaki no	extending from the reel
ito dashite tako	the kite string
kumo no to	reaches the clouds
. . . ni agaru	rising with
harukaze	the spring wind
aratama no	New Year
toshimotatsu chō	has come while
tatsu no mizu	dragon water
uchi watarai shi	spreads around
Suma no shimo	the frost of Suma
hokorika ni	those people who boast
mukashi banashi wo	about their exploits
suruhito e	of the past year
koremiyo ga shi no	should think about their pen names
haru no yutakasa	and the abundance of spring

The writer of the last poem signs himself Shinra Banshō, which means All Things in Nature. This is a pen name of Morishima Chūryō (1754–1808), a famous scholar of Dutch (that is, foreign) studies, and a writer of novels as well as *kyōka* poetry. A gathering that included Chūryō would have been an elegant affair; his presence effectively dates this *surimono* to the Dragon Year of 1808.

1. Keyes 1985, 322.

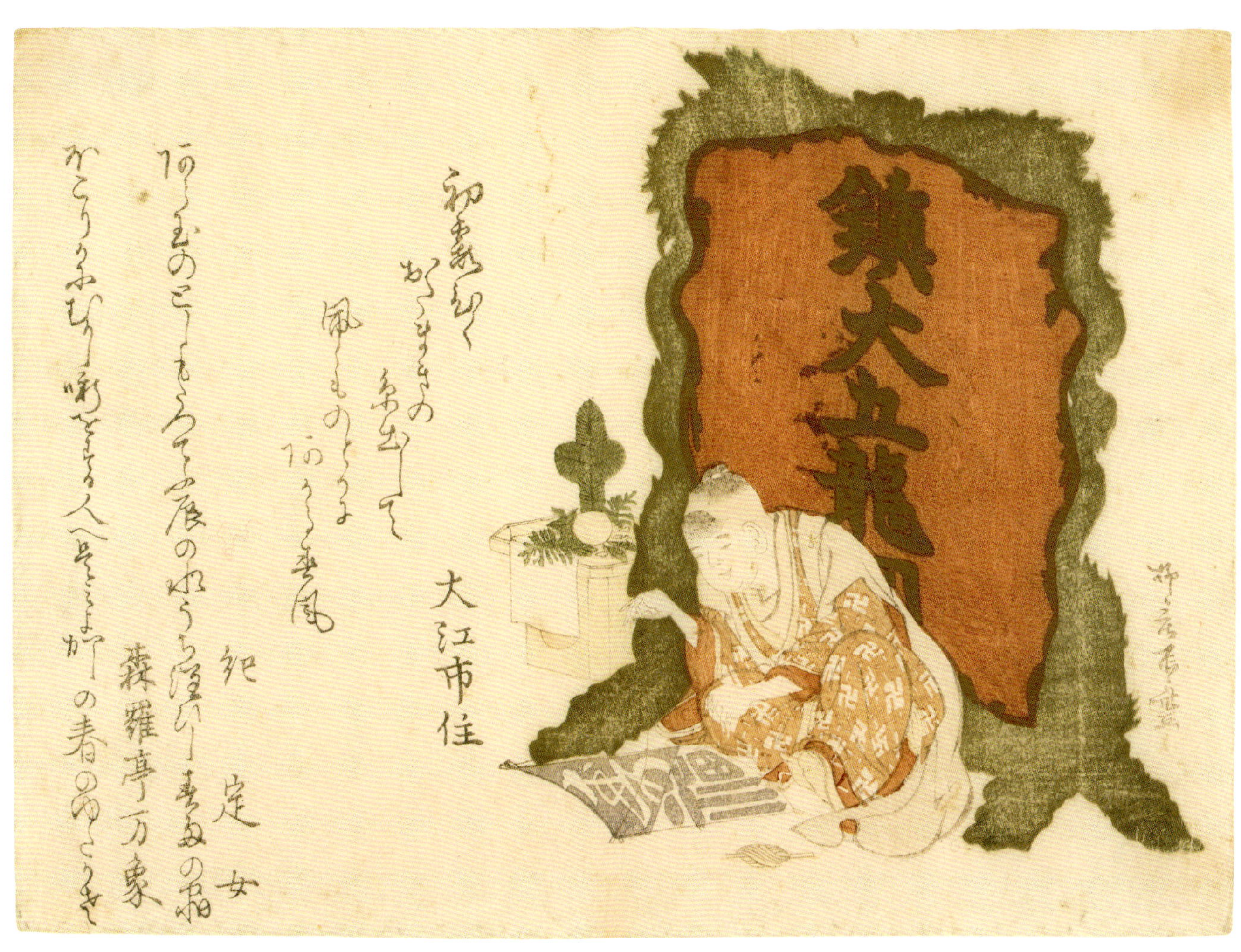
大江市住
定女
森羅亭万象

11

Kites, Hummer, and Inkstone
Ryūryūkyo Shinsai (active 1799–1823)
signed: *Shinsai*
1806 or 1818
surimono shikishiban (20.8 × 18.8 cm)

Shinsai was one of the first *surimono* artists to explore still-life images, a sophisticated development that allowed for allusions to a particular event rather than narrative descriptions. Contrast this and plate 16 with the several expansive Kabuki triptychs of Soga performances in this book. Yet the small-format *surimono,* with its balance and play between image and verses, often includes a vast amount of information.

Here a small *tobi* hawk kite, a larger rectangular kite, a hummer, and a spool of kite-line lie by an ornate inkstone in a lacquer case and a pair of scissors with a tassel. A pine-tree and pine-needle design on the sides of the inkstone are appropriate for New Year. The character on the kite reads *tora,* dating the print to the Tiger Year of either 1806 or 1818; the square format, which Shinsai used almost exclusively in his later work, suggests the latter.

A hummer is a taut bowed string attached to the top of a kite that hums loudly in the wind; it is used on kites throughout east Asia. If not made of string or thin bamboo, a hummer was often made of baleen or whalebone, when it was called *kujira unari,* roaring or howling whale. The first poem plays on the two radicals used to form the character for an orca, or killer whale, with the roar of a zodiacal tiger adding an element to the image. The poem reads:

ōdako no	the big kite's
kujira unariya	hummer
uo hen ni tora chō	a fish [radical] on the left
moji mo umi	and a tiger [radical] on the right
shachihoko	becomes a killer whale in the sea

Shachi is a killer whale and *shachihoko* was the name of the bronze sea-creature placed at roof-corners to protect against fire (see plate 76). The writer has signed himself Arigatei Kagenari, It's Thanks to You, a typically playful name of the kind beloved by *kyōka* poets.

The second poem reads:

medetasa wa	wherever you
izuku mo onaji	are celebrating
nengajō	the same New Year greetings card
senri o hashiru	is carried a thousand *ri*
tora no harukaze	wafted on the tiger's spring wind

The third poem reads:

haru no hi no	the spring sun
. . . yoshi	is fine
Narazumi no	the fragrance of Nara ink
nioi mo . . .	hovers
harukaze	in the spring breeze

Nara *sumi* is the highest quality of ink, and this poem may be a reference to *kakizome,* a celebration of the first calligraphy of the New Year, or *utahajime,* composing the first poem of the year, both possible occasions for the issuing of this print. Celebrations of the first poems of the year are still held in the Imperial Palace today, with commoners invited to join the ceremony as part of the great Japanese family.

The choice of a *tobi* kite with its hawk shape may echo the belief that dreaming of a hawk, Mount Fuji, or an eggplant on the first night of the New Year brought good luck throughout the following year.

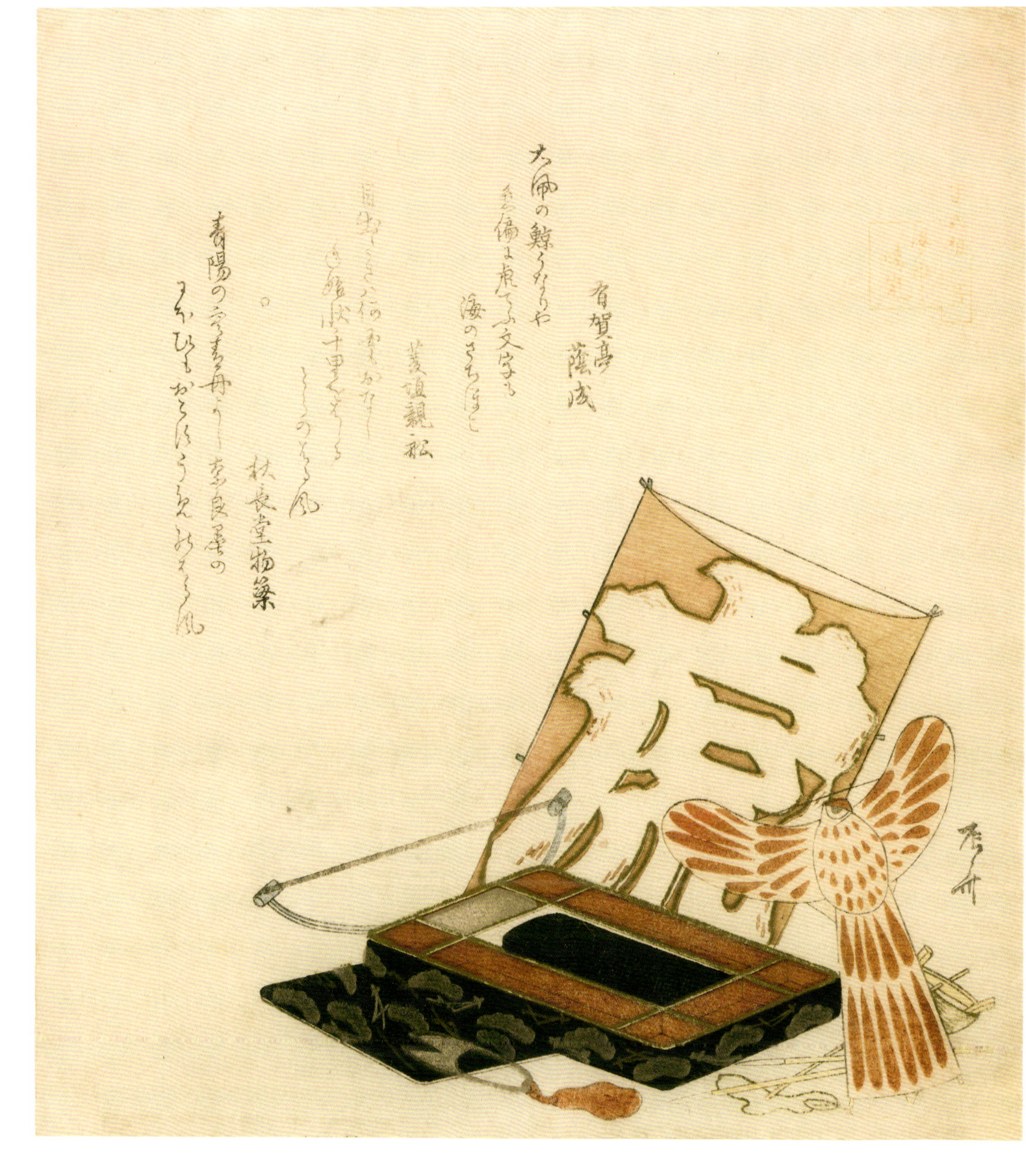

12

Kite with Ichikawa Danjūrō VII
Utagawa Kuniyasu (1794–1831)
signed: *Kuniyasu ga*
c. 1825
surimono shikishiban (20.7 × 18.7 cm)

A man with a single sword instead of the samurai's two confronts the face of the Kabuki actor Ichikawa Danjūrō VII painted on a large rectangular Edo kite. Danjūrō is wearing the heavy *kumadori* makeup of Gongorō, hero of the play *Shibaraku,* both role and play created by Ichikawa Danjūrō I in 1697. The play is named after Gongorō's theatrical shout of *shibaraku*—wait a moment!—as he sees lowlife about to attack townspeople in the street; this is considered probably the most dramatic moment in all of Kabuki. Besides his distinctive makeup, Danjūrō wears the large wig associated with the role and a robe with an outsized design of the Ichikawa clan's *mon* or crest, composed of three concentric squares representing wooden *masu,* rice-measures.

The poem to the right, by a man named Bunōsha Naoki, celebrates the actor in his red makeup:

beniguma no	to the auspiciously
hatsuhi medetaku	red-striped Ichikawa
Ichikawa ni	on the year's first day
. . . no kakaru tako	may a string of good fortune fall
no fukuito	like a long kite-string

Rather than represent Danjūrō directly, the artist shows his face painted on a kite, suggesting the heights to which his popularity rises. The lines are strong and the printing has left deep impressions in the soft paper. The design may have been created to honor Danjūrō before or after a particular performance of *Shibaraku.* The play was a classic example of *aragoto,* rough-style, acting and was traditionally part of the performances held in the eleventh month to open the Kabuki year, when a troupe introduced its team of actors for the new performance season.

The shaved head of the man with the single sword may identify him as Kashima Nyūdō Shinsai, the leader of the thugs, though nominally a priest,[1] that Gongorō accosts in the play. His robe has a multiple-gourd design. Dried gourds were used as containers and were associated with several auspicious sayings, for example, when something apparently impossible happens (such as a horse emerging from a gourd). Another story, however, about trying to catch a catfish in a gourd, suggests ineffectiveness, more appropriate for Gongorō's antagonist. A hollow gourd was used in the definition of the floating world of entertainment (page 8). The standard of one of the sixteenth-century military unifiers of Japan, Toyotomi Hideyoshi, featured a gourd design; Danjūrō VII wore a robe with a gourd design when he played a role alluding to Hideyoshi.

The Danjūrō line of actors dominated Kabuki and were adored by the theater-going public. Danjūrō VII was enormously successful until the government banished him from Edo for leading too luxurious a life. He recreated his brilliant career in Osaka and Kyoto, and was ultimately allowed to return to Edo. His many fan clubs constantly commissioned prints in his honor, and Danjūrō VII is celebrated in *surimono* more than any other actor.[2]

1. *Nyūdō,* meaning literally to enter the Way, is a word used to describe a lay priest.

2. Kuniyasu, who designed this print, was a pupil of Toyokuni and a younger colleague of Kunisada. He designed another *surimono* celebrating Danjūrō VII that is illustrated in Keyes 1985, page 27; a *surimono* of the actor in his dressing-room by Kunisada, who was a close friend of Danjūrō VII, is shown on page 279. Izzard 1993 illustrates many more designs of Danjūrō VII by Kunisada. Bowie 1979 illustrates a large number of *surimono* showing Danjūrō VII and his forebears in *aragoto* roles by a number of different artists (pages 16–23, 54–55, 102–14), including one designed by the multitalented actor himself.

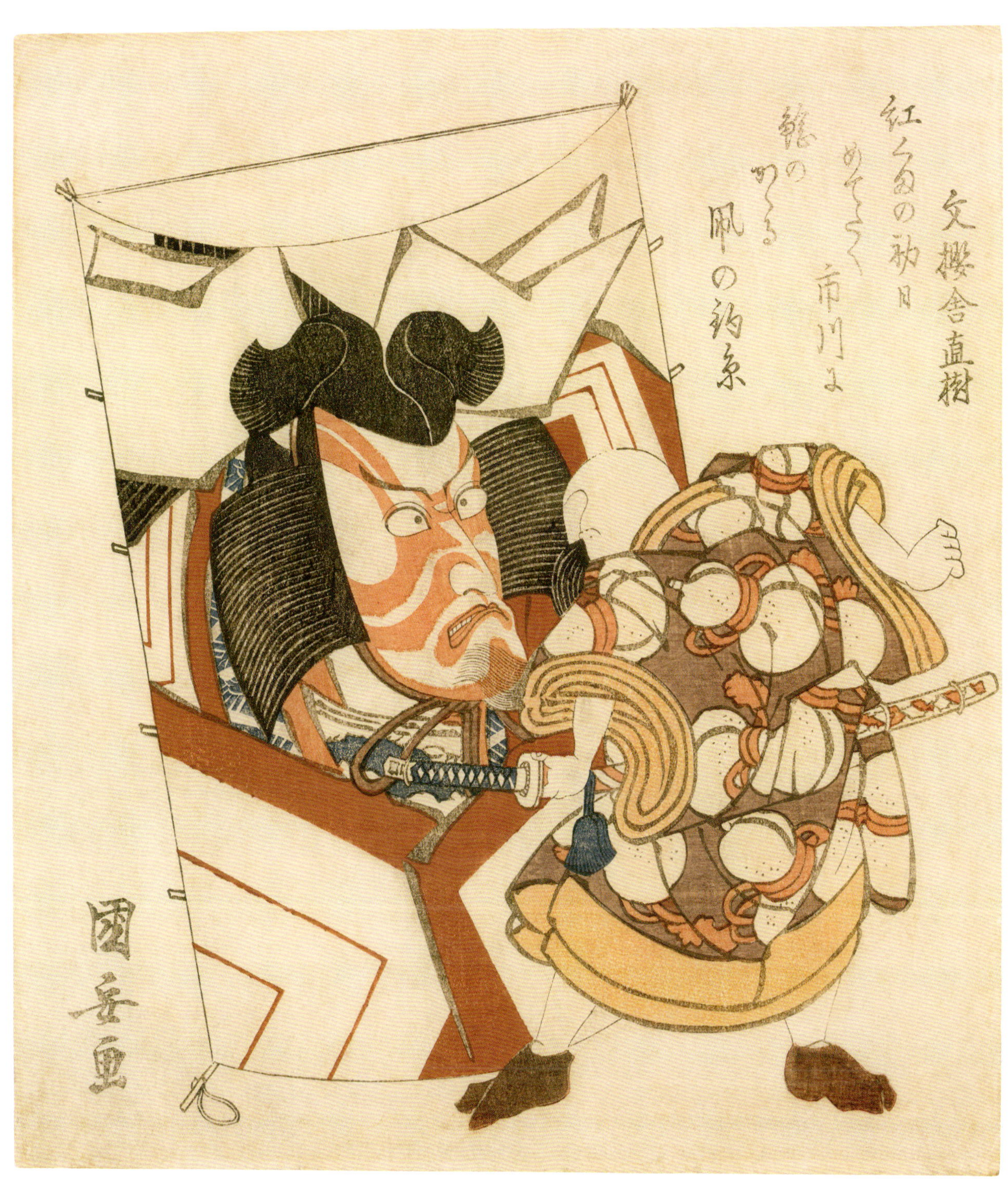
文櫻舎直樹
紅白の初日めでたく市川よ
錦のかゝる凧の釣糸
国安画

13

The Hero Raikō with Shutendōji Kite
Toyota Hokkei (1780–1850)
signed: *Hokkei ga*
c. 1830
surimono shikishiban (21.4 × 18.6 cm)

The tenth-century hero Minamoto no Yorimitsu, known as Raikō, strikes a pose in full armor and with drawn sword. Behind him is a kite bearing the image of one of his many famous adversaries, the giant demon Shutendōji (Drunken Boy), whom he killed with the help of his four retainers. A version of the Shutendōji story was performed each New Year at the Nakamura Theater in Edo; an advertisement for the performance appears in the lively theater-district scene in figure 3 of the Introduction.

The plots of many Kabuki plays and the popular literature of the first decades of the nineteenth century included much violence and horror—lurid ghost stories were especially popular—and this violence is reflected in many woodblock prints of the period. *Surimono,* however, were restrained in their choice and illustration of subjects; the occasion for a *surimono* was usually auspicious, and the direct depiction of a violent scene would not have been appropriate. Here the giant demon, who kidnapped young women and ate his neighbors, is distanced and tamed as a decoration on a boy's kite. The poem also is serene:

sora made ni	a demon kite trails its line
ito yarau oni no	so high in the sky
ikanobori	that even young eyes
wakayagu me ni mo	lose sight of it
miezu kasumeri	in the mist

Nonetheless, this is a powerful and unusual design for a *surimono.* The colors are strong, with a successful frisson between the green and rust-red. Prints in different states exist, suggesting that there was demand for more than one printing and that the design's popularity went beyond its initial publication.[1]

Besides the allusion to a New Year Shutendōji performance and the New Year kite itself, the theme of a defeated demon suggests the *setsubun* ceremony of the last day of the lunar year, when households exorcised evil spirits by throwing beans and shouting, *fuku wa uchi oni wa soto,* good luck in, demons out!

1. An impression with more lines in the demon's curly hair is discussed and the poem translated in Mirviss 1995, plate 21.

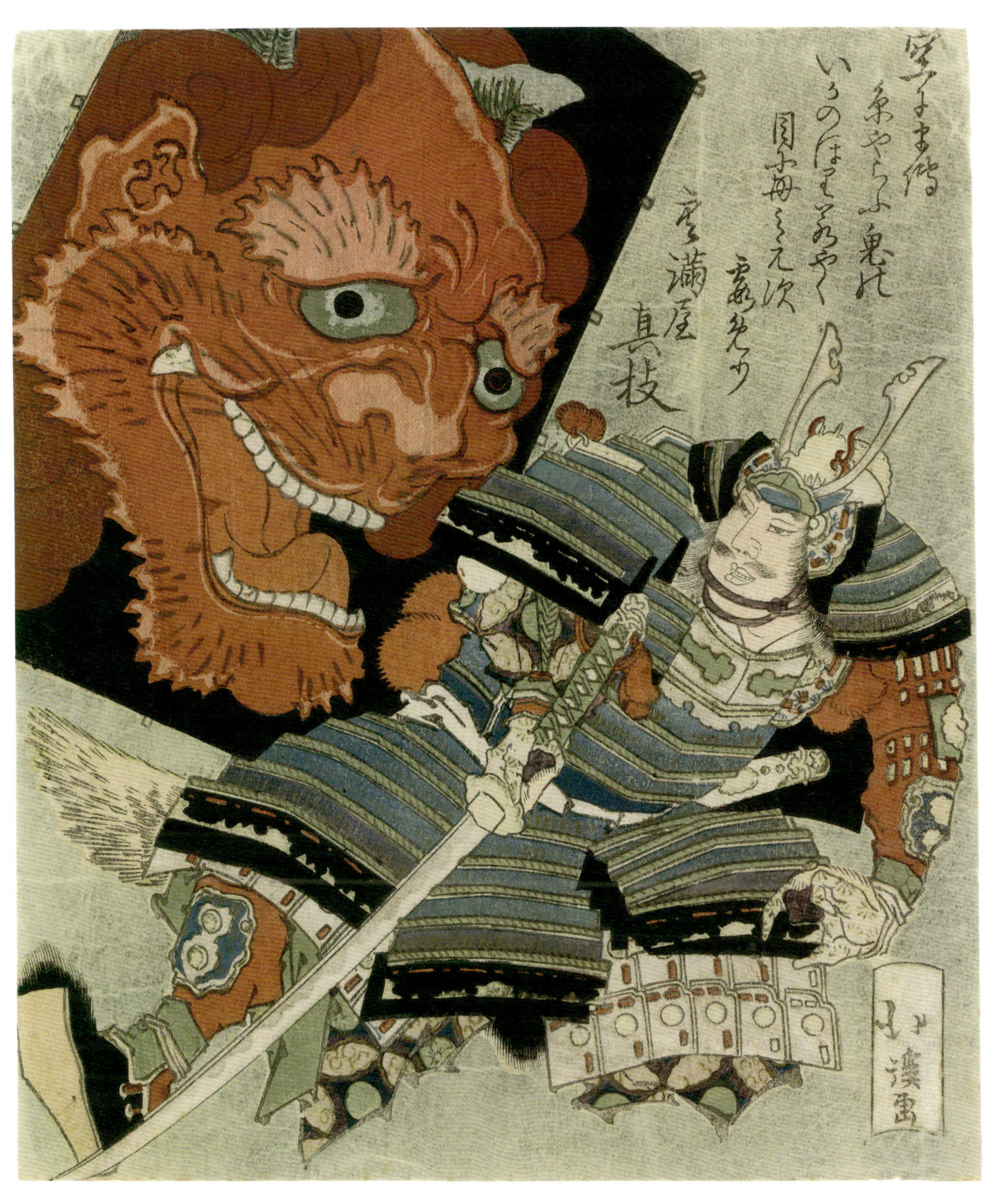

14

Woman with Servant and Danjūrō Kite
Toyota Hokkei (1780–1850)
signed: *Hokkei*
c. 1820
surimono shikishiban (20.8 × 18.5 cm)

A well-dressed woman walks along a riverbank toward a temple. She has bare feet and a geisha's elaborate coiffure.[1] Her servant carries her necessities over his shoulders and holds a kite with the face of Ichikawa Danjūrō VII, painted with the same fierce makeup, wig, and robes that he wore for the *Shibaraku* role of plate 12. The cloth over the man's forearm repeats the square *mon* that the actor wears on his robe, and it is likely that this print was composed in honor of Danjūrō.

The *kyōka* poems read:

uruwashiki	the woman on a pilgrimage
onnareisha no	has a beautiful
Fujibitai	widow's peak
susonoatarino	the bottom of her kimono
komadome no ishi	brushes against the Horse-tie Stone

yukitayou	I wish that
hito no kokoro no	I could tether his heart
komadome to	to the Horse-tie Stone
ishi mo ugokano	so it would not move
miyo no hatsuharu	this New Year

The Horse-tie Stone was a rock near the Mimeguri Shrine by the Sumida River, marking the spot where the Heian general Minamoto no Yoshiie dismounted on his return from a military campaign in Ōshu. Across the river was the Komagatadō Shrine, dedicated to a horse-headed form of Kannon, Buddhist deity of compassion. The woman in the print may be headed toward either sacred place. The ferry at Komagatadō, on the hour-long route from Edo to the Yoshiwara, is associated with a courtesan named Takao, who wrote a famous poem imagining her recently departed lover reaching the ferry. This association gives a lightly romantic air to the print, as does, perhaps, a vague identification of the woman's lover with a stallion. The allusions conjured up by the verses and imagery of *surimono* were often very distant, but appreciated none the less for that.

The Japanese term for the woman's hairline with its allusion to Mount Fuji uses imagery similar to the English "widow's peak." A silvery pigment (probably tin) has been used for the stripes of her kimono. The gray shapes along the riverbank are mooring posts for boats.

Hokkei was an early pupil of Hokusai and also collaborated with the artist Shumman. After Shumman's death in 1820, Hokkei became the most refined designer of *surimono;* here he follows Shumman's style in the face and curious stooped pose of the servant. The spiral mark of the Fundarika poetry group appears in the top right corner of the print and on the cloth wrapper for the load that the servant carries on his shoulders.[2]

1. Keyes 1985, 139, illustrates an *egoyomi* by the same artist with a similar subject, a geisha by a wayside shrine looking over her shoulder at a servant, who holds a rectangular kite and carries a cloth-covered load on his shoulders. That design was produced for the Gogawa poetry circle; see the next entry.

2. Another *surimono* that Hokkei designed for the Fundarika poetry group is illustrated in Keyes 1985, 186.

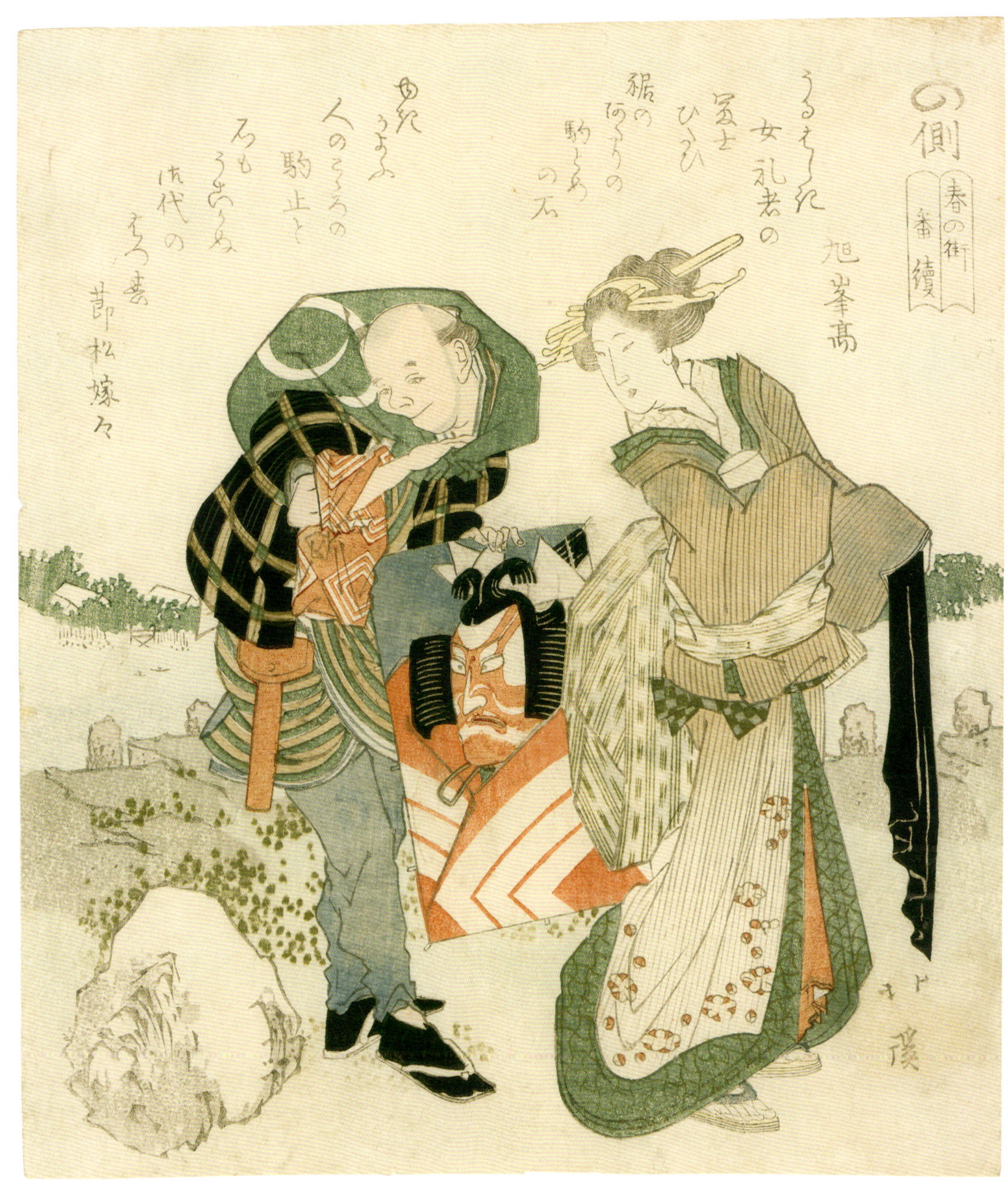

15

Saigyō and Two Boys with a Kite
Toyota Hokkei (1780–1850)
unsigned
original c. 1820 (this may be a reprint of c. 1890)
surimono shikishiban (21.1 × 18.4 cm)

Hokkei often followed the style of his teacher, Hokusai, as he does here in the faces of the boys and the old man. The old man wears priest's clothes and carries a traveling basket and wide straw rain-hat on his back. He is Saigyō (1118–1190), a priest and poet who rambled through the provinces during the late-Heian civil wars. After Yoritomo had defeated the Taira, Saigyō visited him in Kamakura and spent all one night talking with him and composing poems. Yoritomo was extremely impressed with his wisdom and gave him an expensive gift, a cat made of silver. So removed from worldly values was Saigyō that he abstractedly gave it away to some boys playing in the moat as he left Yoritomo's castle. He died soon after at the age of seventy-three.

The poem is narrative:

saku sakura no	under blooming cherry blossoms
Kamakura wo aruku	Saigyō
Saigyō	walks in Kamakura
te ni kiyuru yuki no	holding in his hand
shirogane no neko	a silver-white cat

The character on the kite reads *uguisu,* bush warbler, a bird associated with plum blossom, the first flower to blossom at New Year. The young pine saplings to the right also suggest New Year. There is no plum blossom in the image, but the blossoms of the poem and the character on the kite evoke a feeling similar to the saying "the first robins of spring" (an example of meaning emerging from meaningless phrases, like an English slogan on a Japanese T-shirt).

Hokkei designed this print for the Gogawa, the Group of Five poetry circle, which was dedicated to praising the Danjūrō acting clan. A stylized form of the number five, which looks like an hourglass, in the top right corner of the print represents the group's emblem; it is repeated in a metallic pigment on the robe of one of the boys. As one of the largest *kyōka* circles, with maybe three thousand members around the country, the Gogawa commissioned a great many *surimono* bearing this emblem. The square underneath looks like the character for a well, and also a wooden measuring cup, the basis of Danjūrō's famous crest, also used as a saké drinking cup.

The paper for this exquisitely produced print has a slight hardness, indicating that it was probably made in the Meiji period. The high quality of printing suggests a group of reprints made in Akashi, near Kobe, in the early 1890s.[1]

1. Keyes 1985, 509–21, discusses Meiji copies of early-nineteenth-century *surimono.*

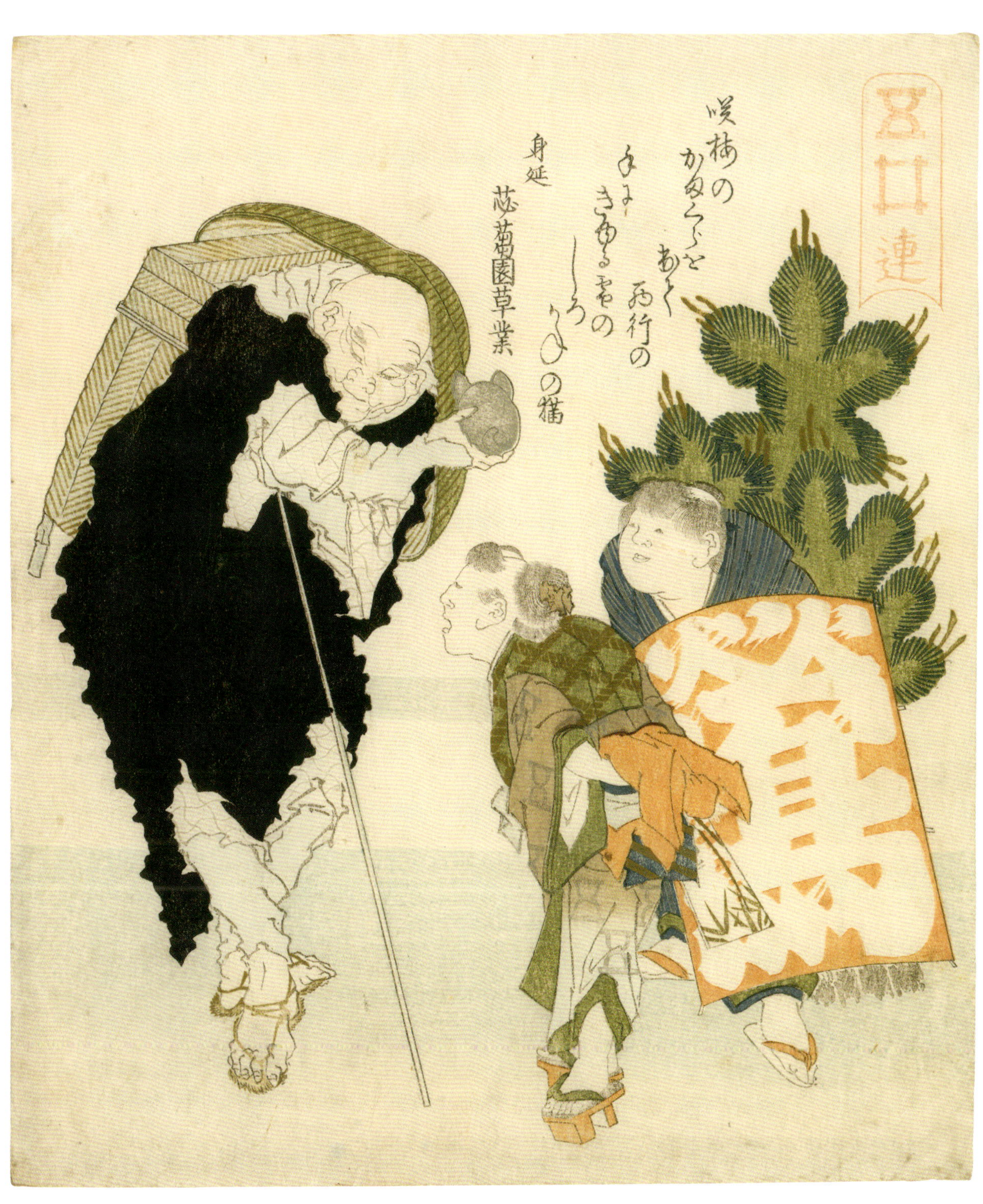

16

Still Life with Two Bird-shaped Kites
Toyota Hokkei (1780–1850)
signed: *Hokkei*
c. 1828
surimono shikishiban (18.5 × 17.2 cm)

This compact still life is simplified almost to abstraction. Two bird-shaped kites are presented as silhouetted forms in restrained colors and with no textural detail. The foreground is subtly graded. The delicate colors are the theme of the verse at upper left written by a poet called Shunyūtei Umeaki:

saohime no	The spring princess
kasumi no koromo ni	her robes of hazy mists
karasudako	compete in color
sometezo haru no	with crow-kites
kiso hajimenari	shaded by spring.[1]

The first phonetic character of the artist's name is cut out of the winding board for the line of one of the kites; the line has been deeply impressed into the paper with a metallic pigment.

Hokkei originally made a living as a fishmonger, but the high quality of his *surimono* and privately published book designs enabled him to become a full-time artist. He studied with Hokusai and collaborated with him on several of his *Manga* volumes. In Hokkei's early *surimono,* the two sides of the first character of his name are about the same length; in the 1820s, the left side of the signature became dramatically longer, as here.

1. An impression with a different seal under the artist's signature is illustrated and the poem translated in van Rappard-Boon 2000, 98.

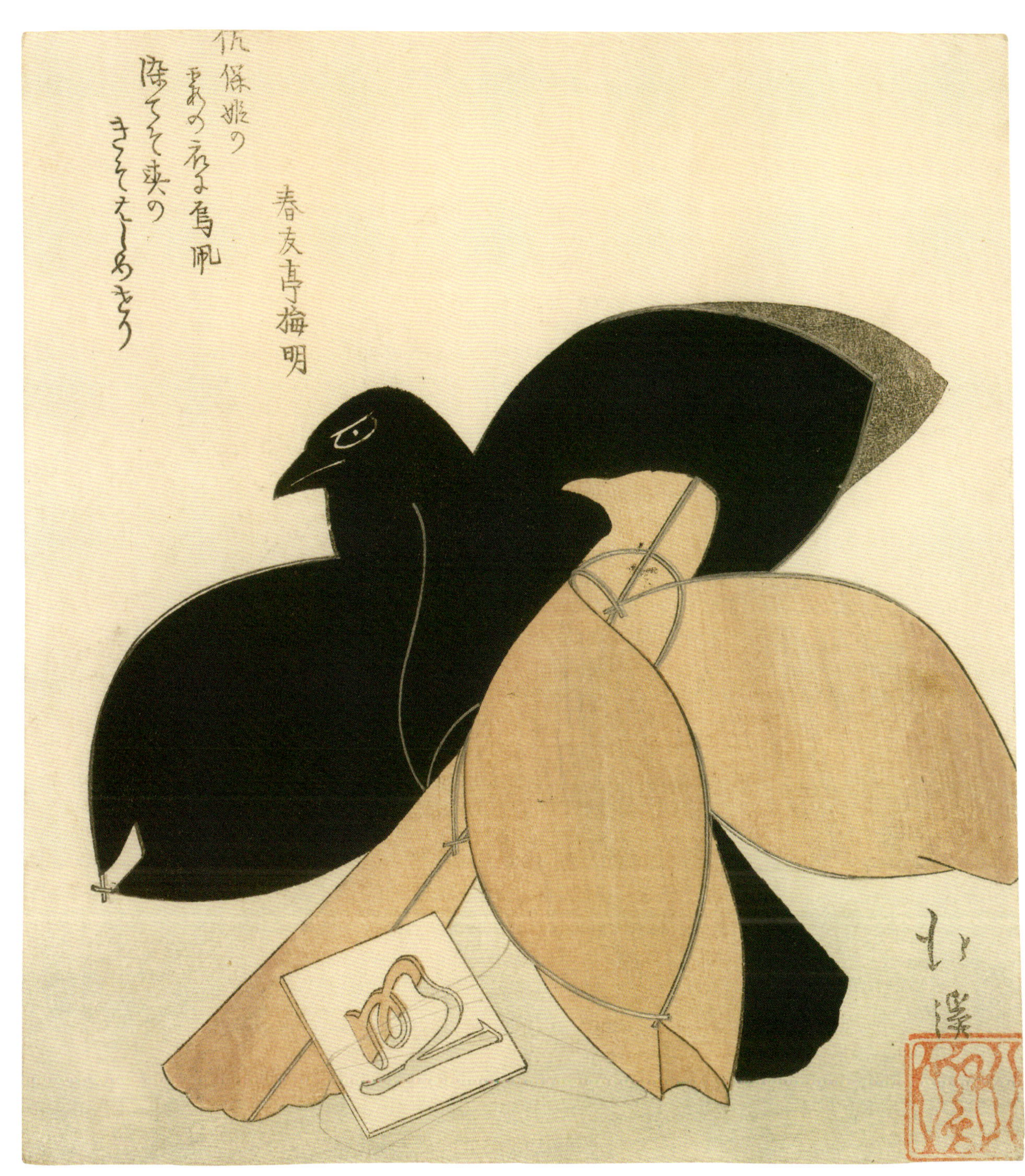
春友亭梅明

17

Geisha with *Yakko* Kite
Toyota Hokkei (1780–1850)
signed: *Go Hokkei*
c. 1830
surimono shikishiban (20.6 × 17.7 cm)

A geisha is returning in her high *geta* from the Yanagiyu, Willow Bathhouse, a towel draped over her shoulder. A *yakko* kite has fallen out of the sky and entwined itself around her, echoing a poem and popular song that compares the string of a fallen kite with the entanglements of love (see plates 32 and 35). She looks down at it in surprise. Rather than a printed black line, the string of the kite is subtly indicated by an uncolored impressed line that reaches round her back.

Yakko were not considered the brightest of men, and were traditionally easily swayed by a woman's charms. The girl here is hitching up her robe, and the conceit may be that this *yakko* has seen her white leg, lost control of himself, and fallen out of the sky. This would have been a parallel with the comic story of Kume no Sennin (a *sennin* was an Immortal who gained supernatural powers through ascetic practices). Flying over the river of his hometown one day, he saw a girl washing clothes by treading on them with sexy bare feet and legs, and similarly lost control. The humor lay in the contradiction between the Immortal's asceticism and his sudden contrary *sartori.*

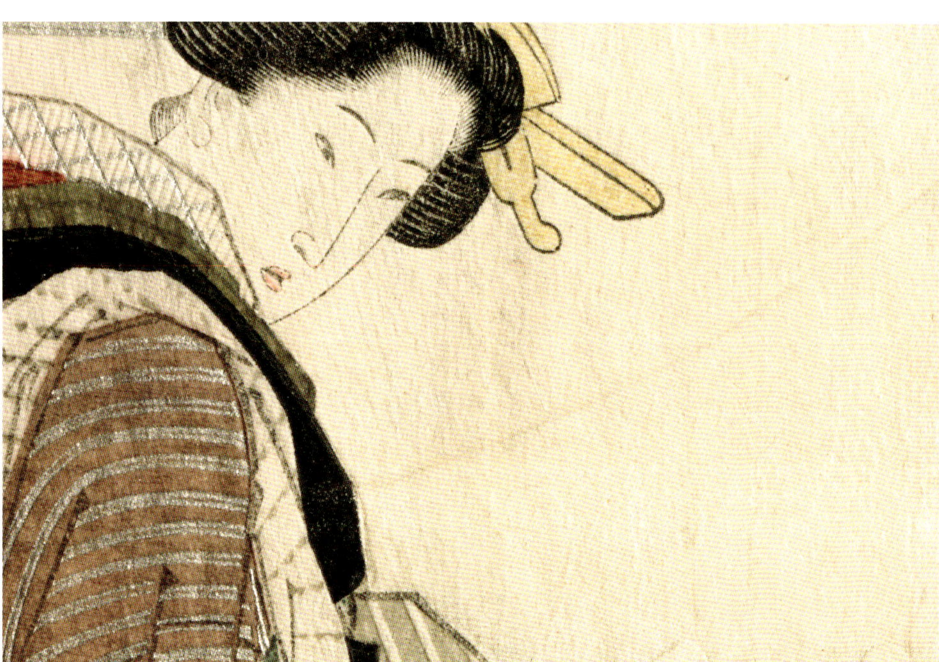

Slender willow branches trail in the colored band to the right of the print. The entertainment network of brothels, teahouses, and houses of assignation was often called the flower-and-willow world. To the upper left is the bathhouse's *noren,* the cloth that hung in an entranceway, decorated with a willow-branch design.

The poet has signed himself Senryūtei Ichiyō, meaning A Thousand Willows One Leaf. His poem reads:

oshiroi no	the smell of her snow-white powder
yuki otoshite	is washed away
suzukaze ni	in a cool breeze
keburu yanagi ya	a willow tree spreads its branches over
yuagari no imo	my love just out of the bath

Suzukaze is a pivot word combining the meaning of a cool breeze with the fresh sound of a wind-chime. There is also a mild pun in the poet's name with the words *karyū,* pleasure quarters, and *senryū,* popular poems. The design's sensual overtones include the bath's hot water and the girl's newly washed skin, and there is a suggestion that without her makeup she is unprotected and open, showing her real self. She smells as fresh as a willow tree.

The left half of the upper character of the signature has the distinct elongation that Hokkei affected from the mid-1820s to the '30s.

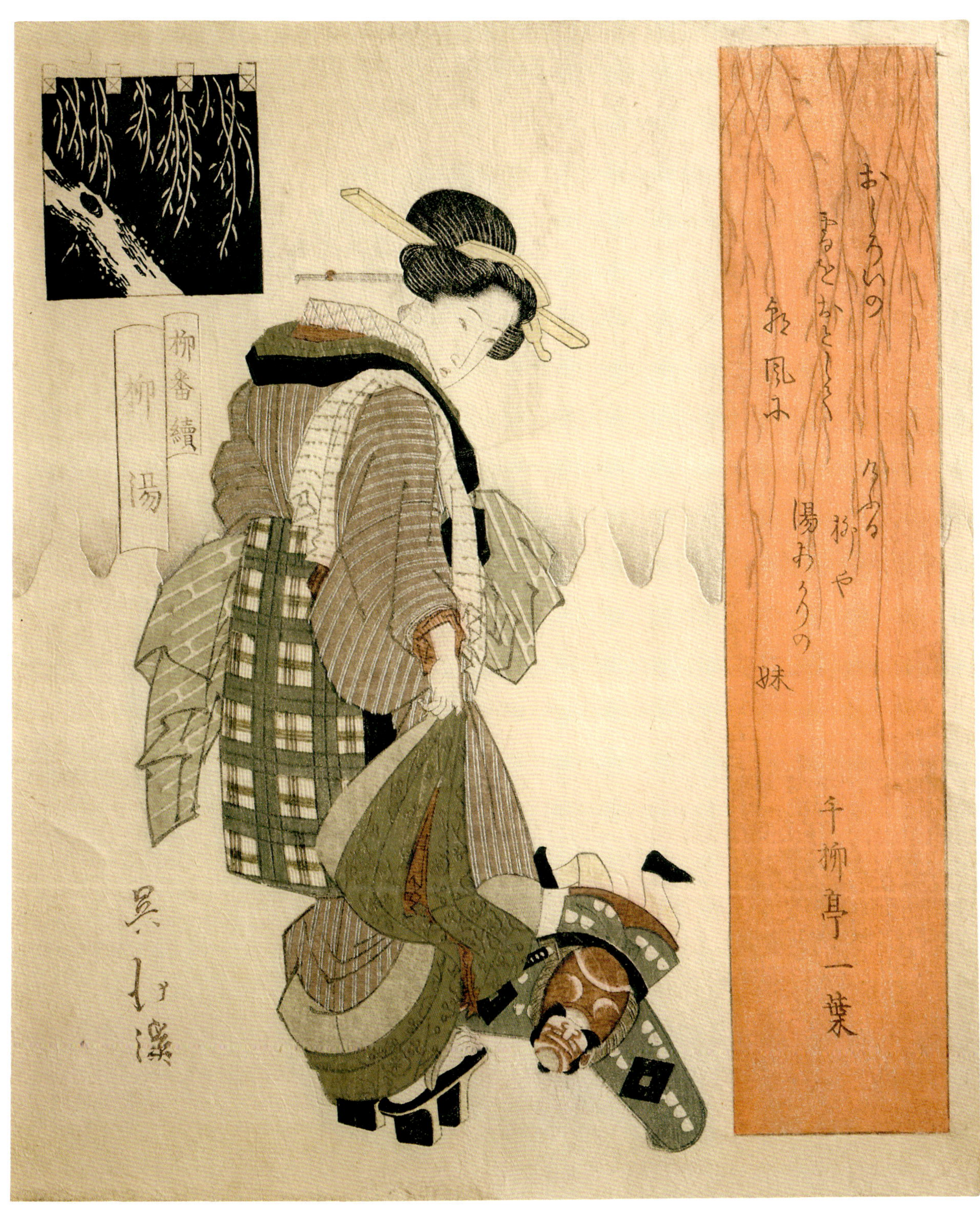
柳番續
柳湯
千柳亭一葉

18

***Bijin,* Boy, and Kite**
Kikukawa Eizan (1787–1867)
signed: *Kikukawa Eizan hitsu*
publisher: Tsuruya Kinsuke
c. 1815
sheet from *ōban* triptych (38.9 × 26.8 cm)

Eizan studied under Hokkei, who designed the *surimono* in plates 13 through 17. His output was not large, but he produced a number of fine *bijin-e,* pictures of beautiful women, tall girls in the style of Utamaro, before the fashion changed in the 1820s to shorter, more round-shouldered figures. Here he shows two young courtesans or geisha wearing their festival best, heavy outer kimonos with several layers of red undergarments and rather flamboyant *obi* sashes. The composition indicates that this is the left-hand sheet of a diptych or triptych. The publisher has repeated his crane trademark as a form of advertisement on the flowered robe of the girl on the left.

Several traditional New Year signifiers define the scene. As one girl coquettishly adjusts a hair ornament, the other holds a battledore, and a boy carries a kite with the character for dragon, which symbolizes masculinity, strength, and the sky. Girls celebrated New Year by playing shuttlecock; boys flew kites. The feathered shuttlecock can be seen at the top of the print, and the kite has a hummer. Behind the group is a large New Year decoration of pine and bamboo, called *kadomatsu,* gate pine; these decorations appear in many of the prints in this book, for example plate 47 and several of Hiroshige's cityscapes.

The round censor's seal *kiwame* (beside the artist's signature), meaning approved, was first required by the shogunal authorities in the ninth month of 1790 to indicate government approval of the design, and occurs in some form on most woodblock prints (except privately issued *surimono* and sexually explicit images) until 1842. After that date, until 1875, other forms of censor seals were used, including a combination of the zodiacal year and a number denoting the month, examples of which we will see later.

This is a lovely print. The lines are crisp—the lines of the hair are a good test of wear, or the lack of it, on a printing block—and the delicate, fugitive colors, derived from natural dyes, are unusually fresh.

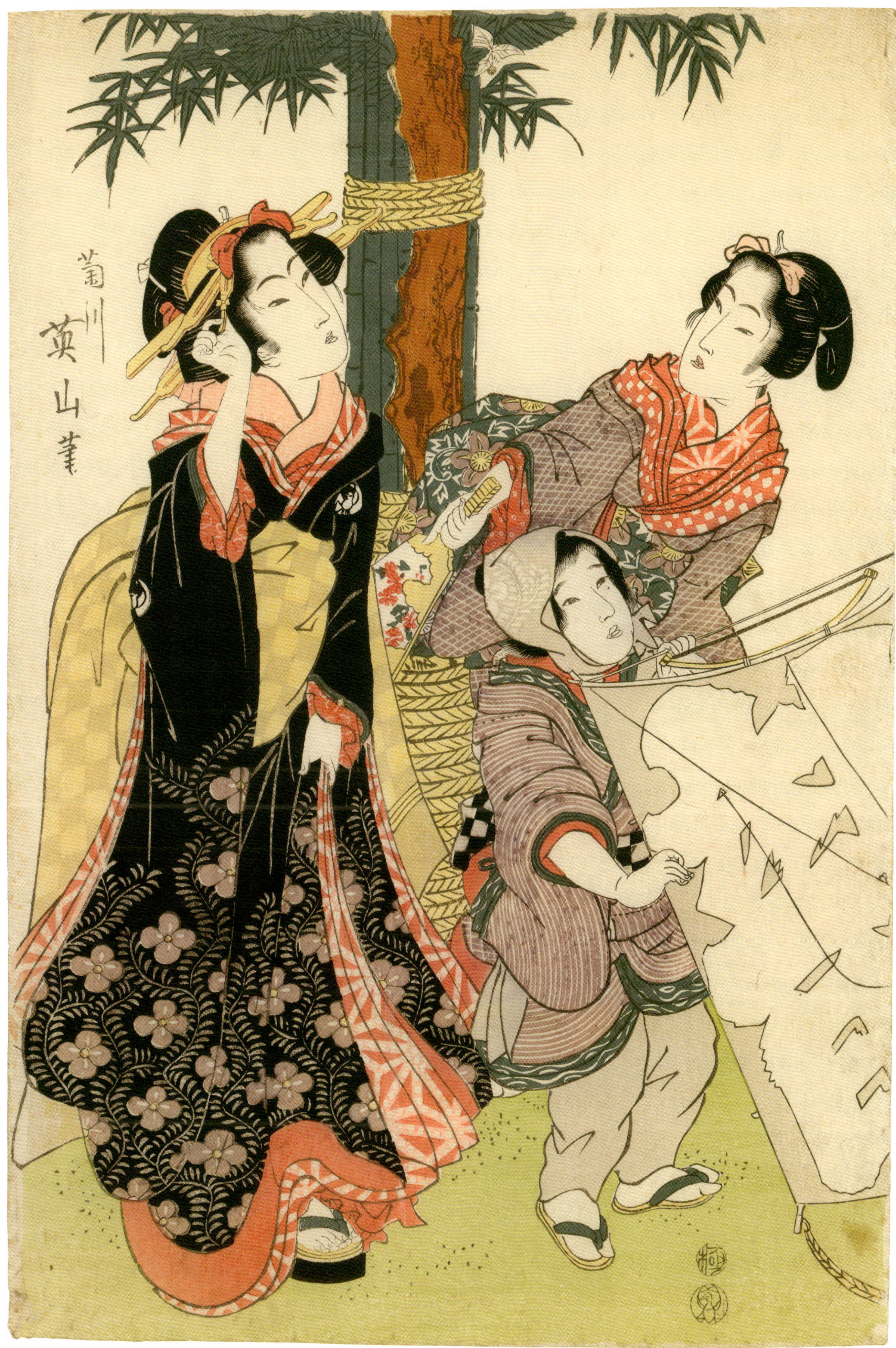
菊川
英山筆

19

Soga Brothers New Year Performance
Utagawa Kunisada (1786–1865)
signed: *Gototei Kunisada ga*
publisher: Yamashirōya Toemon
c. 1815
ōban diptych (each sheet approximately 37.7 × 25.7 cm)

It was an Edo custom to produce plays relating to the Soga Brothers at New Year. Based on a real vendetta at the end of the twelfth century that led to the death of a high-ranking lord, the story of two orphans who plotted the killing of their father's murderer inspired many Kabuki plays.[1] The best known, *Soga no taimen* (The Soga Brothers' Confrontation), was created by Ichikawa Danjūrō I in 1676; it was during the opening performance of this play that the legendary founder of the Danjūrō acting clan first wore the Ichikawa crest of three concentric squares.

These New Year performances were formalized and often departed radically from the traditional Soga Brothers story; for example, Lord Kudō, the villain, became the leading male role and was traditionally played by a troupe's lead actor. The climax was a dramatic face-off between Gorō, the impetuous younger brother, and Kudō. The brothers, waiting for an opportunity to take their revenge, are invited to Kudō's New Year celebrations, where Gorō has to be restrained from hurling his gift's offering-stand at his host.

Visual clues identify the two figures. The robe of the woman on the right bears the butterfly emblem of the younger Soga brother, Gorō. She wears the ornate hair ornaments of a high-ranking courtesan and carries a branch of plum blossom with a poem slip attached. This appears to read *harumusume jōruri,* springtime-girl drama. Kobayashi no Asahina, also known as Asahina no Saburō, portrayed at different times both as Gorō's friend and as Kudō's loyal retainer, catches at the woman's *obi* in an attempt to restrain her. The actor playing the woman is identified as the *onnagata* (male performer of female roles) Iwai Kumesaburō (1799–1836). His father, Iwai Hanshirō V (1776–1847), plays the role of Asahina. Until Kumesaburō's early death, just after he took the name Iwai Hanshirō VI, these two were the dominant performers of female roles in Edo Kabuki. Because of his large, bright eyes, the father was called *senryō yakusha,* actor with eyes like thousand-*ryō* gold coins. There is an echo of this phrase in the title of the print in plate 46, based on a Chinese poem.

Asahina's robes are decorated with his emblem, a circular crane design, and New Year pine seedlings. The legendary Asahina was a heroic strongman and also a comic figure who had many adventures, including a confrontation with Emma, king of the Underworld. He appears in prints and Kabuki plays with heavy red *kumadori* makeup and large sideburns. It is in this guise, along with his customary crane robe, that his face appears on the New Year kite caught in the flowering plum tree. These are also features of a *yakko's* face painted on kites, a visual pun that would have been appreciated by the print's audience. In the original story, Asahina grabs at Gorō's armor: both men are so strong that the leather armor with its silk cords tears apart in Asahina's hands as Gorō pulls away. Asahina's catching at the woman's *obi* here echoes this story.

Kunisada was a prolific artist known for his figure paintings and prints. He changed his *go,* artist name, several times during his career; the artist name he uses here is Gototei, meaning Fifth Ferry Pavilion. He used this artist name often, though far from exclusively, from 1813 to 1844. The name refers to his family's hereditary ferryboat service across a canal in the Honjo district of Edo, which gave Kunisada an independent income when he established himself as an *ukiyo-e* artist. After 1844 he changed his main name from Kunisada to that of his teacher, Toyokuni, and several prints by him shown later in this book are signed *Toyokuni.*

The three-line border of the seal below Kunisada's signature is not Danjūrō's crest of three measuring boxes but a highly stylized Chinese character representing the *sada* of Kunisada's name. Kunisada was a great friend and admirer of Danjūrō VII and modeled this seal on Danjūrō's *mon.*

1. Edmunds 1934 counts twenty-three.

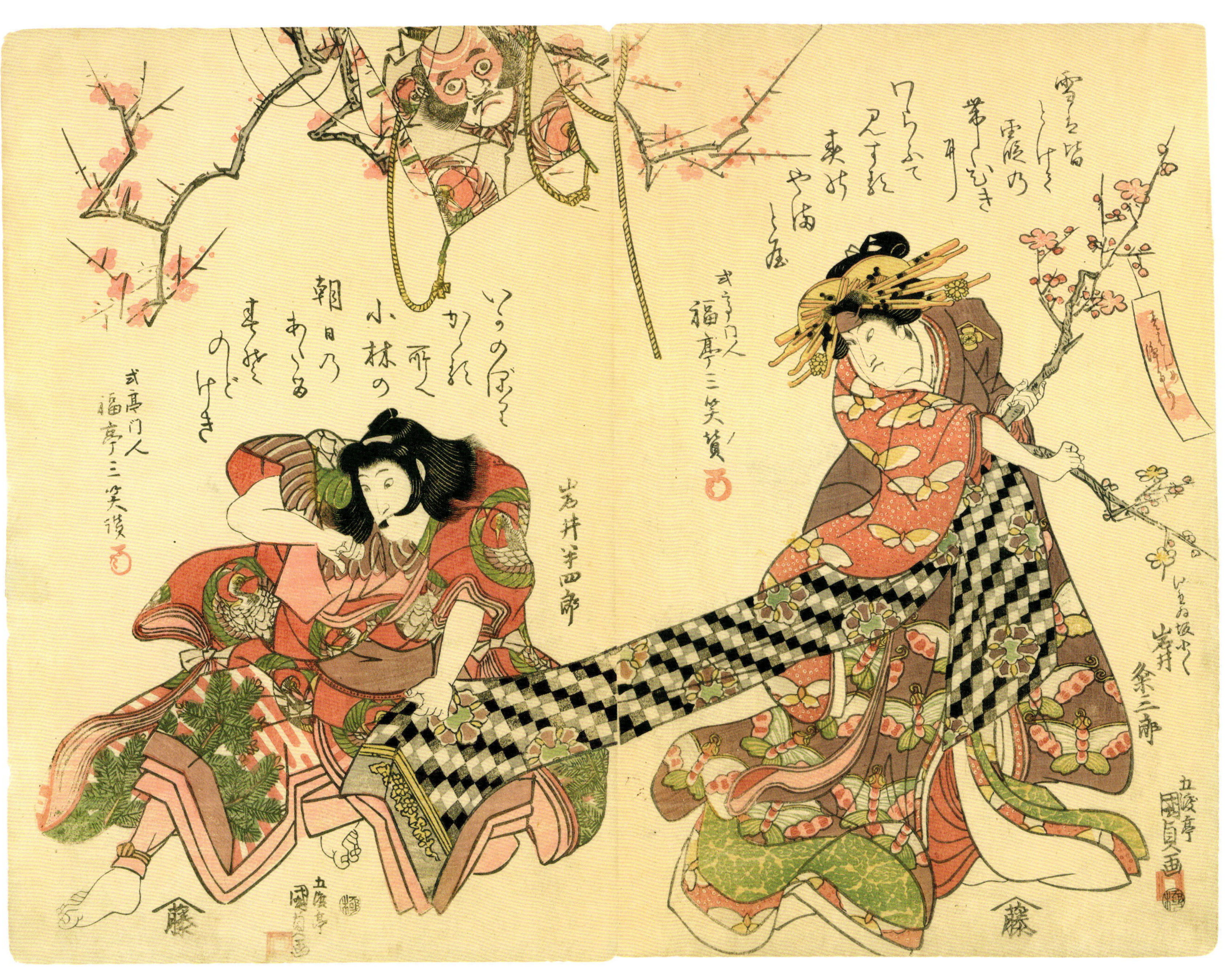
岩井半四郎
岩井粂三郎
五渡亭国貞画

20

Kite Wrapped Round a *Daimyō* Processional Pole
Katsushika Hokusai (1760–1849)
signed: *Saki no Hokusai Iitsu hitsu*
publisher: Moriya Jihei
c. 1820–25
tanzakuban (34.8 × 6.5 cm)

In an echo of the pole in Hokusai's print of Kakegawa (plate 6), a samurai or perhaps a *yakko* (his robe has a *yakko's* diamond-shaped emblem) looks up at a *tobi* kite whose string has wound around the tall pole he is carrying. Hokusai has combined several elements associated with great height: Mount Fuji, a kite, and the ceremonial pole that was carried in procession when a feudal lord moved from one location to another. So far does the pole project into the sky that a high-flying kite has become entangled in it. The New Year season is indicated by the kite itself and the pine decoration past which the samurai is walking. The hawk shape of the kite and Mount Fuji are two of the three objects—Mount Fuji, a hawk, and an eggplant—that it was good luck to dream about at New Year.

Hokusai has chosen an unusual elongated format suited to the composition of this design. The long oblong shape is called *tanzakuban,* after the paper slips that were used for writing poetry and given as gifts or hung on trees and at shrines for good fortune. Fewer than a dozen designs with this format are known from Hokusai's vast oeuvre; tall *hashira-e,* pillar prints, were invented in the 1740s and popularized by Koryūsai in the 1770s, but their dimensions were double those of this print. Though there are *surimono* by Hokusai in this format,[1] and the printing quality here is high, the very thin paper indicates that this was not a *surimono.*

Another unusual feature of this print, besides its format, is the blind embossing in the top left corner. It seems to suggest smoke coming from the top of Mount Fuji. Thin wisps of smoke can sometimes be seen above the snowcapped mountain; it is still considered an active volcano, even though there has been no major eruption since 1707, when Fuji blanketed the city of Edo with six inches of ash.

Unlike the other colors in the print, the red pattern in the kite has been impressed so firmly that it too looks like embossing and adds textural interest. The red at the end of the kite's tail is an indication of what the original unfaded color looked like; this print was framed for some period in its life, protecting the edges from light. The yellow in the wooden legs of the decoration and pole has also faded, but the light indigo blue is a much less fugitive color and probably looks much the same as it did originally.

Hokusai uses the name Iitsu in his signature, meaning One-Year-Old Again. He took this name in 1820 when he celebrated the achievement of his first sixty years of life.[2] The age of sixty, five complete cycles of the twelve years of the zodiac, was a very significant landmark in a person's life and continues to be honored in Japan today. Most of Hokusai's rare *tanzakuban* prints date from around 1830, but the use of the name Iitsu here suggests an earlier date.

1. An example from the Peter Morse Collection is illustrated in Nagata 1993, 182.

2. Keyes 1985, 194.

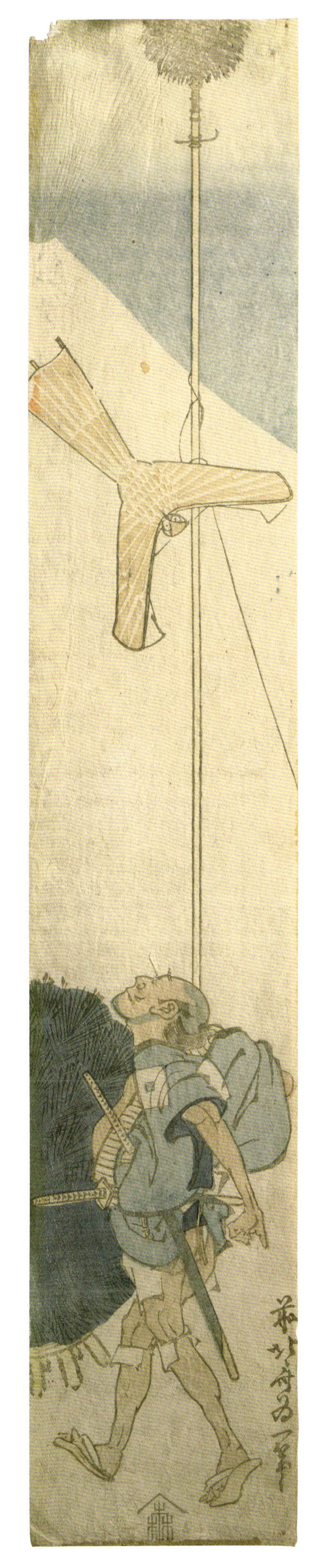

21

View of the Mitsui Stores at Surugachō in Edo
Katsushika Hokusai (1760–1849)
signed: *Zen Hokusai Iitsu hitsu*
publisher: Eijudō
c. 1830
ōban (25 × 37.4 cm)

Kites are prominent in two of the designs of what is perhaps Hokusai's best-known print series: *Fugaku sanjūrokkei* (Thirty-Six Views of Mount Fuji).[1] The title of this design is *Edo Surugachō Mitsuimise ryakuzu* (View of the Mitsui Stores at Surugachō in Edo). Hawk-shaped and rectangular kites fly above a streetscape that leads toward a prominent Mount Fuji. The character on the kite to the left reads *kotobuki,* good fortune.

Repairmen are working on a roof: one throws up material for a colleague to catch, another sits astride the roof-ridge. Mount Fuji is covered with snow, so it is winter (in summer, snow nearly disappears from Fuji's twelve-thousand-feet-high summit), and the kites pinpoint the time as New Year. The Surugachō area was famous for its fine views of Fuji, especially on a clear winter's day.

Surugachō is now Muromachi, north of Nihonbashi, the bridge that marked the center of Edo. In Hokusai's day the area was known for the Mitsui stores, which owed their success to the novel idea of charging cash at the time of purchase. Normal practice was to sell goods on credit, with a bill presented to a customer just once or twice a year; all accounts had to be cleared by New Year. The new method of payment was safer for the store and enabled Mitsui to offer lower prices than its competitors. Here, two stores, each with a hanging signboard bearing the Mitsui symbol of three horizontal lines (the numeral three, *mitsu*) in a square-shaped character for a well (*i*), face each other across the street. The sign outside the building on the right indicates Clothing, the one on the left Braided Cords and Threads. Both signs state the stores' policies: Cash Payment and No Inflated Prices. Today the Mitsui Clothing Store has evolved into Mitsukoshi, Japan's largest and most prestigious department store.

This is an early impression of the Surugachō–Mitsui design, its colors simple but strong. A distinctive feature of this famous series is the printing of outlines in Prussian-blue dye, as here, rather than black, and Prussian blue dominates the palette of all the designs of the series.

1. For a discussion of images of Mount Fuji in Japanese art, see Clark 2001.

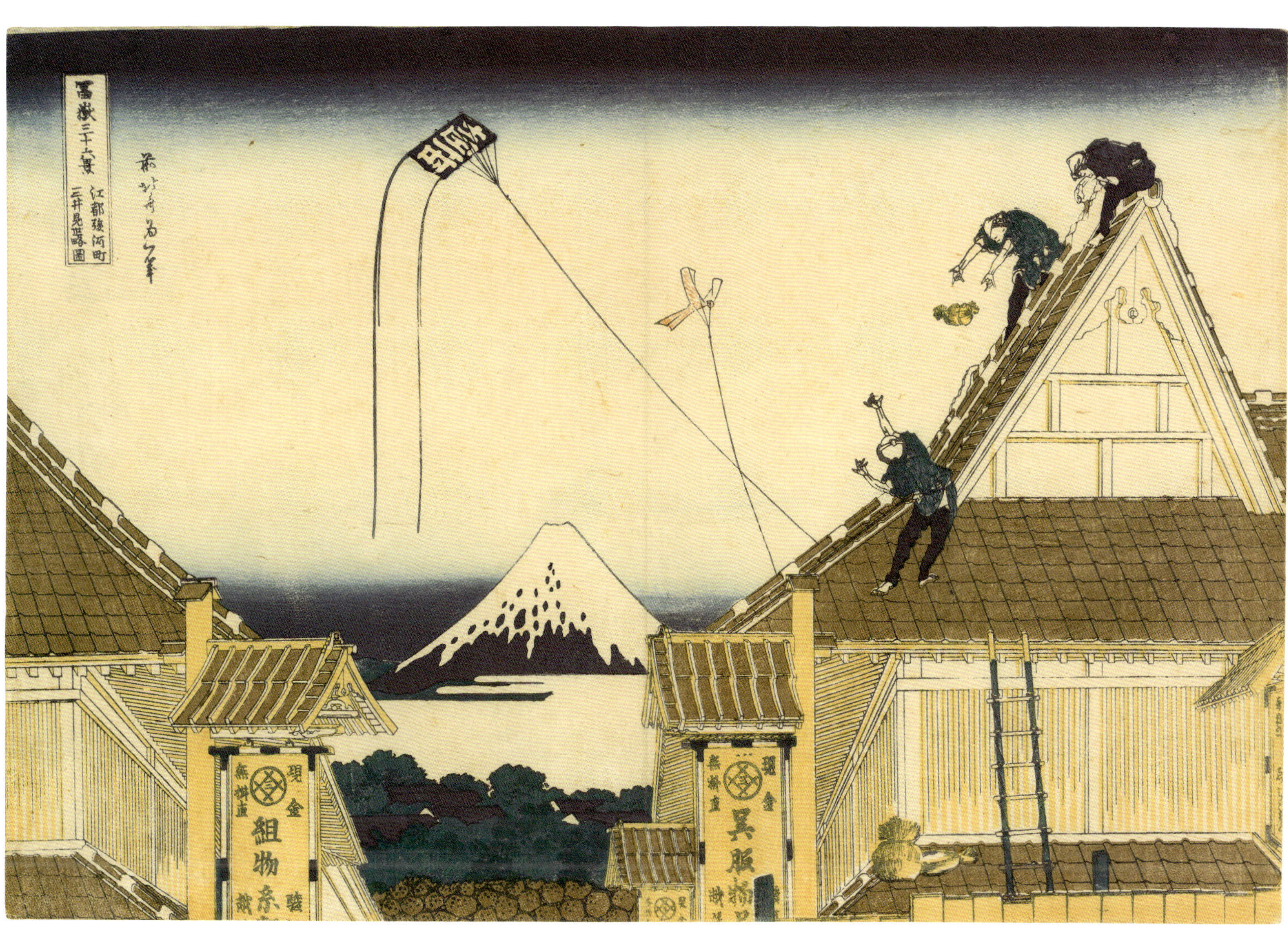
冨嶽三十六景
江都駿河町
三井見世略圖

22

Honganji at Asakusa in Edo

Katsushika Hokusai (1760–1849)
signed: *Zen Hokusai Iitsu hitsu*
publisher: Eijudō
Meiji reprint of c. 1830 original
ōban (23.6 × 35.5 cm)

This is another print from Hokusai's *Fugaku sanjūrokkei* (Thirty-Six Views of Mount Fuji). As in the previous design, a kite hovers over an Edo cityscape with a snowy Fuji majestic in the distance. This time the kite is in the shape of a phoenix, *hō-ō,* an auspicious bird whose arrival signified a virtuous ruler and good fortune for the nation. The shape of the kite here, with its many tail feathers arching in the wind, is very graceful; we can almost hear it flutter. Again, workmen repair the roof of a large building, applying caulking or cement and hauling material up from below. Hokusai was an extremely keen observer of the world around him, and the gestures of these lively workmen echo those of figures in his *Manga* sketchbooks.

The building, with its elaborately tiled roof, is the main hall of Honganji. One of the largest buildings in the city, this temple of the Buddhist Pure Land sect dominated Asakusa, the most densely populated area of old Edo. The district was crowded with the stores of merchants and craftsmen, whose roofs can be seen between the stylized clouds of the scene. At left a scaffolding watchtower for fires rises through the clouds.

Hokusai's series Thirty-Six Views of Mount Fuji was extremely well received and began a vogue for landscape prints (partly because landscapes were safer for artists than pictures of the floating world after prints of actors and beautiful women were proscribed by the puritanical government). His Views of Fuji were printed and reprinted until the wooden blocks wore out and were then recarved. Later impressions used black outlines rather than blue. This recarving happened not only in the early 1830s, when the series was first issued, but intermittently into the Meiji period, several decades later. The design here follows the lines of the original but the paper and coloration are somewhat different. The series cartouche has been removed, the title has been written in new characters, and the print makes no pretense of being other than a reproduction.

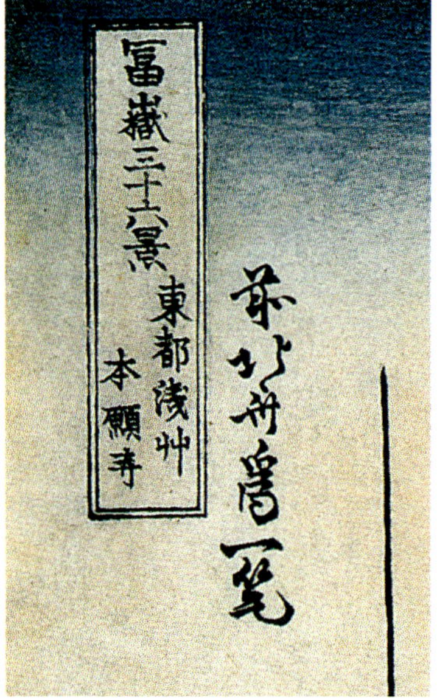

Hokusai's signature and cartouche with series and design titles from the original edition.

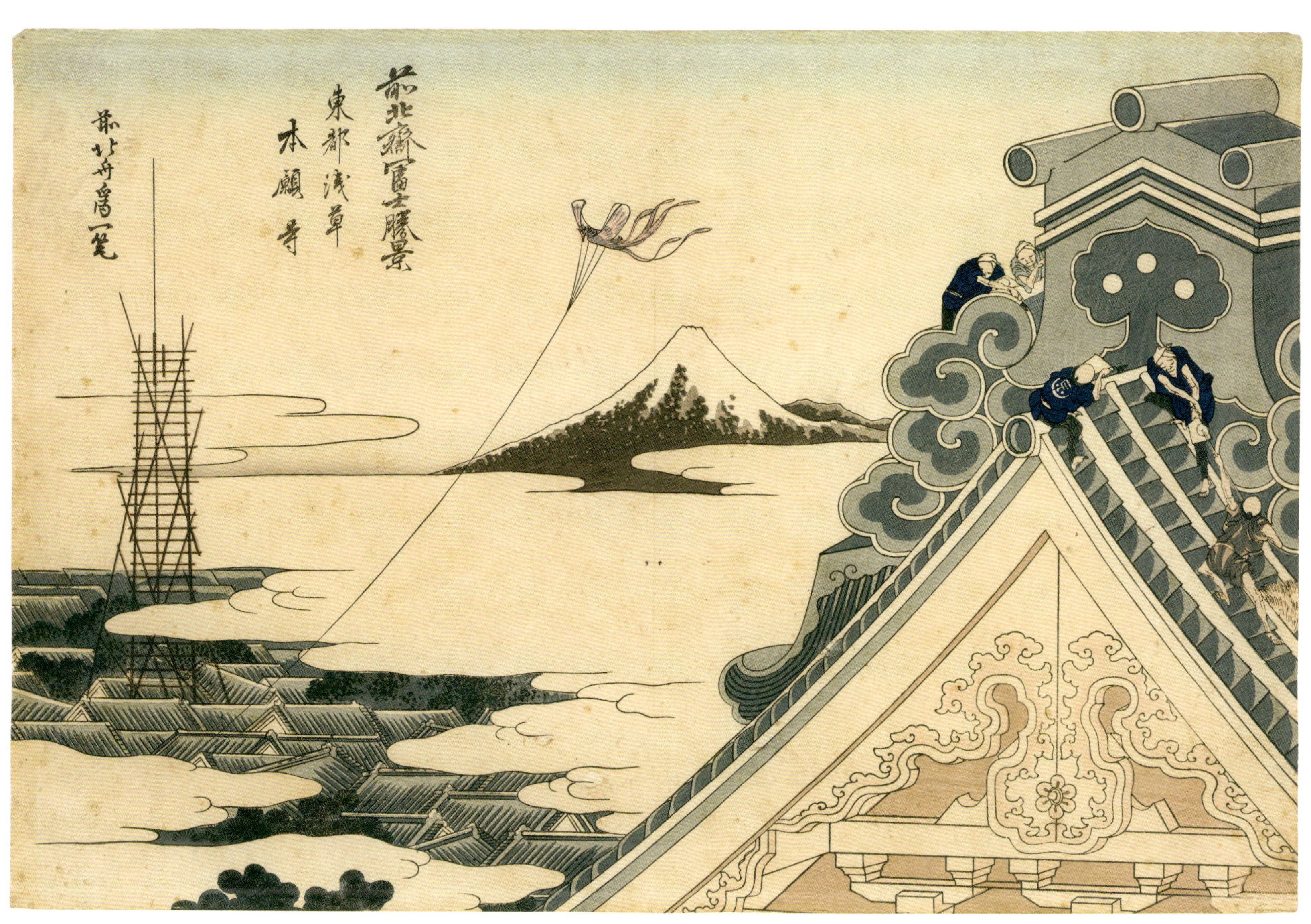
前北齋冨士勝景
東都淺草
本願寺
前北齋為一筆

23

Distant View of Mount Akiba at Kakegawa

Utagawa Hiroshige (1797–1858)
signed: *Hiroshige ga*
publisher: Hoeidō
c. 1833
ōban (23 × 33.4 cm)

Following Hokusai's success with his Thirty-six Views of Mount Fuji, Hiroshige designed his own landscape print series. He took as his theme the fifty-three stations of the Tōkaidō, the resting places along the trunk road from Edo to Kyoto that Hokusai had explored three decades earlier (plate 6). Hiroshige's series *Tōkaidō gojūsantsugi no uchi* (Fifty-three Stations of the Tōkaidō) uses a format twice the size of Hokusai's original Tōkaidō series of 1806 but a similarly restrained palette of colors.

Famous places in Japan tended to become identified with particular characteristics. This design is titled *Kakegawa Akibayama enbō* (Distant View of Mount Akiba at Kakegawa). Kakegawa is the twenty-seventh station, where the Tōkaidō crosses the Tenryū River over a bridge of logs on which earth has been piled. Mount Akiba rises in the background. An old couple bow to a traveling priest and his attendant, and peasants work in the fields. It is a windy day, and Hiroshige features kites in his design of Kakegawa, just as Hokusai did. A young boy standing on the bridge has lost his kite in the high wind: he gestures as he watches it disappear in the distance, its line dipping and fluttering. Another round kite flies from the left. In a confident touch, Hiroshige extends the kite beyond the edge of the design to emphasize its height; later, breaking the edge of a design became a common compositional device, but it was still novel when Hiroshige used it. Less convincing is the bamboo grove at the edge of the fields that bends in a direction opposite to the wind.

Landscapes had been peripheral to the world of entertainment that provided the traditional subjects of *ukiyo-e,* pictures of the floating world, but the success of Hokusai's Fuji and Hiroshige's Tōkaidō series of the early 1830s established landscape prints as a new genre. The many editions of both series, with examples pulled off very worn blocks, testify to their popularity.

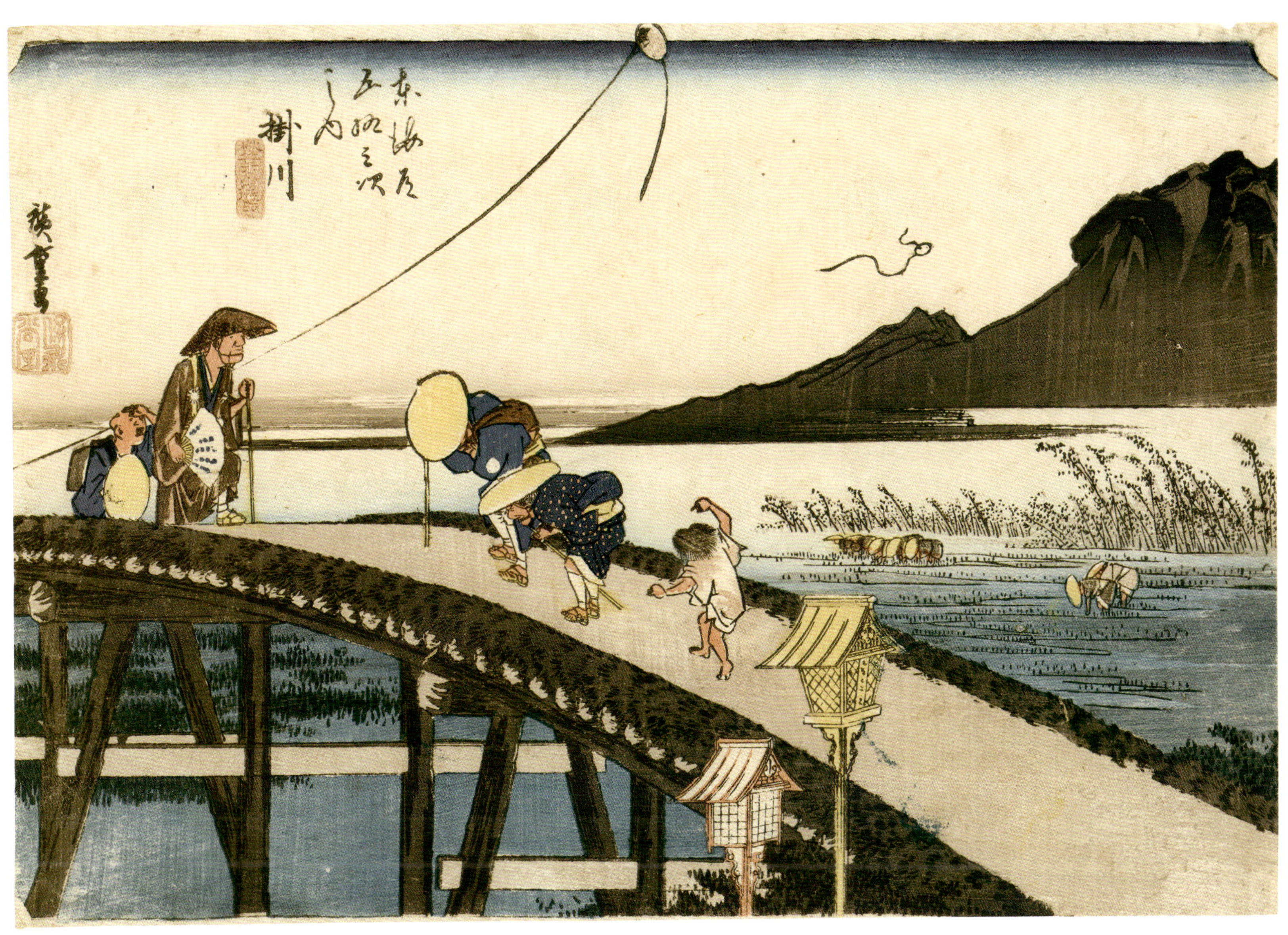
東海道五拾三次之内
掛川
廣重画

24

Distant View of Mount Akiba at Kakegawa

Utagawa Kunisada (1786–1865)
signed: *Kōchōrō Kunisada ga*
publisher: Sanoya Kihei
c. 1838
vertical *chūban* (24.6 × 18.2 and 25.8 × 18.2 cm)

Hiroshige and Kunisada knew each other well. Kunisada was famous for his figure drawing;[1] Hiroshige specialized in landscape prints. Recognizing their separate talents, publishers sometimes commissioned series in which Kunisada drew the figures and Hiroshige drew the backgrounds. Here Kunisada has borrowed outright the designs of Hiroshige's Tōkaidō series as backgrounds for a series of *bijin-e,* pictures of beautiful women. His audience would have immediately recognized the source of the backgrounds, landscapes issued just a few years before; there would have been no thought that Kunisada was passing off the background designs as his own.

A seller of charcoal and firewood rests on her load, a branch of red maple leaves in her hand. She wears a tie-dyed headcloth and unrealistically fine robes, like Hokusai's *Ōharame* (plate 9). Hiroshige's original design of Kakegawa was horizontal; Kunisada has compressed this into a vertical format, using most of the elements successfully, although the gaze of the boy no longer matches the disappearing kite.

Kunisada signs himself *Kōchōrō,* an artist name he took in 1833; he used it in combination with the name Kunisada and also with the name of his teacher, Toyokuni, which he adopted in 1844. He uses the same title as Hiroshige's series, *Tōkaidō gojūsantsugi no uchi,* for his own series, and the same titles for individual designs. His palette is more colorful than Hiroshige's.

A second example of the design in the Skinner Collection is even brighter. The blocks from which it has been printed are rather worn, and the mixture of natural and synthetic pigments suggests that it was made a decade or two after the first, when synthetic dyes were beginning to be imported in greater quantities from Europe and used rather indiscriminately for their novelty value. This implies that the popularity of the series continued for a long time. The green especially is reminiscent of Hiroshige's overprinting of more than one color in landscapes of the 1850s. The second print does not bear the seal of the publisher or the red *kiwame* seal, discontinued in 1842, both of which appear on the original.

1. During his lifetime, it was Kunisada's actor prints that were most appreciated; now he is probably best known for his prints of women.

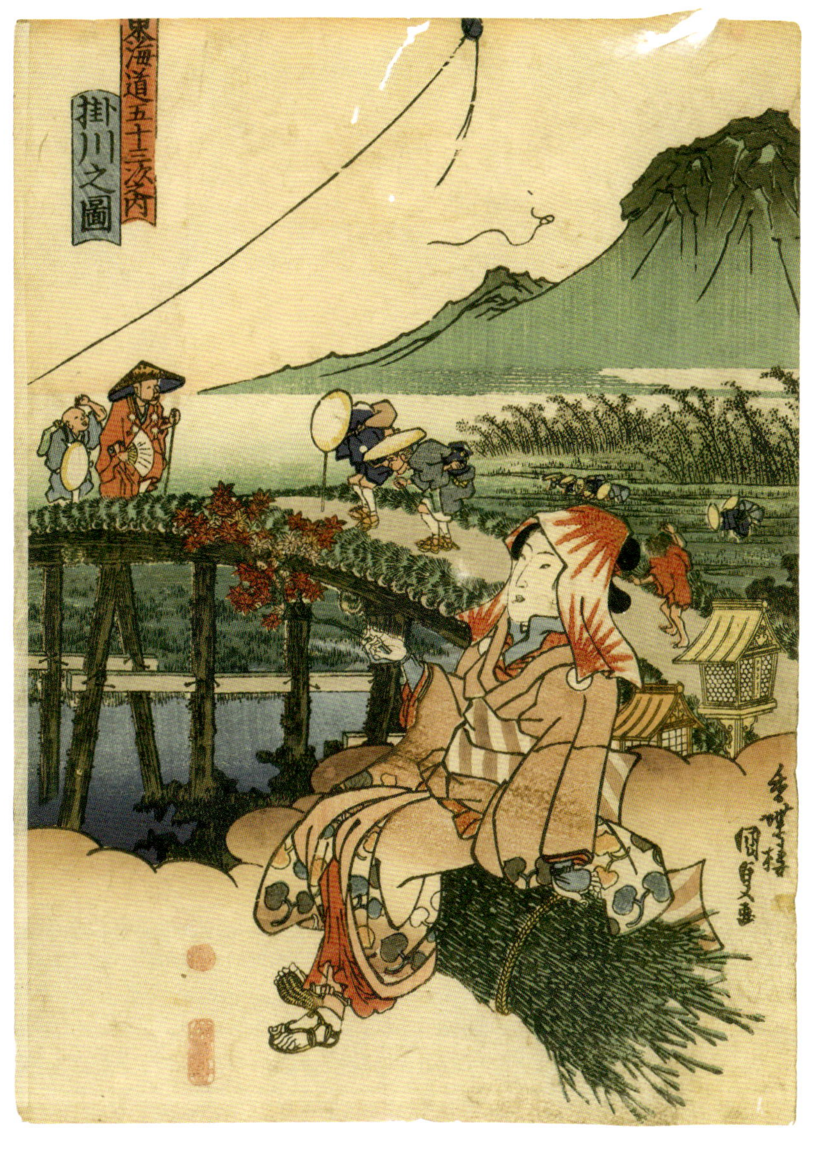
東海道五十三次内
掛川之圖

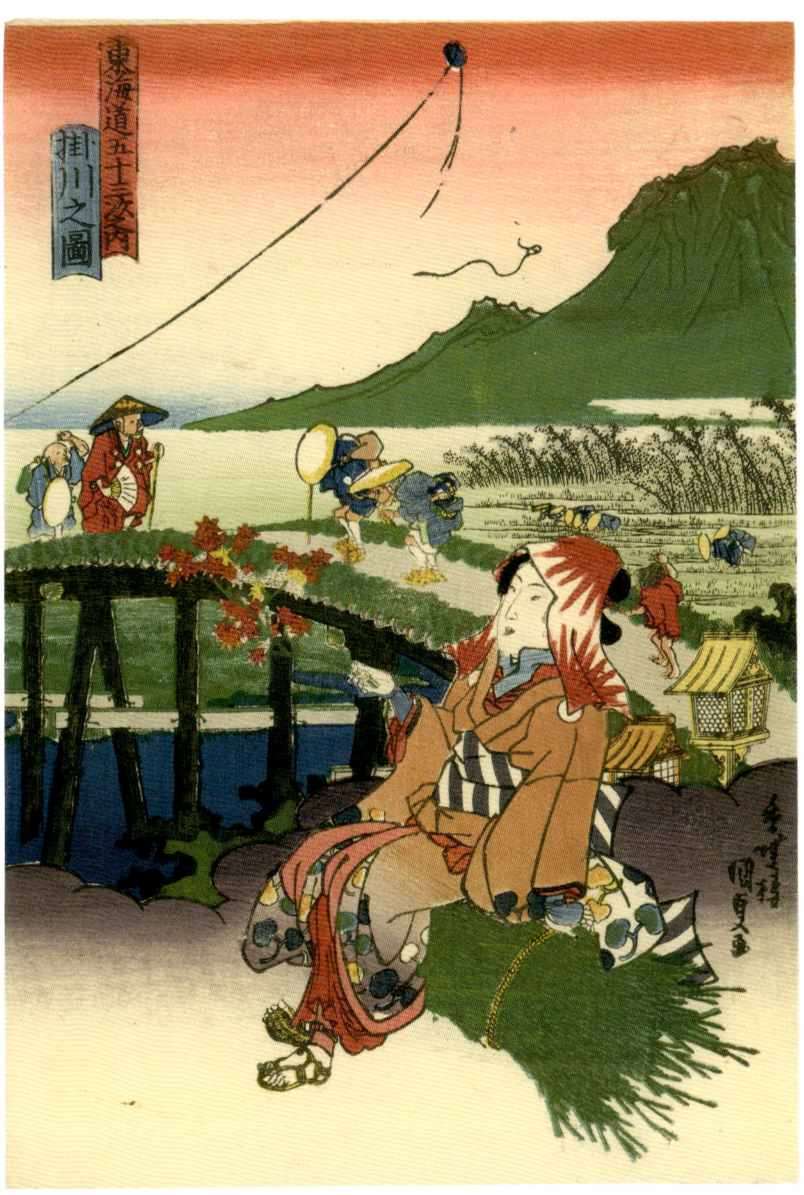
東海道五十三次内
掛川之圖

25

New Year Kite-flying at Yushima Tenjin Shrine
Utagawa Hiroshige (1797–1858)
publisher: Sanoya Kihei
c. 1840
horizontal *ōban* (25.6 × 38.2 and 23.2 × 36.4 cm)

Warmly dressed citizens are climbing steps up to a side entrance to Yushima Tenjin Shrine, indicated by its *torii* gate, on a small hill rising above Shinobazu Pond in the north of Edo; a shrine to Benten can be seen on the island in the middle of the pond. A number of rectangular Edo kites, with their characteristic double tails, fly in a steady wind above a sea of roofs. A samurai strides toward the gate, three women chat, and two tradesmen carry their wares. The blue rectangle carried by one of the women is probably a kite, a present for a little boy rather than something she will fly herself.

After his Fifty-three Stations of the Tōkaidō, Hiroshige produced many landscapes for different publishers, including at least ten different series titled *Tōto meisho* (Famous Places of the Eastern Capital). The public loved these views of familiar spots in their home city. Here are two versions of the same scene, Yushima Tenjin Shrine during the New Year festival, taken from a *Tōto meisho* series dating from about 1840. Not only is the coloration different in each example, but a comparison of details, such as the faces, shows that they were printed from different blocks—one or both sets have been recarved after the original blocks wore down from frequent use. (The upper impression here has more details and is probably the original, or closer to the original, than the lower.) Broken lines, such as the line of the kite on the far left, indicate that the blocks were used even as they deteriorated, to maintain sales of a design that people continued to buy.

To the pine-tree decorations, kites, and warm clothing that we have noted are indicators of New Year are added plum blossoms, seen on the left of the design. The lunar New Year fell during what we call late January or February, when plum trees were beginning to bloom; the Japanese considered the first day of the New Year to be the first day of spring. Yushima Tenjin Shrine was and still is famous for its early plum blossoms. The shrine is dedicated to Sugawara Michizane, a ninth-century nobleman who became the patron saint of learning and the arts and whose best-known poem talked of the fragrance of plum blossoms. The dedication on the *torii* gate pillar (missing on the lower impression) explains that it was donated by a Mr Sakamoto, incense-maker in Kyōbashi.

Characters on the square block at the top of the steps to the right define the slope as male, and therefore steeper than the central stairway, which is described as female; both sets of steps still exist. The building to the right may be selling fortunes. The red paper lanterns outside the building to the left indicate that it is a restaurant; we see similar red lanterns in several of the prints in this book. Temples and shrines remain popular holiday destinations today, places to visit and enjoy at festival times without necessarily strong religious motives, and similar stores and eating places still line the approaches to famous shrines and temples.

The man to the left with a carrying pole is selling *nori* seaweed. Another, with a load on his back, is an *ōgibako-kai,* literally a buyer of fan boxes. Folding fans inscribed with auspicious poems were traditional New Year gifts; this man is recycling unwanted fans, buying them for resale still in their original boxes, complete with their presentation stands, which appear on top of his load. (He echoes the recycling of mandatory gifts, which are still a prominent part of Japanese etiquette.) We will see the *ōgibako-kai* in another design by Hiroshige, plate 54, and several other prints. Utamaro used the figure in a New Year landscape half a century earlier,[1] and the character seems to have become a New Year icon. Hiroshige's frequent use of the figure was doubtless inspired by local peddlers he had seen; print artists were often called on to draw hundreds of designs a year, straining their imagination for novel images, and they held their own idiosyncratic themes in their heads and sketchbooks. Hokusai mined the visual wealth of his *Manga* repeatedly, as we have just seen with the laborers in his Thirty-Six Views of Mount Fuji (plates 21 and 22).

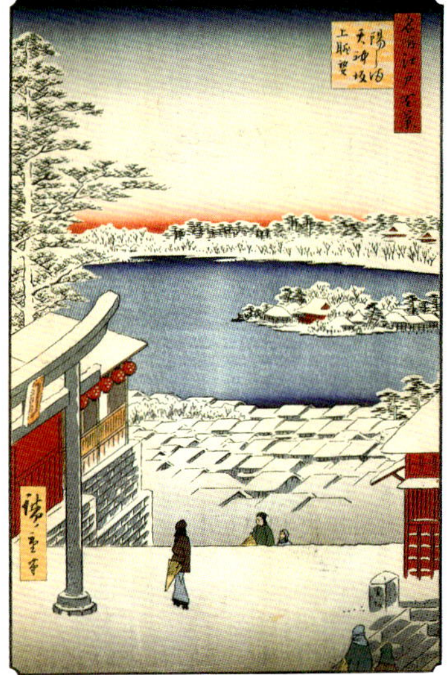

Yushima Tenjin Shrine, from Hiroshige's *Meisho Edo hyakkei* (One Hundred Famous Views of Edo), 1856.

1. Snow scene from the New Year album *Waka Ebisu,* Verses for Ebisu, 1786–89, illustrated in Hillier and Smith 1980, 77, and Kita 1996, 68. An *ōgibako-kai* also figures prominently with boys and a kite in a New Year image from the woodblock book *Saishiki Mitsu no Asa* of 1787 by Kiyonaga, illustrated in Hillier 1987, 393.

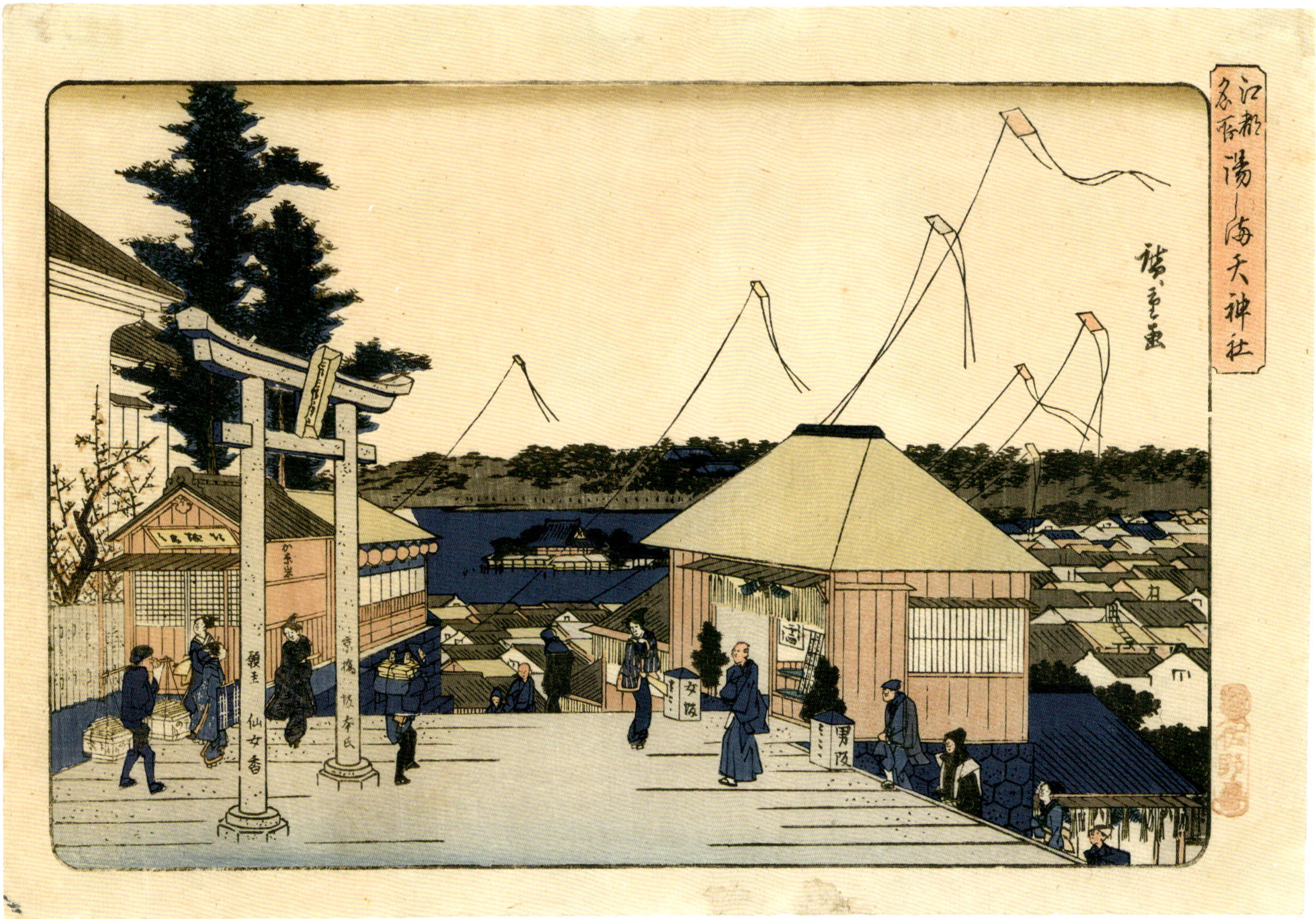

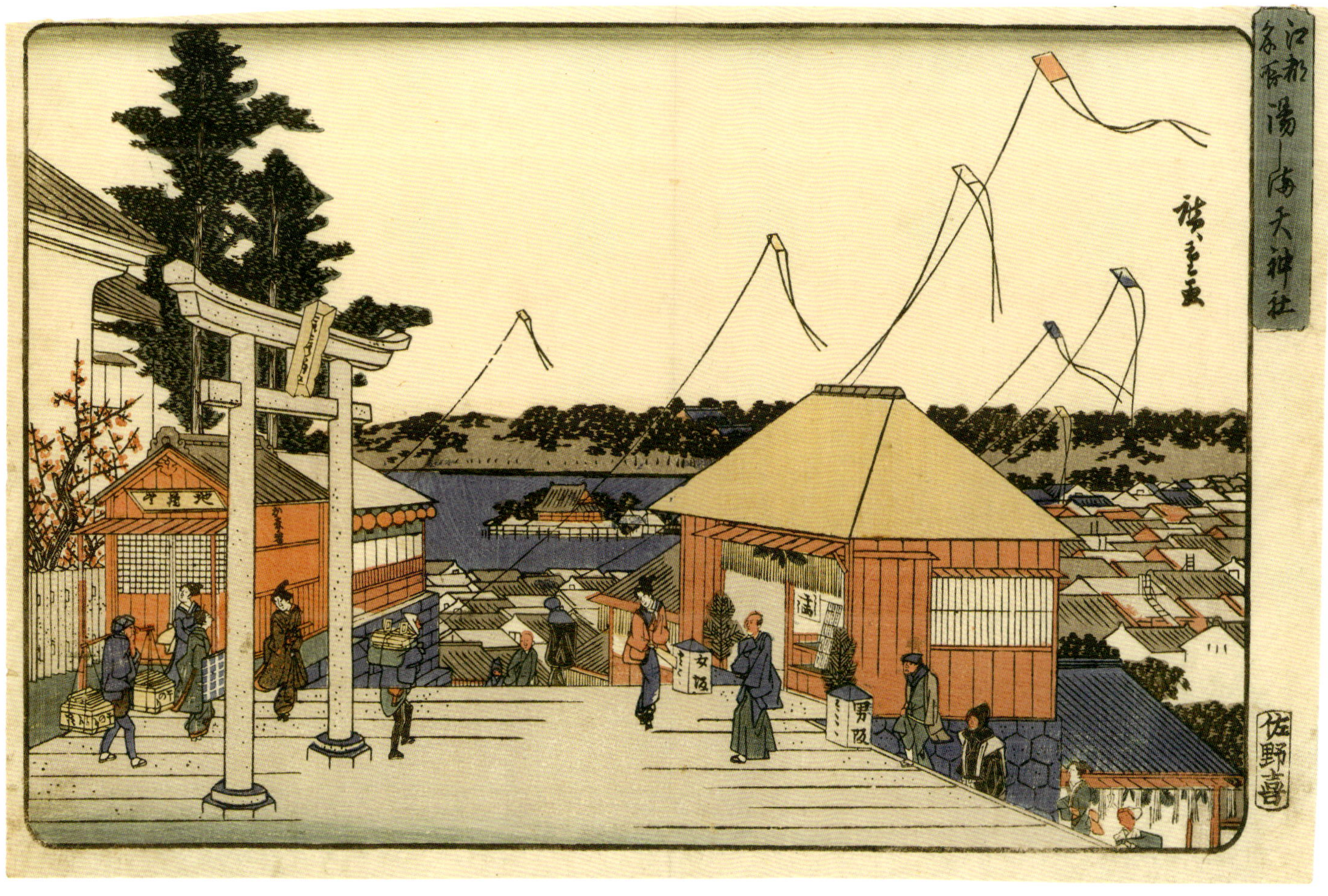
江都名所
湯嶋天神社
廣重画
佐野喜

26

Courtesan with Servant
Utagawa Kunisada (1786–1865)
signed: *Gototei Kunisada ga*
publisher: Fukusendō
c. 1830–35
ōban (36.6 × 25.7 cm)

In this elegant design, a young woman wearing layers of fine robes and a black hood walks with a servant who carries a large load. The combination of warm clothes and bare feet indicates that she is a courtesan; courtesans traditionally went barefoot—compare the girls in plates 30 and 35 who wear *tabi,* socks. The load is her bedding; a high-ranking courtesan would sometimes visit a customer at a house of assignation, *ageya,* rather than sleep on the premises of her establishment. Her semiformal journey as she shuffled regally through the crowd on high *geta* with servant and futon would arouse much interest, both in her and in the identity of her client. Her *geta* made necessary a slow *hachimonji ni aruku,* figure-of-eight walking. If it was raining, her servant might carry her on his back. Here he cocks his head as the servant does in plate 14 and in prints by Shumman. The two stylized bird-shapes forming the *mon* on the girl's flowery blue kimono are *chidori,* sea-plovers.

Kites appear in the cartouche at the top of the print as signifiers of New Year; the *hiragana* script in the cartouche reads *ikanobori,* kites. The characters of the gray-blue kite mean *totonou,* meaning something like "in good shape"; the rising sun on the fan-shaped kite represents good luck. The three-line border of the cartouche is a stylized Chinese character, the *sada* of Kunisada's name,[1] not a form of the crest showing three grain-measuring boxes of the Ichikawa acting clan that we saw in plates 12 and 14; the construction of the character can be seen more clearly here than in the square seal Kunisada uses in plate 19. The censor's seal indicates that this design must have been printed before 1842, but Kunisada was a prolific designer of beautiful-woman prints and there is little information available internally to date this design apart from style.[2]

1. Kunisada showed kites inside a *sada* cartouche again in a series of half-length beauties issued by another publisher in the late 1820s, illustrated Izzard 1993, 101.

2. Many examples of Kunisada's *bijin-e* are available for comparison in Izzard 1993.

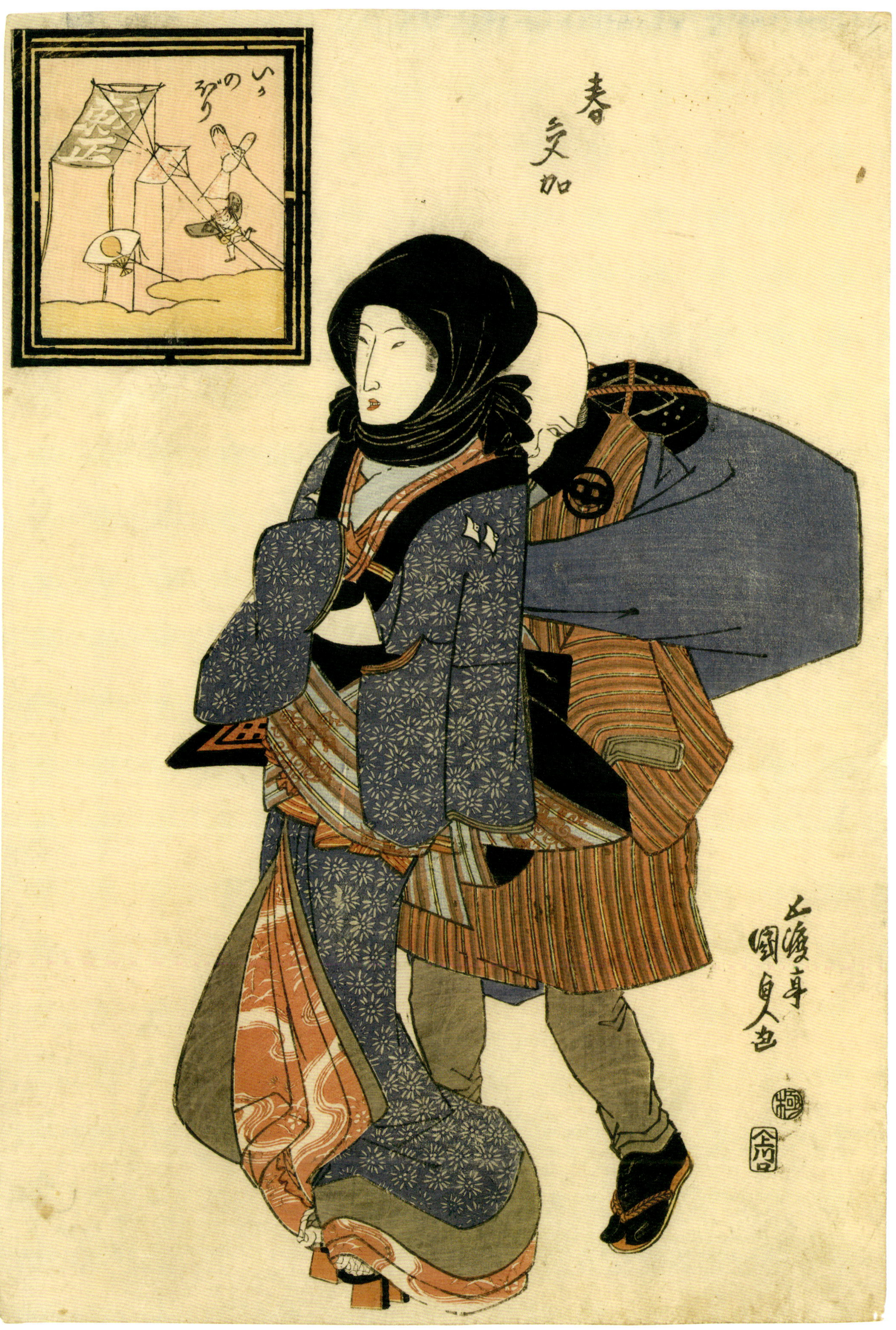
春
いかのぼり
五渡亭国貞画

27

Ōkane Steps on the Line of a Runaway Kite

Utagawa Kunisada (1786–1865)
signed: *ōju Kōchōrō Kunisada ga*
publisher: Kagaya Kichibei
c. 1834
ōban (38.3 × 25.1 cm)

The *Kokon Chōmon shū,* a book of folktales compiled in the thirteenth century, tells of a great warrior traveling to Kyoto who stopped to take a swim in Lake Biwa. Frightened of the water, his horse bolted. No one could stop it until it galloped past Ōkane, a famous courtesan of Omi Province, who stamped on its trailing rope with her high *geta* and brought it rearing to a halt.

The sophisticated Edo public loved parallels and puns, relating folktales and stories from classical Japanese and Chinese literature to their own world. This print parodies Ōkane's story by showing a woman stepping on the line of an escaped kite painted with a design of a galloping horse. The rope dangling at the left of the design is one of the kite's two stabilizing tails. The scene is taken from a Kabuki play and the actor is Iwai Kumesaburō, the *onnagata* we saw in plate 19. His robe features a pattern of the wooden tablets used in a chesslike game called *shōgi.* There is wordplay here: phonetically translated, *shōgi* can mean licensed courtesan.

The inscription in the ornate cartouche, *Hayu Suikoden goketsu hyaku hachinin ikko,* translates as 108 Heroes of the Actors' Water Margin One by One. This is itself a parody of the title of an ancient Chinese novel translated as *Suikoden,* Water Margin. The novel, which recounts the exploits of a group of outlaws whose impregnable base was hidden in the marshes, enjoyed a great vogue when it was translated into Japanese by Takizawa Bakin early in the nineteenth century. Kunisada's great rival, Kuniyoshi, had made his name just a few years before with a wildly flamboyant series of the tattooed heroes of the *Suikoden.*

The double *toshidama* seal below the artist's signature—*toshidama* means New Year jewel—appears on many of Kunisada's designs of the early 1830s. He used the *Kōchōrō* artist name from 1833 to 1844; this design may date from 1834, a Horse Year.

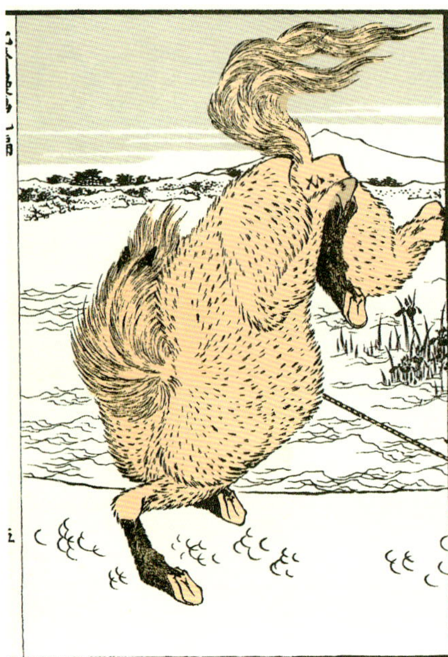

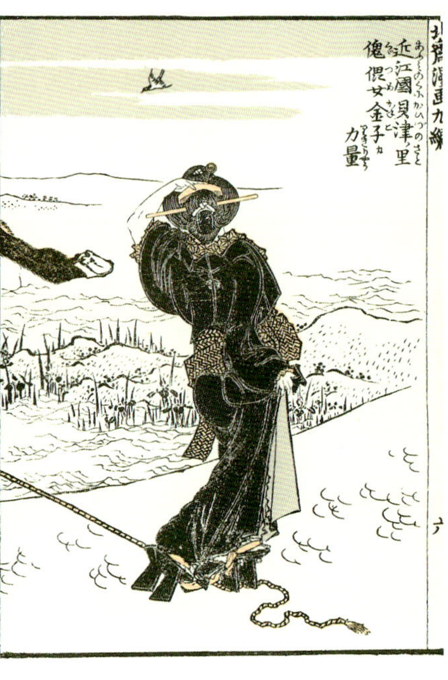

The Strength of Kugatsume Kaneko [Ōkane] of Kaizu in Ōmi Province, Katsushika Hokusai, 1817, adaptation of two pages from volume 9 of the *Manga* sketchbooks, each page approximately 18 × 12.5 cm.

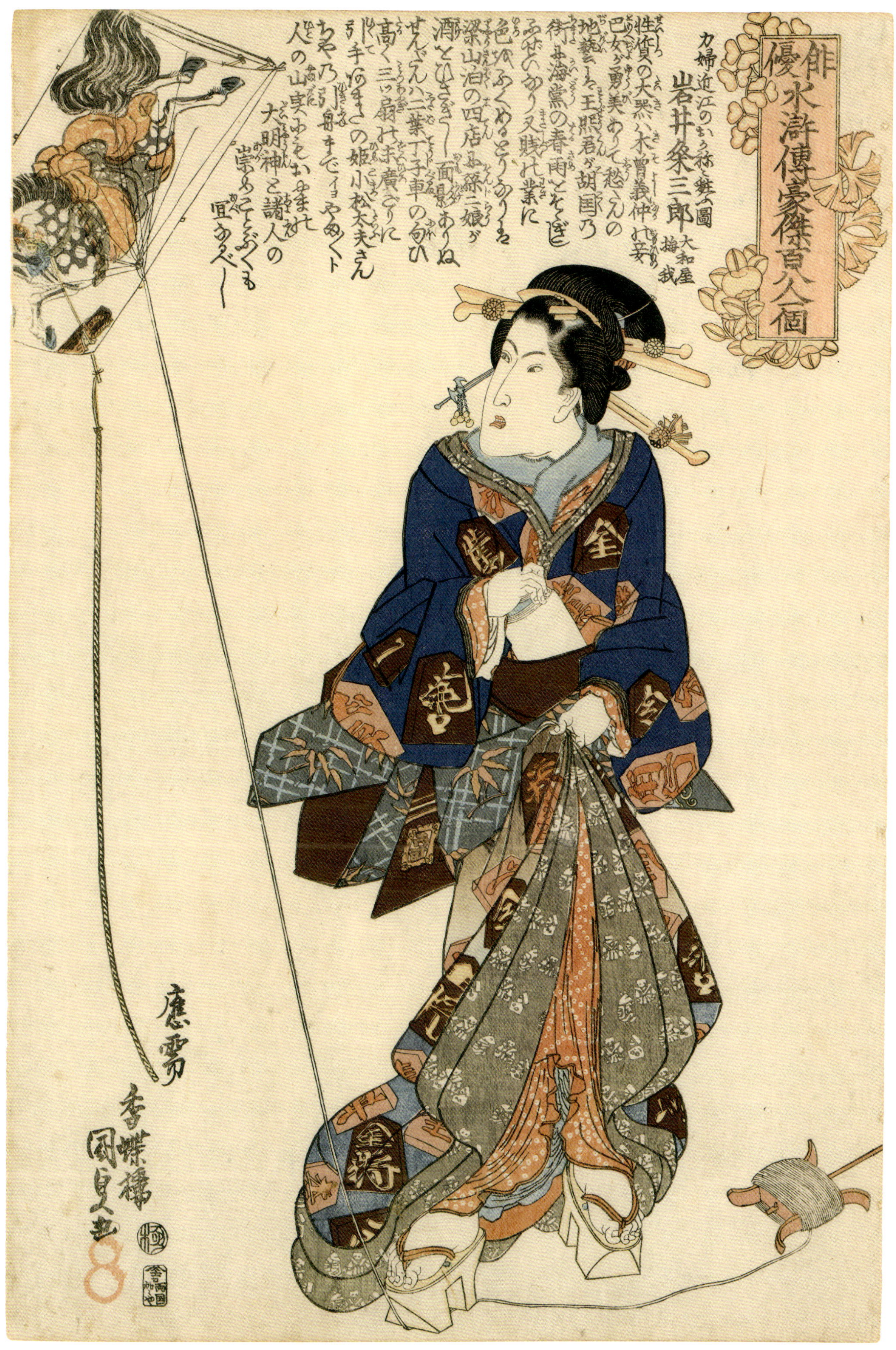

俳優水滸傳豪傑百八人一個
岩井粂三郎
大和屋 梅我
應需
香蝶樓國貞画

28

Kabuki Triptych
Utagawa Kuniyoshi (1798–1861)
signed: *Ichiyūsai Kuniyoshi ga*
publisher: Kawaguchiya Chōzō
c. 1835
ōban triptych (each sheet approximately 36.2 × 24.6 cm)

Three Kabuki actors in magnificent robes dispose of a couple of hoodlums with headbands; the actor's names appear beside them in large black *kanji.* Iwai Shijaku, second son of the great *onnagata* Iwai Hanshirō V, plays the female role on the right. Onoe Kikugorō III takes an imposing stance in the middle, and Ichikawa Ebizō V appears on the left; Ichikawa Ebizō V was the stage name taken by Ichikawa Danjūrō VII in 1832.

The figures stand in front of a cloudlike horizon, and the sky contains an amazing array of kites. Besides a fan kite, a *yakko,* and two bird-shaped and several rectangular kites, there is a kite in the shape of a catfish and another of a spider in its web. There is a crane and a kite in the form of Emma, king of Hell. Some of the kites in these fanciful shapes must have been difficult to fly.

The same face of Emma, almost as fierce as that of the actor himself, decorates Ebizō's robes. Along with a single sword, Ebizō has a *shakuhachi* flute stuck into his flamboyant sash; these are the attributes of an *otokodate,* young man-about-town (see the next entry).

Shijaku's large *obi* has an unusual design of clams. His blue outer robe bears two *hiragana* characters signifying *kira; kira* can mean gorgeous or dazzling clothes (*kira-kira* can mean twinkle, twinkle). The motif of Shijaku's gray inner robe also forms the word *kira* and seems to be a visual pun on the imperial paulownia *mon.*

Kikugorō's robes are decorated with a design of toys that include a good-luck owl, drum, hobbyhorse, and a red sea-bream on a trolley. Sea-bream was a New Year delicacy; this detail on Kikugorō's robe and the flying kites indicate that the occasion is New Year.

The word *mitate,* parody or comparison, appears alone at the right edge of the design, suggesting that this triptych may represent a special occasion rather than a standard Kabuki performance, or even an imagined combination of actors in scenes never actually performed on stage.[1]

1. See Clark 1997 for a discussion of *mitate-e,* sometimes translated as parody or "transpositional" print, and other related terms.

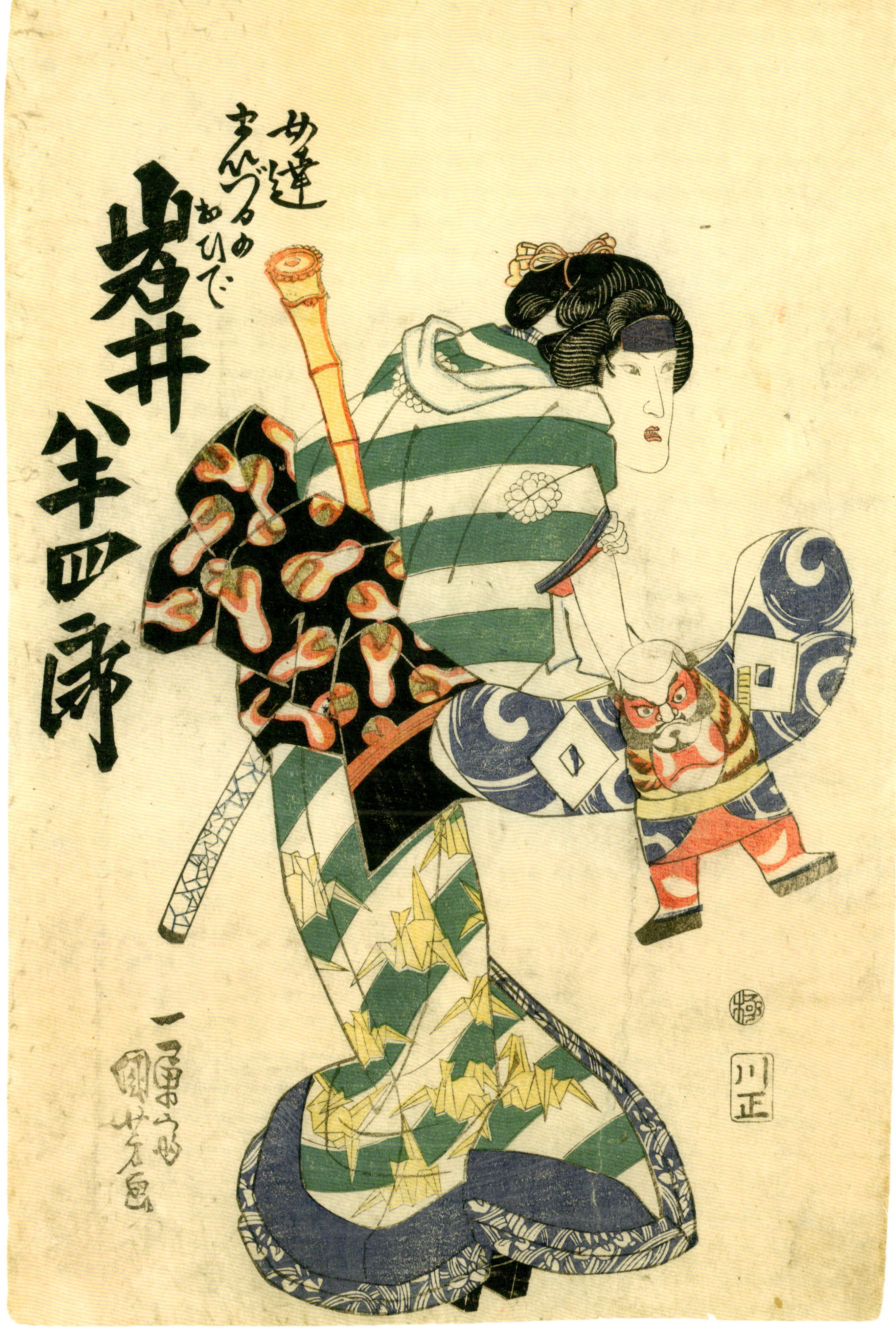
岩井半四郎
一勇斎国芳画
極
川正

30

Girls Playing Shuttlecock at New Year
Utagawa Kunisada (1786–1865)
signed: *Gototei Kunisada ga*
publisher: Sano-Ki
late 1830s
ōban (37 × 25.1 cm)

A *tobi* and several double-tailed rectangular kites soar over the Edo rooftops on a clear winter's day. Mount Fuji rises in a glorious backdrop to the west; the mountain is covered with winter snow and the evening sky is dyed red. The line of houses is pierced by a stack of drying bamboo in a lumberyard and a ladder, used for firefighting and lashed to the side of a house.

Two girls play *hanetsuki,* a game traditionally associated with New Year in which a feathered shuttlecock (*hane*) is hit back and forth with battledores (*hagoita*). The latter are often painted with bright designs, such as a favorite Kabuki actor or a rebus made up of daily objects (see plate 33). The game originated during the Heian period (794–1185) as an exorcism ritual; by Muromachi (1336–1568), it had become a pastime primarily for girls. The girls here in their *tabi* socks are probably two well-dressed sisters of the *chōnin,* merchant class. They wear beautiful, elaborately decorated robes and elegant platform *geta.* Besides the game of *hanetsuki,* their warm clothing and the kites indicate the season.

This sheet is probably part of a triptych. Its colors are unusually bright and fresh; most are traditional vegetable or mineral pigments, but the purple of the cloud-horizon is probably an early example of a foreign synthetic dye. Japan's isolation after the government banned most overseas trade in 1639 was far from watertight. In the 1820s, Prussian-blue dye began to be imported into Japan by Dutch traders and was quickly used on woodblock prints by publishers who were always looking for something novel to attract the buying public. At first the rarity and expense of these dyes restricted their use, but within a few decades imports of synthetic pigments from Europe had entirely changed the palettes and color balance of woodblock prints.

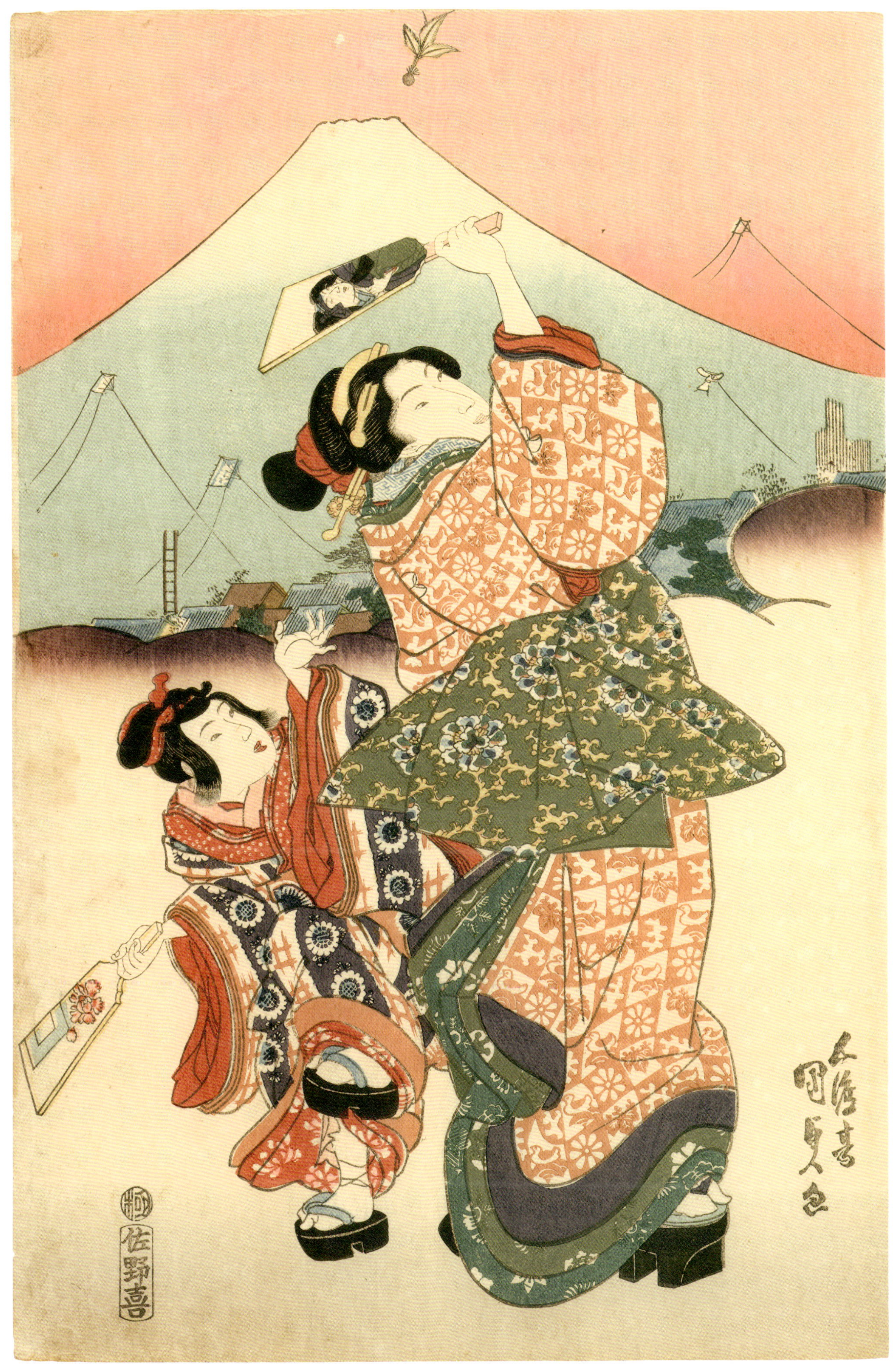
応需国貞画
極
佐野喜

31

Today's Kept Woman
Keisai Eisen (1790–1848)
signed: *Keisai Eisen ga*
publisher: Izumiya Ichibei
1830s
ōban (38.5 × 25.9 cm)

A young courtesan and a little boy, probably her son, are walking at New Year. She wears several layers of fine clothes, including an outer robe with a pine-needle decoration, and carries a bundle wrapped in a cloth with a sea-plover and swirling-water design. The boy carries a kite bearing the character for dragon and a spool of line. The young woman is richly dressed in a robe with a maple-leaf and pine-needle design and red undergarment; in a sensual gesture typical of Eisen she holds a knotted kerchief between her teeth. She turns her head as if looking at the round cartouche, which shows an old lady with a wrapped bundle holding a hairpin that she may be offering to a fortune-teller at a shrine.

The print forms part of a series whose title is given not in the cartouche, as would be usual, but in the characters to the girl's right: *Gokusaishiki segata no utsushi-e* (Multicolor Pictures of Transformation). The meaning probably plays with the word *utsushiyo,* meaning this transient life, which has similar connotations to *ukiyo,* the floating world (of transient pleasures). Instead of the series title, the cartouche states the subject of the design, with characters that read *Kakoime no genzai* (Today's Kept Woman). The word *kakoi* means enclosure; a mistress was sometimes called a *kakoimono,* enclosed thing, implying a woman kept for one man's pleasure, not a sensitive term.

The round cartouche with vignettes of aged people is repeated in other designs of the series. If the idea is that the courtesan is glancing into her inevitable future, this is an unusually black subject for a woodblock print. Prints, especially those of Edo, were usually bright and auspicious, aiming to induce positive reactions in a viewer—but Eisen was an eccentric character. He is best known for his sensual *bijin-ga* and was very much part of the demimonde that he portrayed. For a while he ran a brothel in the Nezu district of Edo, using his employees as models for his prints and paintings; the professional women of Nezu were much more direct and straightforward than the expensive women of the Yoshiwara, whose attractions were beginning to become formalized and less stylish. Eisen's establishment was destroyed by fire, however, and he was forced to disappear for a while when it was found that he had misappropriated another man's seal and incurred substantial debts. Several stories describe his taking a down-payment from a publisher and spending it all on women and wine, then being found dead drunk and in no condition to complete the commission.

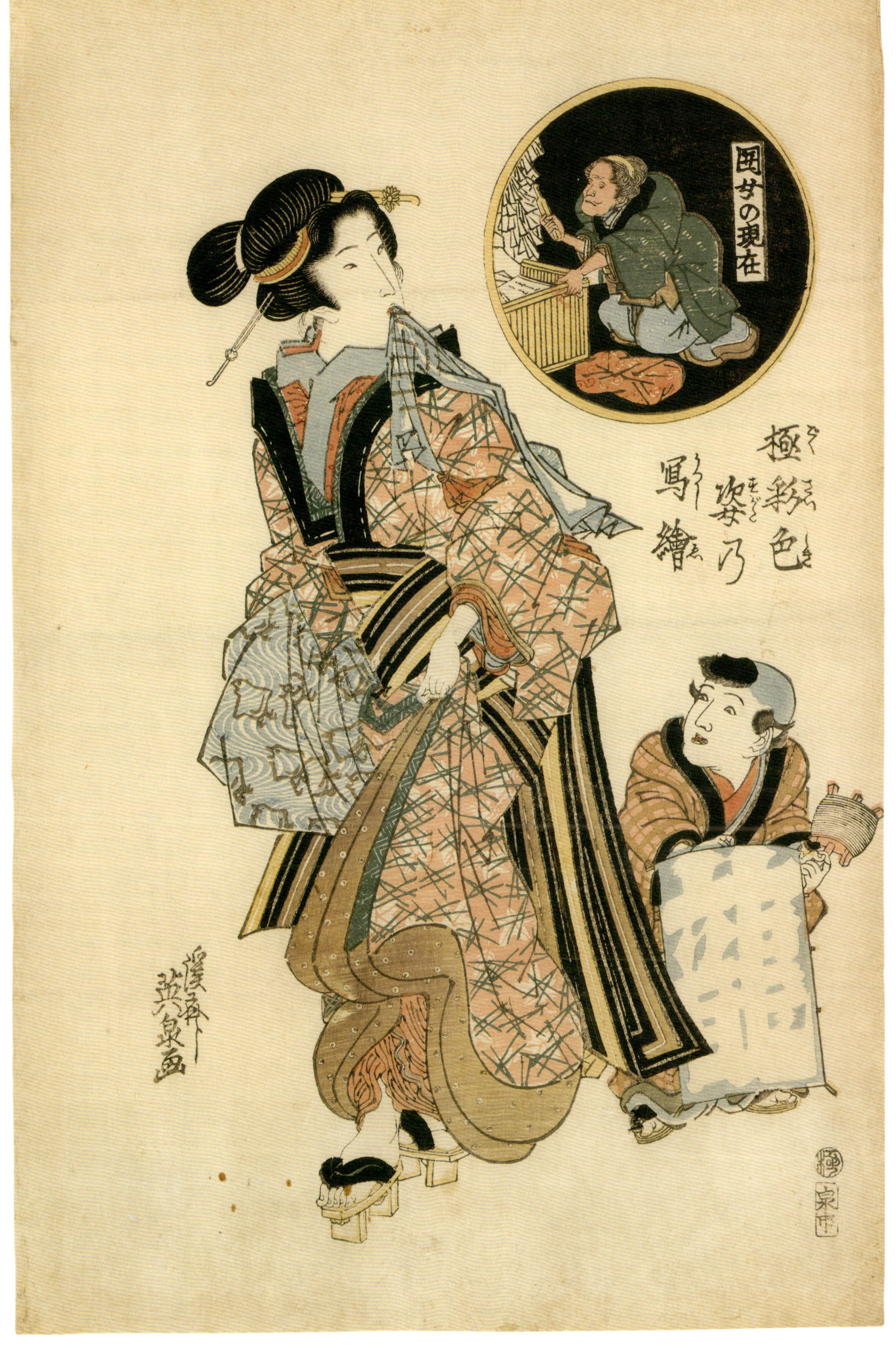

囲女の現在
極彩色姿乃写絵
渓斎英泉画

32

First of the Five Festivals
Utagawa Kuniyoshi (1798–1861)
signed: *Ichiyūsai Kuniyoshi*
publisher: Enshūya Matabei
1843–46
ōban triptych (each sheet approximately 36.5 × 25.5 cm)

Three young women are celebrating New Year with their sons or the boys of the neighborhood. The center of attention is a large Daruma kite. At least three young boys can be made out holding up the kite as the network of strings connecting its face to its main control line are separated and arranged for flight. Another boy, at the left, is laying out the two groups of heavier ropes attached to the bottom corners that form the kite's stabilizing tails when it is flying. Every detail has been carefully drawn and is technically accurate, down to the knots in the ropes.

The fierce face of Daruma as he struggled to gain enlightenment was a favorite decoration for kites. Daruma, called Bodhidarma in Sanskrit, was the Indian teacher who brought Chan (Zen) Buddhism to China in the sixth century. Kuniyoshi's stylized representation of his hairy foreign features and round eyes is skillful. Daruma spent nine years meditating in front of a wall until the wall crumbled, a story that led to an irreverent comparison with courtesans, who owed their employers ten years of servitude. A subtheme of *ukiyo-e* showed Daruma disporting himself in the clothes of a courtesan and courtesans dressed as holy men (see plate 69).

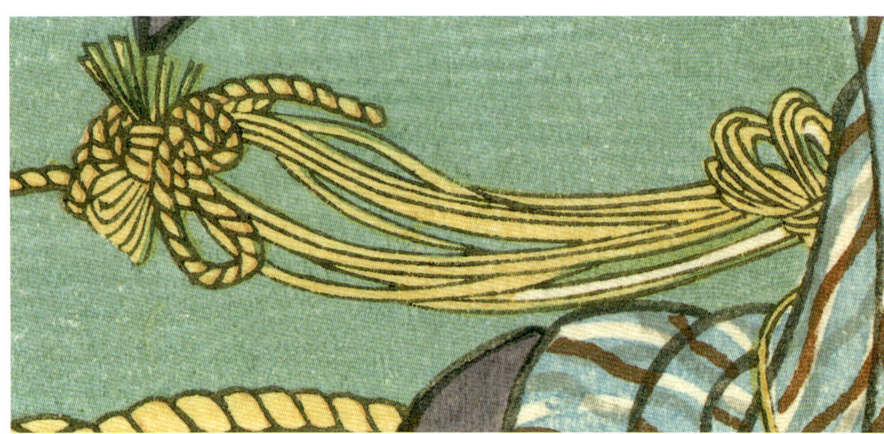

In the background are Mount Fuji covered with snow, New Year pine-tree decorations, and casks of saké wrapped in straw coverings, all indicating the season. The pine-tree decorations stand outside the premises of the Mitsui store (see plate 21); above them is a sign advertising sundry goods. Two laborers bend their backs to haul a cart heavily laden with bales of rice.

The colors of this print are bright and fresh and the carved lines of the women's hair and Daruma's beard are extremely crisp. The barefoot girls are beautifully dressed, the layers of robes artfully turned back so that their full luxury can be appreciated. The girls are probably courtesans or geisha, and their establishment is probably located behind the black fence at the right, which is not typical of a normal residence. One girl wears a housewife's apron; perhaps they are geisha playing at being housewives. Two wear red silk undergarments, a color thought to protect women and young children against harm; to catch sight of a woman's red undergarment was considered mildly titillating. One of the girls holds a shuttlecock and battledore; a young girl dressed in her best hangs onto her arm. In a reference to a love poem, another of the girls finds herself entwined in the line of a fallen *tobi* kite (see plates 17 and 35). The little boy she carries on her back holds a tiny toy *yakko* kite on a stick.

The title of the triptych is *Gosekku no uchi mutsuki* (Five Festivals: Mutsuki); *mutsuki* was the name of the first of the five major festivals of the Edo year. The whole forms an idealized image of prosperity and good fortune ushering in the New Year.

33

The Shiba Shrine during the First-month Festival
Utagawa Kunisada (1786–1865)
signed: *Kōchōrō Toyokuni ga* and *Kunisada aratame nidaime Toyokuni ga*
publisher: Kagaya Yasubei
1844
ōban triptych (each sheet approximately 38.1 × 26.1 cm)

After Kuniyoshi's interpretation of Mutsuki, the first of the five great festivals of the Edo year, here is Kunisada's. Both are triptychs of very high quality, in excellent condition, made at about the same time.

The title of Kunisada's triptych is *Tōto meiri yuran mutsuki Shiba shinmei* (Tour of Edo's Famous Places: The Shiba Shrine during the First-month Festival). Three elegant young ladies of the merchant class dressed in gorgeous robes for the festival stroll demurely during the New Year holiday outside the Myōjin Shrine at Shiba. The gateways of the shrine appear at the left. The sky is filled with kites, including an aerodynamically challenging group of bird shapes (see plate 7)—branch-train kites like this are very hard to fly. A *yakko* kite flown by a little boy has become entangled suggestively within the robes of one of the girls, echoing the theme of a popular song. Like the woman in the next print, she carries a New Year gift in a *furoshiki* cloth. The girl at the right carries a battledore painted with objects that make up an auspicious rebus. The first is a cherry blossom, indicating the syllable *sa;* the other objects are the hat and raincoat of invisibility and gold jewels, all part of the Myriad Treasures associated with the Seven Lucky Gods (see plates 79–81), whose ship comes into harbor on New Year's Day.

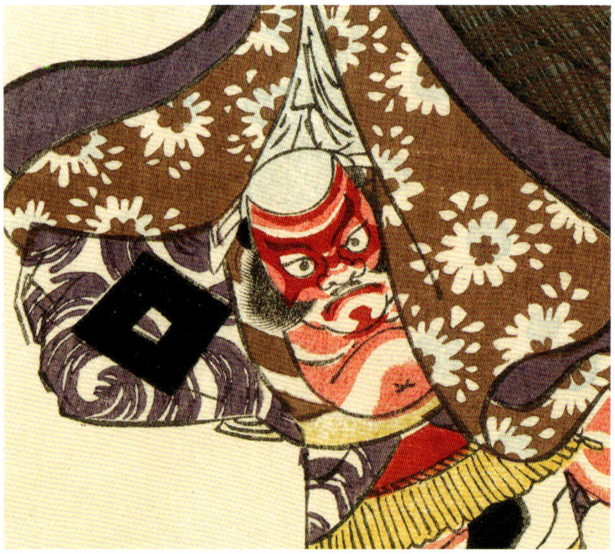

Pine-and-bamboo New Year decorations stand outside the line of houses in the background. The symbol of the publisher and Kunisada's round *toshidama* seal are used whimsically on the sides of two of the buildings. The title cartouche is also in the form of a *toshidama.* The *mura* seal of the censor Murata Heiemon appears on each panel of the triptych, dating it to between 1843 and 1846; in other years his seal was used combined with those of other censors. The date can be further pinpointed: two of the sheets are signed *Kōchōrō Toyokuni ga,* but the central panel is signed *Kunisada aratame nidaime Toyokuni ga.* This means, "drawn by Kunisada who changes his name to Toyokuni II," and marks the artist's confident appropriation of his master's famous name on the seventh day of the New Year, Kōka 1 (1844). It is unlikely that the artist would have used this form of signature for more than a few months, by which time his name change would have become generally known.

Foreground and background are delineated by the same purple cloud-line we see in the next two prints. The purple, used also in the girls' robes, is probably an imported pigment. The natural dyes of the rest of this print are delightfully fresh and unfaded, and the color balance is simple and sophisticated.

In the 1830s, '40s, and '50s, the Utagawa print school was split into two branches, one headed by Kuniyoshi, the other by Kunisada, who was considered in his own time as the greatest *ukiyo-e* artist ever. Kunisada was best known for his figure designs; Kuniyoshi specialized in warrior prints and scenes from history, as well as genre prints showing scenes of everyday life. Both designed actor prints. This and the preceding triptych, both interpretations of the Mutsuki New Year festival, provide a direct comparison of their work. Their rivalry was productive and both triptychs are very fine.

A young woman dressed in heavy, fashionable robes watches her son play with his New Year *tobi* kite, which is balanced by the auspicious crane in the round cartouche. The characters in the cartouche read *Mitate fukujinko takarabune* (Parody, or Comparison, of Lucky People and Children and the Treasure-boat); the title's intention is perhaps to give a general sense of good fortune rather than a literal meaning. The *takarabune,* treasure-ship of the Seven Lucky Gods, was believed to sail into harbor on New Year's Day laden with the gods' traditional myriad treasures.

The boy's robe has an *origami*-crane design, perhaps an echo of the cartouche, and his head is shaved in the manner of a five- or six-year-old. The woman's bare feet suggest that she is a courtesan or geisha. Her outer robe is a fashionable plaid. Her *obi,* sash, is a huge affair, decorated with Genji-chapter motifs, with a bow at the back hanging almost to her ankles. She holds up her robes with her right hand as she steps in her elegant high *geta;* the blue cloth she holds under her left arm is probably a New Year gift wrapped in a *furoshiki.* The design has been stamped by the censor Hama Yahei, whose circular seal, *hama,* appears by itself on prints from 1843 to 1846 and later in combination with the seals of other censors.

The palette of the print is limited to a few colors. The back of the print shows a brighter yellow than the color that now appears in the shoes and the vertical cartouche; yellow was also used in the *obi,* distinguishing it from the other blues in the print before it faded. The original color of the horizontal cloud-line can be seen at the extreme left, which was at one time shielded from light.

34

Courtesan and Boy with Hawk-kite
Utagawa Kunisada (1786–1865)
signed: *Kōchōrō Toyokuni ga*
publisher: Fujiokaya Keijirō
1843–46
ōban (37.6 × 25.5 cm)

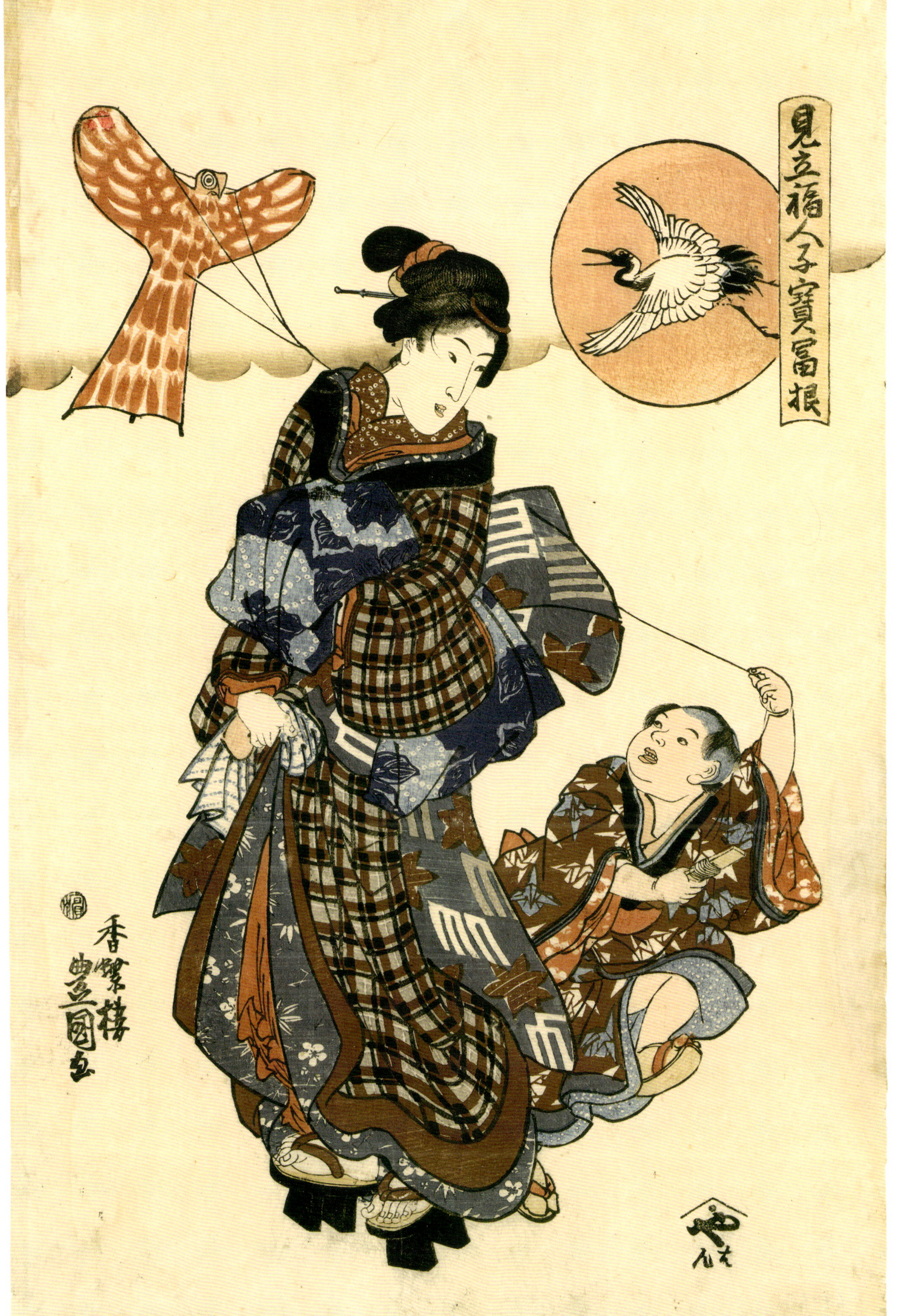
見立福人子寶富根
香蝶楼
豊国画

35

Girl and the String of a Fallen *Tobi* Kite
Ichieisai Yoshitsuya (1822–66)
signed: *Ichieisai Yoshitsuya ga*
c. 1845
ōban (37.2 × 24.9 cm)

In this charming design, the line of a *tobi* kite falls across the shoulders of a beautiful girl, a reference to a love poem and a popular song. In an ancient tradition that goes back long before the Edo period and which has Buddhist origins, string or thread symbolizes destiny and the ties between human beings, which include the entanglements of love. A married couple are imagined as being tied together with string. Following a spool of thread looms large in the plot of *Imoseyama onna teiken* (The Exemplary Woman of Mount Imo [representing a woman] and Mount Se [representing a man]), a Kabuki play that originated in Osaka in 1771 before becoming very popular in Edo. See also plate 17 for a more ribald comment on the kite-line story.

The girl's robes have the long sleeves typically worn by an unmarried maiden; her hairstyle includes the hair ornaments of a teenager; and she wears *tabi,* socks: this is the daughter of a merchant family. The cartouche reads *Gosekku no uchi* (The Five Festivals); this print depicts the first festival, New Year, and she holds a New Year battledore and a ball made of tightly woven thread. The objects painted on the battledore, which include the hat of invisibility, form a rebus. Her robe has a *hanaguruma,* flower-wheel, pattern. Her *obi* is distinctly oversized and similar to the *obi* of the woman in the previous print. There is no censor's seal to date the print, but Edo fashions changed quickly and the similar *obi*s suggest that this and the previous print were made at about the same time.

The stylized cloud-line that appears across the background of both these sheets and the previous triptych suggests that there also was a certain fashion in print designs. All three designs are by artists of the Utagawa school, which dominated *ukiyo-e* at this time. The school was divided into two rival branches: Kunisada was the leading teacher of one branch, Kuniyoshi the other. The previous two designs are by Kunisada himself; this design is by one of Kuniyoshi's best students, Yoshitsuya.

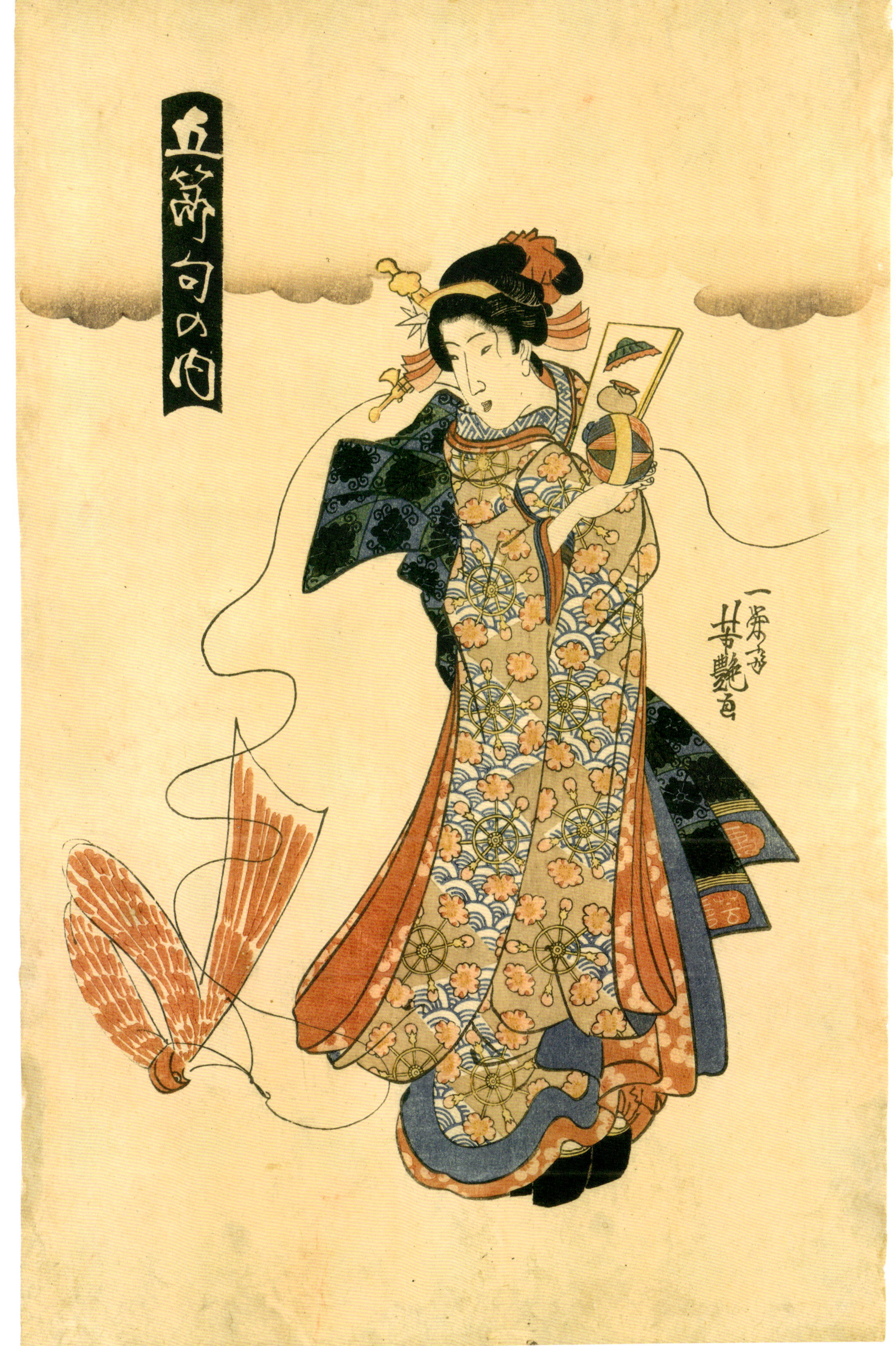
五節句の内
一英斎芳艶画

36

Kabuki Actors, Cherry Blossoms, and *Yakko* Kite
Utagawa Kunisada (1786–1865)
signed: *Ichiyōsai Toyokuni ga, Toyokuni ga,* and *ōju Toyokuni ga*
publisher: Yamagushiya
1847–48
ōban triptych (each sheet approximately 36.1 × 24.5 cm)

37

Trapping the White Fox
Utagawa Kuniyoshi (1798–1861)
signed: *Ichiyūsai Kuniyoshi*
publisher: Ibaya Senzaburō
1847–48
ōban triptych (each sheet approximately 36.4 × 23.9 cm)

As we saw in plate 19, it was an Edo custom to perform a scene from a Soga Brothers play at New Year. The performance usually focused on the climactic moments of the play *Soga no taimen,* when the two brothers confront their father's murderer, Kudō no Suketsune, at his New Year celebrations. Gorō has to be restrained from throwing the offering-stand for his gift at his host. This basic theme was interpreted in many ways, with the sexes of the protagonists and other details changed, often radically. Gorō, the younger and more impulsive of the brothers, acts in the bombastic *aragoto* style and wears bold *kumadori* makeup; his brother, Jūrō, acts in the more restrained *wagoto* style.

These Kabuki triptychs by the two most important print artists of their day bear similar date seals but depict different interpretations of the story. In Kunisada's version, the figures have been changed to a handsome young man and two women. Soga no Gorō's emblem was a butterfly, which can be seen on the young man's robe. Jūrō's emblem was a *chidori,* sea plover; the *chidori* design on the robe of the woman in the center indicates that she represents Jūrō. The two figures are also related by the similar stylized treatment of the butterfly and plover designs. The robe of the woman holding a knife bears emblems of the villain, Lord Kudō. The young man (Gorō) appears to be presenting the woman with a New Year *yakko* kite on an offering-stand like the one Gorō tries to hurl at Kudō in the traditional play, and the young woman (Jūrō) offers a shuttlecock and battledore, also placed on an offering-stand. The battledore bears the same auspicious hat and raincoat of invisibility that we saw in plate 33. Plum blossoms indicate the season, as they do in the artist's diptych of a Soga Brothers performance thirty years before (plate 19). The *yakko* kite bears a crane motif, emblem of Gorō's friend Asahina, as in the earlier diptych.

Kuniyoshi's triptych has a similar format of confronted figures; the roles (but not the actors) are identified in the yellow cartouches. A number of details show that the two designs are related. Gorō Tokimune at the left, wearing *kumadori* makeup and a robe with a butterfly design, faces the villain Kudō Suketsune, who holds a fox mask. Kudō's rich brocade robe bears a single example of his personal emblem. The woman is identified as Asahidayū, a courtesan of the highest class; there is doubtless a reference to Asahina Saburō, Gorō's friend, also known as Kobayashi no Asahina. To complicate the nomenclature, the man behind Gorō is identified as Kobayashi Tsurukichi. He holds a kite decorated with a New Year crane, *tsuru* (a pun on his name), like the crane on the *yakko's* shoulder in Kunisada's print. The same military crests that appear on the tent cloth in the background appear on the sashes of the figures in Kunisada's print; one is the emblem of the publisher of Kuniyoshi's design.

Kunisada's print is untitled but appears to be more closely related to the traditional Soga story. Kuniyoshi's print is titled *Tsurigitsune wana no kangiku* (Trapping the White Fox) and is an example of the imaginative nature of Kabuki plots and subplots, where a playwright could pursue a flight of fancy that took him far away from the original story. Smaller characters in the title cartouche of Kuniyoshi's triptych mean three days and three nights at the Daiichiza, Great Theater. The scene is set in the *Ukiyo kuruwa no zensei* (Floating-world Brothel at the Height of Prosperity) where the performance continued for three days and nights.

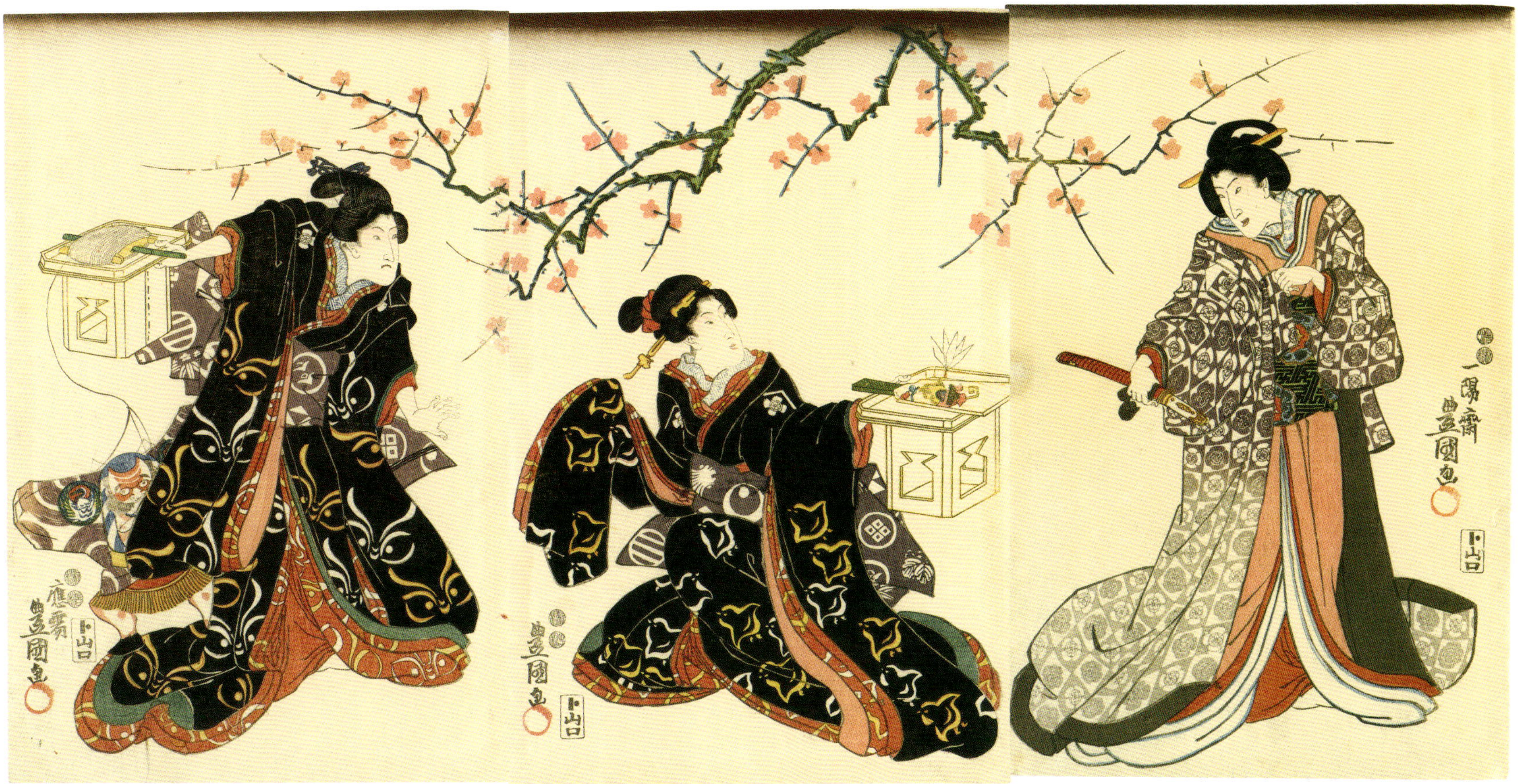

一陽斎豊国画

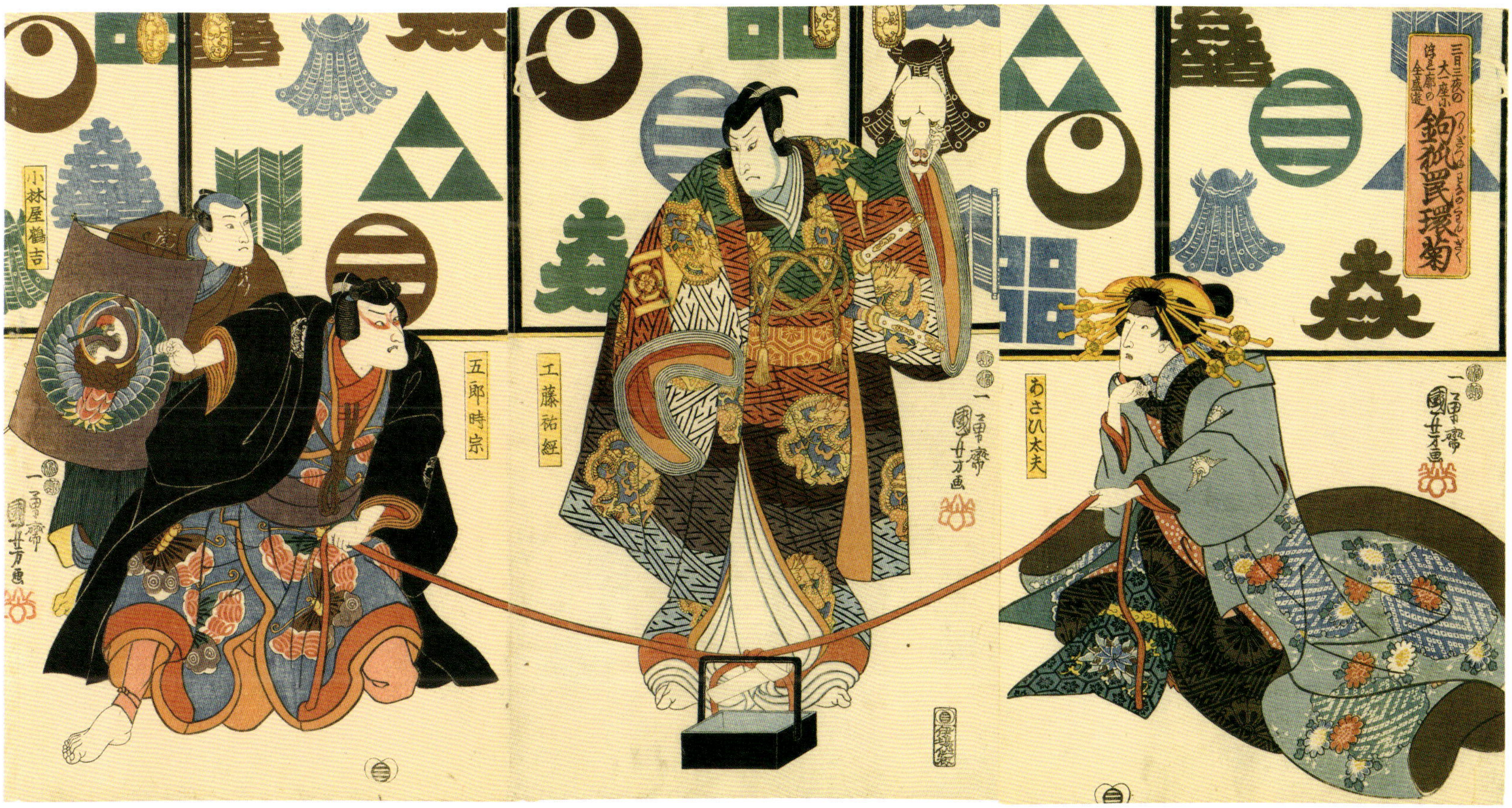

三月三夜の 大一座ふ 蓬莱廓の 全盛遊 鉤瓶罠環菊

小林屋梅吉

五郎時宗

工藤祐経

あさひ太夫

一勇斎国芳画

38

Spring Festivities
Utagawa Kuniyoshi (1798–1861)
signed: *Ichiyūsai Kuniyoshi*
publisher: Waka-u
1845–50
ōban triptych (each sheet approximately 35.7 × 25.8 cm)

Besides producing Kabuki and historical prints depicting scenes of high moral intensity, Kuniyoshi took a delight in everyday life that was shared by Hokusai before him and Kyōsai after, but not perhaps by his more restrained contemporary, Kunisada. This triptych is titled *Haru no nigiwai* (Spring Festivities). Like plates 32 and 33, it celebrates New Year festivities, but it is of a different quality. The colors are simple and the carving quite crude, and the design's appeal lies in its details and its vigorous portrayal of people enjoying themselves rather than expensive printing or an uplifting moral story. It aimed at a different segment of the market than Kuniyoshi's more formal and finished Kabuki prints.

Starting at the right, as a Japanese viewer would have done (it is unusual to have the title cartouche on the left), we see a *nori* seaweed vendor standing with a shoulder-pole in front of a large New Year pine-and-bamboo decoration. Two *daikagura* performers, one with a drum, sing as a townsman dances; a boy supports him and he is probably drunk. Behind them a boy flies a New Year kite and four others gather round a candy-seller's portable stall; one of the boys carries a Daruma kite. The candyman is making blown-sugar treats, similar to glass-blowing. These fragile objects could be eaten right away or used as toys for a while; the craft is still alive at temple fairs today. In the background a boy tries to bring down his friend's kite with a stone attached to a string.

To the left, musicians and a lion-dancer amuse a group of young boys. With typical playfulness, Kuniyoshi shows the lion pretending to bite the head of one of the boys; this was considered good luck for the child. A dog joins in the fun. The background consists of snowy Mount Fuji and a sky-full of kites. The characters on the kites in the central panel mean fish and dragon; an octopus kite flies in the distance.

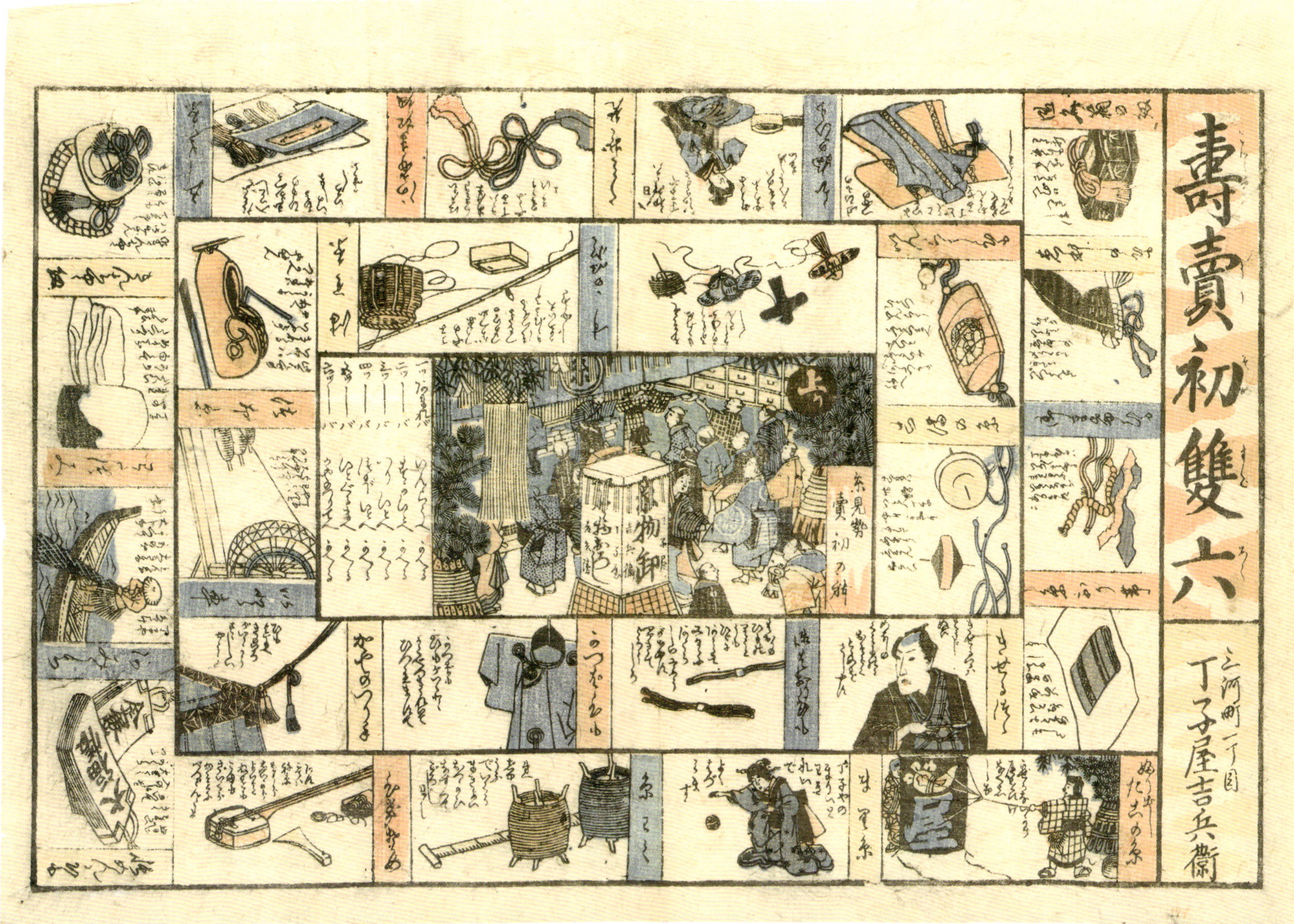

壽賣初雙六
三河町一丁目
丁子屋吉兵衛

40
Kite Designs
Utagawa Yoshifuji (1828–87)
unsigned
publisher: Kazusaya Iwakichi
1843–46
ōban (35.6 × 24.5 cm)

41
Kite Designs
anonymous
c. 1845
ōban (34.4 × 23.8 cm)

42
Newly Printed Sheet of a Kite Collection
Utagawa Yoshifuji (1828–87)
signed: *Ichieisai ga*
publisher: Seijō
1847–48
ōban (36 × 24.8 cm)

43
Newly Printed Sheet of a Kite Collection
Utagawa Yoshikazu (fl. 1850s–60s)
signed: *Ichiyūsai Yoshikazu ga*
publisher: Kinseidō
1849–53
ōban (37.1 × 26 cm)

Kites were a young boys' sport and were associated with Boy's Day, the fifth day of the fifth month. These four sheets show legendary Japanese heroes alternating with large stylized characters, or, in one case, firemen's standards. An Edo boy growing up in a culture steeped in tales of Japan's rich history would have immediately recognized these figures; each was a model of courage, strength, perseverance, or some other manly virtue. The rectangles, both of figures and Chinese characters, could be cut out and used as toys or models or even as tiny kites themselves.[1]

The two unsigned sheets are by different hands, though both are drawn in the bombastic manner of Kuniyoshi's school. The center of one sheet features the ferocious stare of Daruma, the Zen patriarch we saw in plate 32. Benkei with his hood and huge mallet appears in the other sheet, along with Kintarō, the Golden Boy, wrestling with a carp in a waterfall; Kintarō was a model of strength for young boys (see plates 2 and 3). Above them fly three cranes of immortality with auspicious poem slips (as in plate 7).

The two signed sheets are by Yoshifuji and Yoshikazu, students of Kuniyoshi. Both designs are titled *Shinhan tako zukushi* (Newly Printed Sheet of a Kite Collection). They show Japanese heroes with their distinctive attributes. Satō no Tadanobu, for example, in the bottom left corner of Yoshifuji's signed print, can be identified by the thick wooden *go* board that he turned into a lethal weapon. Benkei, with his heavy hood and mallet, glowers. In the top right panel of Yoshikazu's print, Kintarō throws beans at a little green demon on New Year's Eve. Below him appears Jiraiya, bandit and toad magician. Jiraiya was a folk hero derived from an Indian ascetic who became the protagonist of a wildly successful Kabuki play called *Jiraiya gōketsu monogatari,* which debuted in 1852. Danjūrō VIII was the actor who made it famous, shortly before his untimely death (plate 49).

In Yoshifuji's print, plate 42, the heroes' faces alternate with *matoi,* firemen's standards. Firemen too were heroes in Edo, notorious for boisterous and daredevil behavior. So common were fires in the city's crowded wooden houses, and so colorful the conflagrations, that they were called, with typical Edo bravado, *hana no Edo,* flowers of Edo. Each district had its band of firemen, which had its own distinctive tall standard made of paper and leather, used for signaling when the noise and heat of the fire made other communication impossible. Though often raffish, firemen, like generals and other heroes, had qualities of bravery and strength to offer as models for growing boys.

The large flamboyant characters, which are kite designs in their own right, include the words for dragon, eagle, storm, orchid, treasure, and good luck. There is also the character for fish—perhaps the idea is that, like squid and octopus (and carp and catfish; see the following designs), they "swim" in the sky, and flying them is like playing a fish at the end of a line. The center panel of Yoshifuji's unsigned print, plate 40, reads *matoi,* like the ones he depicts in plate 42.

1. The art of making tiny kites, which pick up the slightest breeze and can be flown even indoors, is continued in Kyoto today by Nobuhiko Yoshizumi, who travels often to proselytize his craft.

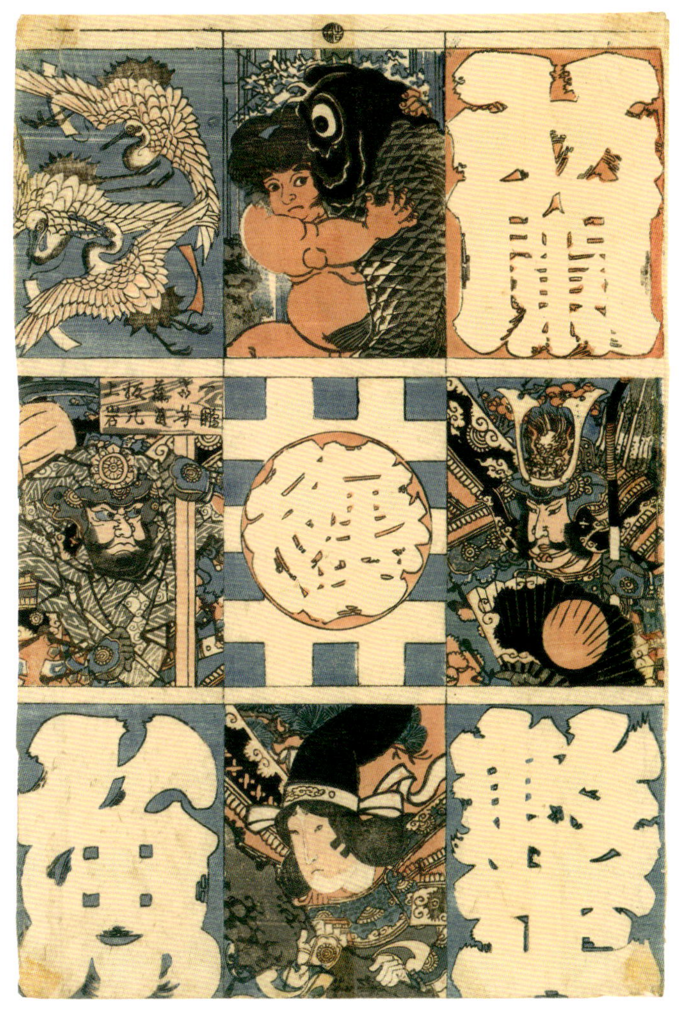

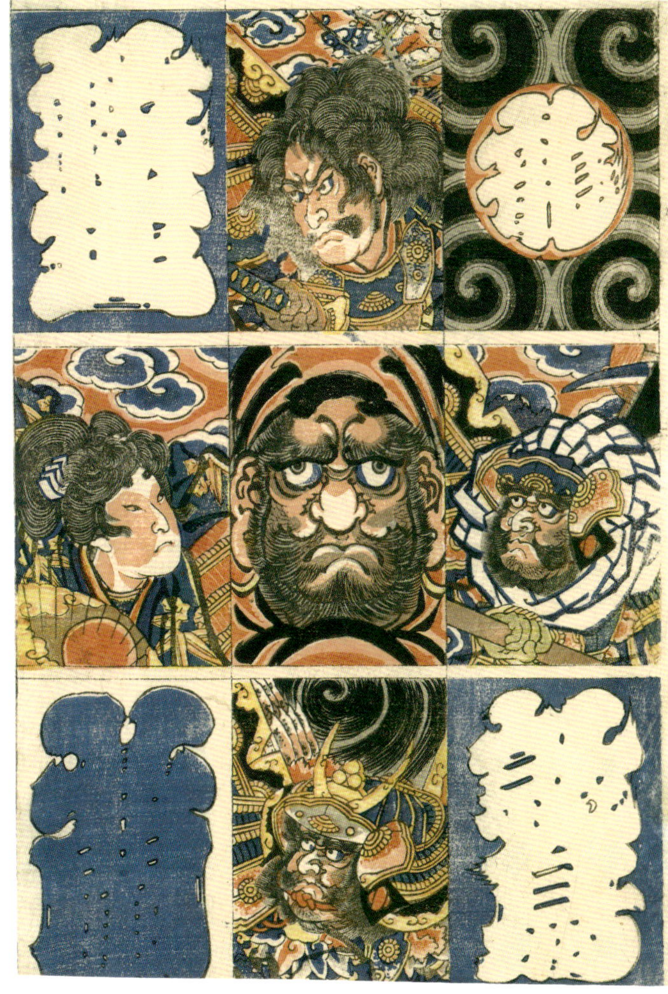

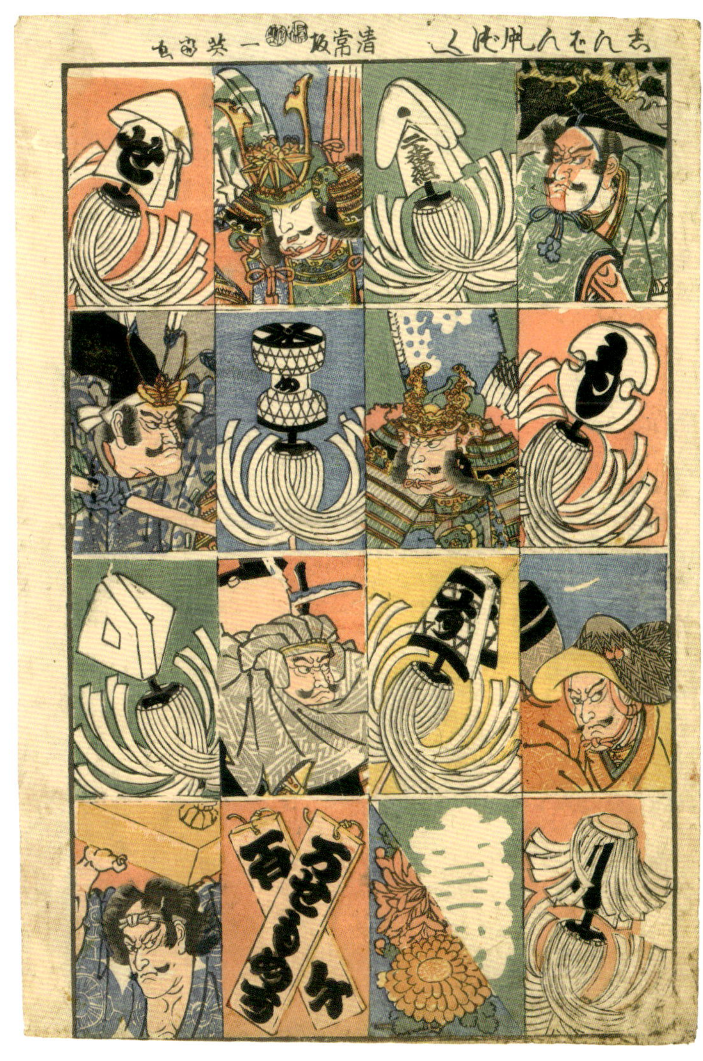
清常板
一英斎画

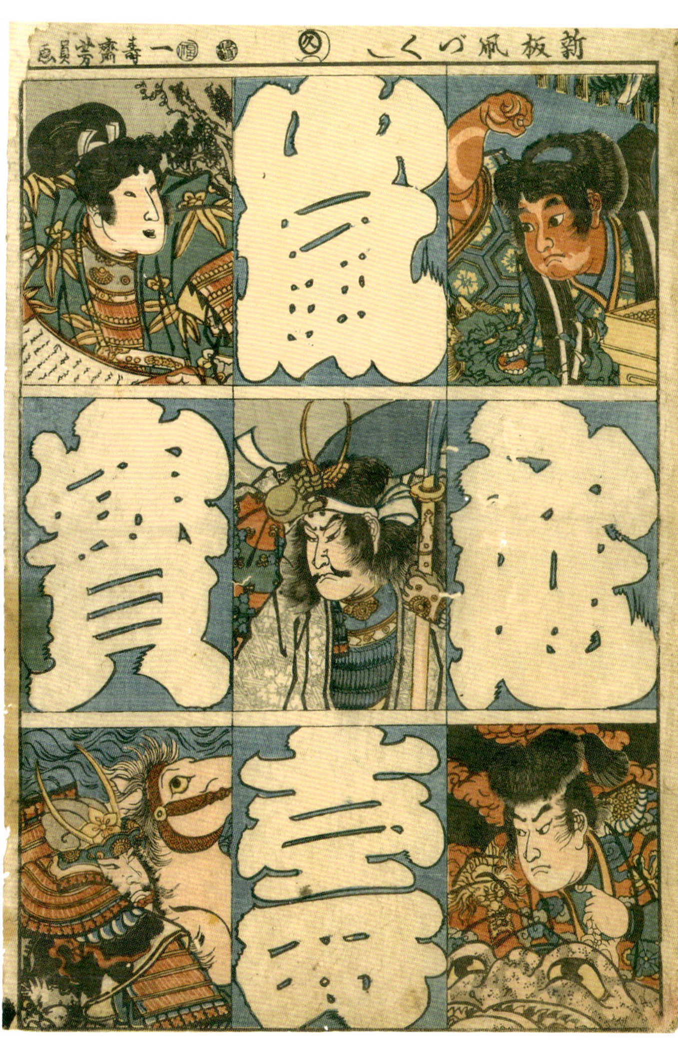
新板凧づくし
一寿斎芳員画

44

New Edition of a Collection of Kite Shapes
Utagawa Yoshifuji (1828–87)
signed: *Ippōsai Yoshifuji ga*
publisher: Tsujiokaya Bunsuke
1849–53
ōban (37.5 × 25.1 cm)

The title of this print is *Shinban katachi tako zukushi* (New Edition of a Collection of Kite Shapes). The tabs on some of the designs show how they were intended to be cut out and used as toys. A big-bellied *tanuki* badger at lower right has a separate tail to be attached; the *hiragana* next to it says *tanuki no shippo,* badger tail. Hokusai designed similar sheets of cutouts for making toy buildings, bathhouses, and shops.[1]

The range of designs is impressive. Included are a phoenix and a cicada; a *yakko* kite next to one in the form of a workman; an octopus at the top and a squid at the bottom; a rising-sun fan and a gourd. The design at upper right, shaped rather like a Suruga kite, is decorated with a bag of treasures and the hat of invisibility. There is a long-tongued lantern ghost and next to it the tofu-loving goblin, his tongue licking a block of tofu, who likes to scare children—he is holding an account book for tofu purchases. The entertainer named *saru mawashi,* monkey trainer, below them is provided with a separate tongue to cut out and attach.

Unlikely shapes for kites include a shop lantern and a warrior's helmet. The catfish banner on the right is a reminder that Edoites believed earthquakes were caused by the wriggling of a giant catfish deep under the ground. Next to it is Fukusuke, the large-headed dwarf who brings good luck. The star actor Danjūrō himself appears at the bottom, bowing behind his huge sleeves in the *Shibaraku* role that we saw in plate 12.

1. Tobu Museum of Art 1993, 104–5.

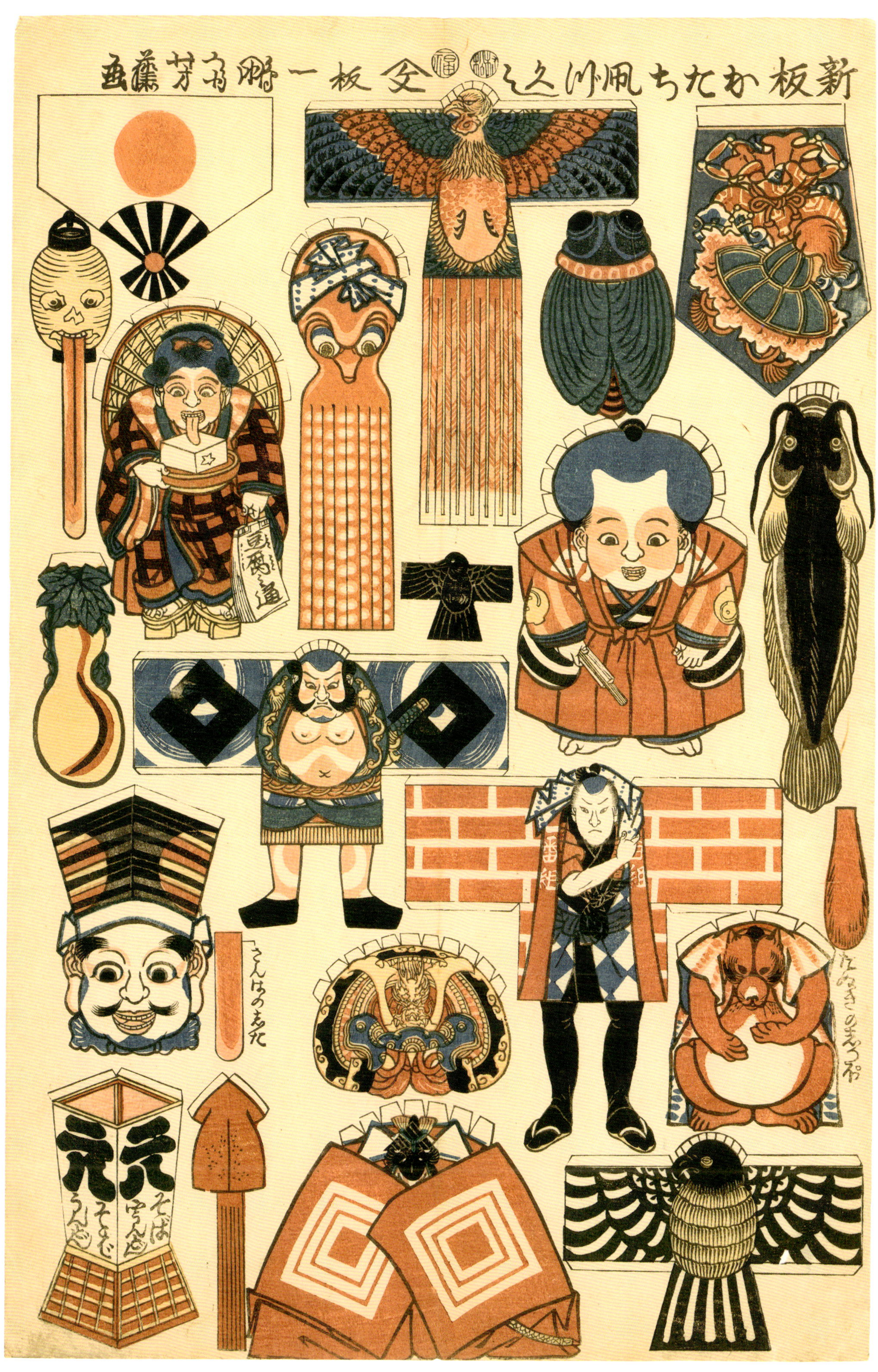
新板かたち凧づくし
全板
一鵬斎芳藤画

45

New Edition of Collected Kite Cutouts
Utagawa Yoshifuji (1828–87)
signed: *Ippōsai Yoshifuji ga*
publisher: Tsujiokaya Bunsuke
1849–50
ōban (37 × 24.7 cm)

This print has a title similar to the previous one, *Shinban kirinuki tako zukushi* (New Edition of Collected Kite Cutouts). Though not in good condition, it is included because it shows more of the fanciful kite designs of late Edo, all with auspicious or symbolic significance. There is a lucky bat and a lucky rabbit; another badger at bottom left, another phoenix, and an armored warrior; another *yakko* kite and one in the form of a tattooed workman. The *tanuki*'s tail has been printed to be cut out separately, as has the tongue of the *saru mawashi,* monkey trainer, at center right, who brings good luck with the entertainment he provides to households at New Year.

Some of these shapes must have been very difficult to fly—for example, the one-legged umbrella ghost at upper left. Like many inanimate household objects, umbrellas were believed to become mischievous spirits when they wore out. Ghost stories described travelers spending the night at abandoned houses where everyday objects assumed a life of their own at nightfall, partying till dawn and preventing the tired but unintimidated traveler from sleeping. Umbrella ghosts figured in early nineteenth-century Kabuki plays and still haunt modern comic books.

The carp at the right is a sort of banner that was flown at the top of a post like a windsock on Boy's Day, the fifth day of the fifth month. Following a Chinese story of determined carp who leaped waterfalls at the Dragon Gate on the Yellow River and became dragons themselves, carp were considered symbols of strength and perseverance, appropriate models for young boys to emulate. These banners were not strictly kites but were included in a print of kite designs, like the catfish toward the right of the previous print.

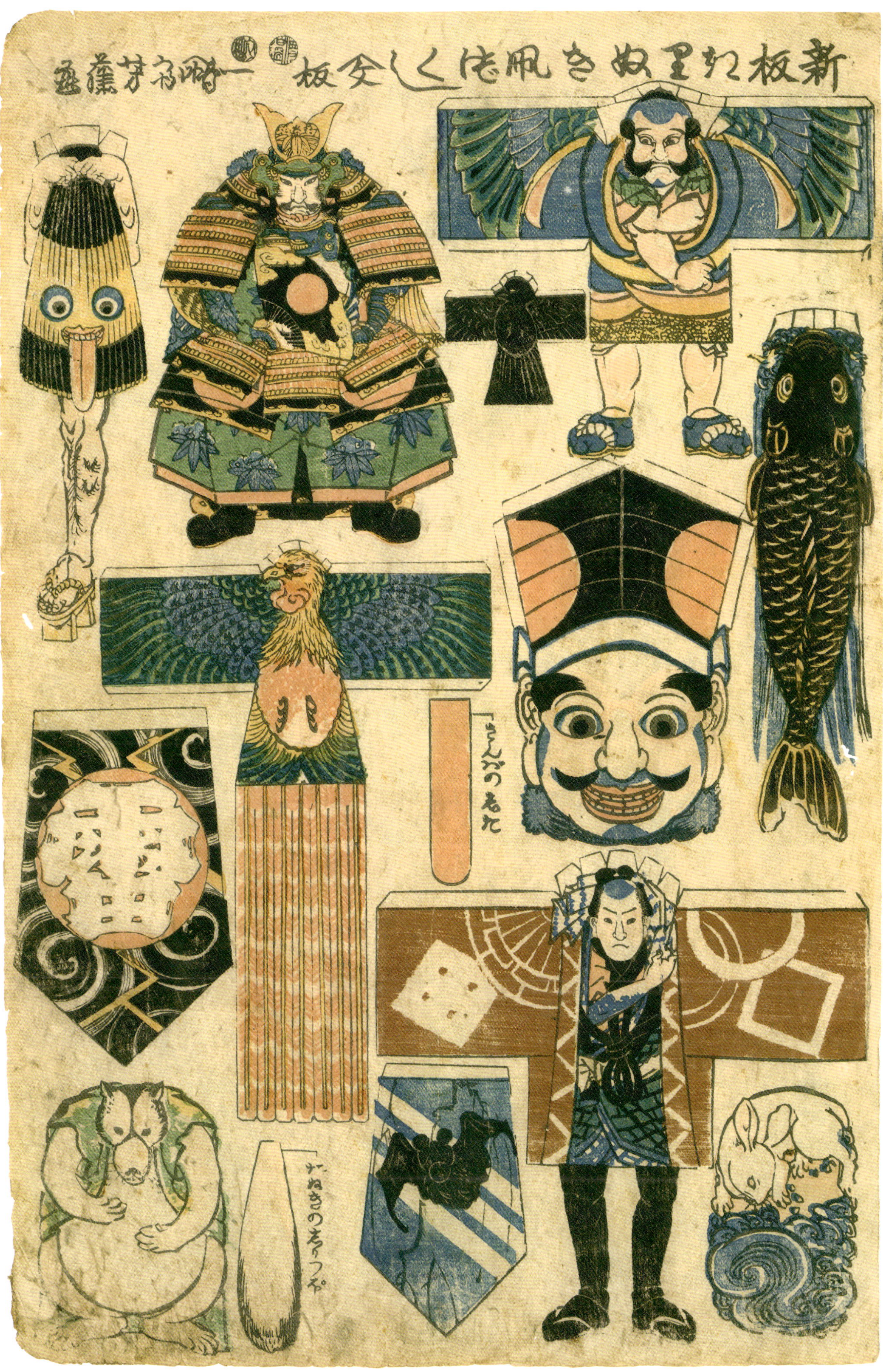

一鵬斎芳藤画
たぬきのしつぽ

46

Spring Worth a Thousand Gold Pieces
Utagawa Kunisada (1786–1865)
signed: *Kōchōrō Toyokuni ga*
publisher: Wakasaya Yoichi
1847–53
ōban (36 × 24.9 cm)

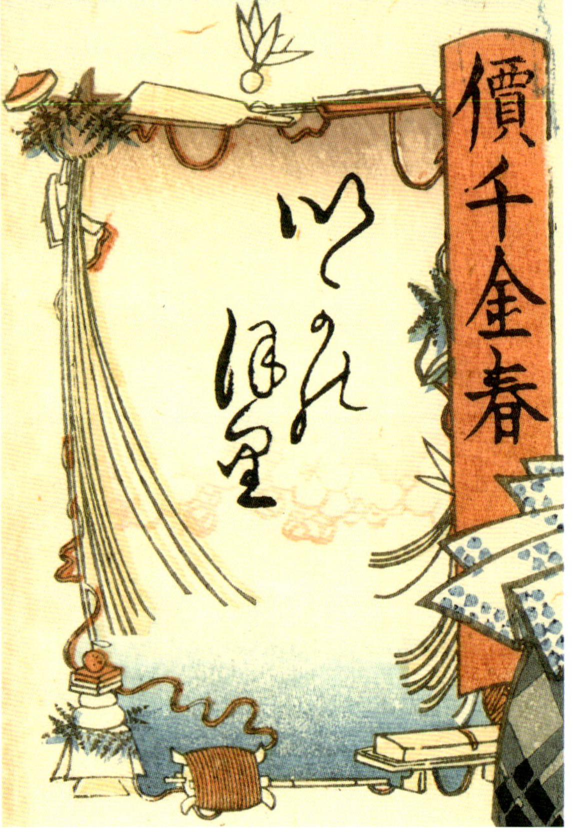

Kites hang in a small store and a customer takes down a couple for inspection. With a *tenugui,* hand towel, slung over his shoulder, he is at his ease in his neighborhood; perhaps he is returning from the local bathhouse. His face, bulk, and demeanor suggest a Kabuki actor.

One kite he is holding has the character for thunder, *kaminari,* set against a bold design of black clouds, appropriate for a kite. The other shows the head of Daruma, the perennially popular Zen patriarch, in his red cowl. The kite underneath bears the character *shibaraku,* wait a moment!, which we have seen in plate 12 was the title of a Kabuki play made famous by the Danjūrō line of actors. Other kites on view include a *yakko* and a realistic octopus. These kites would have been professionally painted and fairly expensive, made for festival time; most kites were simple homemade affairs. This print shows some of the most popular shapes among the wide variety available for purchase in the mid-nineteenth century.

Characters in the red cartouche read *atai senkin no haru* (spring worth a thousand gold pieces), a stock expression for a prosperous New Year. The phrase derives from a poem by the twelfth-century Song-dynasty poet Su Shi that describes a spring evening being as precious as a thousand gold pieces.

In the larger cartouche appears the word *ikanobori,* meaning kite. *Nobori* means banner and generically something long and thin; a different character also pronounced *nobori* means an ascent. *Ika* is written in the cartouche in *hiragana* script; *nobori* is written in three *kanji,* Chinese characters used here for their sounds—*no, bo, ri*—not for their Chinese meanings. A more common word for kite is *takonobori.* The sounds *ika* and *tako* also mean squid and octopus, and an octopus kite is included among the kites for sale.

The border of the cartouche is formed of a miscellany of objects associated with New Year: a spool for kite-line, a shuttlecock and battledore, a spinning top, a gift fan in its box on a presentation tray, and a *hōraidai* (see plate 10) complete with *mochi* riceballs. The poem beneath talks of a big kite bringing in the winds of New Year.

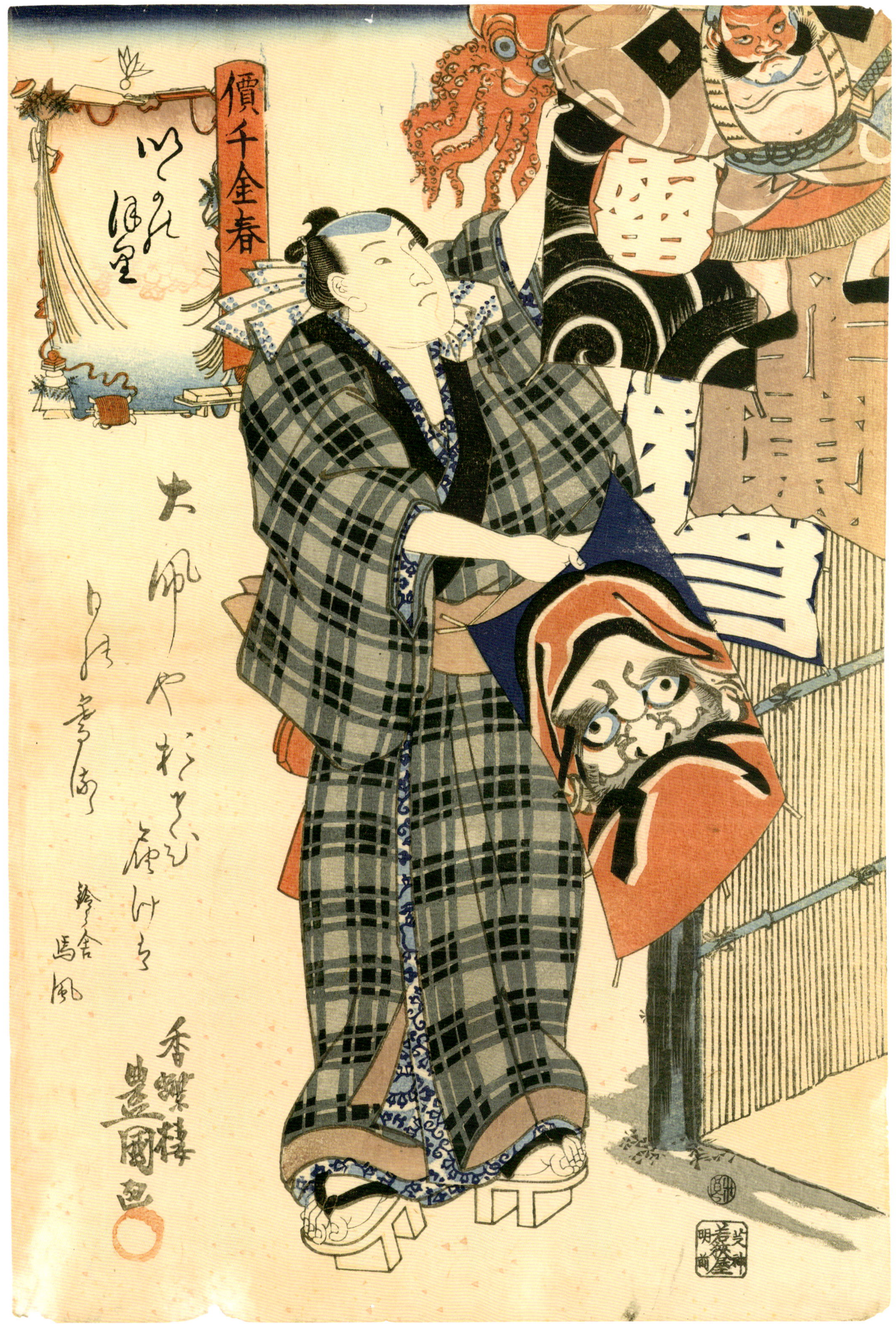

47

Spring Dawn
Utagawa Kuniteru II (1829–74)
signed: *Sadashige Kuniteru ga* and *Ichiyōsai Kuniteru ga*
publisher: Shōrindō
1847–53
ōban triptych (each sheet approximately 37.8 × 25.3 cm)

The title of this triptych, given in the upper right corner, is *Haru no akebono,* literally Spring Dawn; the first day of the New Year was considered the first day of spring. Three beauties perched on fashionable high *geta* watch the boys of the neighborhood prepare to launch a kite. Two of the girls hold feathered shuttlecocks and battledores, the third carries a New Year pine branch. The kite is painted with a scene of the young Soga Brothers, Jūrō and Gorō, as they approach their destiny, the assassination of their father's murderer. It is a dramatic design, though the kite is much too large for the boys to handle in a high wind. Jūrō is identified by the sea-plover design on his robe, Gorō by the butterfly antennae on his. The brothers have traveled through a dark, rainy night, indicated by the burning torch that Jūrō carries, to reach their sleeping victim.

Details such as the knots on the kite's tether rope and tail are clearly depicted. The boy holding the right side of the kite can just be distinguished by his hair and fingers. Many other boys are out playing on this New Year morning and the sky is filled with kites, including *yakko* and *tobi,* a five-sided *beka* and rectangular kites, a multiple-bird train kite, and one in the shape of an octopus.

New Year pine decorations appear at the right and left edges of the triptych. Two more can be made out in front of a house seen in the distance through the figures on the left-hand panel, giving depth and perspective to the street scene. The building on the right appears to be a *yose,* a small theater used by comic storytellers. The names of the performers hang behind the ticket-seller, bent over in a corner of his booth, and seasonal potted plants have been placed in the window behind bamboo slats. Some of the names, such as *Tarō,* suggest courtesans, and the girls with their bare feet are entertainers rather than daughters from the neighboring households. The signs for lobster on the shoji screens and the grain-measure *mon* on the battledore of the girl in the center panel suggest an association in this print with the actors Danjūrō VII or VIII. The face on the right of the central kite may be that of Danjūrō VIII, though the features are not as distinctive as in prints by other artists (see the next design). The building in the background of the central panel is a large storehouse. The scene gives a lively impression of New Year festivities in a *chōnin* residential district of Edo.

The colors of the print are bold and attractive and seem quite fresh, but they have lost much of their original yellow, one of the more fugitive of the vegetable dyes used on woodblock prints during the Edo period. The colors seen from the back of the print, which has presumably not received direct light over the last century and a half, show a stronger yellow. Green was often achieved by overprinting blue with yellow, and the green of the pine trees, for example, would have been much brighter when the print first came off the blocks.

48

Ichikawa Danjūrō VIII, Kite, and Lobsters
Utagawa Kunisada (1786–1865)
signed: *Kōchōrō Toyokuni ga*
publisher: Ebisuya Shōshichi
1847–50
sheet from *ōban* diptych or triptych
(36.3 × 24.2 cm)

A warmly dressed Kabuki actor with his small-bowled pipe sits by a glowing charcoal brazier with two long chopstick-like fireirons. Behind him is a fishmonger's stall piled high with lobsters; above the stall is a sign reading *Narita.* A companion carries a New Year kite with the characters *ō-atari,* big hit, appropriate for a Kabuki actor. Note the kite's hummer. Neither actor is named, but the seated smoker has the long face and distinctive features of Ichikawa Danjūrō VIII (1822–1854).

Lobsters, *ebi,* were a traditional New Year delicacy and a symbol of good luck and longevity. Here they are also a pun on the name Ebizō, which Ichikawa Danjūrō VII (1796–1859) took as his stage name in 1832, becoming Ichikawa Ebizō V. He used the occasion to introduce his young son, then aged ten, into the acting family as Ichikawa Danjūrō VIII; the son also used the name Ebizō, acting under the name Ichikawa Ebizō VI. The word *ebi* also plays on the names of the publisher of this print, Ebisuya Shōshichi, and Ebisu, the popular god most associated with New Year, who is often depicted with a fishing rod and red sea-bream (see plates 28, 80, and 81), which, like lobster, is another auspicious food served at New Year. Ebisu's mallet appears on the chest of the standing actor's robe and as a motif on his inner-robe.

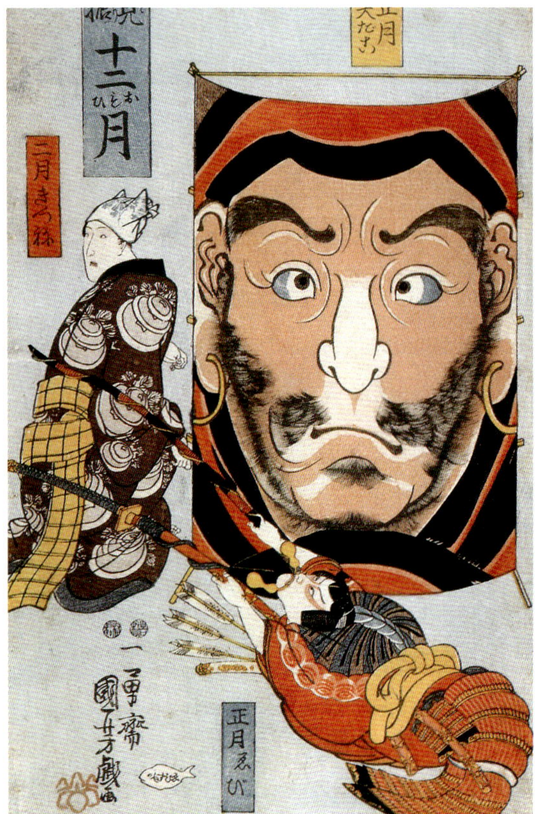

Danjūrō VIII's father was an immensely successful actor and led a flamboyant lifestyle. He flagrantly flouted the sumptuary laws by which the shogunate attempted to restrict conspicuous consumption by commoners. In 1842 the governor of Edo, seeking to blame the economic difficulties of the period on high-living actors who turned the social order upside down, exiled Danjūrō VII from the capital. This sort of persecution was not unique. The star Osaka actor Nakamura Utaemon III was prosecuted for high living in 1817 after a tour of Edo that is an example of the close relationship between the theaters of the capital and the Kamigata region. In exile, Danjūrō VII successfully rebuilt his career in Osaka and Kyoto.

The artist of this print, Kunisada, was extremely close to the Danjūrō family. During the Bunka era (1804–17), Kunisada became secretary to one of Danjūrō's many fan clubs, and he accompanied three of Edo's leading actors (including Iwai Hanshirō V, plate 19) on an extended tour of Osaka in 1820. Danjūrō VII was also a gifted poet and playwright, and Kunisada often included Danjūrō's poems on his prints of the actor. He illustrated a novel written by Danjūrō VII in 1824. Danjūrō VII is the most frequently depicted actor in Kunisada's vast output of Kabuki prints. Kunisada also designed many prints of Danjūrō VIII during his abbreviated career.

The two censors' seals on this print, *mera* (for Mera Taichirō) and *murata* (for Murata Heiemon) appear together only on prints published from 1847 to 1850. Danjūrō VII was not allowed to return to the capital until 1850, where he resumed his position as the dominant actor of his generation. Meanwhile his son's good looks were making him the most popular actor in Edo. During his father's exile the young man was honored by the city authorities for his filial piety, which sent his reputation even higher. Then, in the eighth month of 1854, he committed suicide, an event that rocked the nation.

Daruma kite and actor in the form of a lobster. Utagawa Kuniyoshi, 1847–48, *ōban* woodblock print, 35.2 × 24.4 cm. Private collection.

Kuniyoshi enjoyed designing puzzle prints in which silhouettes of common objects seen against a screen turn out to be carefully contrived assemblages of shapes. Here, a Kabuki actor with the makeup and butterfly-design costume of Gorō no Soga tucks in his armor of layered lacquered leather and becomes a New Year lobster. The print is from a series of the twelve months; the kite and lobster represent the first month, the catlike actor the second month. To avoid the prohibition against portraying living people in prints imposed by a government that wished to minimize potential sources of controversy, Kuniyoshi has thinly disguised the face of a popular actor as a Daruma kite.

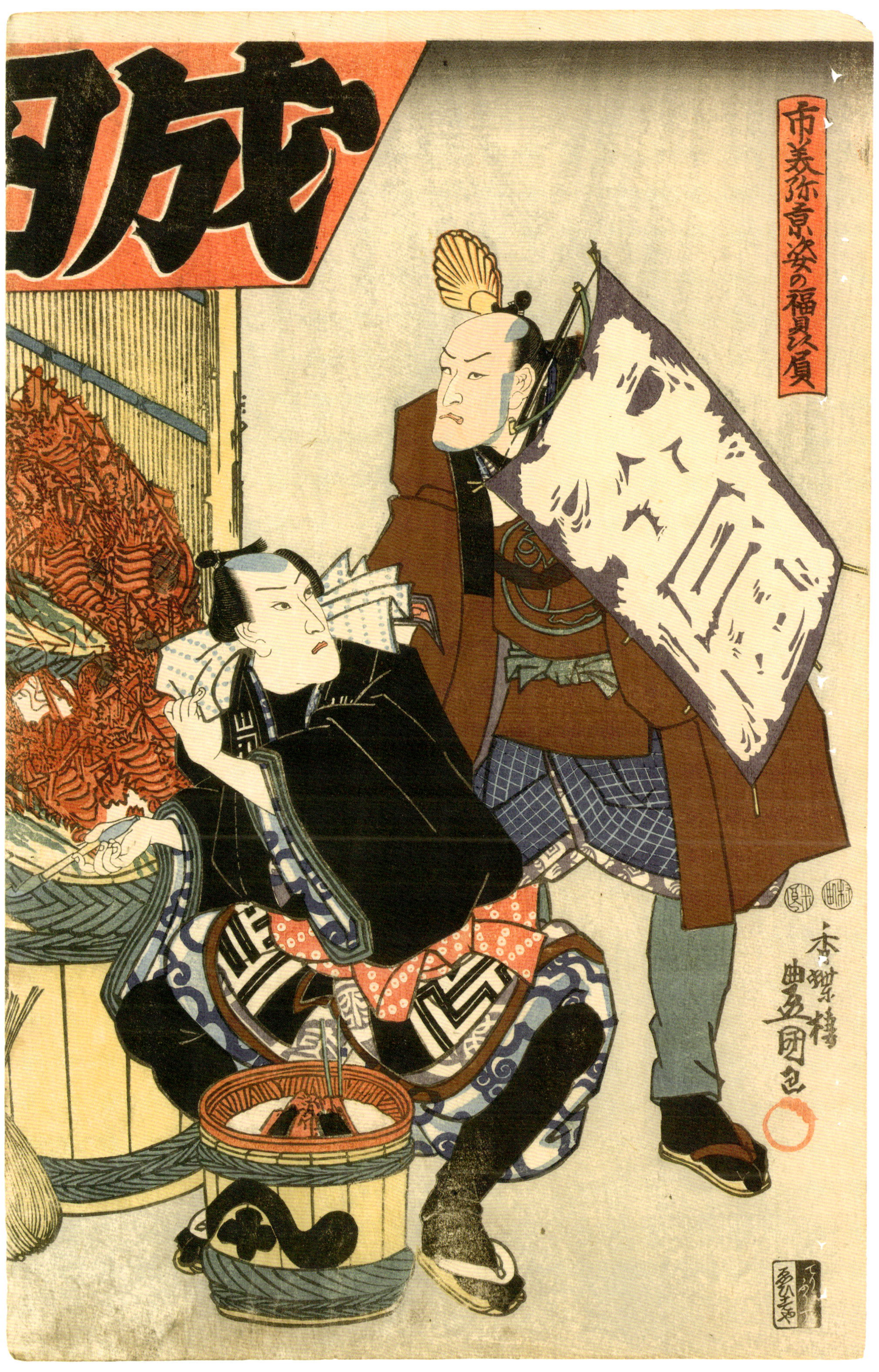
市美弥京姿の福貝次眉
香蝶楼豊国画

49

Memorial to Ichikawa Danjūrō VIII
Utagawa Kuniyoshi (1798–1861)
unsigned
1854
ōban (37.1 × 25.3 cm)

In Osaka, in 1854, Ichikawa Danjūrō VIII, eldest son of the leading Kabuki actor of the day and himself an immensely talented actor, handsome and adored, slit his throat, for reasons that are still unclear. The whole country was shocked, and many *shini-e,* death pictures, memorializing him were issued. Besides his skills as an actor, Danjūrō VIII's good looks and attractiveness to women were legendary, and he was idolized throughout Japan. He was equally at home with the Ichikawa family's *aragoto,* "rough stuff," style of acting and playing the roles of *nimaime,* young, handsome, sometimes effete lover characters. He created, for example, the role of Yosaburō in *Genyadana kirare Yosa,* with its climactic speech beginning, "Love and passion have been my worst enemies . . ." A famous story tells how the water that had touched him when he got into a barrel while playing Sukeroku in *Yukari no Edo zakura* was sold to hysterical fans.

Here Danjūrō rises into the sky like a kite as a horde of mourning women try to hold him back. Some haul on ropes as if they were kite lines. The lines themselves twist and form the *hiragana* characters *munen dayō,* meaning approximately, "My hopes are over" or "It's so regrettable." Danjūrō's name, *hachi daime,* Eighth Generation, appears above him, together with his Buddhist name, his age (thirty-two), and the date of his death (the sixth day of the eighth month).

The women come from every walk of life. Their occupations are identified in small characters: matron, widow, maid, house-servant, candy-seller, nun, shrine attendant, teahouse girl. They call out to Danjūrō, "Don't go," "Please wait, I have something to tell you," "Don't rush away," "Hey, Hassan [number eight], don't go," "Do you really, really have to go?" and "Oh catch him quick."

A poem at top left reads,

sasowaruru	beckoned by
mujō no kaze ni	the wind of death
karehisago	an empty gourd
hiiki no hana no	a favorite flower cut down
kiruru kanashisa	sadness

This print is unsigned but is by Kuniyoshi. A cat, one of Kuniyoshi's favorite motifs, joins in the frenzy to the right of the pyramid of ladies. Fans clearly recognized their favorite actors' likenesses when they were drawn in prints; here we see the same features in Danjūrō VIII's face as in the previous print, drawn by Kunisada. Memorial prints for famous actors (and sometimes *ukiyo-e* artists) were common, but they were normally formal and restrained. Danjūrō VIII's suicide was an extraordinary event and inspired unusual memorials, such as this.[1]

1. A similar anonymous memorial showing women of all ages and walks of life weeping in front of a hanging scroll bearing Danjūrō VIII's portrait is illustrated in Keyes 1989, 184. A diptych by Kuniyoshi showing women attempting to prevent a demon-messenger from the King of the Underworld, who grips Danjūrō VIII's wrist as he drags him away, is illustrated in Inagaki and Isao 1991, 97. Another, rather cruel, diptych by Kuniyoshi shows the actor's privacy being invaded by a group of grotesque women; Inagaki and Isao 1991, 96.

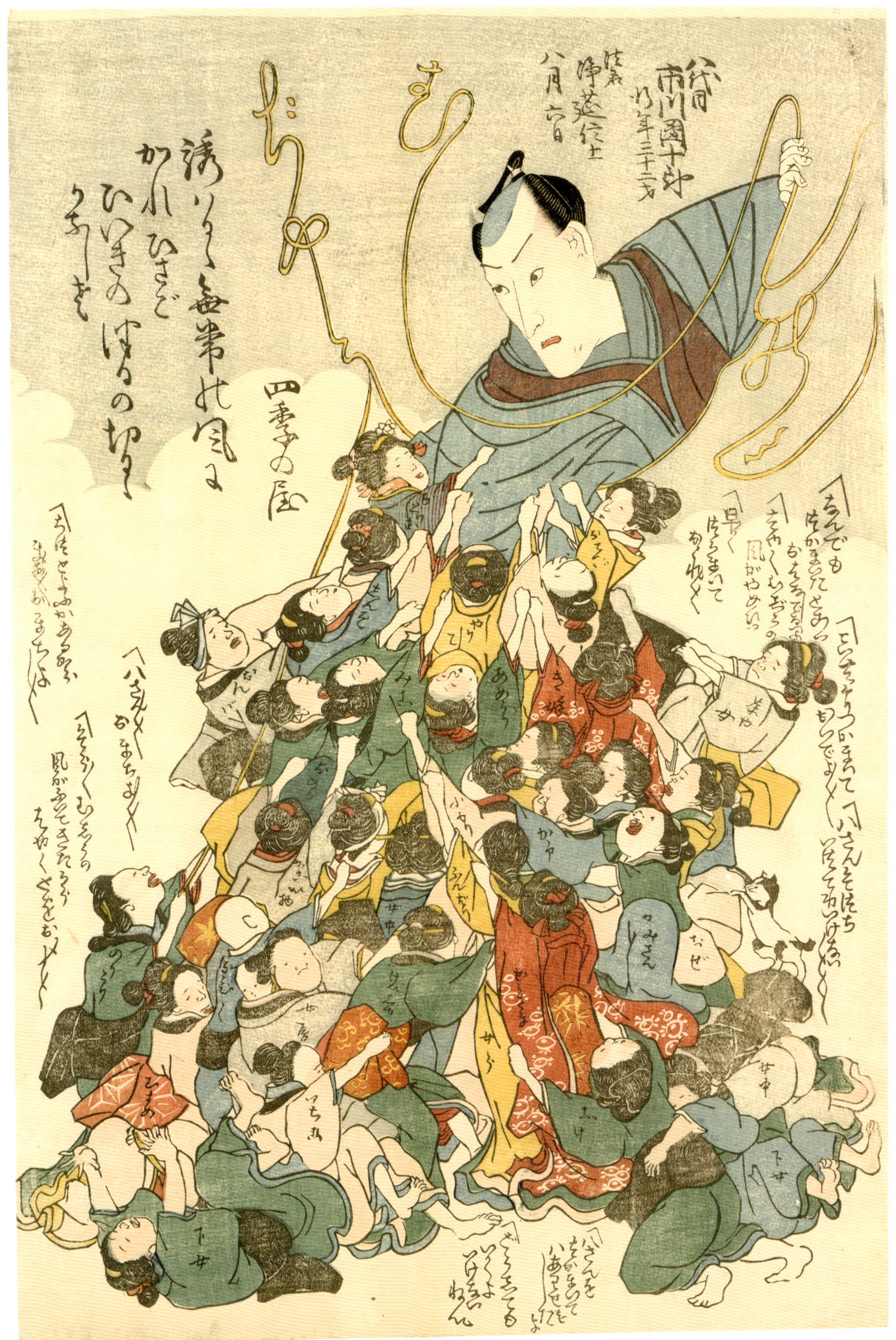
八代目
市川團十郎
行年三十二才
法名
浄蓮信士
八月六日

50

View from Honganji
Utagawa Kunisada (1786–1865)
signed: *Toyokuni ga*
publisher: Iseya Sōiemon
engraver: Hori Mino
1854
uchiwa-e (23 × 29.2 cm)

A geisha in fashionable winter clothes and stylish coiffure is portrayed against a background clearly inspired by Hokusai's design of Honganji in his series Thirty-Six Views of Mount Fuji (plate 22). We see the same temple rooftop, the same Fuji, the same city roofs, and a slightly less ornate kite. Kunisada, now signing himself Toyokuni after his teacher, has borrowed the designs of Hokusai's series as background for a series of beautiful-women fan prints. His series is titled *Fukaku bōke* (Alternative Views of Mount Fuji) and this design is subtitled *Honganji kara miru* (View from Honganji). The print-buying public would have appreciated the novel way the artist incorporated a popular series from twenty years before and there would have been no thought of condemning the appropriation. Kunisada was known for figure prints, and publishers commissioned him for a number of series where he designed the figures and another artist (notably Hiroshige) designed the background landscape. The background here is rather crudely drawn and was probably the work of one of Kunisada's students.

The colored area of the design is shaped like an *uchiwa* round fan on a stick (not a folding fan). Unused fan prints like this are fairly rare; most were cut out and pasted onto a frame to make a fan, and ultimately thrown away. The drawing is rather stiff, but the bright colors give the design an air of luxury; note the heavy use of Prussian blue, still expensive though no longer as rare as a couple of decades earlier. Grading such as the red in the sky and the blue of the mountain were extra touches of luxury, though they are rather heavy and unsubtle here. The girl wears sumptuous robes and has a roll of tissues tucked in her *obi,* something of a symbol of her profession.

There are several rather obtrusive identifying marks on this small design. The circular censor's seal *aratame,* meaning examined, that appears above the artist's signature on the right was used from 1854 to 1857. The approximately heart-shaped cartouche on the left was used specifically on fan prints in association with the *aratame* seal from 1854 to 1857; this example contains the character *tora,* tiger, for the Tiger Year of 1854, and *ni,* two, for the second month. Below the heart-shaped cartouche appears the mark of the publisher, Iseya Sōiemon. The yellow cartouche at bottom right contains the name of the engraver, Hori Mino (*hori* means to carve). It was fairly unusual for the carver of the blocks to be given credit in this way; his was a craft, not an art. The artist himself was considered no more than a craftsman. *Surimono* apart, woodblock prints were produced for sale to a commercial mass market; their creators were regarded as artisans, and there was little concept—except in the heads of certain star-designers (such as Utamaro and Kunisada)—of prints as high art.

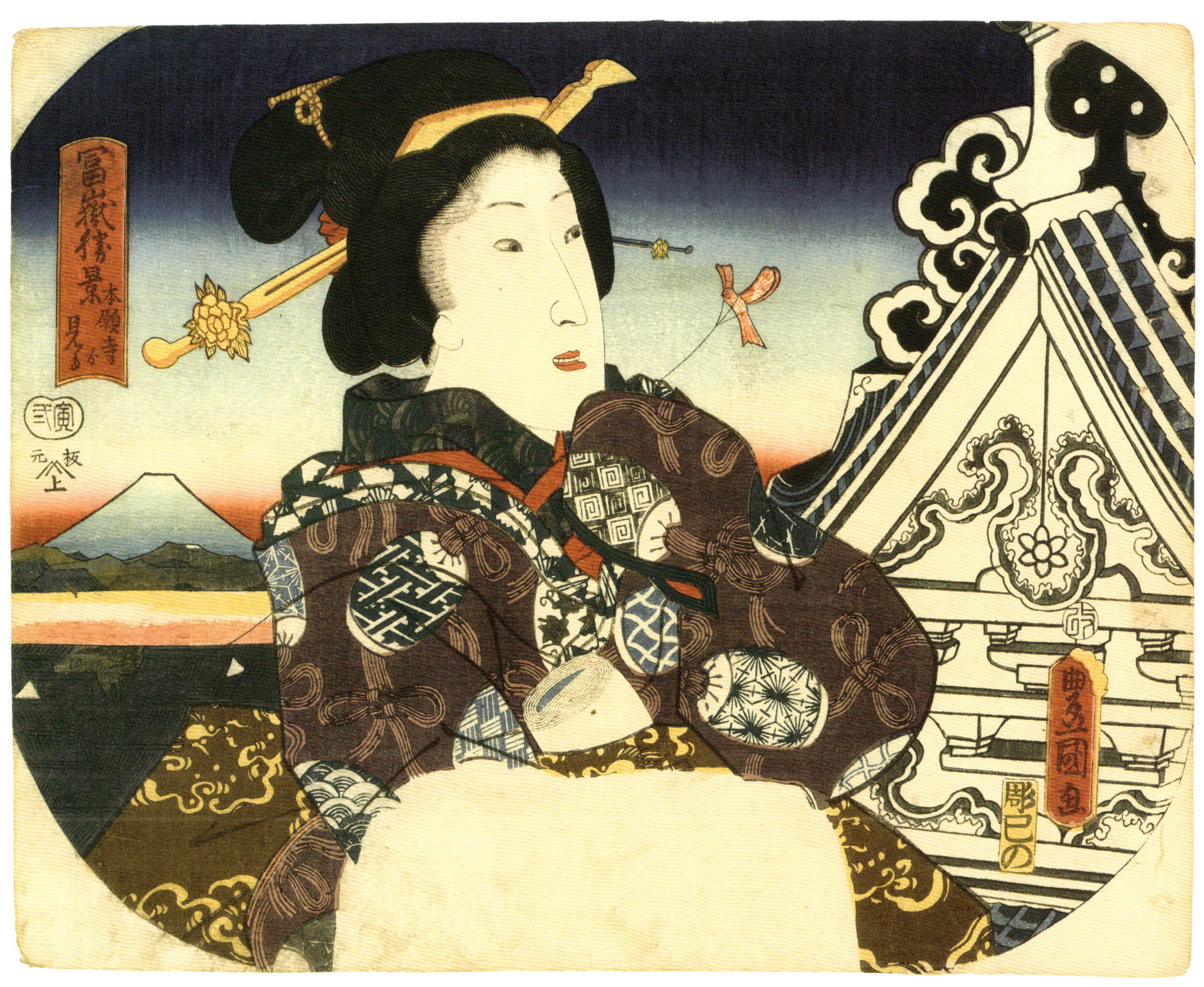
本願寺ゟ見る
元板
上
豊国画
彫巳の

51

Fifty-three Views: Fukuroi
Utagawa Hiroshige (1797–1858)
series: *Tōkaidō*
signed: *Hiroshige ga*
publisher: Jukakudō
1850–51
horizontal *ōban* (21.8 × 34.3 cm)

52

Fukuroi
Utagawa Hiroshige (1797–1858)
signed: *Hiroshige ga*
publisher: Tsutaya Kichizō
1855
vertical *ōban* (35.3 × 23.8 cm)

In plate 6 we saw an early landscape from Hokusai's series of the stations of the Tōkaidō, the main road that ran from Edo to Kyoto. To illustrate Kakegawa, station 27, Hokusai used the theme of flying kites. Hiroshige also chose a kite theme to illustrate Kakegawa in his own Tōkaidō series of 1833. The landscape at Fukuroi, a few miles down the road from Kakegawa—Fukuroi in the Enshū district is station 28 on the Tōkaidō—does not appear to have been very dramatic. Hiroshige's depiction of Fukuroi in the 1833 series shows travelers resting at a roadside teahouse next to flat, harvested rice fields on a calm autumn day, with no hint of hills or mountains.

But in plates 51 and 52, Kakegawa's wind has blown on to Fukuroi, inspiring a much more lively design. In the first design, travelers walk along the road, which is set on a dike above rice fields, toward a distant village. There was little or no wheeled traffic along the Tōkaidō; commoners walked and the more wealthy rode horses or were carried in palanquins. The most original element of this design is the viewpoint—we are taken high above the countryside and hover a few feet from a kite painted with the auspicious design of a Chinese lion-dog playing among peonies, a favorite motif of Hiroshige's. The other kites are equally auspicious: a crane, symbol of immortality, flying in the clouds, and a New Year sun rising behind waves.

Hiroshige designed at least seven sets of views of the Tōkaidō. The red title cartouche of this horizontal series is titled simply *Tōkaidō;* the series is sometimes known as the *Reisho Tōkaidō* after the formal calligraphy of the cartouche. Here the characters *Gojūsan tsugi Fukuroi,* Fifty-three Views: Fukuroi, appear to the left of the cartouche, and the number twenty-eight is added. The seal under Hiroshige's signature is a simplified form of *Hiro.* The characters *meibutsu,* famous product or specialty, to describe Fukuroi kites appear in both the small red cartouche to the right of this print and in the yellow cartouche of the next: kites were a specialty of Fukuroi.

Hiroshige often contoured the corners of his landscapes, as in plate 25. The margins of plate 51 have been trimmed, giving the corners a rounded appearance that the original prints in the series do not have. (Prints were often trimmed by owners or dealers if they became damaged, a smooth edge being preferred over the maximum original paper available, the modern preference.)

In plate 52, from a vertical Tōkaidō series titled *Gojūsan tsugimeisho zue* (Famous Views of the Fifty-three Stations), Hiroshige shows us a different view of Fukuroi. It is spring, when the winds traditionally blow hard. Peasants work in the fields, their postures and groupings providing Hiroshige plenty of material for a lively composition. Rice seedlings are being brought to the fields in baskets; the landscape is open and peaceful. Though it is not New Year, two young men haul on the rope of a large kite with a crane decoration and an ornate tail; two young children follow them excitedly. Perhaps

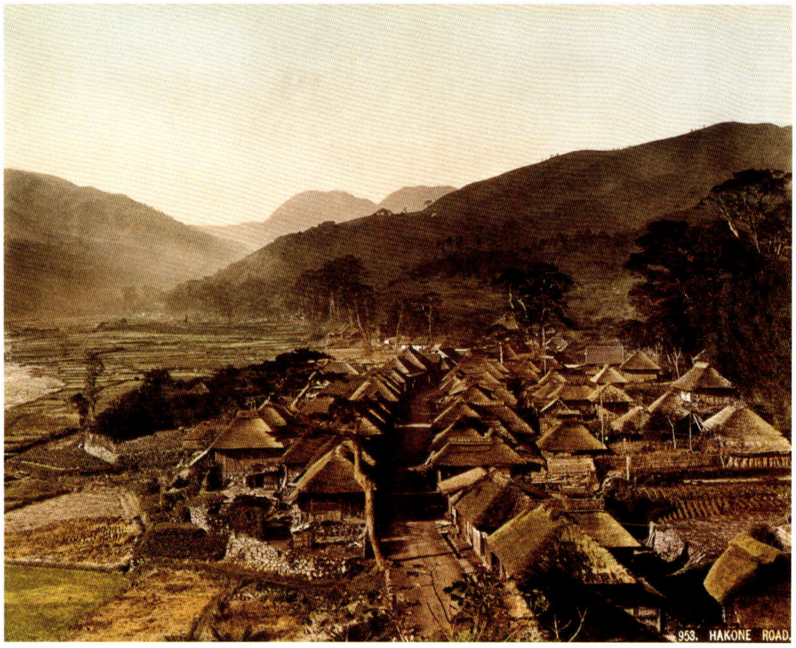

The Tōkaidō at Hakone, station 11, c. 1880.

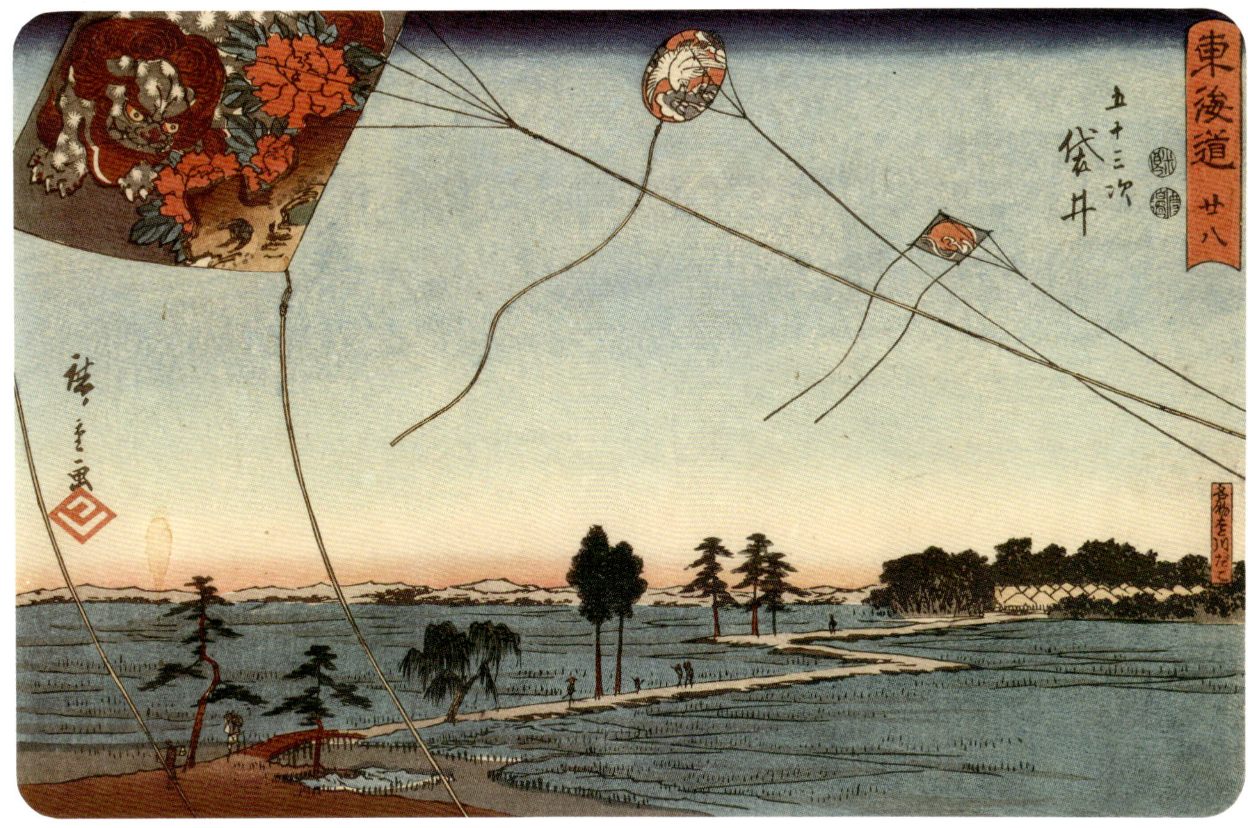

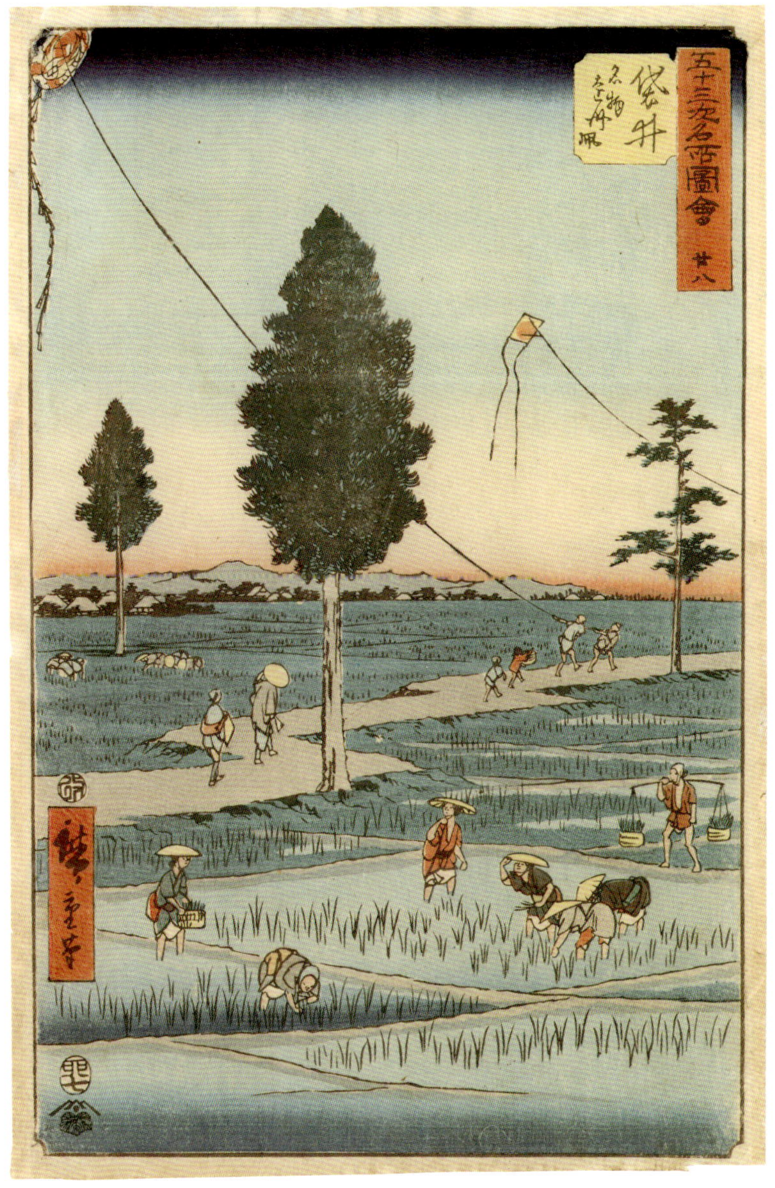

it is Boy's Day, the fifth day of the fifth month, which was associated with transplanting rice and its overtones of fertility. It would be unusual for two able-bodied young men to be flying kites for pleasure rather than assisting in the rice fields—when villagers worked in the fields, everyone worked. Perhaps flying kites here signifies more than having a good time, and the kite-flyers are asking the gods for good weather and an abundant harvest or wishing for the health of the boys of the community.

It is curious that the characters in the yellow cartouche read *Fukuroi meibutsu botandako,* Fukuroi: Famous-Product Peony-Kite, when the kites shown in the previous and next design show peonies and this design shows only a crane. Hiroshige must have assumed that his audience would be widely acquainted with folklore and traditions.

The same trees grow in both prints and the same hills rise on the horizon. Both impressions are well printed, with strong lines and fairly good registration, but the colors are faded. Yellow is one of the first colors to lose intensity, leaving the rice fields here more blue than green; compare the fresh colors of the following print.

53

Distant View of Akiba and Enshū, Fukuroi Kites
Ichiryūsai Shigenobu (Hiroshige II) (1829–69)
signed: *Hiroshige ga*
publisher: Uyoa Eikichi
1859
ōban (36.1 × 24.8 cm)

On Hiroshige's death in 1858, his best student, Shigenobu, married his master's daughter and took the Hiroshige name, signing his prints with an almost identical signature. His designs are neither as prolific or as imaginative as Hiroshige's, but they can be very good, especially when they were printed to the same high standards as the best of Hiroshige I's work. All the elements for a successful print are here: a well-drawn design with striking composition, strong colors, and skillful printing off fresh blocks. Together with the intensity of the Prussian blue at top and bottom and the graded red at the skyline, the heavy overprinting of green and gray in the fields gives a sense of opulence.

The source of Hiroshige II's design is clear—his master's horizontal print of Fukuroi on the Tōkaidō of nine years earlier (plate 51)—but the student's treatment is more dramatic. He gives the scene a vertical format, increasing the sense of height; adds a shower of confetti released from a bag placed halfway up the kite's line; and makes the scene less anonymous by including a group of young men flying another kite. The artist has even copied the rising-sun design of the smaller kite in the picture from his master's design. These kites must be large: the kite the young men are flying requires two to control the line, with a third looping the line into a basket. As in the previous two prints, farmers are transplanting rice seedlings. It is possible that the confetti is auspicious, scattering blessings over the fields.

The print is from a series titled *Shokoku meisho hyakkei* (One Hundred Famous Views of the Provinces), published by Uyoa Eikichi who commissioned Hiroshige's great series One Hundred Famous Views of Edo (plates 54 and 56). It is subtitled *Enshū Akiba enkei Fukuroi tako,* meaning Distant View of Akiba and Enshū, Fukuroi Kites. Though the design is obviously based on his teacher's design from the Tōkaidō series, there is no mention of the Tōkaidō: the location is described as a scenic spot in its own right. Hiroshige II appears to have taken liberties, however; for example, the mountains are larger and more imposing than in his teacher's designs.

The round kite shows a Chinese lion-dog playing among auspicious peonies. Its shape is unusual, and very difficult to fly. The traditional round kite of Japan is the *wanwan* of Naruto; during the 1920s and '30s the largest kites in the world may have been Naruto *wanwan.* Perhaps these round kites were the specialty kites of Fukuroi in Hiroshige's time but they are absent now, for example at the annual Hamamatsu festival held nearby. The squarish kite here with a stick extending from the bottom is typical of the fighting kite of Hamamatsu. This kite, called *machijirushi,* is flown by neighborhood teams at the festival to celebrate children born in the last twelve months.

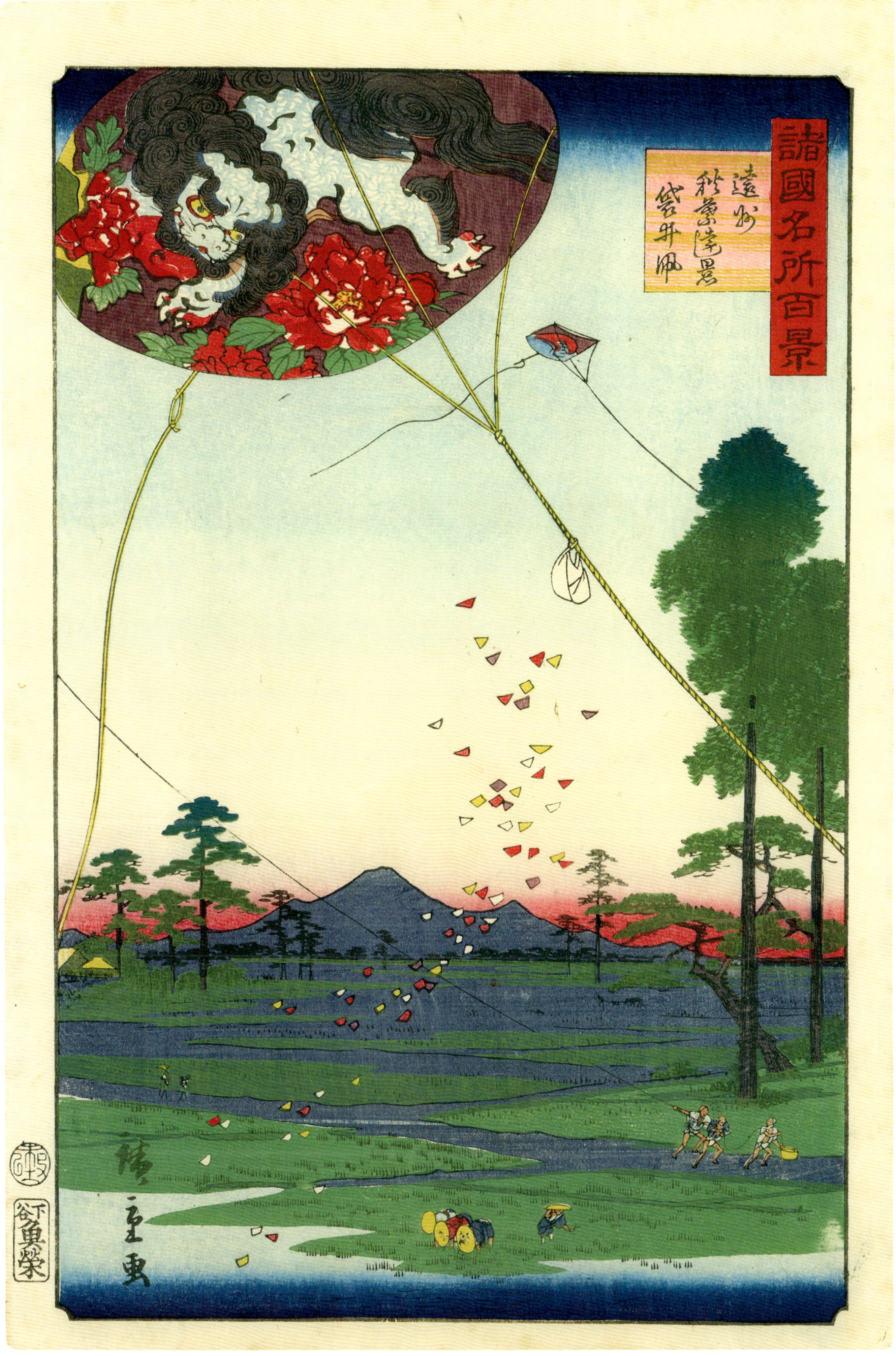

諸國名所百景

遠州
秋葉遠景
袋井凧

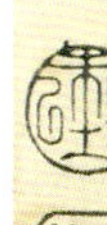

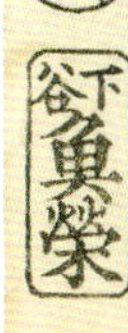

54

Kasumigaseki
Utagawa Hiroshige (1797–1858)
signed: *Hiroshige ga*
publisher: Uoya Eikichi
1857
ōban (36.9 × 25.2 cm)

The culmination of Hiroshige's career was his series *Meisho Edo hyakkei* (One Hundred Famous Views of Edo). Having dominated landscape prints for twenty years, Hiroshige and his publishers now offered the public a series unprecedented in its number and its rich print qualities. The first design was a snowscape of Nihonbashi, the geographical center of the country. Designs two and three of this great series both show New Year kites flying merrily above Hiroshige's native city. This is an appropriate start to the One Hundred Famous Views, which eventually numbered 118 designs.

Here we look eastward down a road lined with *daimyō* mansions on Kasumigaseki Hill, toward a sky where dawn adds a band of red to the horizon of Edo Bay. Many people are already up and about on this fresh, cold festival morning (early impressions of this design[1] are much more heavily inked and darker than this, giving a stronger notion of a crisp early morning). Kites hang in the morning sky; the kite closest to us bears the character for fish, *uo.*[2]

Besides kites, several other elements indicate that the time is New Year. A pine-and-bamboo *kadomatsu* dominates the right edge of the print, with smaller decorations on the left. A little girl with her mother holds a New Year battledore. Two *manzai* performers are dressed as priests; they will visit households and perform New Year dances to spread good fortune. In the middle of the print a group of *kagura* performers, who will also offer good-luck skits and dances for the New Year, approaches. The original *kagura* dancers came from Ise Shrine, and the ceremonial pole that this group carries probably bears the name of Amaterasu, the sun goddess enshrined at Ise (plate 1).

A *hatamoto,* his high rank marked by a much taller ceremonial pole, climbs the slope with his entourage. In another view that Hiroshige designed of Kasumigaseki, part of a *tanzaku*-format series of 1838 titled *Tōto meisho* (Famous Places of the Eastern Capital), the artist shows a similar group with their long pole descending the slope in the other direction.[3] Print artists often returned again and again to some visual detail that had caught their attention; a *hatamoto's* formal procession would have been a common sight in this neighborhood but one never devoid of interest. The *ōgibakokai,* fan-box buyer, whom we saw in plate 25, heads down the hill from the right. The tradesman to the left carries piled trays of sushi. The low perspective lengthens the foreground, emphasizes the height of the *kadomatsu,* and increases the steepness of the incline.

The swirling masks in the foreground have been left by a *baren,* the bamboo-leaf pad used to rub the back of the paper hard during the printing process.

Though he designed prints on other subjects, Hiroshige acknowledged his reputation as a landscape artist. His lighthearted *jisei,* death or farewell poem (see also plate 49), translates, "Leaving my brush behind in Edo, I travel to see the famous views of Heaven."

The *kasumi* of the title of this print means haze, evoking thoughts of distant views long gone; today the views from Kasumigaseki are obscured by Tokyo's tallest building.

1. For example, see Smith 1986, plate 2.

2. Smith 1986, caption to plate 2, points out that *uo* was part of the name of the publisher of this series, Uoya Eikichi, and that the use of the character on the kite was probably a form of advertisement. We have also seen in plates 38 and 43 that the character for fish was more widely used to decorate a kite. Fish were auspicious creatures; perhaps there was also an idea of fish swimming in the sky, like octopus and squid (homonyms for kite). And controlling a kite is a little like bringing in a fish on a line.

3. Izzard 1983, 56.

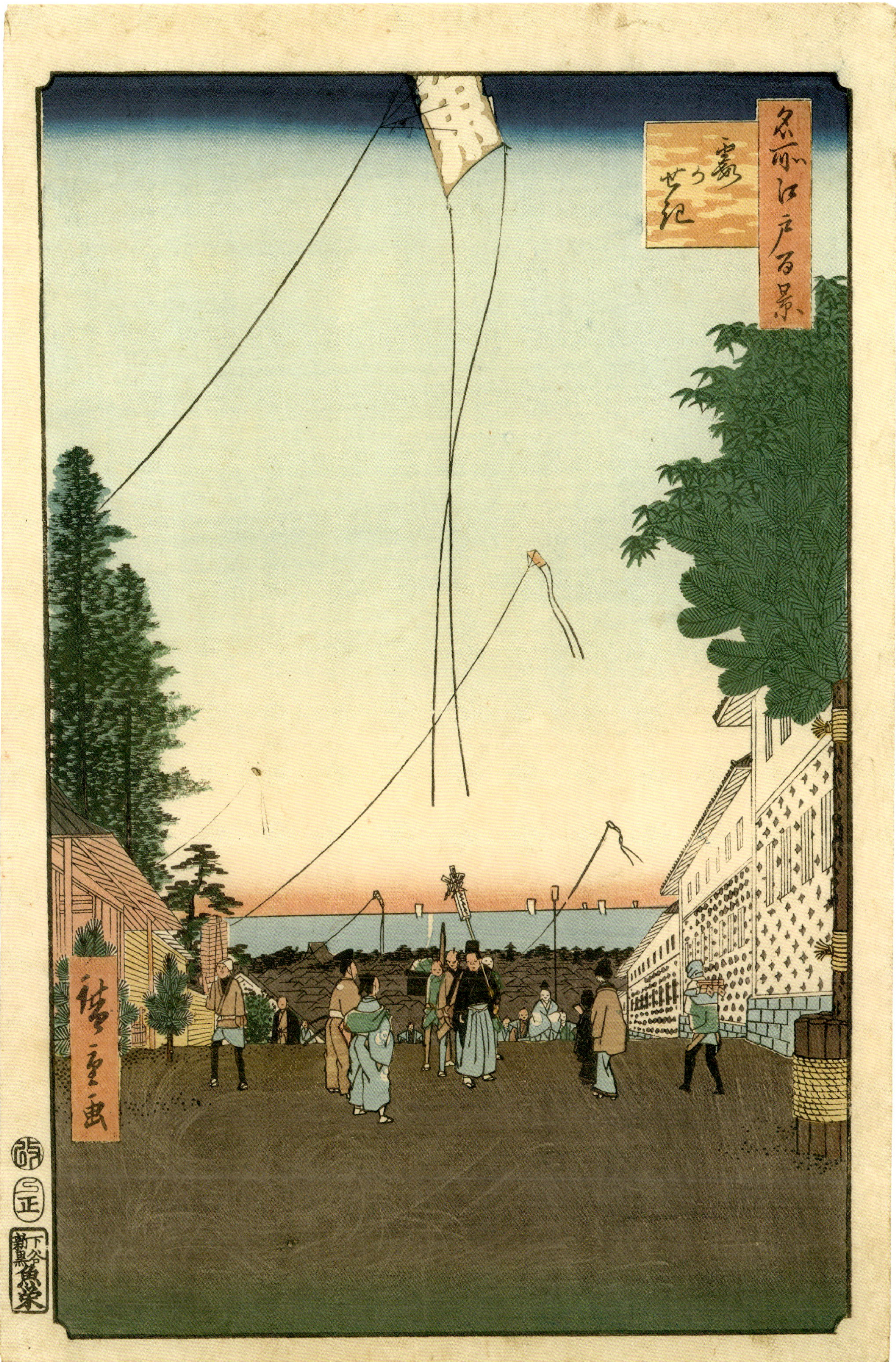

名所江戸百景
霞かせき
廣重画

55

Riverbank in the Yamashita District in Edo
Utagawa Hiroshige (1797–1858)
signed: *Hiroshige ga*
publisher: Sano-Ki
1852
chūban (18.3 × 24.8 cm)

This design of the Yamashita district in Edo forms part of Hiroshige's 1852 small-format series *Fuji sanjūrokkei* (Thirty-six Views of Fuji), and the artist clearly conceived the design originally as a view of Mount Fuji, not the city of Edo. Five years later he used the design as a model for his much better known image of the Yamashita district in his *Meisho Edo hyakkei* (One Hundred Famous Views of Edo). An artist was often under great pressure to produce an image for a publisher quickly and was obliged to recycle ideas from his head or his sketchbook. Many of Hiroshige's sketches of people and places have survived; he was a great draftsman.

The characters in the top left corner read *Tōto Yamashita-chō kashi* (Riverbank in the Yamashita district of the Eastern Capital). It is a clear New Year's day and kites fly over this aristocratic corner of old Edo, where Hiroshige grew up in a firemen's barracks near Edo Castle. Samurai walk on the embankment by the moat that surrounds the castle, home of the shogun. Behind them rise the vast residence of the lord of Shirakawa and the even more imposing mansion of the Nabeshima clan of Saga, with its red façade. The front of each is decorated with a pair of huge, three-story-high *kadomatsu* New Year pine-and-bamboo constructions. Kites and their lines echo perfectly the slope of a snowy Mount Fuji looming in the distance. Ducks or seabirds bob in the moat.

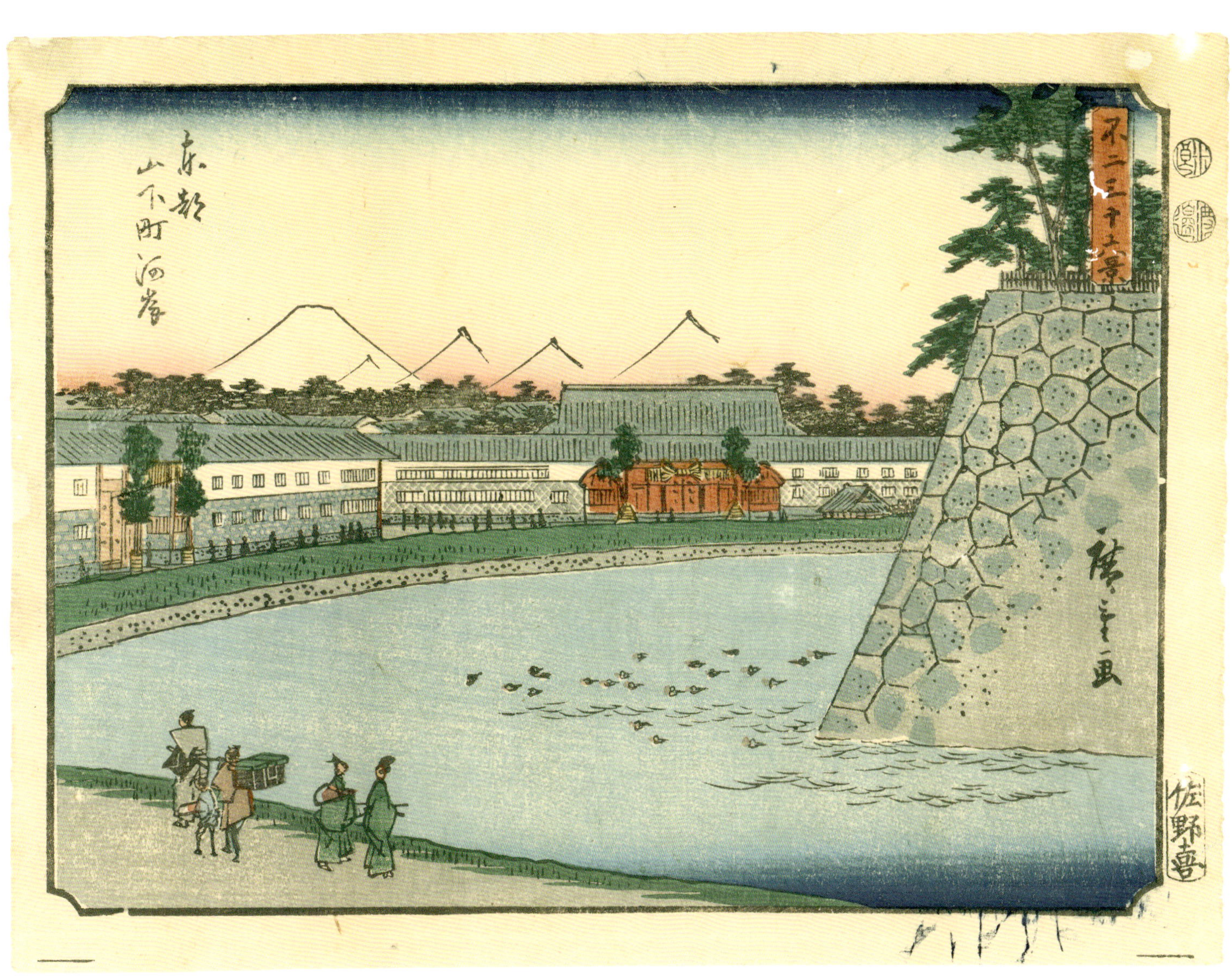
不二三十六景
東都
山下町河岸
廣重画
佐野喜

56

Hibiya and Soto-Sakurada from the Yamashita District
Utagawa Hiroshige (1797–1858)
signed: *Hiroshige ga*
publisher: Uoya Eikichi
1857
ōban (37.2 × 25.3 cm)

This design, number three of Hiroshige's *Meisho Edo hyakkei* (One Hundred Famous Views of Edo), follows immediately after the design of Kasumigaseki and is subtitled *Yamashita-chō Hibiya soto Sakurada* (Hibiya and Soto-Sakurada from the Yamashita District). It provides another view of Edo at New Year, and seasonal details dominate the print. In an extreme close-up—a specialty of Hiroshige's that has led to speculation that he was aware of early photographs[1]—two battledores held by figures just out of sight hit a feathered shuttlecock back and forth. One battledore bears a painting of bamboo, the other an *onnagata* Kabuki actor. Two huge *kadomatsu* pine-tree decorations stand in front of the *daimyō* mansion facing the viewer, which belonged to the Nabeshima clan. The branches of another decoration are even closer than the battledores—we look right through them. Kites fill the sky, the nearest being a *yakko* kite, dramatically cut off at the top. One kite has become entangled in another's line.

Watchtowers for fires rise above the residences, a motif close to Hiroshige's personal experience. The hereditary duty of Hiroshige's samurai father was to oversee one of the shogunal firefighting organizations. Hiroshige grew up in the Yayosu barracks of the shogunal firefighters close by Edo Castle, near the scene of this design—a few years before, when he was a boy, one of the kites here might have been his. His father died when Tokutarō (Hiroshige's childhood name) was thirteen, and Hiroshige inherited his position. He continued to fulfil his administrative duties even while he worked as an artist, until 1832, when he passed the post to an adopted son. He lived in the barracks, where thirty samurai supervised three hundred often rowdy firemen, until he was forty-three.

We are now looking west toward Mount Fuji, and the red glow on the horizon is the sunset (insofar as it is more than a cliché in Hiroshige's landscapes). Details such as Fuji and the birds on the moat indicate that Hiroshige followed his earlier print (plate 55), or perhaps an image in his sketchbooks. The *bokashi* color gradation and heavy use of pigment, especially the overprinted green, are typical of the best impressions of the series, yet the break in the block in the center foreground shows that this impression was not printed early from the blocks. Continued sales of deluxe printings from worn blocks suggest how very popular this series was—if the product was moving well, flaws in the blocks as they became worn could be ignored.

1. Smith 2000 analyzes the compositions of Hiroshige's landscapes, in which the artist would "frame a shot" in ways that appear to foreshadow photography and the cinema. Smith concludes that Hiroshige was clearly not inspired by photography. He points out as a very basic reason that mid-nineteenth-century cameras did not provide the kinds of compositions that Hiroshige created, especially extreme foreshortening in a close-up view.

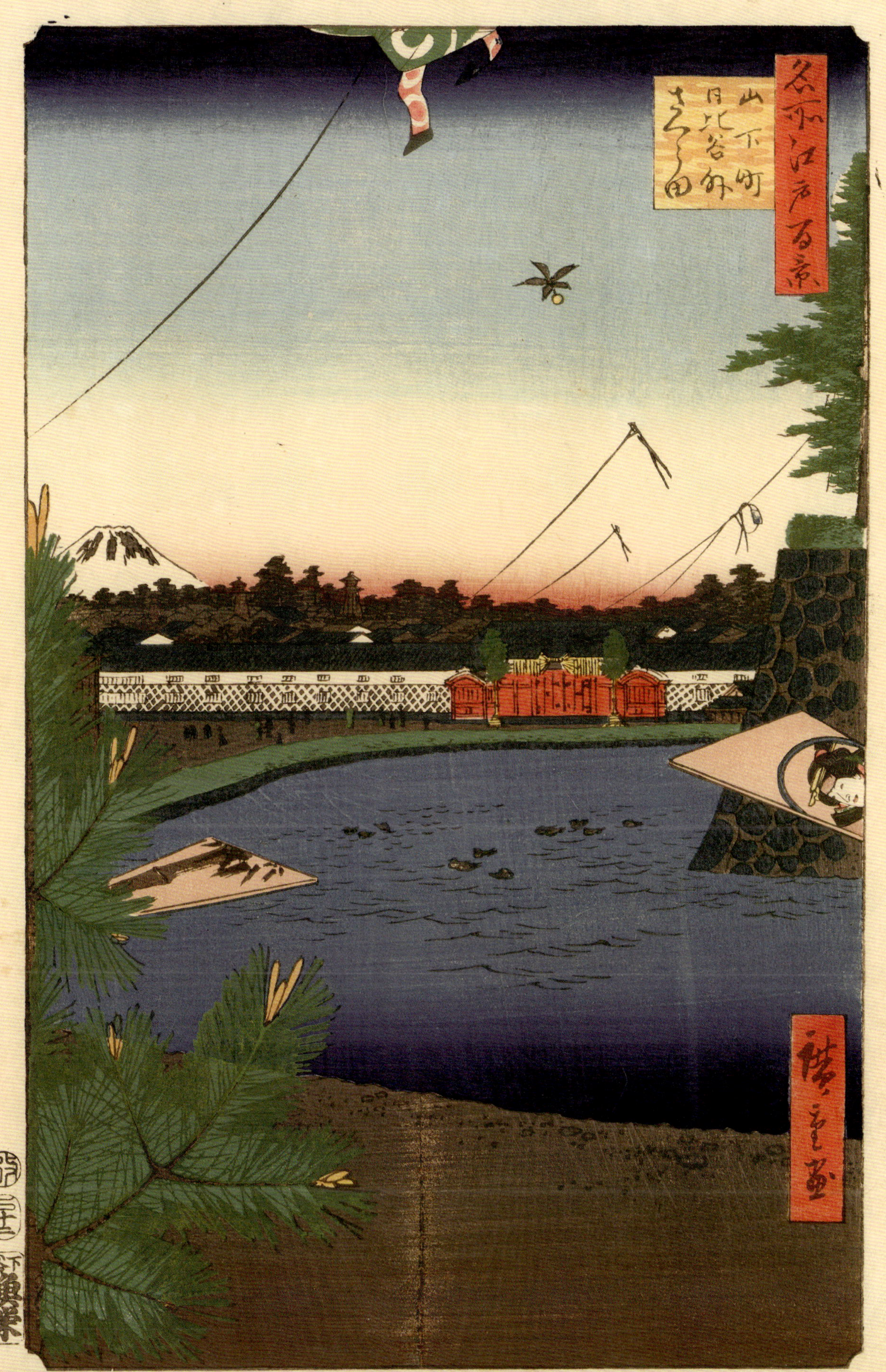
名所江戸百景
山下町日比谷外さくら田
廣重画
下谷魚栄

57

Bishamon's Messenger
Utagawa Hiroshige (1797–1858)
signed: *Hiroshige ga*
1853 eleventh month
horizontal *ōban* (24.2 × 35.4 cm)

A third design showing kites from Hiroshige's One Hundred Famous Views of Edo (see inset) is not included in the Skinner Collection, but this precursor from 1853 is. The scene is the Shinto shrine to Bishamon on Atago Hill to the south of the city; Bishamon was the northern and most important of the Four Guardians of Buddhism and became one of Japan's Seven Lucky Gods (plates 79–81). The title of the series from which this design is taken is *Edo meisho* (Famous Views of Edo) and appears in the vertical cartouche to the right. The square cartouche reads *Shiba kichirei Atagoyama shōgatsu mikka Bishamon no tsukai,* which may be translated, "Auspicious ceremony at Atagoyama in Shiba on the third day of the New Year, Bishamon's messenger."

On the third day of the New Year festivities,[1] this peculiar figure—not a priest but the proprietor of the Atagoya teahouse near the shrine—presided over the Heaping Rice Ceremony. His outrageous costume consists of objects associated with New Year, including *urajiro* ferns and *daidai,* bitter orange, and he is festooned with paper prayer slips. He carries a huge rice pestle, signifying prosperity, with which he strikes a large chopping block and commands his audience, "Eat, eat," to which they reply, "We will, we will."[2]

Atago Hill is not very high, but it is steep and was known for its uninterrupted views of the city and Edo Bay (see plate 65 for a wider view). Morning mists separate the shrine from the sea of low houses, and New Year kites fly overhead. The board under the complex eaves of the gateway lists the names of donors to the shrine.

1. Edmunds 1934, 299, says the third day of the sixth month and gives a detailed description of the unusual ceremony.

2. Smith 1986, caption to plate 21, traces the particularity of this figure to an image in a sketchbook by Hiroshige titled *Teppōzu tōrō ryakuzu* of 1849.

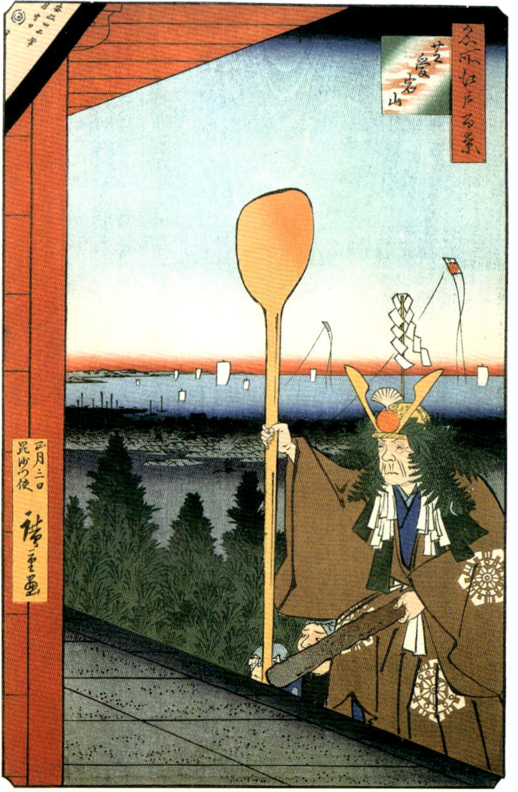

Atago Hill, Shiba, from Hiroshige's *Meisho Edo hyakkei* (One Hundred Famous Views of Edo), 1857.

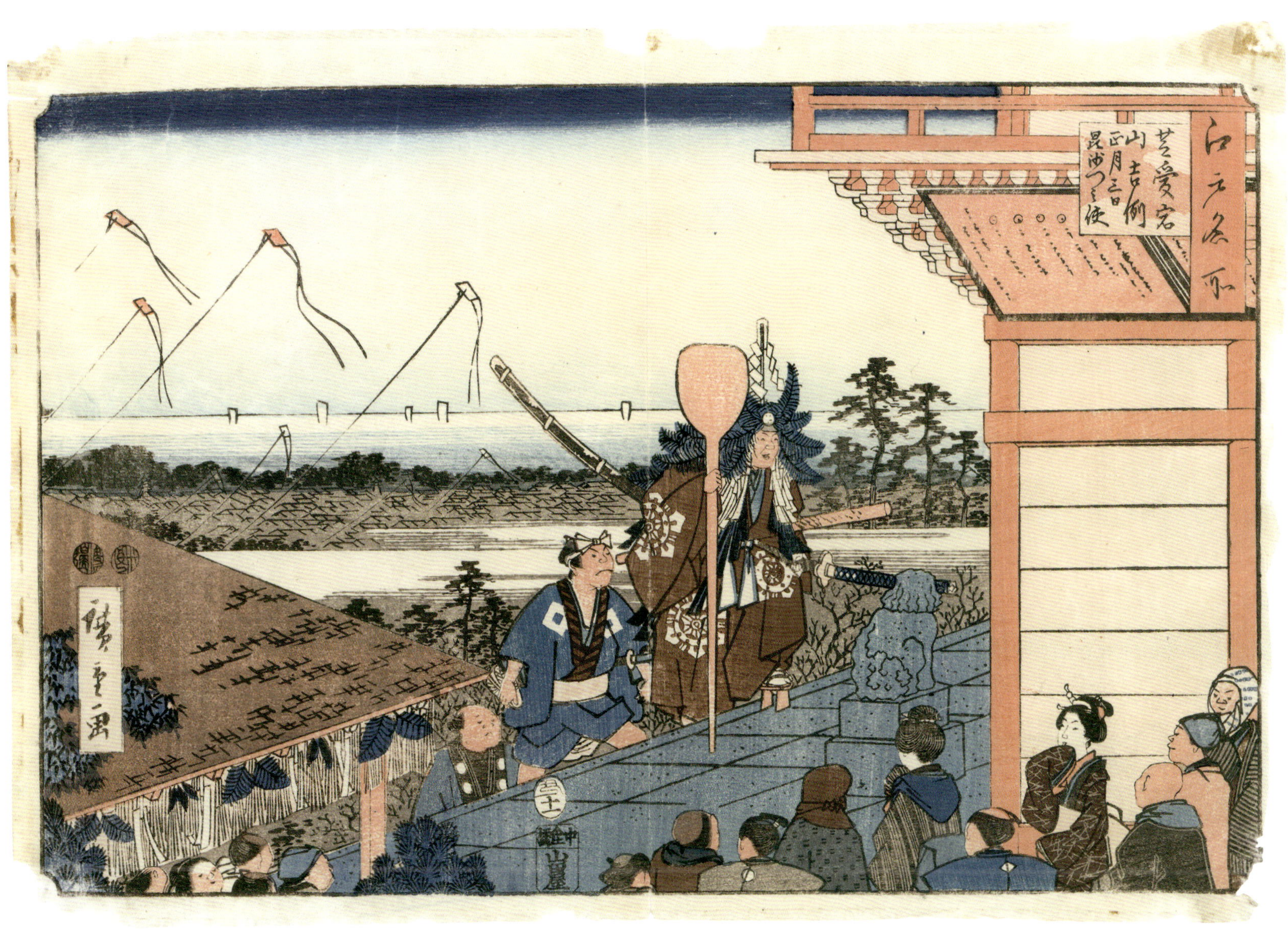

江戸名所
芝愛宕山吉例
正月三日
毘沙門の使
廣重画

58

***Yakko* Kite and Fuji**
Utagawa Kunisada (1786–1865)
signed: *Toyokuni ga*
publisher: Maruya Jimpachi
1857 first month
two sheets of *ōban* triptych (each sheet approximately 36.3 × 25.2 cm, lower right sheet missing)

59

***Yakko* Kite and Kabuki Actors**
Utagawa Kunisada (1786–1865)
signed: *Toyokuni ga*
publisher: Kinshōdō
1857 first month
ōban triptych (each sheet approximately 35.5 × 25.2 cm)

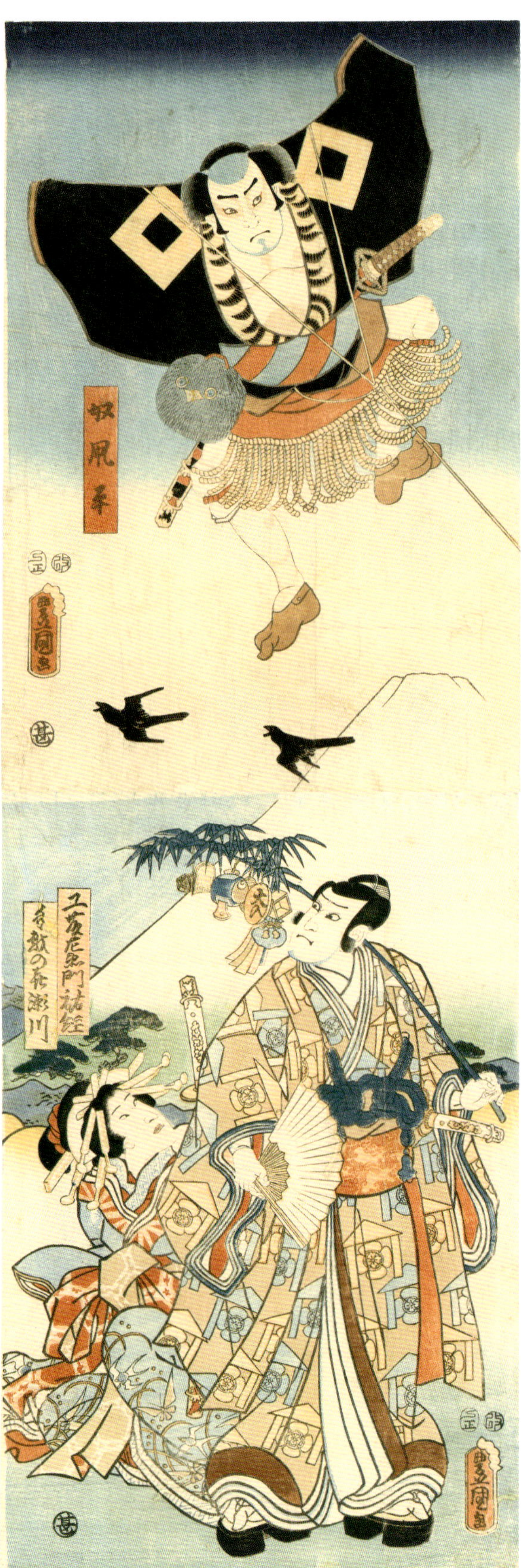

Here are two versions of a New Year Soga Brothers play. Both are in the very unusual format of an L-shaped triptych. The names of the characters, given in the red and yellow cartouches, and the date—first month of the Snake Year—are basically the same in each design. It appears that Kunisada was commissioned by two different publishers to illustrate the same New Year performance.

In each design, a Kabuki actor plays the part of a *yakko* kite flying above actors playing the roles of Lord Kudō no Suketsune and a female companion. The roles are identified in the vertical cartouches and are slightly different in the two versions. The actors' names are not given; often both role and actor are identified on a Kabuki print. Kunisada has, however, caught the actors' distinctive facial features, which are the same in each design and would have been recognizable to their fans. The actor playing Kudō no Suketsune, who wears a robe with Kudō's family motif in each design, appears to be Ichikawa Ebijūrō I.[1]

The differences between the two interpretations include Mount Fuji as a dominant feature in one but not the other. Crows fly in one design, geese in the other. New Year is indicated in one design by the bamboo branch, dangling with New Year treasures, that Kudō carries over his shoulder, and in the other by the pine saplings in the background, which suggest the New Year tradition of pulling up pine seedlings as symbols of longevity. In one, the woman's outer robe has a pattern combining sea plovers and butterflies, the signifiers of the two Soga Brothers; in the other, her robe has a chrysanthemum pattern (see plate 74).

The kite role is identified as Yakko Takohei, Mr Yakko-Kite, a character with no relation to the original Soga Brothers story but one who came to figure large in the New Year performances. The figure flying the kite/actor in plate 59 is the comic strongman Kobayashi no Asahina; he wears his trademark crane robe, exaggerated *kumadori* Kabuki makeup, and facial hair as bushy as a *yakko*'s. In the traditional story, Asahina helps the brothers obtain an invitation to Kudō's New Year celebrations.

In the bottom right panel that is missing in plate 58, a very similar Asahina, with one sword, heavy sideburns, and the same *kumadori* makeup, flies the *yakko* kite with one hand and holds a large spool of line in the other. Single sheets of these designs appear from time to time but never an upper-right sheet; it seems that these really are L-shaped triptychs, not tetraptychs.

1. See Shindo 1993, 121.

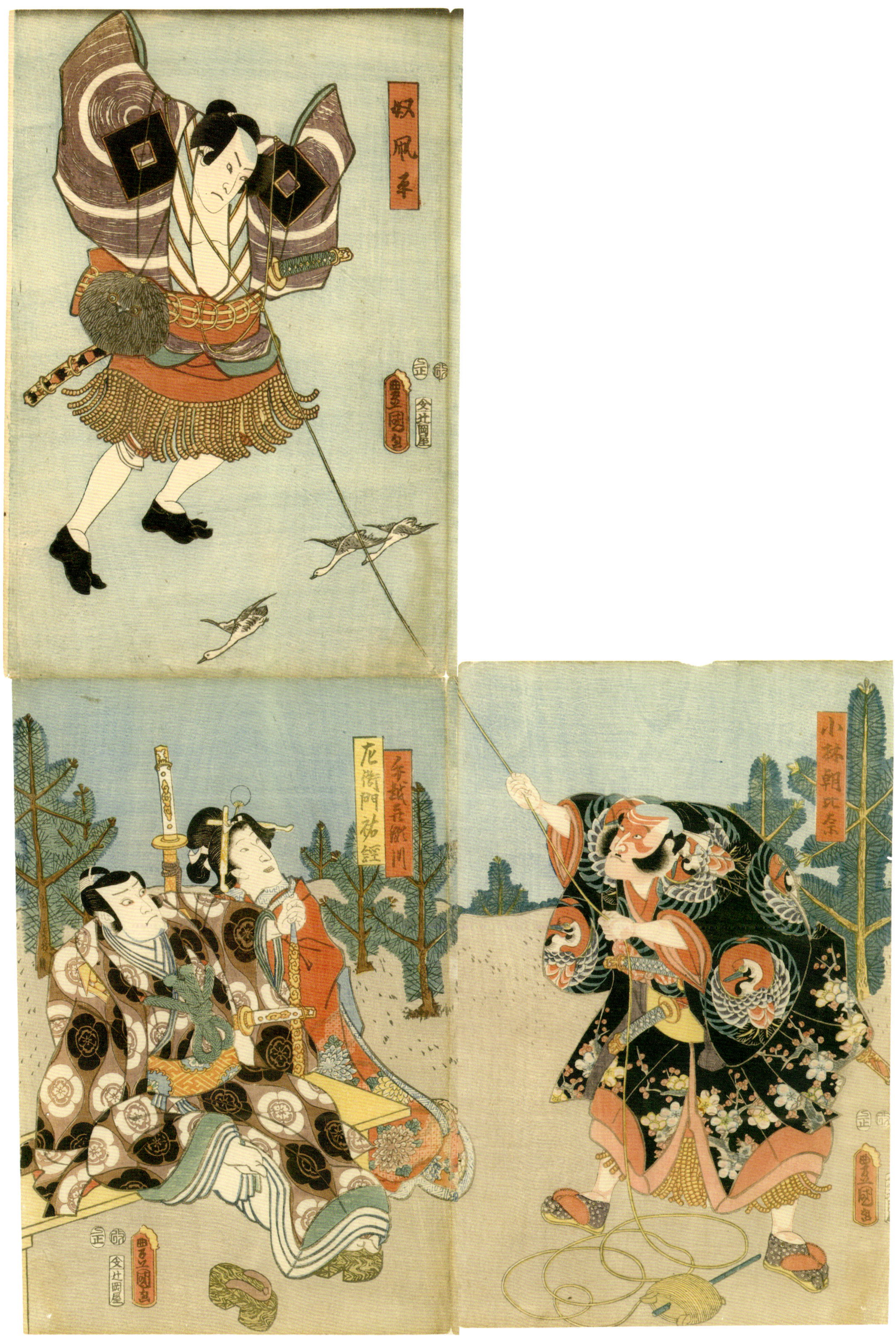

奴凧平
豊国画
左衛門祐経
小林朝比奈

60

A Demon Kite at Night
Uehara Yoshitoyo (1830–66)
signed: *Yoshitoyo*
c. 1858
chūban (23.3 × 17.1 cm)

A samurai and his servant, traveling through the rain at night, feel something fall across their shoulders and glimpse a demonic face—a kite decorated with a *hannya,* female demon, has caught in a tree and they have run into its tail-lines. They fall back terrified; the servant loses his sandal and his paper lantern catches fire. Rain is indicated by straight lines running across the design. The print is from a series titled *Kokkei Naniwa meisho* (Comic Famous Views of Naniwa) and the location is described as *jōnan sugiyama,* south of Cedar Mountain Castle; a distant castle building is suggested by dark shadowy shapes.

Yoshitoyo was a pupil first of Kunisada and then of Kuniyoshi, who were rival leaders of the two main branches of the Utagawa school. He worked both in Edo and Osaka—the Naniwa of the series title is the old name for Osaka—and this design is set in the Osaka area. This is an unusual subject: most prints made in Osaka were associated with the Kabuki theater (see plate 62). Apart from the Osaka school and a few other regional traditions, woodblock prints were overwhelmingly an Edo phenomenon.

The people of Naniwa were famous for enjoying jokes, and the two figures are depicted in the exaggerated comic style that we saw in plate 1 and will see again in plates 61 and 66. The subject material of woodblock prints ranged widely, and a significant subgenre included humorous scenes from daily life.

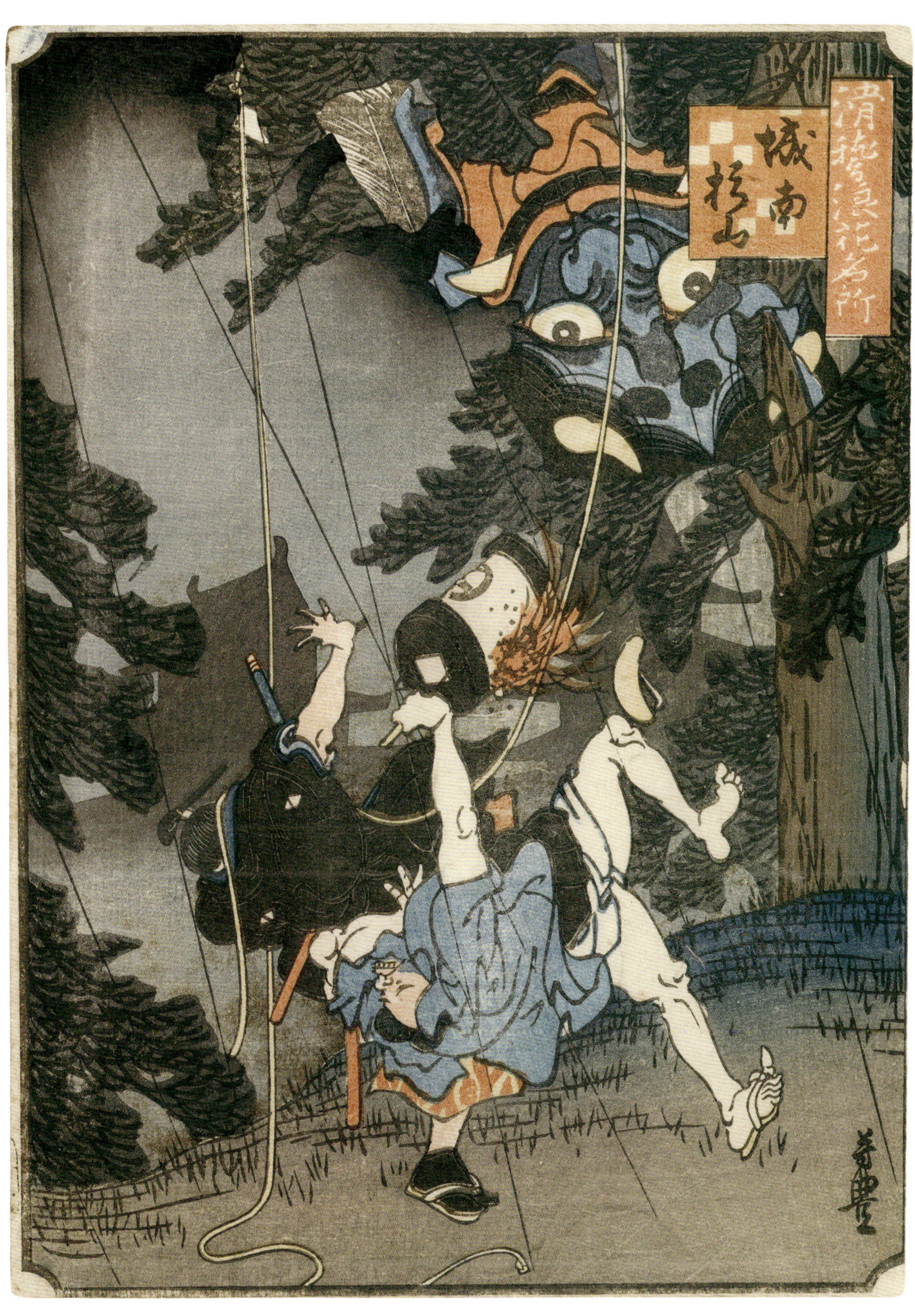
滑稽浪花名所
城南杉山
芳豊

61

The Willow Well at Soto-Sakurada
Utagawa Hirokage (fl. 1855–65)
signed: *Hirokage ga*
publisher: Tsujikaya Bunsuke
1860
ōban (32.9 × 22.9 cm)

As in the previous print, though with less optical credibility, an escaped *hannya* kite causes comic consternation. The kite has caught in a budding willow tree and its painted demon face reflected on the surface of a well scares three men, who appear to be wearing uniforms, gathered at the well with a dipper. The print is from Hirokage's rather crudely produced series *Edo meisho doke zukushi* (Famous Places of Edo with Humorous Scenes), and the scene is identified as *Soto-Sakurada yanagi no i,* The Willow Well at Soto-Sakurada. Soto-Sakurada was and still is the location of the main police station of the capital, close to Benkei Moat outside Edo Castle, near where Hiroshige placed his kite-and-battledore image in the One Hundred Famous Views of Edo (plate 56). A *daimyō* mansion and the watchtowers of the district can be seen in the background.

By using the reflection of a demon's face, the artist, a pupil of Hiroshige, recalls the story of Taira no Koremochi and the demon of Mount Takao. Hiking in the mountains outside Kyoto to see the red maple leaves one fine autumn day early in the tenth century, Koremochi met a beautiful woman. They happily shared saké together and admired the beautiful scenery, until he noticed that her reflection in the saké cup showed the face of a *hannya* demon. Reflections always reveal a person's true nature, and Koremochi quickly drew his sword and cut her down.

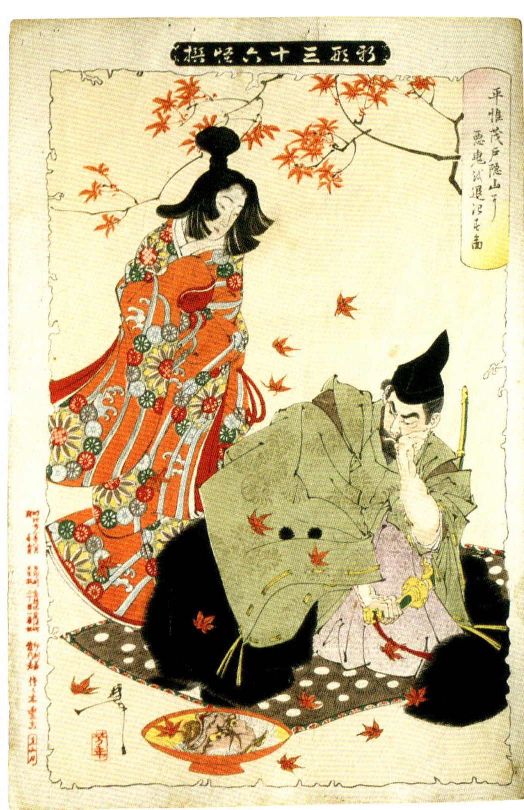

Taira no Koremochi notices the demon's reflection, from Taiso Yoshitoshi's *Shinkei sanjūrokkaisen* (New Forms of Thirty-six Ghosts), 1890.

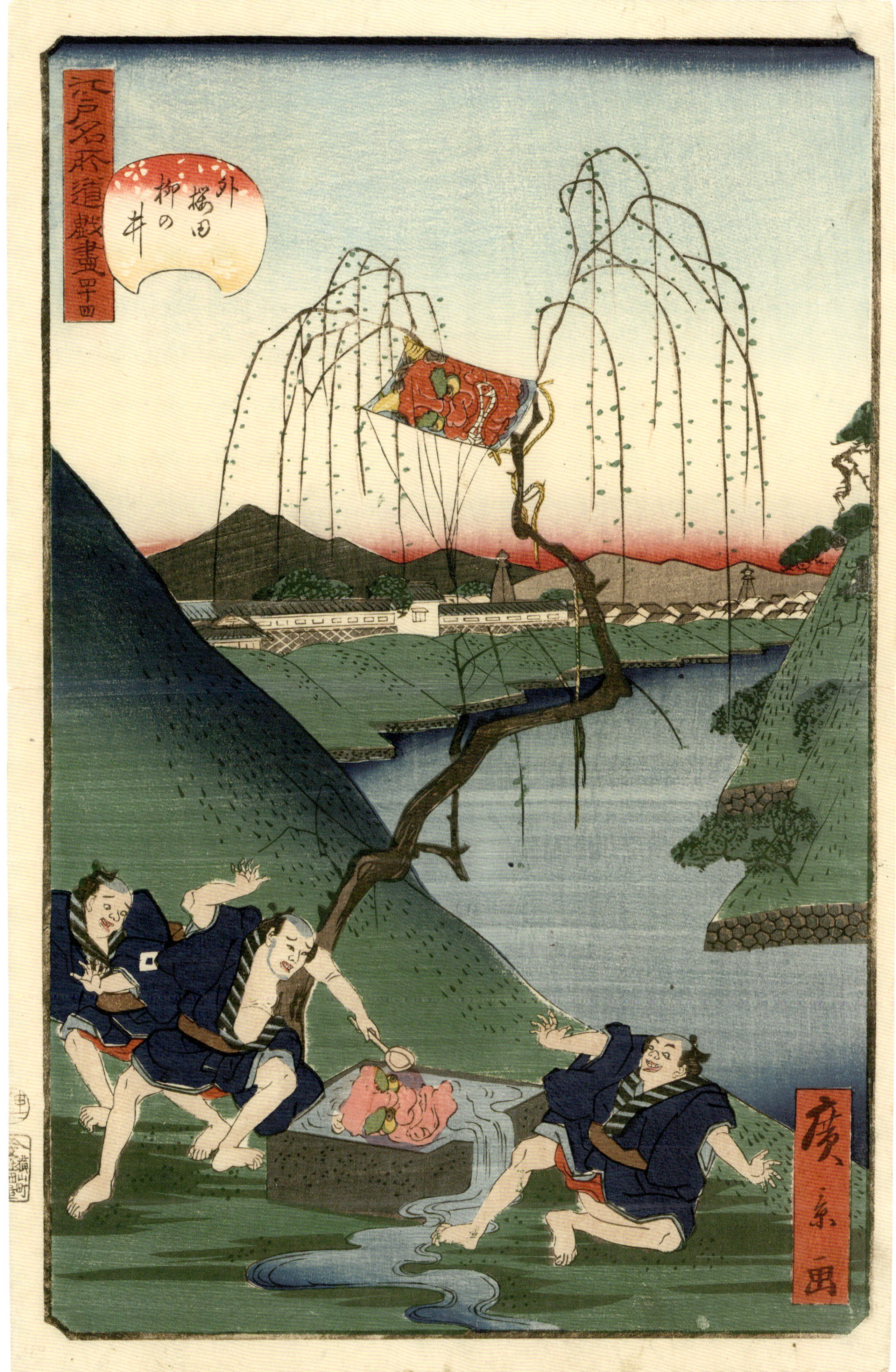
江戸名所道戯盡 四十四
外桜田柳の井
広景画

62

Hundred-Eyes Yonekichi and a *Tobi* Kite in a Plum Tree
Kinoshita Hironobu (active 1851–70)
signed: *Ashinoya Hironobu*
c. 1855–60
chūban diptych (each sheet approximately 24.4 × 17.3 cm)

Two members of the popular Arashi line of Kabuki actors in Osaka face each other in a Kabuki performance. Arashi Rikan III holds the line of a *tobi* kite that has caught in a flowering plum tree. His role of Hyakume (Hundred-Eyes) Yonekichi is given in the light red cartouche to his right. Appropriately for his nickname, he wears a jacket with a striking design of half-masks, the eyebrows of each arched in a different way to suggest a different emotion. The metal fitting of his carrying case, which bears the characters of his name, is also in the form of a half-mask.

The other actor, Arashi Rikaku II, is identified as Kikudōji, Chrysanthemum Boy. This person was an exile from the Chinese court who created the elixir of life when he wrote a magic Buddhist phrase on chrysanthemum leaves and floated them down a mountain river. He reclines on a dais in Chinese robes and holds a Chinese-style fan. Two butterflies, symbols of the souls of the living and dead, flutter between the two actors; their presence indicates that someone is about to arrive, or that a death will take place, or that a death has occurred.[1] When butterflies were part of the plot of a Kabuki play, an attendant dressed completely in black (and therefore invisible to the audience) would hold out a long pole with a model butterfly at the end.

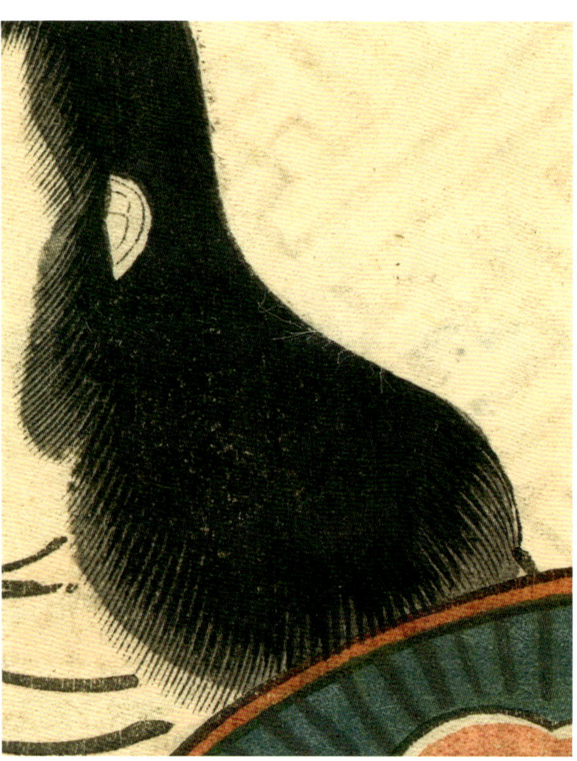

The overwhelming majority of prints made in Osaka illustrate Kabuki performances. After about the 1830s, most were made in the half-sheet *chūban* format, with a design often made up of many sheets; the composition suggests that this may be a triptych with the right sheet missing. The technical qualities of Osaka prints are usually very high, often higher than those of Edo. The carving of the block for the hairline of each actor here, for example, is extremely fine. The white of the trousers of the reclining figure has been embossed using a piece of closely woven linen, and the background has a heavily embossed swastika pattern.[2] The dais has been dusted with mica powder that lightly glitters when the print is turned. Brass- and tin-based pigments, first used on prints in the 1810s, have been used to simulate gold and silver. None of these luxurious touches were unusual in later Osaka theater prints, which are often small gems of the printer's art.

1. When the tenth-century usurper Taira no Masakado was preparing a rebellion in Kyoto, an unusually large swarm of butterflies invaded the city, frightening the people, who considered them to be the spirits of those soon to be killed in battle. (The idea of a general surrounding himself with doubles, used in the film *Kagemusha,* literally Shadow Warrior, originated with Masakado.)

2. This pattern is often associated with the Danjūrō line of actors—is Ichikawa Ebizō V (Danjūrō VII) posing in a missing right-hand sheet? Even after his return to Edo from exile in Osaka in 1850, he performed regularly on the Osaka stage from 1853 till 1858.

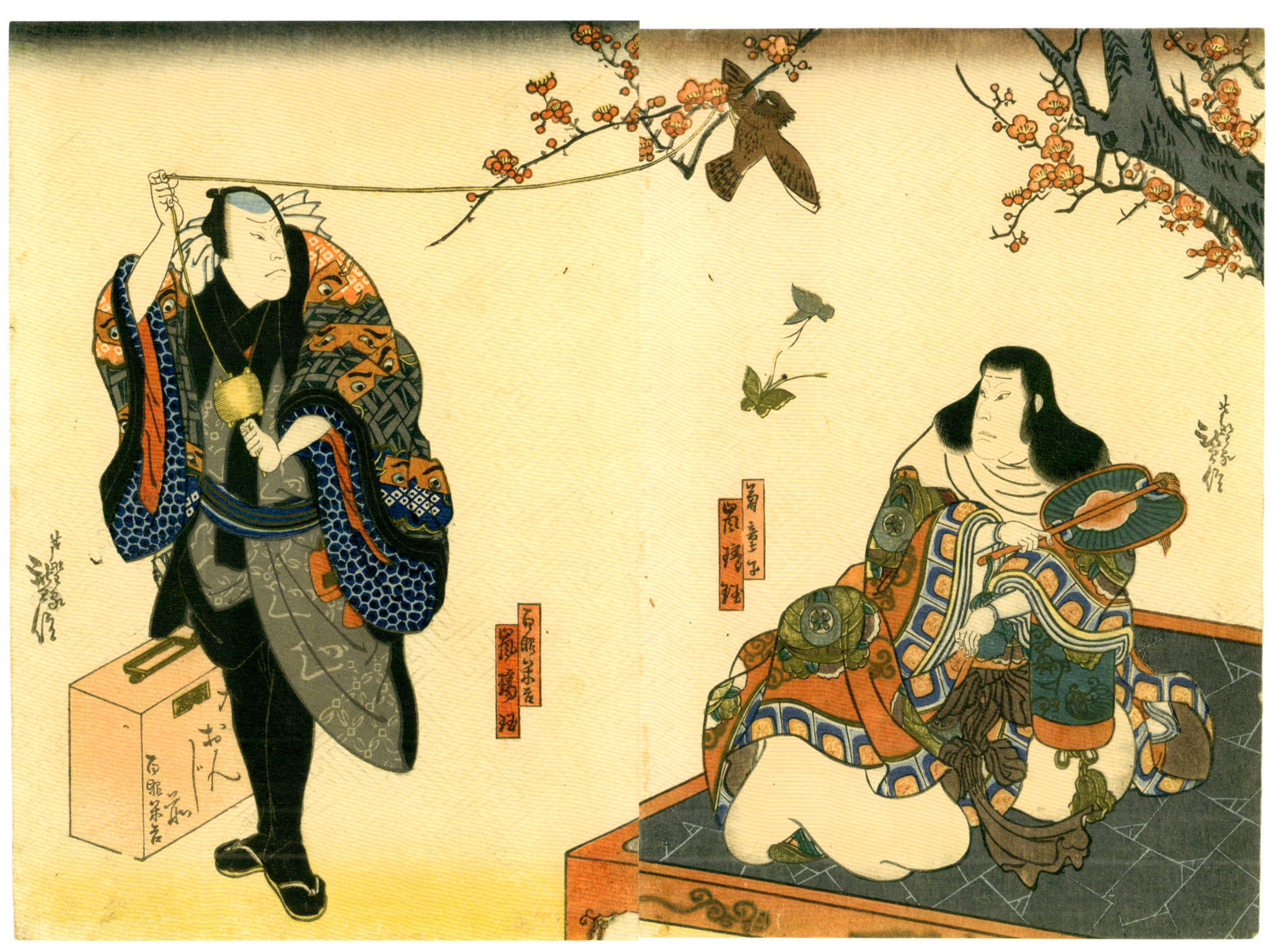

63

Two Worldly Men Going Around the Pleasure Quarters
Utagawa Kunisada (1786–1865)
signed: *Ki-ō Toyokuni ga*
engraver: Matshima Horimasa
publisher: Kaijudō
1862 first month
ōban diptych (each sheet approximately 35.2 × 24.3 cm)

The Kabuki actor Nakamura Tsurusuke IV rides on a suspended *tobi* kite pursued by a *yakko* played by Ichikawa Ichizō III. They are playing the roles of Musōbei and Takohei (Mr Kite), in the play *Mata meguri kuruwa no irotako,* performed at the Morita Theater in Edo at New Year, 1862. The title may be approximately translated as Two Worldly Men Going Around the Pleasure Quarters; *mata meguri* means to go around and around, and there is a pun on the word *mata,* crotch. We have seen a Mr Yakko-Kite as a Kabuki character in the two triptychs of plates 58 and 59; he will fly with Musōbei again in plate 66 and appears twenty years later in plates 85 and 86.

The design is a fascinating example of complex Kabuki stage effects, and this is probably an accurate depiction of the mechanical theater props set against a painted background. The two crows are intended to give the viewer an impression of being high in the sky. The distinctive five-story pagoda of Asakusa, part of the plot of the play, appears in the background, along with another temple building in the right sheet (see also plate 74). Early plum blossoms are blooming in the temple grounds.

Kunisada's signature includes the phrase *ki-ō,* happy old man: he was well into his seventies. Print fashions had changed, but Kunisada was regarded in his lifetime as the greatest of all woodblock-print artists, and at a time when sixty was considered a satisfactory old age, he continued to design until his death early in 1865 when he was in his seventy-ninth year. This print is somewhat static and wooden, lacking the flair of some of Kunisada's earlier figures and compositions. The block-carver's name, Matshima Horimasa (*hori* means to engrave), is given in the yellow cartouche, a rare honor for a carver that is not particularly well deserved here.

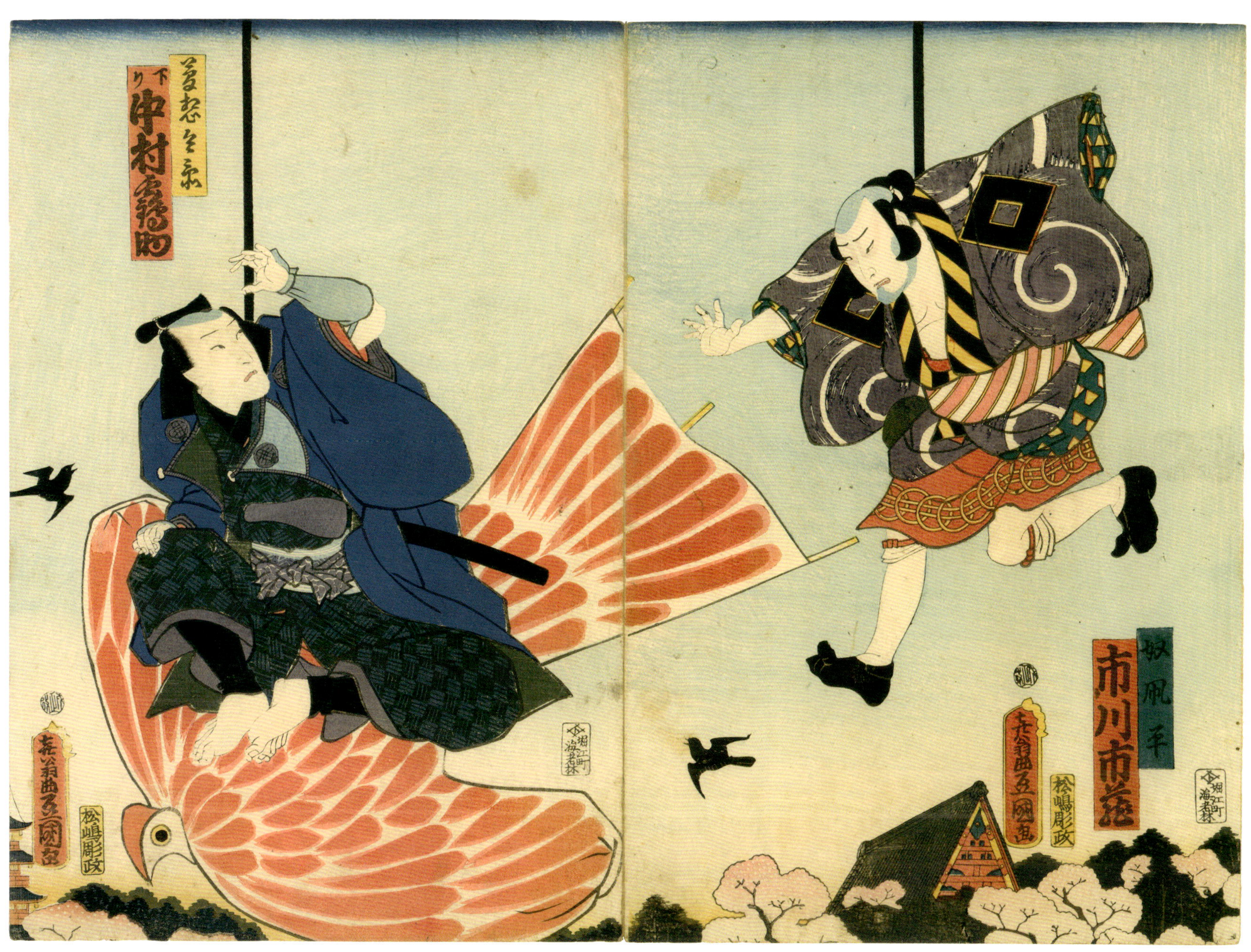
下り
中村
七十九歳豊国画
松嶋彫政
奴凧平
市川市蔵
七十九歳豊国画
松嶋彫政

64

Beauty with Dragon Robe
Utagawa Kunisada (1786–1865)
signed: *Nanajukyūnen Toyokuni hitsu*
1864, second month
ōban (37 × 25.8 cm)

A courtesan with ornate hair ornaments, a roll of tissues, and a toothpick in her mouth looks out from the verandah of a fine restaurant. Restaurants traditionally hung large red lanterns under their eaves; here the lanterns are decorated with a *toshidama* circle, Kunisada's mark, which is repeated under his signature. She wears a magnificent outer robe with a complex design of a rectangular dragon-kite. Carefully drawn tail-lines dangle down from the kite across a design of cherry blossoms and cracked ice, a motif that suggests sex between an older man and a younger woman. That the dragon kite is tangled in a blossoming cherry tree tells its own story.

The cartouche under the lantern reads *Ensugata hana no jūnishi* (Voluptuous Portraits of Flowers of the Twelve Signs of the Zodiac), indicating that the design is part of a series exploring the theme of the twelve signs of the zodiac; this sheet illustrates the Dragon. Though the young woman fits the panel naturally, the composition suggests that this may be the right panel of a triptych. Kunisada's pupil, Utagawa Kunihisa II (1832–91), has been allowed to draw and sign the fan-shaped cartouche of a mansion, with its fine roofs and fire-buckets, at the upper right.

This is another print in which Kunisada refers to his advanced age: the signature translates as, "painted by Toyokuni in his seventy-ninth year." The fact that the Japanese regarded a person to be one year old as soon as they were born and two as soon as they passed their first New Year explains the mathematics. This was the last year of Kunisada's life: he died on January 12, 1865, shortly before the next lunar New Year, still signing himself (for example in his death poem[1]) as being seventy-nine. The design must have been popular, as the lines show considerable wear of the printing block. Most of the colors here are imported synthetic pigments and are faded; many natural dyes also faded quickly in light, but here only the dark blue of the natural indigo at the top of the print retains its depth.

1. His death poem translates, "I have entrusted everything to Amida; my soul is at ease; whatever happens—homage to Amida Buddha!"

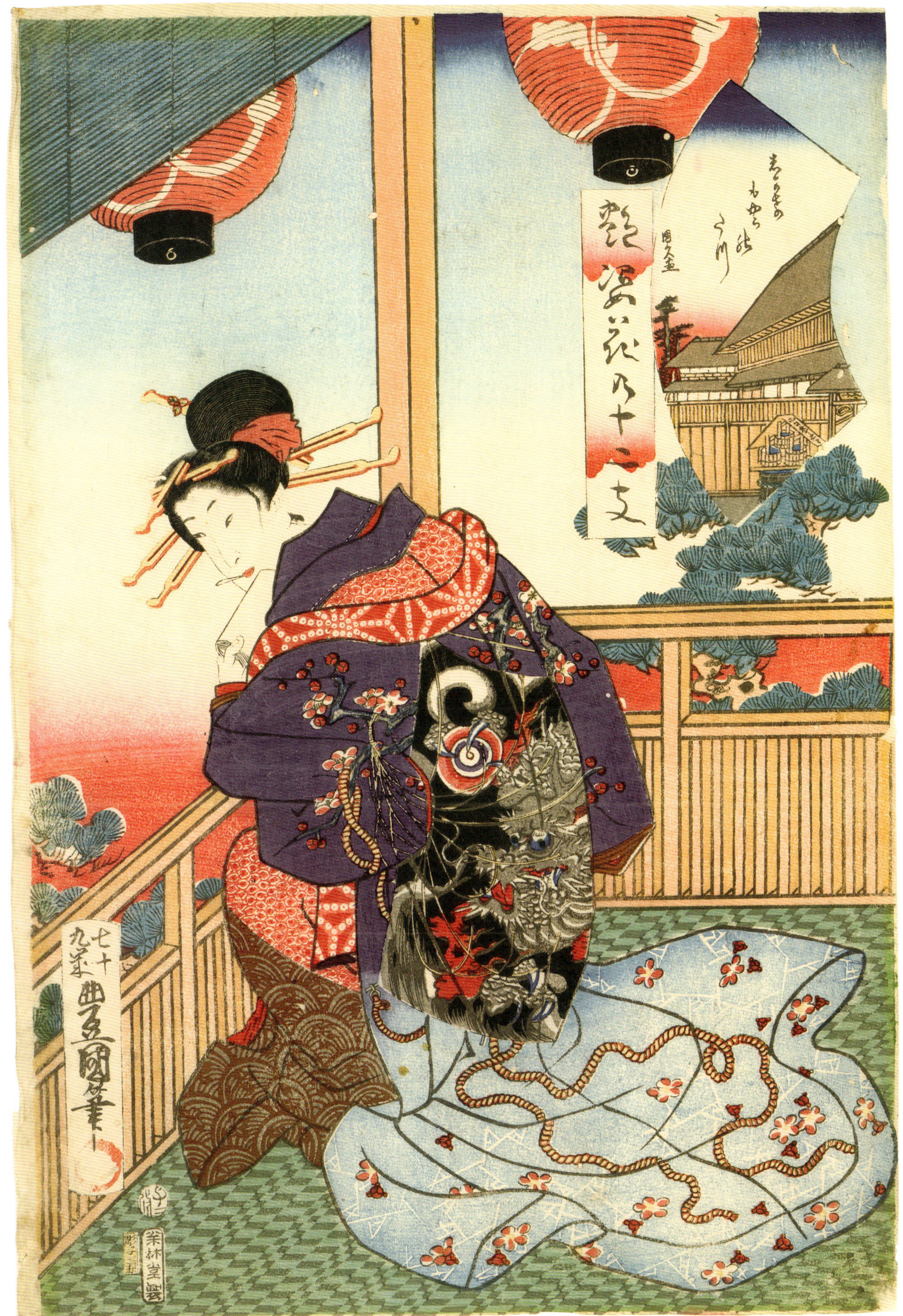
艶姿花乃十二支
七十九歳豊国筆

65

Atago Hill
Ichiryūsai Shigenobu (Hiroshige II)
(1829–69)
signed: *Hiroshige ga*
publisher: Aeto
1862
ōban (35.8 × 24.3 cm)

After Hiroshige's death in 1858, his son-in-law continued to offer the public landscape prints in his master's style; his signature is a direct copy of Hiroshige's. Here he shows us Atago Hill, pulling back from Hiroshige's close-up setting in plate 57 and giving us a wider view. The rust-red cartouche with the series title reads *Tōto sanjūrokkei* (Thirty-six Views of the Eastern Capital). The name of the location, *Atagoyama,* appears in the fan-shaped cartouche, which has color grading and is embossed with clouds. Atago Hill was less than a hundred feet high but gave an uninterrupted view of the low-lying city as it spread to the northeast.

Again it is a New Year morning and the sky is full of kites. The character on the rectangular kite at the top means dragon and the one on the kite to the left means fish, like Hiroshige's design in the kite in plate 54. To the right is the gate of the shrine to the Shinto deity Bishamon, with a large wooden plaque on the side listing donors. Next to it are two restaurants, lined with the red lanterns of eating places, open to the breezes and the magnificent view. Customers sit on raised platforms; kettles sit on small stoves. Mists over the sea of houses lighten and simplify the design. Stylized cloud-bands, a formal painting convention often used by Hiroshige, appear in yellow and pink at the bottom of the design.

The people illustrated are too small to make out faces, but each group relates in natural ways. They include a little boy with two swords at the right lagging behind his samurai father and a servant, and another child gesturing to its parents. There is a palpable peace and charm to this simple print.

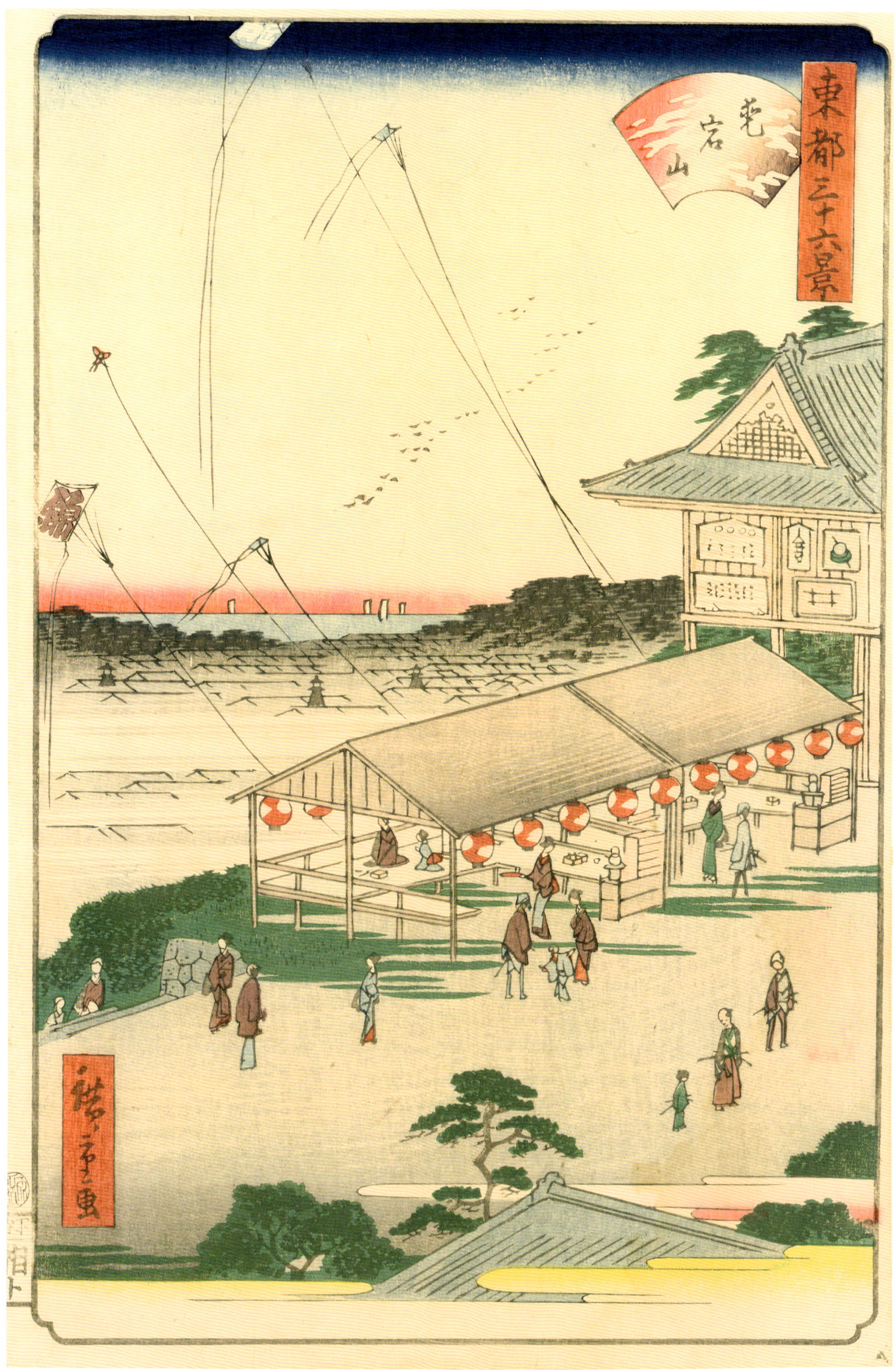
東都三十六景
愛宕山
廣重画

66

Pictures of Edo Flowers and Scenic Spots
Utagawa Kunisada (1786–1865),
Ichiryūsai Hiroshige II (1829–69),
Kawanabe Kyōsai (1831–89),
Tsukioka Yoshitoshi (1839–92),
Kiyokuni, Shunkai
signed: *Toyokuni ga, Toyokuni hitsu, ōju Hiroshige ga, Ōkō Yoshitoshi hitsu, Seisei Kyōsai, Kiyokuni hitsu, Shunkai*
engravers' signatures: *Hori Mino* (right), *Katada Hori Chō* (center), *Hori Uemura Yasu* (left)
publisher: Kato-sei
1863 twelfth month
ōban triptych (each sheet approximately 35.6 × 24 cm)

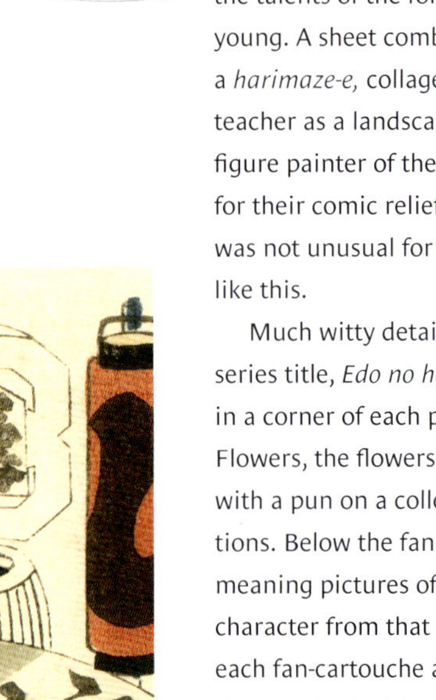

For this ambitious triptych, from a series that provides a small compendium of Edo life, the publisher commissioned the talents of the foremost print artists of his day, old and young. A sheet combining different subjects like this was called a *harimaze-e,* collage picture. Hiroshige II, heir to his great teacher as a landscape artist, and Kunisada, the dominant figure painter of the day, are joined by Kyōsai and Yoshitoshi for their comic relief, along with two lesser-known artists. It was not unusual for a publisher to commission joint designs like this.

Much witty detail is contained in these three panels. The series title, *Edo no hana-e,* is given in the fan-shaped cartouche in a corner of each print. This means literally Pictures of Edo Flowers, the flowers referring in this case to Kabuki actors, with a pun on a colloquialism meaning fires, as in conflagrations. Below the fan cartouche are the characters *meishō-e* meaning pictures of scenic spots (the *shō* being a different character from that used in the more common *meisho*). Above each fan-cartouche an Edo district is identified by a *matoi,* the standard of the local firefighting troop. Below, specialties of the district—saké, soba, candy—are named and illustrated in tiny detail. Edoites enjoyed local specialties, as Japanese travelers do today, and including them in a print would probably have boosted sales of the print; it is also possible that they were a form of paid advertisement.

Besides the title groupings, tours de force of printing in themselves, each sheet is divided into three panels drawn by different artists. One panel on each sheet contains a Kabuki actor drawn by Kunisada; the names of the actors are given in the heavy, florid style used on Kabuki posters. Another panel on each sheet shows a landscape. Two of the landscapes form backgrounds for accidents involving kites that are treated in a lighthearted way. In one, the Kabuki character Musōbei (see plate 63) falls out of the sky from a *tobi* kite; in the other, an Ōkame kite falls onto a startled itinerant musician, to the glee of a little boy who looks up her robes. In Kyōsai's brilliantly drawn panel at the bottom of the center panel, two New Year performers rush to help the falling Musōbei.

The overall design is held together by the line of a *yakko* kite that stretches across the triptych; the kite is flown by a boy dressed as a young prince. The actor playing the *yakko* is identified as Onoe Tamizō, probably Onoe Kikugorō V, who would have been nineteen at the time and already manager of the Ichimura Kabuki theater. His role is identified as Yakko Takohei of Akasaka. The black pole above his head indicates that he is suspended over a theater stage—as the same character is in plate 63. The kite lines attached to his shoulders sag realistically: there is no tension in them because he is suspended.

The other two actors both belong to the Ichikawa acting family. The one beside the little prince stands in front of a deep-blue Edo kite, dressed in a bear-fur robe and holding a spool of kite-line. He is Ichikawa Danjūrō IX, younger brother of the ill-fated VIII (see plate 49), playing the role of Imai Shirō Kanehei. The other actor, Ichikawa Ichizō, is dressed as a lay priest and holds a bell and a model of a shrine; the three borders of the panel around him form the traditional Ichikawa Danjūrō *mon.*

The landscape panel by Hiroshige II on the right side of the right sheet illustrates a gate in Akasaka. The panel on the left shows a restaurant called Yamanoi, Mountain Well. The text recounts a flirtatious conversation between a woman and Yakko Takohei using wordplay on different characters for fish. There is a much-used pun, for example, on the word *koi,* which can mean either carp or love, depending on the character; also *aitai,* meaning I want to see you, and *tai,* meaning red sea-bream, a New Year delicacy. The center sheet shows another Akasaka landmark, Hikawa Jinja, a Shinto shrine.

The triptych is fresh and the lines are crisp. The quality of carving is very high; the extraordinary detail (see inset) would be lost without it. The engravers, different for each sheet, are named in small, unobtrusive cartouches.

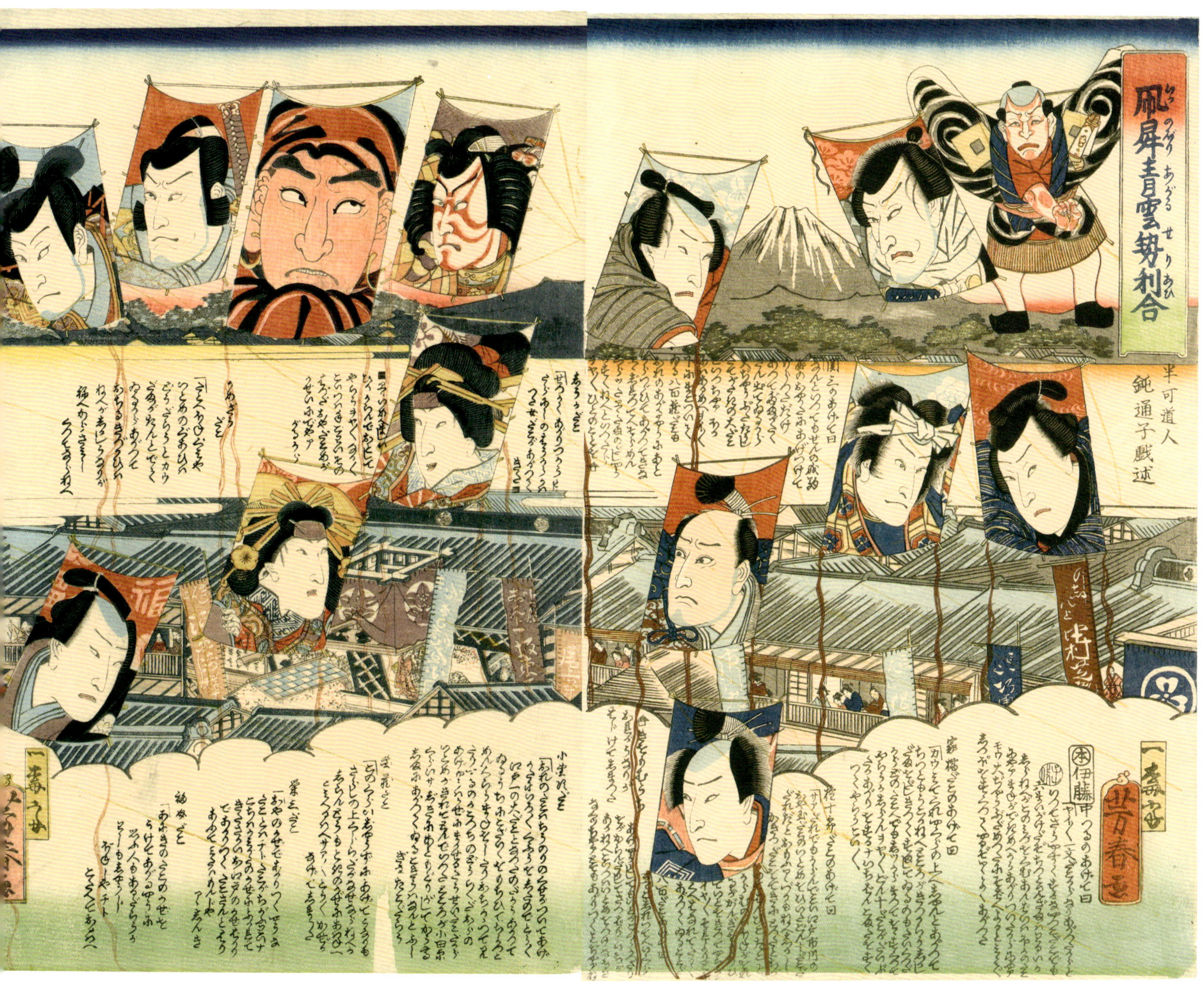

thinking person who believes he knows it all." He claims he is quoting the actors. The statements of each actor, filled with slang, are written in a mixture of *hiragana* and *kanji* and are a minor tour de force of engraving; the print quality of this triptych is very high. All the major actors are here, their faces immediately recognizable to their fans. They are not named formally but are identified by nicknames, with swaggering statements such as "They say they are Number One in Edo, but I think I am," prefaced by *Umezō iwaku,* or *Shirō iwaku* (Umezō states, or Shirō states).

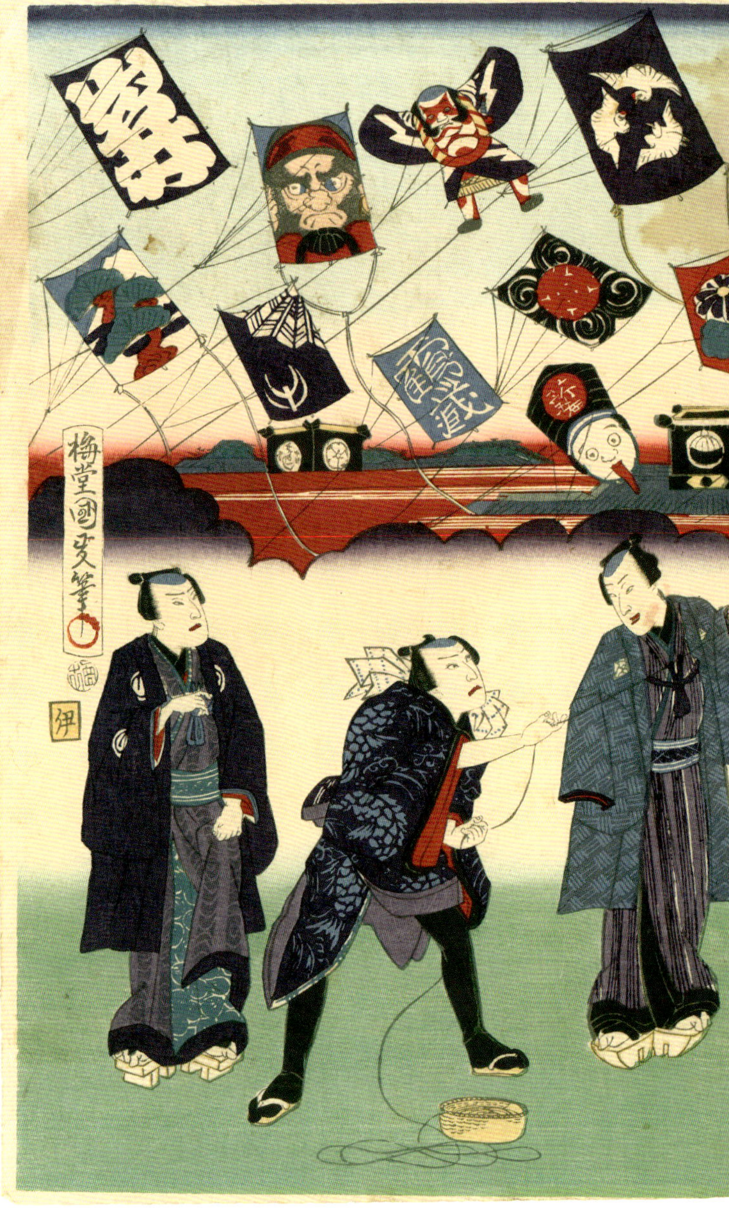

68

Kabuki Stars Rising in Popularity Like Kites
Kunimasa II?
signed: *Umedō Kunimasa hitsu*
publisher: Maruya Tetsujirō
1873
ōban triptych (each sheet approximately 36.1 × 24.5 cm)

This triptych is based on a concept similar to that of the previous one, with actors flying kites that rise into a sky full of a large range of kite-shapes. One showers the city with auspicious confetti. The same *yagura* drum tower that we saw in the previous print appears, along with two others, one for each of the three theaters in Edo's Kabuki district, above a stylized line of clouds. Small boys join the fun; kites were very much a young boys' sport.

The title cartouche reads *Takonoburi agari hanagata* (Kabuki Stars Rising in Popularity Like Kites). The actors are not named as they are in most representations of Kabuki scenes and the drawing is not good enough for us to recognize the actors, as it is in many other prints in this book. The kite in the top left corner reads *Iwai,* the name of the *onnagata* acting family that we saw in plates 19, 27, and 28. The kite of the little boy in the right sheet reads *Ichikawa,* for the Danjūrō line of actors. The whole image of kites and Kabuki actors had propitious, happy overtones, and the triptych is useful in showing a range of kite designs popular in early-Meiji Japan.

Nevertheless, this is not a beautiful print. The quality of the drawing and printing has deteriorated badly since Yoshiharu's triptych of a decade earlier. The design is pedestrian and the blocks have been clumsily carved. The colors are garish; there was a great temptation to overuse the bright synthetic dyes

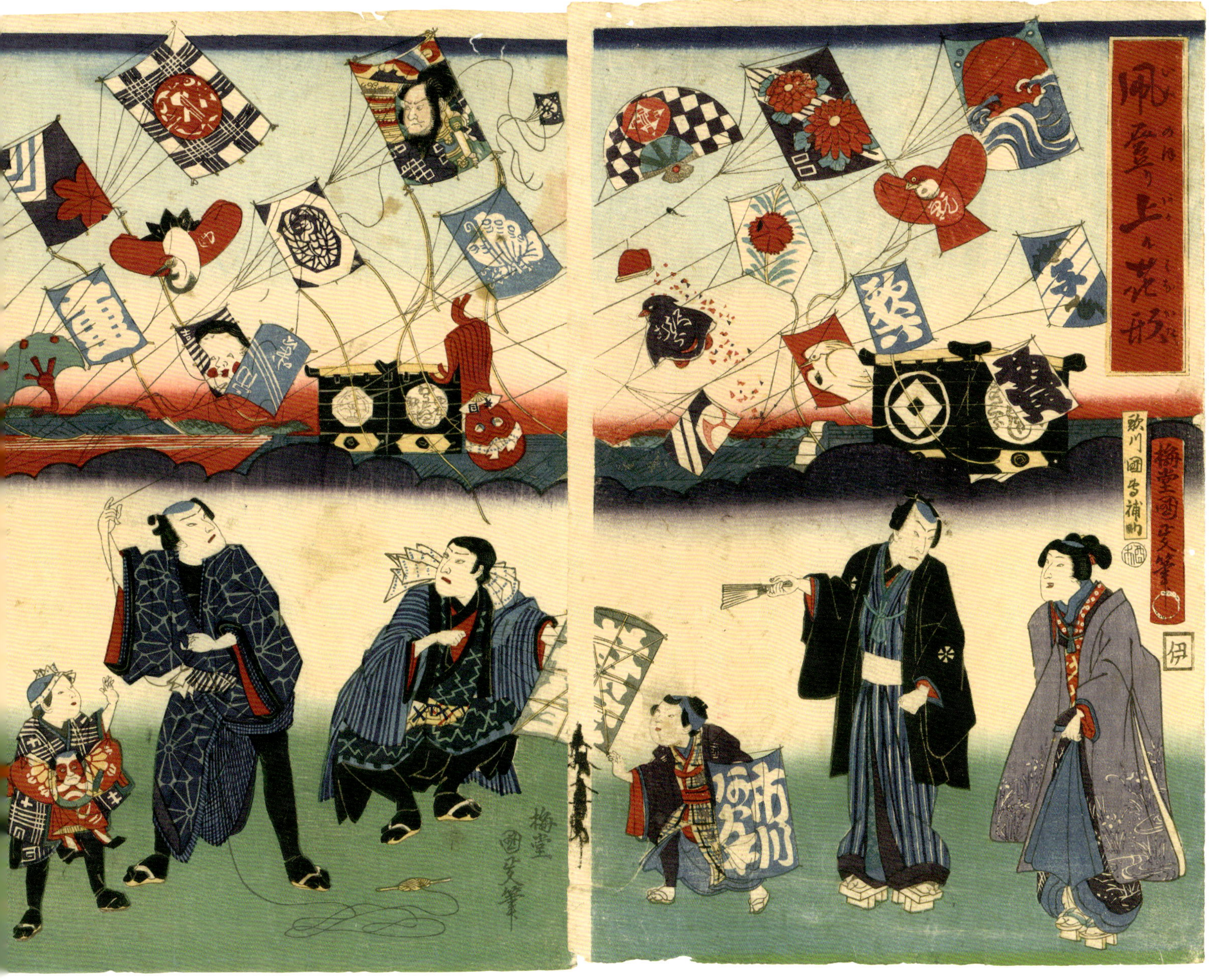

imported as international trade increased after the Meiji Restoration. At the same time, the dislocation resulting from a decade of unrest and the change in government damaged the economy, and the early 1870s were very hard years for many in the capital. In these troubled times, publishers could not maintain high standards of woodblock printing (plate 74 is a stunning exception), nor could the public afford expensive prints.[1]

1. See Keyes 1983, 27–28 and 120–33, for details of how the distressed times affected one woodblock artist, Taiso Yoshitoshi.

69

Modern Parody of a Kite Store
Toyohara Kunichika (1835–1900)
signed: *ōju Kunichika ga*
engraver: *Katada Hori Chō*
publisher: Iseya Tōkichi
1865 eleventh month
ōban triptych (each sheet approximately 36.4 × 24.2 cm)

A well-dressed matron with her little son and a servant visit a kite store. The proprietor, wearing a bandanna, demonstrates how to gather the many strings that attach to a kite, their function being to keep equal tension over its face and maintain stability. The kite's complex frame is visible from behind. The way lines are looped is shown in the kite held by the servant. Objects in the store include thick hanks of line on the floor, scissors for cutting the line, balls of thinner line lying on a *hibachi* brazier, and another *hibachi* with fire-tongs in the lower right corner (it is presumably winter, and the kite is being purchased for New Year). The walls appear to be bamboo laths, similar to the wall in plate 46.

The word *mitate,* parody, in the title—*Tōsei mitate tako shidashi* (Modern Parody of a Kite Store)—suggests that the scene is a witty fiction based on Kabuki actors and roles rather than a literal depiction of a kite store. The features of the proprietor are those of Ichimura Uzaemon XIII (later Onoe Kikugorō V).[1] The kite he is holding bears the word *matoi,* fireman's standard, and he seems to be dressed as a fireman. Most of the kites are decorated with Kabuki scenes and actors, several with recognizable features, for example, the demon kite and an octopus named Aizō in the top left corner. Danjūrō in a Shibaraku role appears at the left and the villainous Kudō no Suketsune at the right, behind the store-owner's shoulder. Chikashige, a student of Kunichika who must have assisted his master in the design, has been allowed to inscribe his name on the Lord Kudō kite.

Other kites show creatures typical of Edo urban culture. There is Tofukozō, the Tofu Boy, a goblin of whom children must beware. A *yakko* figure appears not only in its usual outstretched form but also painted on a rectangular kite. A bewhiskered Daruma in his red robes takes center stage, as he does in Kuniyoshi's triptych, plate 32, and in different circumstances in plate 77, also in the cutouts of plates 41 and 42: Daruma must have been among the most popular kite designs. His fierce expression conveys the intensity of his concentration as he focuses on achieving enlightenment. In the center of the left panel a kite shows a courtesan wearing Daruma's red robe, a comic comparison of Daruma's nine-year meditation and a courtesan's ten-year contract with her brothel. Behind the visiting matron a kite shows a woman clasping a phallic mushroom festooned for a festival. The *tobi* kite has a mackerel clutched in its talons; behind it is a long-tongued goblin kite. Kintarō throws New Year beans at little *oni* demons.

Though the composition is overly crowded—doubtless like the shop—and the print is not in good condition, this triptych is valuable as a cornucopia of the kites available to a young Edo boy at festival time.

1. See Shindo 1993, 113, 122.

70

Today's Rising Kites
Mitani Sadahiro (active 1864–1876)
signed: *Sadahiro*
1866
ōban diptych (each sheet approximately 35.6 × 24.6 cm)

The title of this witty Osaka print is *Tōsei nobori ika,* Today's Rising Kites. The word used for kite, normally *tako* (which can also mean octopus), is *ika* (which can also mean squid). *Ka* is also the word for price, so the title sounds similar to "Today's rising prices." The figures in the bottom right corner are saying, "Going up, going up."

Each of the many kites shown has a character on it for a household item or service. Everything for daily life is here: paper, oil, tea, *tabi,* knives, raincoats, vegetables, *miso, geta,* lipstick, books, brushes, shoe repair, lodging, tailoring, goldsmithing, *azuki* beans, lumber, horse fittings, *nori,* houseplants, *udon,* New Year *mochi* and New Year *zenzai.* Some of the objects are roughly grouped: the characters for theater and musical instruments fly next to each other, as do carpenters and manual labor. Appropriately, the last two are depicted as male figures: *yakko* kites. The money market, *zenisoba,* lies supine on the ground.

In the waning decades of the shogunate, the Japanese economy became highly unstable. Tensions escalated between supporters of the shogunate and modernizers who used the emperor as a figurehead. The result was civil war and the "restoration" of the teenage Meiji emperor in 1868. As an indication of the disruptions of the period during which this print was made, half of Edo's population of at least a million deserted the city during the 1860s, 300,000 in 1867 alone.[1]

This diptych bears neither publisher's mark nor censor's seal and, because of its political content, may have been a *kawaraban,* literally roof-tile print, a privately distributed broadsheet. The date is given as Tiger, second year of the Keiō era. The artist, Mitani Sadahiro, was a student of Maruyama-style painting, and the design is closer in style to the Shijō than the *ukiyo-e* school. He took the name Sadahiro II on the death of his teacher Hirosada, a leading designer of Kabuki prints in Osaka, the commercial capital of Japan.

1. Jansen and Rozman 1986, 347.

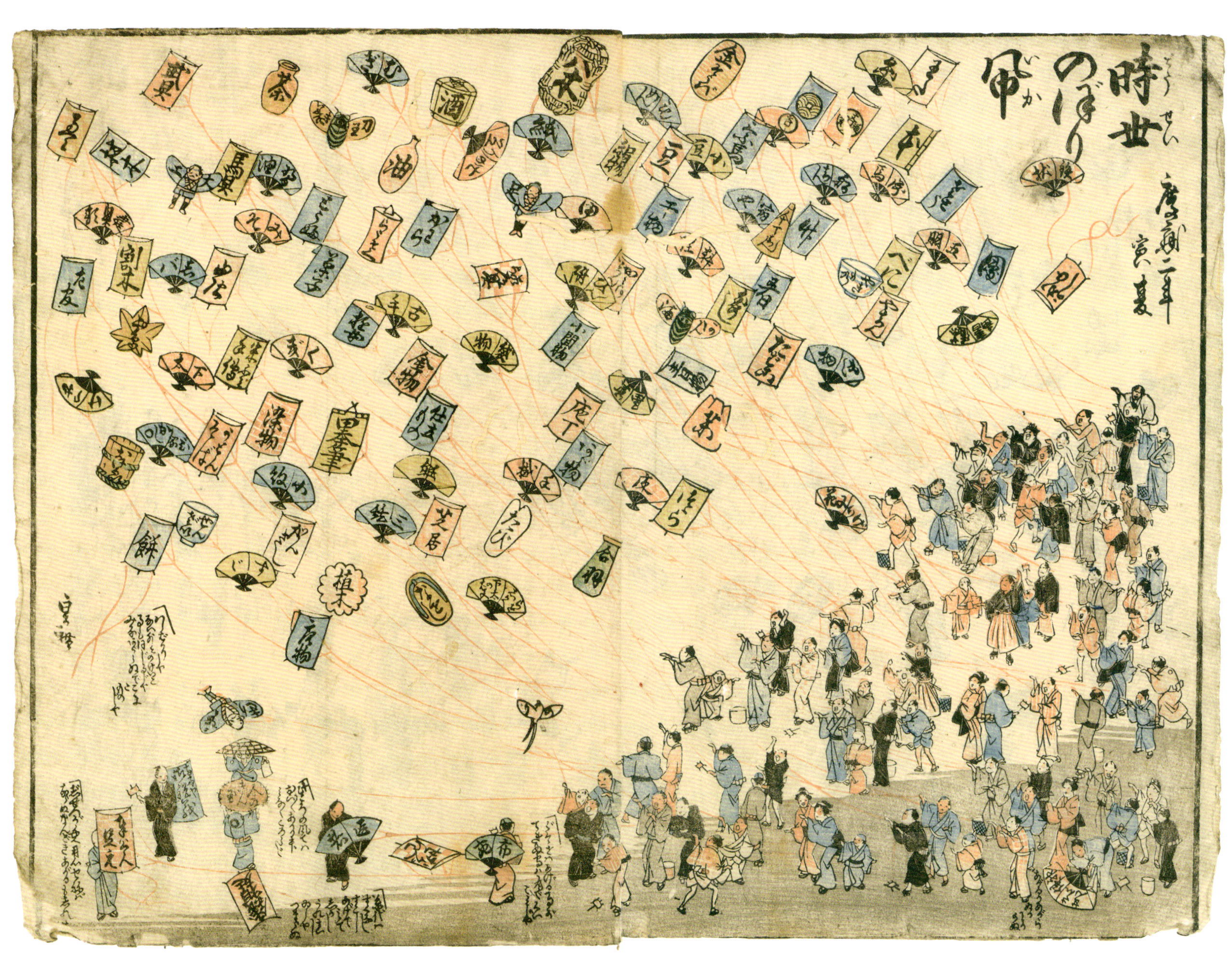
時世のぼり凧

71

Children's Play, Kite Games
Taguchi Yoshimori (1830–84)
signed: *Ikkōsai ko-Yoshimori ga*
publisher: Kagaya Katsugoro
1868
ōban, right-hand sheet of a triptych
(36.4 × 24.3 cm)

The title of this print is *Kodomo asobi tako no tawamura* (Children's Play, Kite Games). Young boys, the two smallest with their mothers, fly kites, and there is a strong sense of boyish rivalry. The *hiragana* characters give an excited barrage of comments such as "Pull a little, make the kite go lower," "Look at the wind blow that kite," "I've got to pull, the balance is off, it's unstable," and so on. The design is full of energy and competitive good humor.

Yoshimori, who signs himself Little Yoshimori here, was a pupil of Kuniyoshi; he worked first in Edo and later in Yokohama. Yokohama, a port and commercial center just south of Edo, had no famous Kabuki theater or entertainment center, and this genre print of everyday people would have been a natural subject for Yoshimori. Some trouble has been invested in the production of this print: the design is lively, the carving strong, and the colors—a mixture of imported and traditional dyes—bright. The market for this design would not have been Kabuki aficionados or elegant customers of the entertainment quarters, yet the quality of its printing suggests that it would not have been inexpensive. Compare it, for example, with the game board in plate 39, which contains fascinating social information but was produced as cheaply as possible.

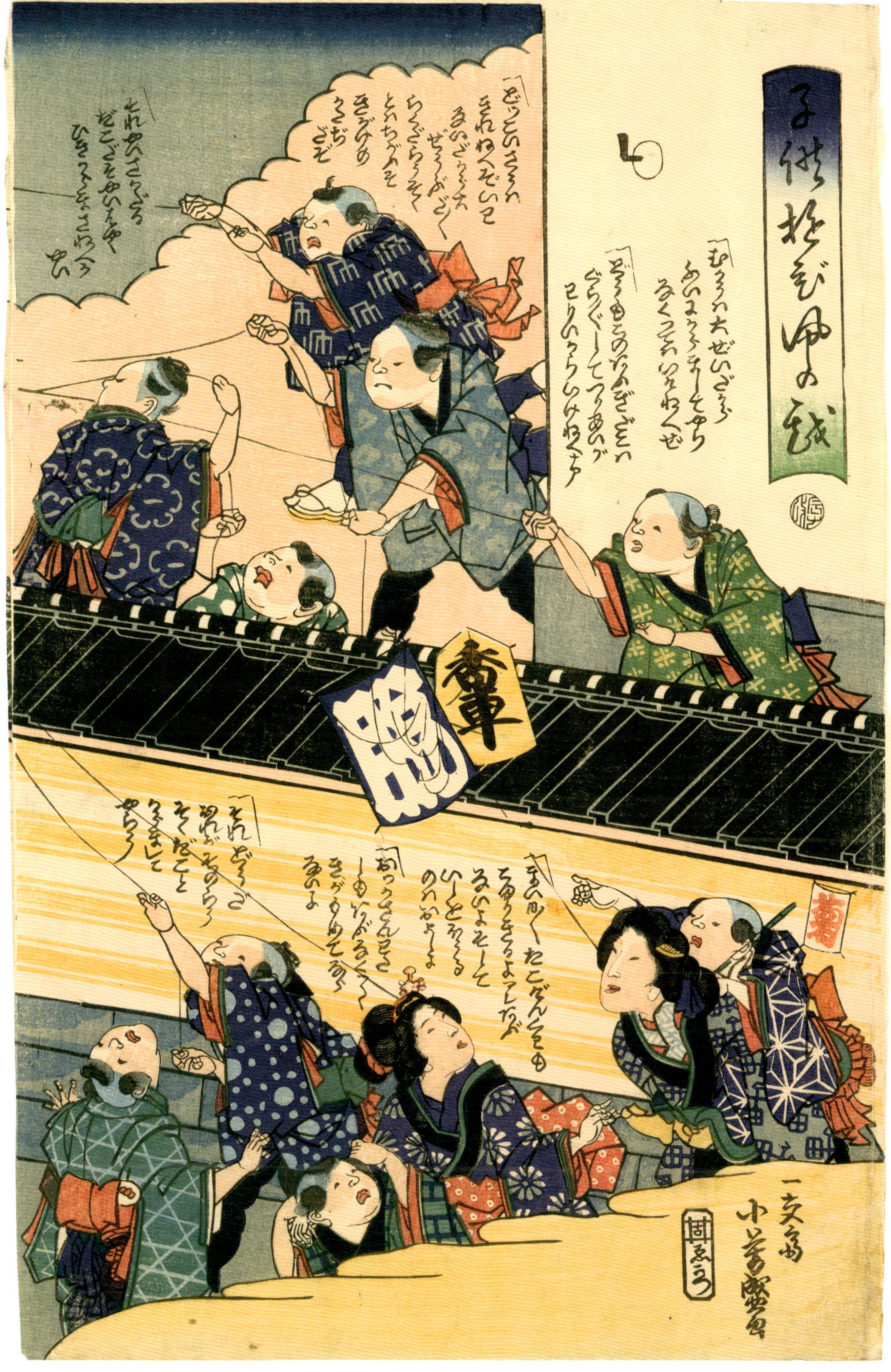

72

Kite-flying at Ueno Hirokōji
Utagawa Hiroshige III (1843–94)
signed: *Hiroshige hitsu*
1869 twelfth month
ōban (36.4 × 24.3 cm)

It is New Year, and boys are taking advantage of the open area near Ueno—an uncharacteristically empty public space in the crowded city of Tokyo—to fly their kites. A Daruma kite with a trailing tail-rope, seen close-up in the top left corner, frames the scene. Each of the modest shops in the background has a pair of small New Year pine-tree decorations at the entrance. Our friend the fan-box buyer carries his load in the foreground and provides another indication of the season. A high-ranking lord rides a horse; a servant carries his tall ceremonial pole. Two *manzai* performers, one with a drum on his back, watch two boys with kites; the characters on the kite we can see read *atari,* big hit. The character on the kite just below the series cartouche reads *itamoto,* meaning published, perhaps an attempt at a pun.

There is no hint of the recent disturbances in the area. The climactic battle of the Meiji Restoration had been fought at Ueno only seven months before. Two thousand troops loyal to the shogun armed with traditional pikes and spears made a last stand at Ueno and were massacred by the modern equipment of the reformist imperial forces. The artist Yoshitoshi (plate 66), who witnessed the battle with one of his students, was almost alone over the next several years in producing designs of the violence (perhaps as personal exorcism of the horrors he had seen). Regulations banning prints that depicted contemporary political events were still in force, and most artists and the buying public focused on traditional subjects such as the Kabuki theater and, increasingly, scenes of daily life.

The design by this student of Hiroshige's student is rather crudely drawn and static (the horseman's attendants seem to have stopped in their tracks, and the figure groups appear arbitrary). The print is part of a series by Hiroshige III titled *Tōkyo meisho zu-e* (Pictures of Famous Places in Tokyo); the yellow cartouche describes the scene as kite-flying at Ueno Hirokōji. The censor's seal indicates the twelfth month of the Dragon Year, corresponding to early 1869. This was the second year of Meiji, and Japan was still using the traditional lunar calendar. The country changed to the Gregorian solar-based calendar by imperial fiat when December 3, 1872, by the old calendar was decreed to be the first day of 1873. Inevitably there were complaints that the government was stealing a month of people's lives.

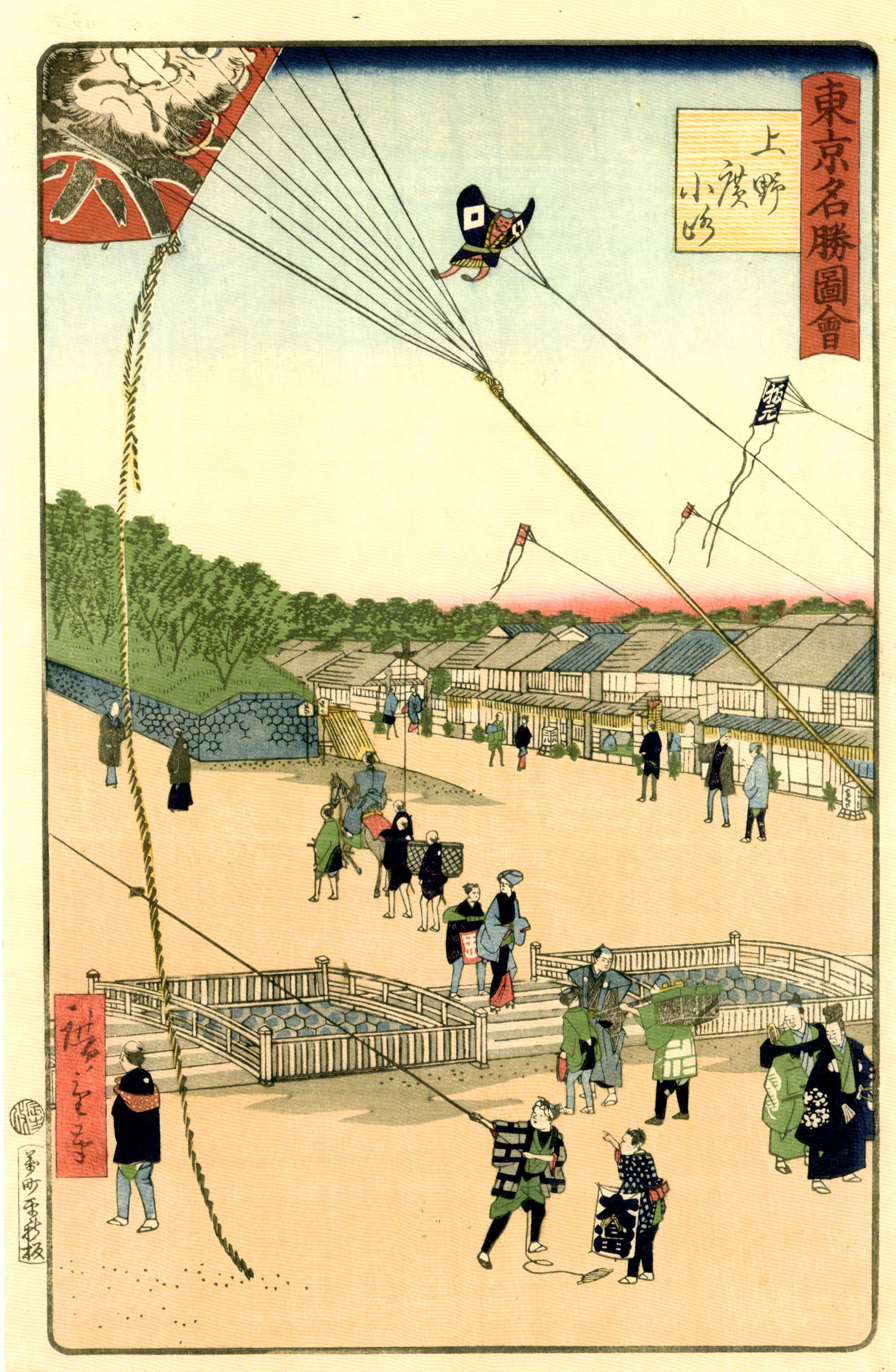
東京名勝圖會
上野廣小路
廣重筆
萬町平新板

A girl with an umbrella wears a striking kimono with a *yakko* kite decorating the shoulder; her *obi* is fashionably oversize. A towel is thrown round her neck and perhaps she is returning from a bathhouse, like the geisha in plate 17. The kimono has designs within a design: the *yakko's* costume is decorated with a carp-and-waterfall motif and playing cards depicting the *hyakunin isshu,* one hundred poems by one hundred poets. Both kites and the card game are New Year pastimes and indicate the time of year, suggesting that what the girl carries is a resin-protected umbrella, not a summer parasol.

The hard-edged *yakko* design contrasts with the soft colors and lines of the rest of the print, partly the result of the kimono's dark color. The eye's attention naturally focuses on the woman's face, especially as it is framed in the radiating spokes of the umbrella, but the strongest element in the design is the direct gaze of the *yakko,* with his aggressive sideburns and moustache. The result is an unusually unbalanced, almost disturbing composition.

The characters in the cartouche read *Yanagi hikari hōki kurabe* (Competition between Youthful Radiant Willows—that is, female beauties). The *hiragana* in the small red cartouche on the left read *yakko.* Prostitutes and *yakko,* the lowest-ranking retainers of samurai, traditionally often had relationships with each other. Perhaps *yakko* was this girl's nickname and her reason for wearing this kimono. Professional women had nicknames intended to be memorable to customers; among the most famous was Jigokudayū, Lady from Hell, Ikkyū's fifteenth-century protégé, who wore robes decorated with scenes of Hell.

The engraver's name is given in the cartouche in the bottom-right corner, an addition indicating a high-quality publication, as engravers were not normally credited with their names on prints. Printers too were almost always anonymous, yet the success of a woodblock print depended to a great degree on the skill of these artisans.

73

Competition between Youthful Radiant Willows
Toyohara Kunichika (1835–1900)
signed: *Kunichika hitsu*
engraver: Hori Yasu
1870
ōban (36.6 × 25.3 cm)

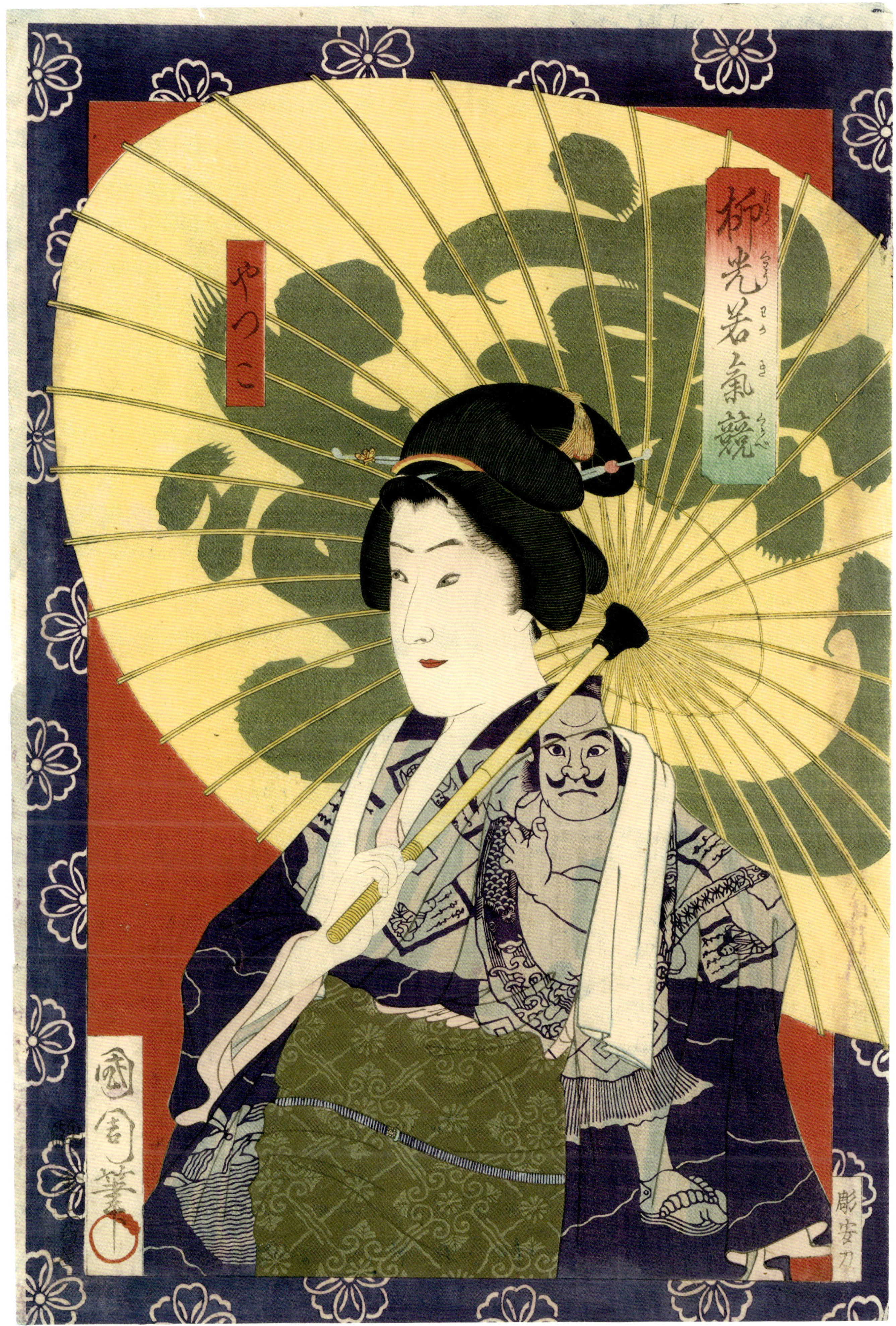

柳光若氣競
やつこ
國周筆
彫安刀

74

Fan Print

Toyohara Kunichika (1835–1900)
signed: *ōju Kunichika hitsu*
1871 fourth month
ōban diptych (each sheet approximately 37.2 × 24.9 cm)

The actor Onoe Kikugorō V (1844–1903) looks out over the rooftops of Edo toward the five-story pagoda of the Asakusa Kannon temple. The *kumadori* makeup of this role, which we saw in plate 37 (conventionally lighter than, for example, the makeup used for the role of Gongorō in *Shibaraku,* plate 12, or Asahina, plate 59), and the stylized butterfly pattern on his robe indicate that he is playing the role of Gorō, the younger of the Soga Brothers. He holds his body-armor, the object of a tussle between him and Asahina in which the two young men are so strong that the armor is torn apart.

Plays relating to the Soga Brothers saga, usually single scenes, were performed in Edo at New Year, and even though the date in the censor's seal indicates the fourth month, Kunichika has included several New Year kites in this print. The cartouche above Kikugorō's head extends the reference to kites. The actor says that he humbly presents his fans a new interpretation of the Soga Brothers story, in which he takes the role of Yakkodako (*yakko* kite) and is suspended, *chūnori,* over the stage. Plates 63 and 66 give an idea of what he may be intending. This design is an intriguing combination of two traditional New Year characters, Gorō no Soga and Yakkodako, showing the freedom with which Kabuki material was adapted by playwrights and actors.

Chrysanthemums, *kiku,* decorate the background along with imitation metallic squares sprinkled over the paper (see also plate 84). Besides being a pun on the actor's name, *kiku* were appropriate symbols of winter; chrysanthemum competitions were held in Edo to determine the most colorful and flamboyant blooms.

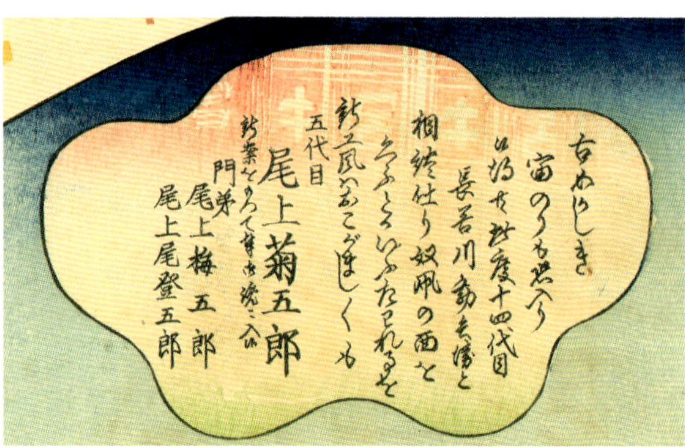

The image is drawn within the shape of a folding fan, *ōgi,* not a round fan as in plate 50. Fan prints were enjoyed as designs in their own right and were also cut out and pasted onto frames to make real folding fans. The size of this example, spread over two *ōban* sheets, is unusual. A fan made from this design would have been large—not impossibly large, but it is likely that the function of the format here was to create a striking design rather than to make an actual fan. The indentation on the sides of the double-fan shape, as if one is laid on top of the other, would have been awkward for a real fan. Also, much care has been given to the background, which would have been cut off and thrown away in the making of a fan, and it includes the artist's name, which he would usually want to appear on the fan itself.

This impression, one of the most luxurious in the collection, is beautifully printed. The lines are crisp and the pigments rich and strongly applied. Distinct ridges were created in the thick, high-quality paper by the woodblock-printing process, which gives texture to the print. There are three beautifully controlled examples of *bokashi,* color grading—purple, red, and indigo blue. The cartouche to the upper left has a very delicate embossed pattern that also includes *bokashi.* Black details of Gorō's robes and armor and the black sides of the buildings in the background have been burnished and reflect oblique light as the print is turned; there is even a subtle burnishing of the black on the sides of the buildings. Both embossing and burnishing required that a pattern be carved into separate woodblocks. In the case of the blind embossing, the paper was placed face down on the block and the back rubbed hard with the flat surface of a *baren,* bamboo pad. For the burnishing, the carved block was placed behind the finished print, with the pigments already applied, and the surface areas were rubbed with a smooth object such as a saké cup. Another method of achieving this effect was to use lacquer as if it were a separate color; this technique was used in plate 84. At a time of economic dislocation after the Meiji Restoration, this was an expensive print to produce.

There is no publisher's mark on this diptych, though there is a censor's seal, and it may have been issued semiprivately to commemorate the event mentioned in the cartouche.

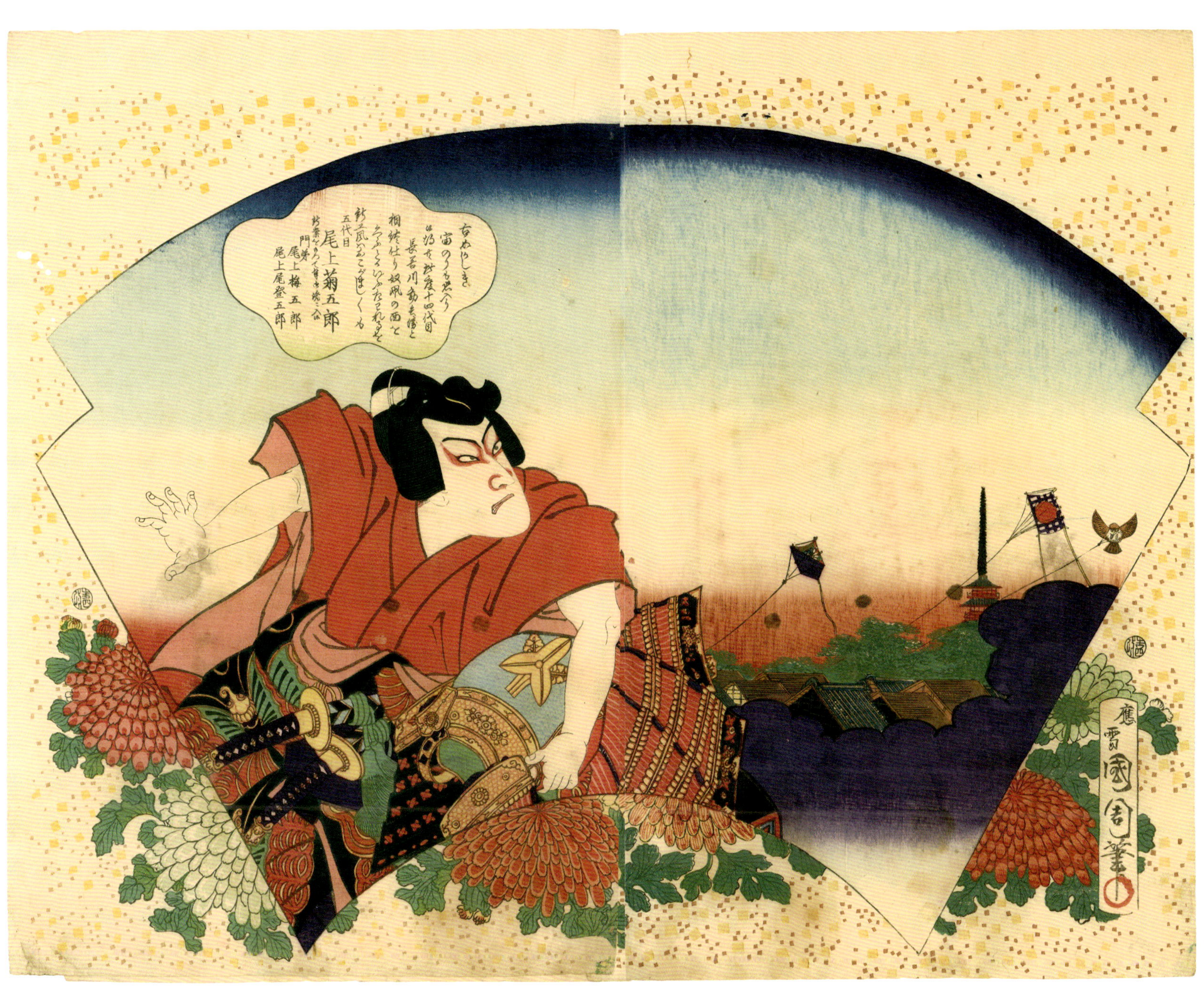
五代目
尾上菊五郎
門弟
尾上梅五郎
尾上尾登五郎
應需國周筆

75

Flying Kites at Sujichigai Gate
Isshōsai Ikkei (fl. 1870s)
signed: *Shōsai Ikkei hitsu*
publisher: Tsutaya Kichizo
1871 seventh month
ōban (37.2 × 25.1 cm)

A small but lively crowd celebrates New Year at Sujichigai Gate in central Tokyo as kites fly overhead. A group of young men prepare to launch a six-foot-high rectangular Edo kite painted with a rising-sun-and-waves decoration. Its framework and the knotting of its heavy line are shown in detail. A hummer is attached to the top of the kite; the line will be fed out of a basket. A boy with his own small kite approaches the basket; another boy points out the action to his mother with delight. The design is fresh and cheerful. A man has spread out small items for sale on a cloth, and covered stalls are shown in the middle distance. Close to the large stone gate with its fishy roof-ends (see the following print) is a rickshaw, a contraption believed to have been invented in Tokyo by an American missionary just two years earlier than this print, making it an object of novelty that an artist would naturally like to include.

The design is from a series titled *Tōkyo meisho shijūhakkei* (Forty-eight Famous Views of Tokyo) by Ikkei, a student of Hiroshige III who followed the landscape tradition of the Hiroshige school. The cut-off composition made popular by Hiroshige was a constant source of creative novelty, which Ikkei has used to good effect, showing only part of the young man at the left of the design and focusing interest on the kite. When woodblock prints were first brought to the West, the freedom of their composition was much appreciated by the French Impressionist painters. As early as 1869, before this print was made, the writer Ernest Chesneau coined the term *dysymétrie* to describe what he perceived to be a dislike of symmetry in the creations of Japanese print-makers.[1]

The print is titled *Sujichigai-gomon uchi tako asobi* (Flying Kites at Sujichigai Gate). This was a gate of Edo Castle located in the northeast corner of today's 1-chōme Kanda Sugachō in Chiyoda-ku. The open area was a favorite place for kite-flying; in the previous year, the third year of Meiji, it had witnessed the last officially approved duel in Japan, between swordsmen of the Mito feudal clan. The three hoods pushing each other at the right are wearing the latest western fashions, including jackets and trousers. Like several other figures in the picture they appear to be carrying swords; by 1873 swords were outlawed by the Meiji government, even for samurai, and only the new conscript military was allowed to bear arms.

1. Spate 2001, 72.

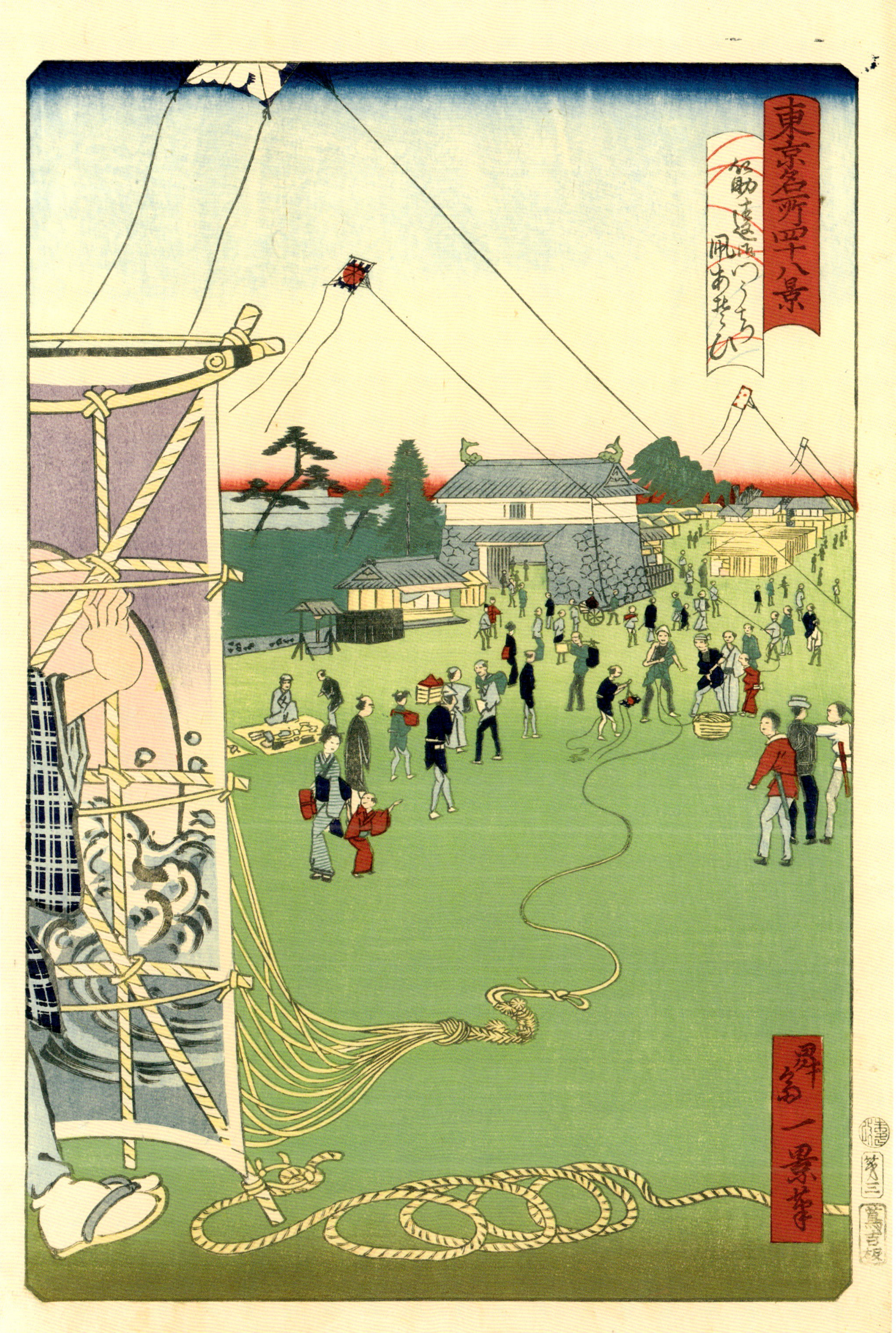
東京名所四十八景
昇斎一景筆

76

The Mitsui Bank Building
Utagawa Hiroshige III (1843–94)
series: *Tokyo kaika sanjūrokkei*
signed: *Hiroshige ga*
c. 1875
ōban (35.9 × 24.6 cm)

Woodblock-print artists tried to be on the cutting edge of things novel and fashionable. After the Meiji Restoration of 1868, western styles came into vogue throughout the country, especially in the capital, renamed Tokyo. Knowledge of what was happening in the West entered Japan from a variety of sources, including foreign books, traveling officials, and returning students, and affected all aspects of life, including architecture. The new Meiji government actively encouraged westernization, inviting foreign architects to visit and teach and even entering the construction business itself.

This print, from Hiroshige III's series *Tōkyo kaika sanjūrokkei* (Thirty-six Views of Modern Tokyo), shows Mitsui Bank, one of the earliest western-style buildings, built in stone by the architect Shimizu Kisuke in 1874. Comparison with early photographs shows that the representation of the building here is accurate, from the French windows, balconies, and metal drainpipes to the large bronze *shachihoko* at its apex. This mythical water creature was believed to protect against fire, and from about the end of the sixteenth century images of it were often placed at the corners of *daimyō* castles.

The brimmed hat, red jacket, and western overcoat of the two men on the lower balcony show the rapid acceptance of western clothing besides western styles of architecture. The western flagpole with the striped flag of the Mitsui Group appears in other prints of this building—much has changed since Hokusai's design of the Mitsui stores half a century before (plate 21). The traditional elements with which the artist anchors the design are limited to details such as the battlements of Edo Castle, a distant Fuji, and New Year kites. The character on the rectangular kite reads *atari,* big hit, as in plate 72.

In the 1890s this exuberant, naïve construction, along with the First National Bank building (see the next design), which was also built by Shimizu Kisuke, became "a public embarrassment"[1] and was torn down.

1. Finn 1995, 17.

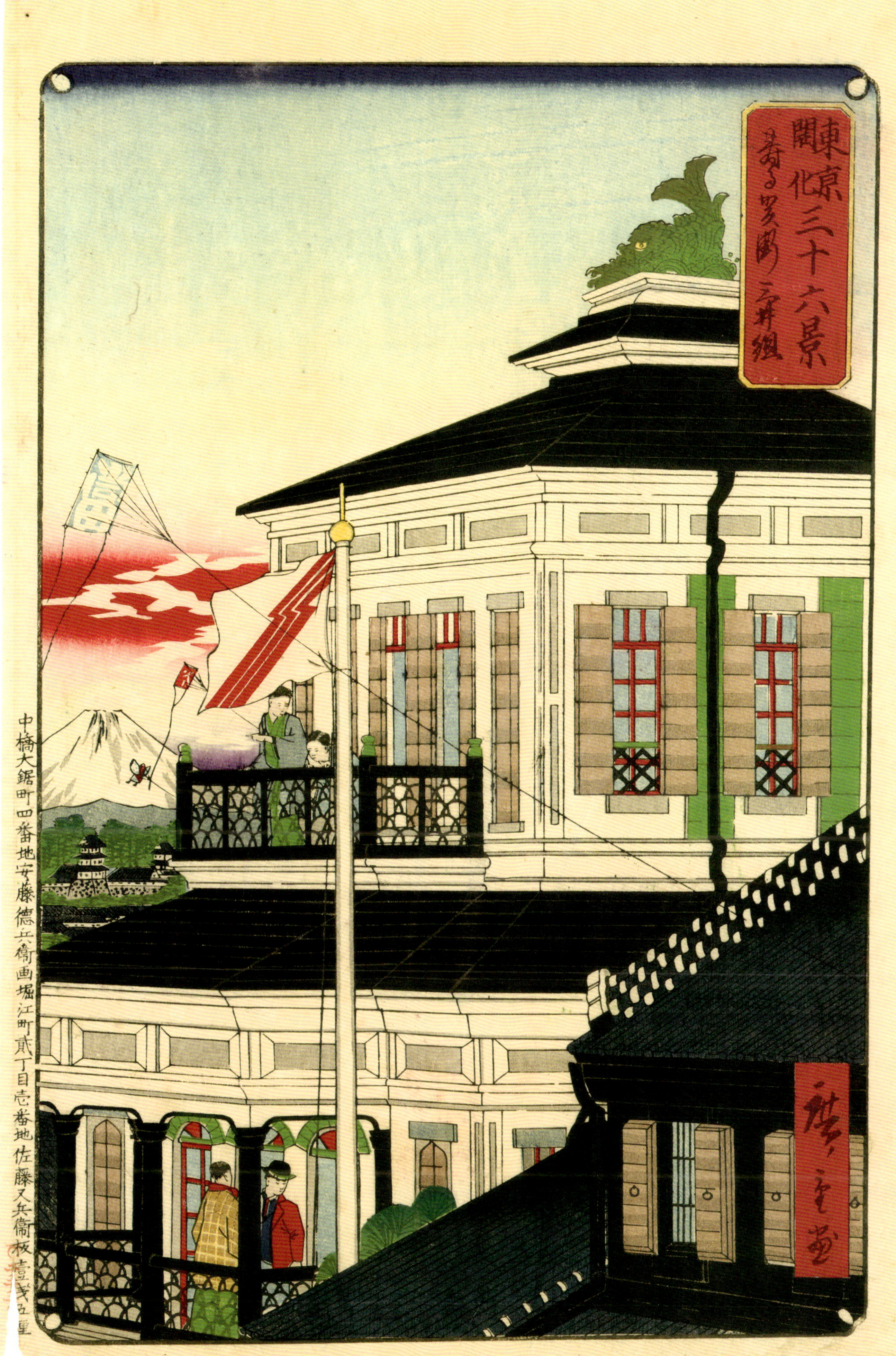
東京開化三十六景
中橋大鋸町四番地安藤德兵衛画堀江町貳丁目壱番地佐藤又兵衛板壹弐五壐
廣重画

77

Festivities on the First Day of the New Year
Utagawa Kunitoshi (active 1847–99)
signed: *Baiju Kunitoshi ga*
publisher: Hasegawa Shinkichi
engraver: Yamamura Seisuke
1878 first month
ōban triptych (each sheet approximately 36.8 × 24.5 cm)

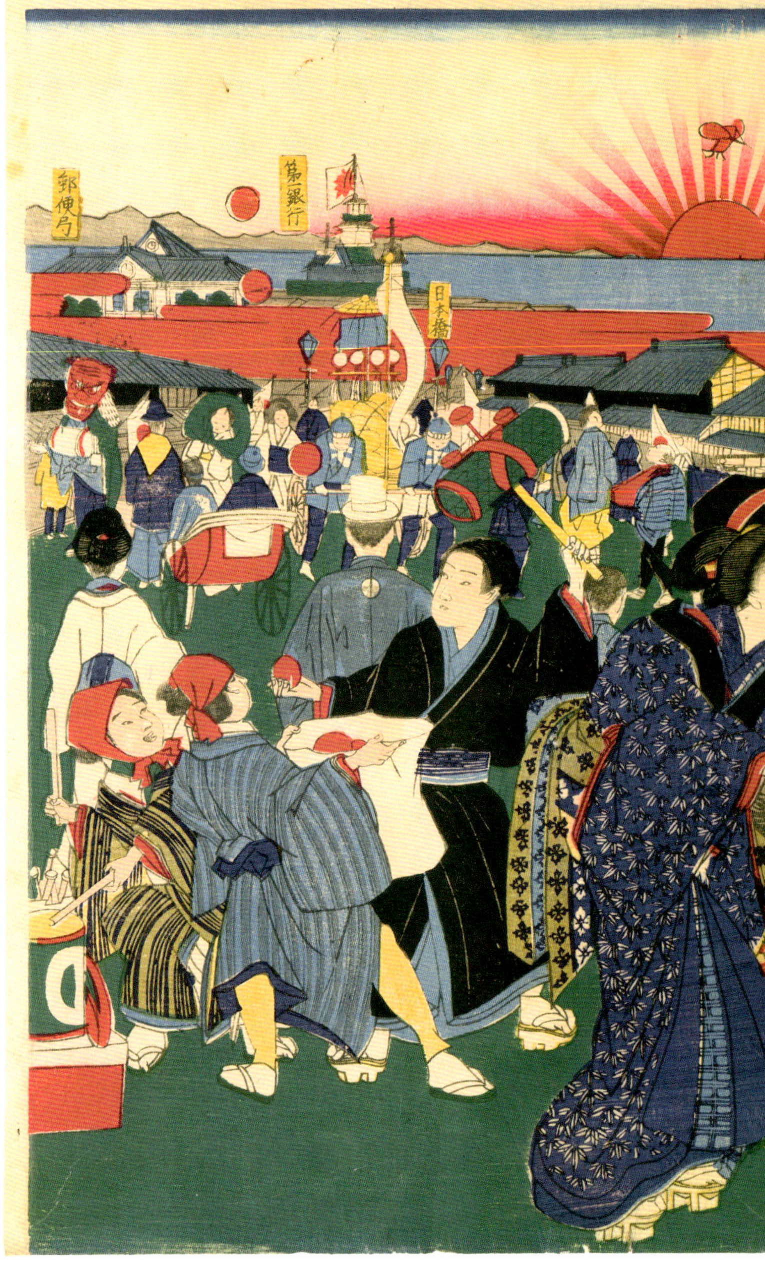

Kunitoshi, an obscure pupil of Kunisada and Kunitsugu, presents the central area of Tokyo on the first day of 1878, a decade after the Meiji Restoration had established a new government intent on catching up with the West. The scene is an extraordinary mixture of old and new. Around the traditional theme of three beauties playing shuttlecock in front of a large Daruma kite, like Kuniyoshi's triptych of plate 32, the artist has introduced a multitude of innovations to showcase the new city. He titles it *Tōkyo jiman jūnikagetsu no uchi mutsuki ganjitsu no nigiwai* (Tokyo's Pride through the Twelve Months—Festivities on the First Day of the New Year).

Mount Fuji rises as always in the background, but is balanced by an enormous sun rising over Tokyo Bay, its rays announcing a new direction for the nation. As kites fly over the houses, western sailing ships appear on the horizon. Major new city landmarks are labeled with small yellow cartouches. They include the Mitsui Bank (which we saw in the last print) on the right and the First National Bank building on the left, two of the first and most fanciful interpretations of western architecture to be built in Japan. To the left of the First National Bank is the new Post Office; in front and to the right is Nihonbashi, the bridge that marked the center of the capital. On the middle sheet a puffing train approaches the new Railway Station. To the right is a large building labeled Echigoya, the business that morphed into Mitsukoshi, the most prestigious department store in Japan today. The only building in the street behind the *bijin* to be given its own large, legible sign is a restaurant advertising meat. This would have been as amazing to a visitor from the provinces as any architectural novelty, as meat was simply not part of the Japanese diet (following a Buddhist tradition) until Meiji, when the government encouraged meat-eating as a way to physically strengthen the population.[1]

In the left panel a rickshaw passes a lion dancer and other traditional entertainers; this form of conveyance now seems typical of the China and Japan of a century ago but was the invention of a Christian missionary to Japan. In the right panel two firemen perform balancing acts on a bamboo ladder, a contribution to the New Year celebrations by the local firemen's troupe, whose white *matoi,* standard, can be seen below them; firemen still sometimes put on shows like this at New Year. On the extreme right, a large band of uniformed soldiers marches, part of the conscript army that the year before had put down the Satsuma Rebellion. This was a last-ditch attempt by traditionalists and dissident *daimyō* to stem the Meiji reforms, and was fought with great ferocity and loss of life; woodblock-print artists who never saw a battle kept the capital in a state of high excitement for months with violent designs of the confrontation.

Most of the clothes being worn are still traditional, perhaps because it is New Year. The only exceptions are a couple of western hats in the left panel and a man leaving the meat

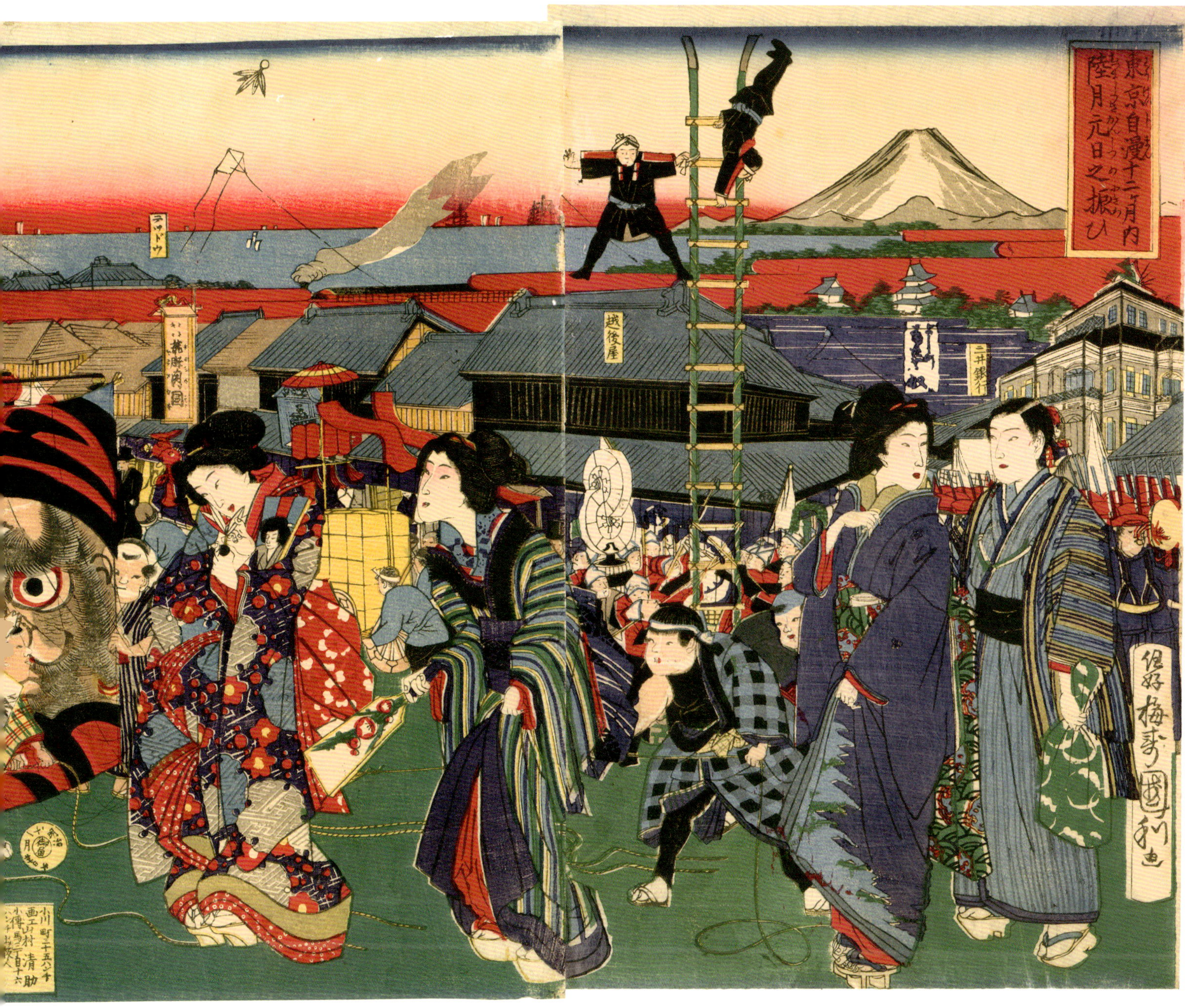

restaurant. The man in the foreground of the right panel, however, has a disconcerting western parting in his hair along with his kimono.[2] His *furoshiki* bears the Utagawa school *toshidama,* a final flicker of Kunisada's ghost.

The quality of this triptych is not good; the composition is overly crowded, the drawing and engraving are mediocre, and there are serious registration problems. The artist has succumbed to heavy use of the violent red and purple pigments newly available in quantity from European chemical factories. The coloration and design of the fabrics, often a major element of a print's appeal, compare poorly with earlier triptychs in this book (or later that of Shuntei, plate 90). Yet as an illustration of some of the radical new concepts with which the Japanese people were coping—banking, railways, a postal service, a conscript army, new forms of clothing, new foods—this design is extremely informative.

1. Kyōsai (plates 79–81) punned on this in an illustrated book of 1871–72 when he signed himself *Seiseijin Gyūsai,* "Born-again Meat-eater"; Clark 1993, 122.

2. Already by 1869, only two years after the Meiji Restoration, thirteen percent of the men in Tokyo had cut their hair in the western style, and by 1890 it was difficult to find a man in the cities with a traditional haircut; Jansen and Rozman 1986, 461.

78

Picture of the New Year
Toyohara Chikanobu (1838–1912)
signed: *Yōshū Chikanobu hitsu*
publisher: Morimoto Junsaburō
engraver: *Muneoka tō*
1885
ōban triptych (each sheet approximately 35.4 × 23 cm)

Chikanobu, a pupil of Kunichika (plates 73 and 74), has filled this idealized street scene with details of a traditional Edo New Year. The skyline of the capital and the clothes of its citizens have changed radically since the Meiji Restoration of 1868, when Edo became Tokyo, and this print from the series *Edo sunago nenjū gyōji* (Annual Celebrations in Edo) is an exercise in nostalgia. The print is titled *Gantan no zu* (Picture of the New Year).

The scene is set near Edo Castle, from which the shogun is leaving in a magnificent procession, crossing the bridge over Benkei Moat. Mount Fuji towers in the background with its benign majesty. Girls play shuttlecock and boys fly kites—the sky is filled with them. Besides old favorites, such as *yakko* and Daruma, we see Kintarō the Golden Boy (see plates 2 and 3) holding a square box of beans: people cleansed their households of demons on New Year's Eve by throwing beans and shouting, "Demons out, good luck in." The battledore of the little girl in the center is decorated with the face of a favorite Kabuki actor; to her right is a battledore with a bamboo decoration, a popular seasonal motif used also in plate 56. A little boy in the center carries a small *yakko* kite.

To the right, a monkey trainer and a group of *shishimai* lion dancers gather. Two street musicians with straw hats and *shamisen* walk to the left. They are *torioime,* literally bird-chaser-girls, entertainers who visit houses and sing "bird-chasing" songs for money, especially at New Year. There is something of the idea of caroling outside houses at Christmastime for treats, though *torioime* were usually available for more than singing. The right and left edges of the design are framed by large New Year pine-and-bamboo decorations.

If a print became damaged, it would often be trimmed to make it more tidy; the edges of this triptych have been cut away, which explains why brushstrokes that stretch across the panels do not line up. The margins would have included date and publishing details; this print is part of a series issued in 1885. The drawing is delicate, and the artist has not been seduced by the over-enthusiastic palette of early Meiji.

The composition and choice of detail forms a fascinating contrast with the raucous energy of the previous triptych. Compare this also with the robust pre-Meiji street scene of plate 47 and the juxtapositions of fashions in plate 84. The world of old Edo was already gone, and was apparently already missed. Self-conscious and artificial, this triptych is a Disneyland of traditional elements thrown together—charming though they are, the *torioime* girls would have been inappropriate in an earlier print of a formal shogunate procession. Compare Hiroshige's cityscapes in plates 54 and 56, which have the quality of scenes from real life.

82

Street-scene Board Game for the Beginning of Spring
Utagawa Yoshifuji (1828–87)
signed: *Yoshifuji ga*
publisher: Higuchi Gintarō
1886
ōban (35.9 × 23.4 cm)

Two decades after the Meiji Restoration, Japan and especially its renamed capital had been radically transformed. This game board, titled *Haru no hajime ōrai sugoroku* (Street-scene Board Game for the Beginning of Spring), is a marvelous mix of traditional pastimes and novel developments. Ebisu, the god of wealth with his red sea-bream, presides over a series of New Year vignettes, riding on a float bearing the character for saké and flanked by western-style flags and buildings, even street lights. The character *agari* beside him marks the game's goal, and the figures in the little red circles indicate dice numbers; some mean you go backward.

Contrasts in the street scenes abound. At top left a fireman performs a traditional balancing act on a ladder against a backdrop of Mount Fuji and New Year kites; at top right, an officer in smart westernized uniform rides a white horse against a backdrop of newly popular rising-sun flags. The center panel with its horse-drawn tram on rails also features a street light (electric lighting had first been installed in the Ginza four years before); a family gawks at the conductor in his new uniform. At bottom right a boy rides a newfangled tricycle. Rising-sun flags fly with the kites in the panel marked *takoage,* kite-flying, to the right and in the panel with New Year entertainers in red head-scarves at the bottom.

Traditional elements include a woman carrying New Year treats on her head, accompanied by a *torioime* singer. A boy flourishes a top; another smears ink on a friend's face, the forfeit for allowing a shuttlecock to fall in the game of *hanetsuki* (see plate 90). A boy wearing a western-style scarf carries a branch of New Year treasures, including Daikoku's *daikon* (see the previous print); the characters in the panel read *ehōmairi,* lucky direction, echoing the taboos of centuries (see plate 5).

This game board is a fascinating contrast with the simple elements and coloration of the sheet that the thread wholesaler Chōji Kitchibei gave away to his customers forty years earlier (plate 39), both featuring New Year kites.

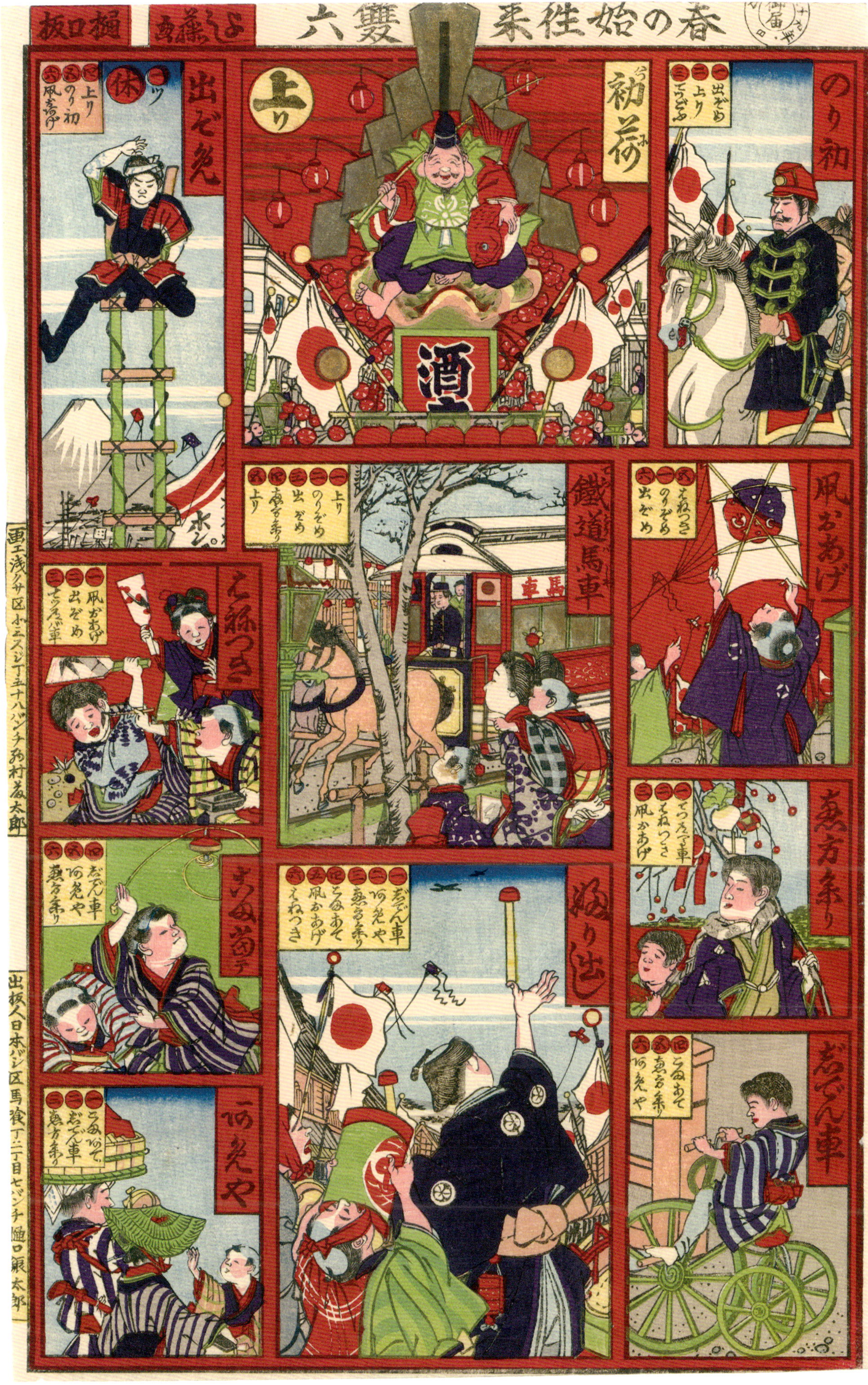

春の始往来雙六
樋口板
上り
初荷
酒
のり初
出ぞめ
鐵道馬車

83

Triumphant New Year War Games
Baidō Kunimasa (Utagawa Kunisada III) (1848–1920)
signed: *Sho Kunimasa*
publisher: Onishi Shonosuke
1887 first month
ōban triptych (each sheet approximately 36.7 × 24.5 cm)

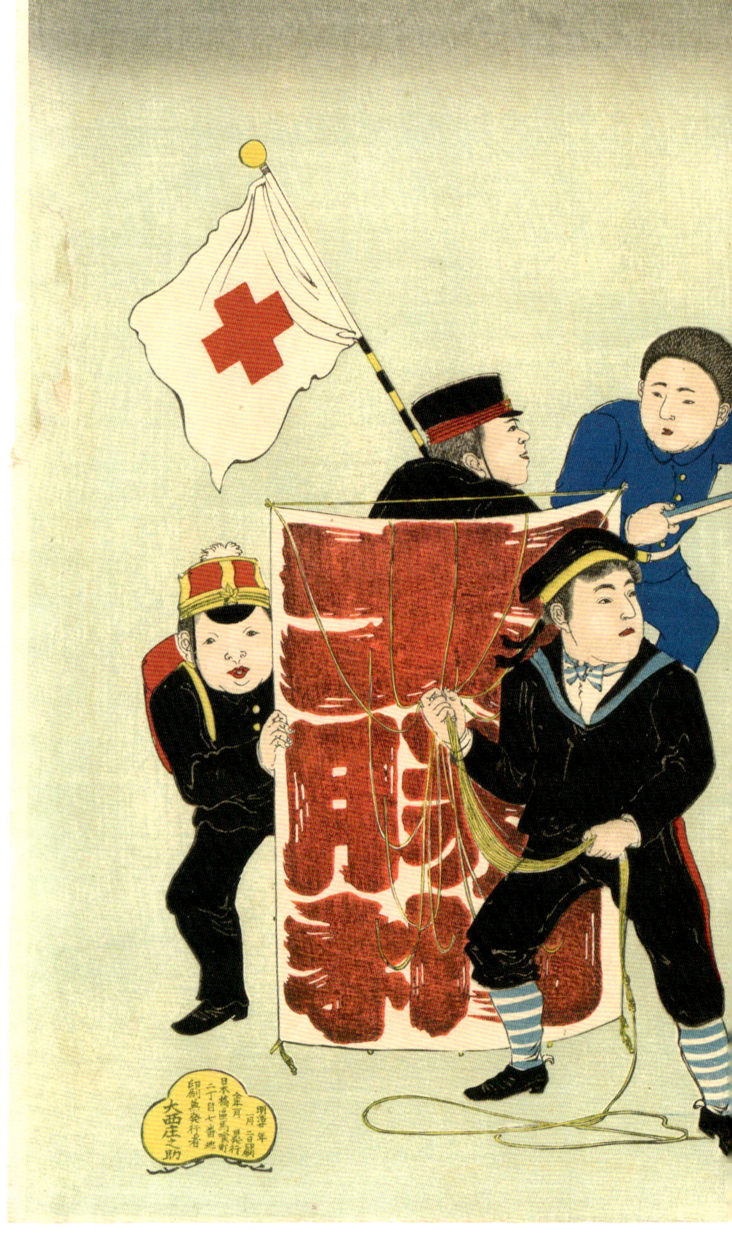

This triptych is titled *Shunyu shōri no tawamure,* Triumphant New Year War Games. Boys play at being military Red Cross officers, and a boy on a hobby-horse flourishes a sword at a balloon painted with a worried-looking face. Another boy runs off holding a flag with a Chinese dragon—he is the enemy. A little boy with a military cap and a Japanese rising-sun flag invites his mother to watch the fun, tugging at her western-style shawl, which has a stylized New Year lobster design. A boy and girl dance in the center. In the foreground three boys, one in army uniform, two in naval costumes, play with a kite. Rather than the traditional Dragon or Good Fortune, the characters on this kite read *Dai shōri,* Big Victory. Delicate plum blossoms incongruously decorate the title cartouche.

Along with foreign fashions, Japanese nationalism flourished after the Meiji Restoration as the country turned its back on the isolationism of the Tokugawa period. Samurai lost their right to carry swords, and a modern military based on conscription was established with the German army and

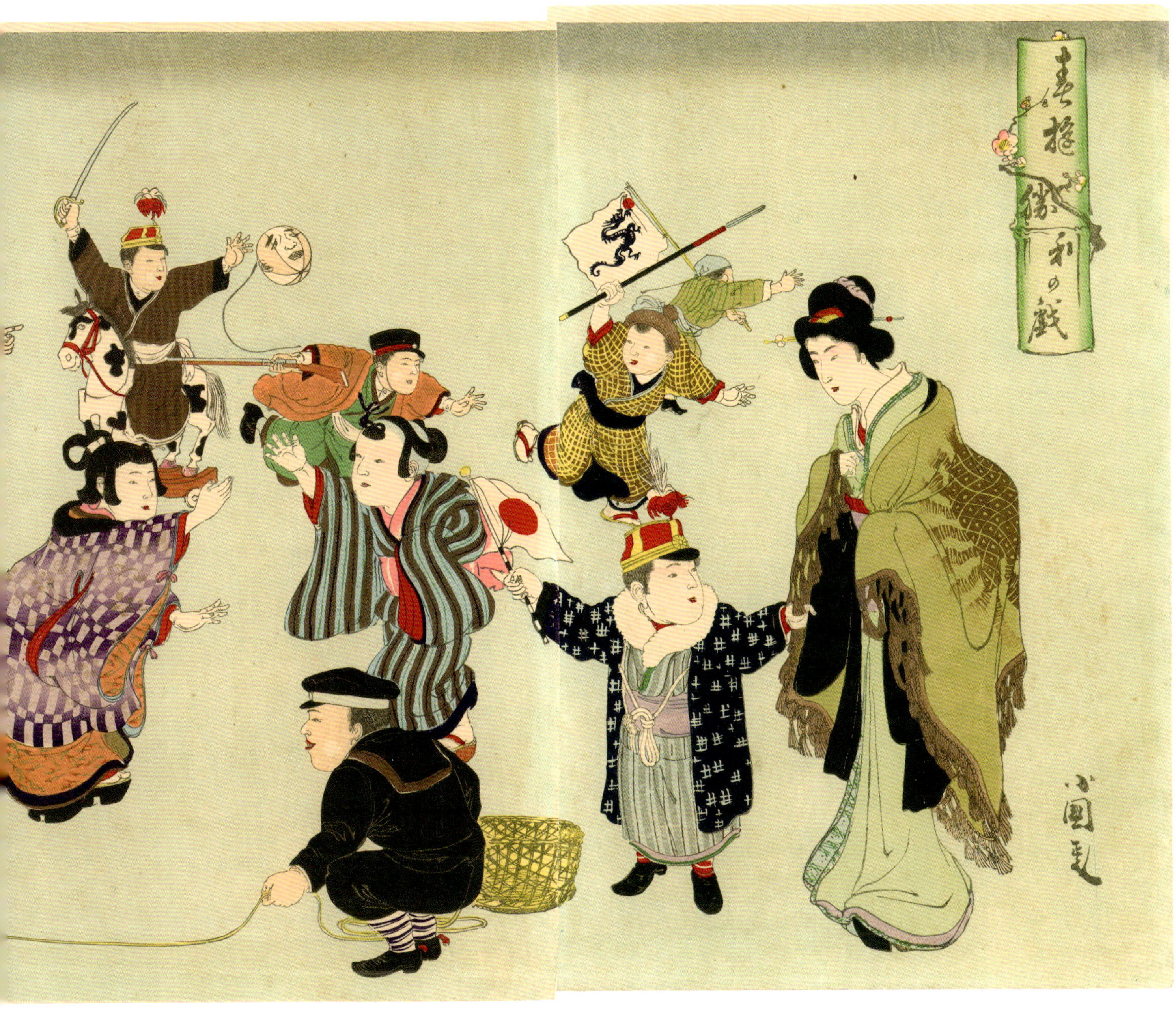

British navy as models. Colonies were part of the new world order: less than a decade after this print was made, Japan found a pretext for war with China and annexed Taiwan. Ten years after that, Japan went to war with Russia in Manchuria, destroyed the Russian fleet in a single engagement, and became the first Asian country to defeat a western colonial power. Having neutralized competing Chinese and Russian interests, Japan infiltrated Korea and assassinated its queen, formally annexing the country in 1910 and inaugurating a period of extremely brutal colonization. (Japan's behavior in Taiwan was somewhat more benign, reflecting differing national attitudes toward Korea and China that go back at least as far as Hideyoshi's devastation of Korea in the 1590s.)

The children in this triptych are playing very different New Year games from those their parents played. Kites are all they have in common, and these too have been subverted by the budding new imperialism.

84

Variety
Ogata Gekkō (1859–1920)
signed: *Gekkō ga*
publisher: Hayashi Kichizō
1887 twelfth month
ōban diptych (each sheet approximately 36.8 × 25.2 cm)

By the time this print was made, Meiji Japan had been open to the West for nearly two decades, consciously absorbing western ways, from clothes to education to methods of organizing a navy. This diptych is titled *Torimazete,* meaning Mixture or Variety, and deliberately combines old and new elements to create a New Year pastiche. It is a fascinating hybrid, portraying traditional Japanese New Year celebrations in a rather delicate westernized style. Gekkō absorbed new styles of drawing and won a gold medal for illustration at the St. Louis World Fair in 1904. Compare his quiet interpretation of Daikoku and his rats here with Kyōsai's robust treatment in plate 81, produced in the same twelfth month of 1887.

In the left panel, a matron in western clothes points out a traditional lion-dancer to her two sailor-suited sons and her little daughter, who wears a pink bonnet and dress. Another mother, in Japanese kimono and holding a shuttlecock, turns to her daughter, who wears a Japanese robe over a long plaid dress and has a westernized hairstyle. In the background a Japanese kite flies beside a western flagpole.

To the right, a woman and two boys join two New Year performers. The woman's kimono has a pattern of shuttlecocks and battledores; the yellow-and-red patterns on the robe of one of the boys are auspicious gold coins. One performer holds a blossoming branch with paper good-luck charms. The other is a puppeteer; he manipulates a dancing *sanbasō* figure with a fan through holes in the box slung in front of him.

In the center, Daikoku with his huge earlobes (denoting wisdom) reclines on a straw-wrapped keg of saké attended by two of his rat companions; the robe of one is decorated with Daikoku's *daikon* radishes. Behind him is a small table with a New Year offering and a huge treasure bag; gold coins and jewels are strewn on the floor. Late-winter flowers, camellia and plum blossoms, appear behind the three differently shaped panels. New Year ferns decorate the title cartouche.

This diptych was expensive to produce. The dark squares of the right panel are a metallic pigment that has oxidized: when the print was first made, these squares would have shone brightly. (The background pattern in plate 74, a luxury print of a different era, strove for this effect in a cheaper way.) Black areas, including clothing and Daikoku's hat, have been lacquered to give a burnished look (a different technique from that used in plate 74). The lacquer required its own carved block and was applied as a separate pigment. The blocks for this diptych were finely engraved and the printing was precise, with time-consuming embossing effects and color grading—look at the complexity of the camellia blossom and the green subtleties of the leaves. The coloration is subtle and restrained. The red, for example, which in many contemporary prints was overwhelming, is limited to small areas, balancing the greens and violets. To get an idea of the artist's effective use of red to highlight and contrast, try to imagine the print without its reds by blocking them out with your hand.

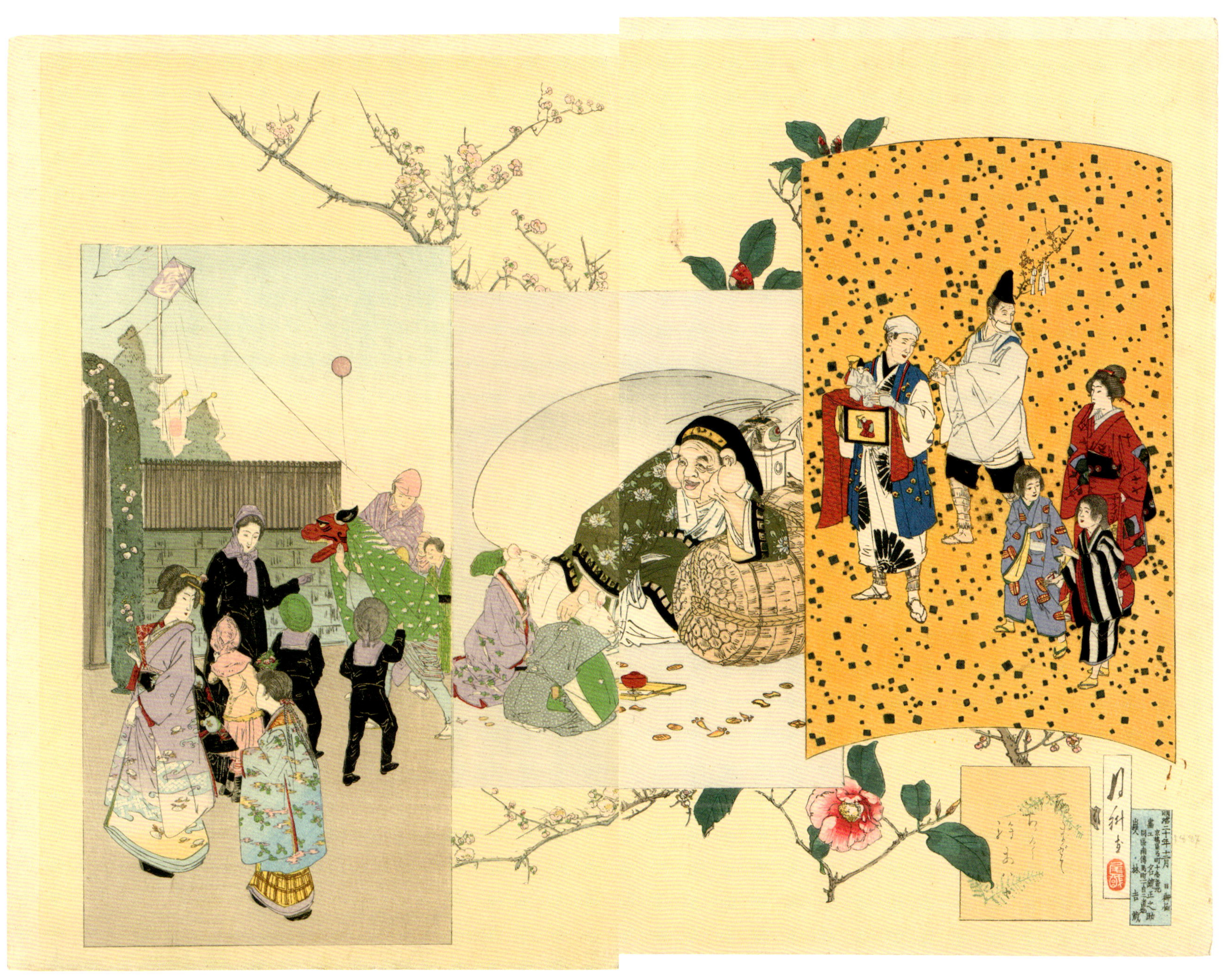

85
Onoe Kikugorō V in One Hundred Roles
Toyohara Kunichika (1835–1900)
signed: *Kunichika hitsu*
1893
ōban (34.7 × 23.4 cm)

86
Yakkodako Flying in the Spring Breeze
Utagawa Kunisada III (1848–1920)
signed: *Kōchōrō Toyomasa hitsu*
1892 twelfth month
ōban triptych (each sheet approximately 37.3 × 25 cm)

These two prints by different artists both show the actor Onoe Kikugorō V (1844–1903) in a New Year kite dance titled *Yakkodako kuruwa no harukaze* (Yakkodako Flying in the Spring Breeze at the Pleasure Quarters), performed in the first month of 1893. The dance is described on the triptych as being adapted from a Kabuki play based on the last work of the Meiji playwright Kawataka Mokuami. Kikugorō is wearing almost identical costumes in each design; they bear almost the same date; and they both almost certainly depict the same performance.

The single sheet is from an ambitious series dedicated to Onoe Kikugorō V and titled *Baikō hyaku shu no uchi* (Baikō in One Hundred Roles). Onoe Baikō was a poetry name of Onoe Kikugorō I, founder of the Onoe acting clan, and was used as a stage name by several of his successors, including Onoe Kikugorō V. With Ichikawa Danjūrō IX, Onoe Kikugorō V was the most popular actor of the last decades of Meiji. The two young men in the upper left corner of the sheet are part of the Kikugorō acting family; one holds a large spool of kite-line.

Kunisada III, signing himself Toyomasa, uses the large triptych format to create an impressively monumental design, almost like a poster. A fan kite flies to the left. The inscriptions to the right and left of the triptych have been brushed, carved, and printed in the large flamboyant characters used on Kabuki fliers and the signs outside Kabuki theaters. The characters on the right read *Kabukiza jōruri* (Ballad Drama at the Kabuki Theater); the characters on the left read *Yakkodako Onoe Kikugorō.* Yakkodako, Mr Yakko-Kite, was a comic role associated with New Year Soga Brothers' performances that we have seen several times in this book. In plate 63, Mr Yakko-Kite flies suspended over a Kabuki stage; in plate 66 he carries on a punning conversation with a woman in a restaurant; and in plate 74 a youthful Onoe Kikugorō V introduces a new Yakkodako dance to his many fans.

An associated triptych in the Skinner Collection by Kunisada III, also published in the twelfth month of 1892, is similarly titled *Yakkodako kuruwa no harukaze.* It includes the same characters as plate 85—Kikugorō and two boys—plus two courtesans wearing the butterfly and sea-plover robes of the two Soga Brothers. Kikugorō was forty-eight and at the height of his popularity at this time; this must have been a very special performance to be memorialized so extravagantly.

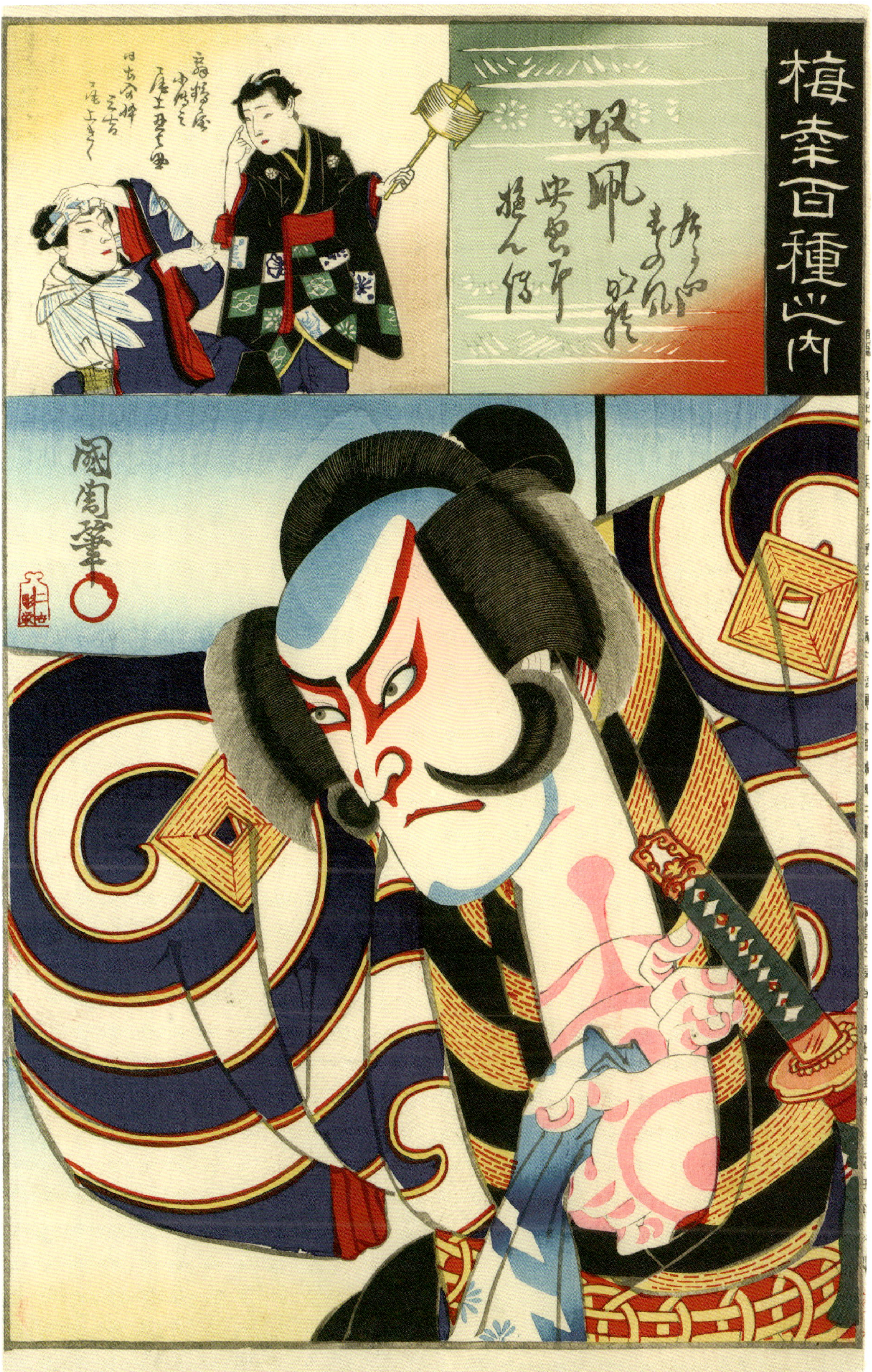
梅幸百種之内
國周筆

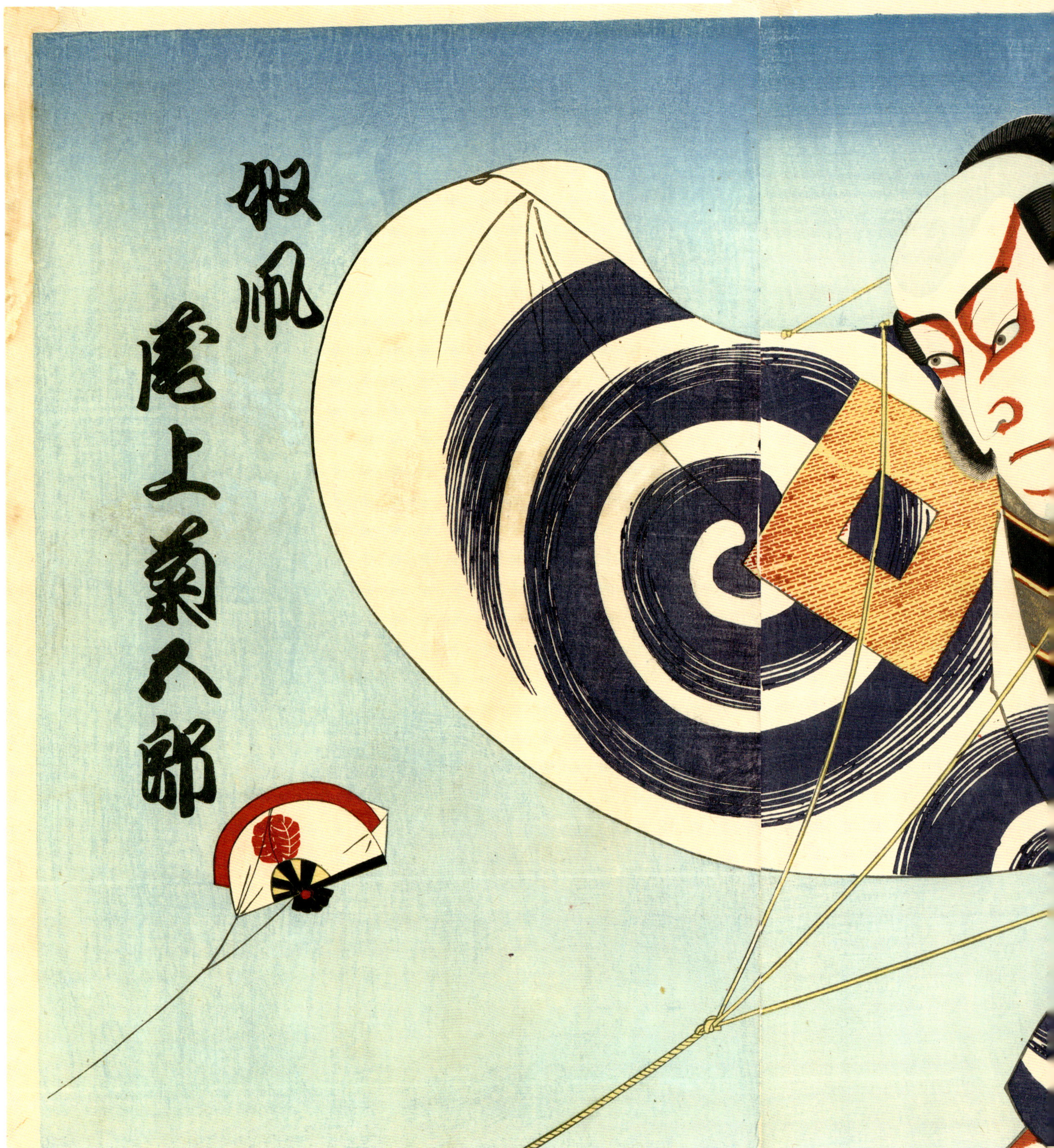

似凧
尾上菊五郎

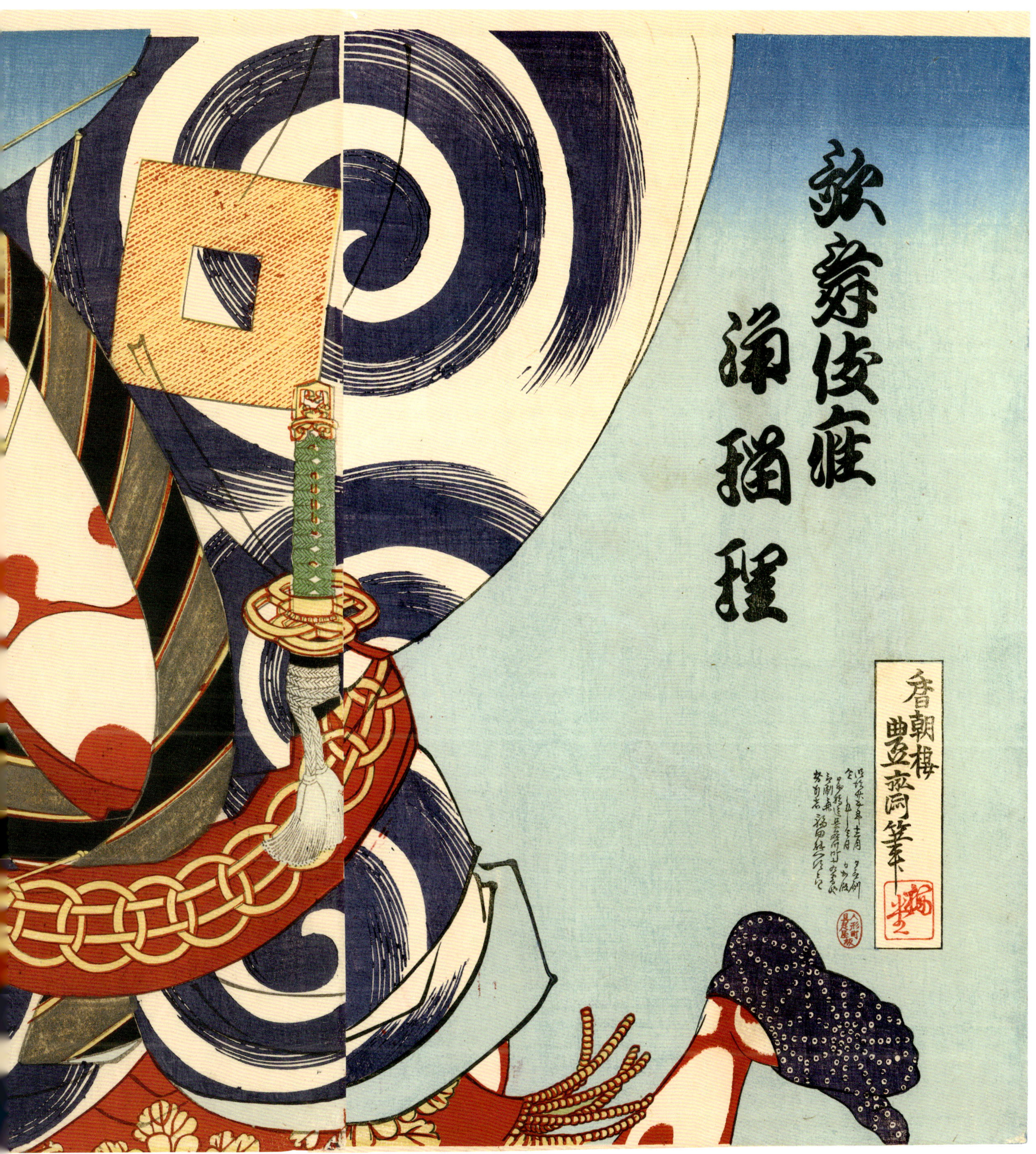
歌舞伎座
浄瑠璃
香朝楼豊宣筆

87

Entertainer and Demon Kite
Shigemitsu
signed: [*Kyo*] *Shigemitsu saku*
c. 1895–1900
book frontispiece (22 × 28.5 cm)

Echoing themes seen earlier in the book, a boy's kite with a *hannya* female-demon design falls out of the sky onto a startled street entertainer; we have seen demon kites in plates 60 and 61 and falling kites in plates 17 and 32. The girl is a *torioime,* literally a girl who sings bird-chasing songs, with a hint of the connotation of scarecrow. She is an entertainer who comes to people's gates, especially at New Year, with her *shamisen*—the archetypal instrument of a geisha—and sings in return for money. It is always possible that she is available for more than singing. Here she holds her *shamisen* and a plectrum for plucking the strings; she wears a farmer's broad straw hat and a kimono with a line-design like one of the girls in plate 78. To be hit on the head by a hideous demon kite is not a good New Year omen for this girl. A similar image appears in plate 66, harsher than the theme of the *bijin-e* of plate 35 with its implications of a love poem.

Many types of *kadozuke,* gate visitors, still existed fifty years ago but are now gone from Japan, at least in the cities, just as the custom of groups of children or adults visiting every house along a street singing carols for a small donation at Christmastime has largely disappeared in the West. (*Kado* means gate, as in *kadomatsu,* gate-pine, the New Year decoration we have seen placed outside residences throughout this book.)

The thin paper and format of the print with its two vertical crease lines indicate that this was the woodblock-printed frontispiece of a novel, folded and tipped into the front of the book. The word *saku,* work of, in the signature also indicates a book illustration. Both the style of drawing and the print's color palette have a delicacy typical of late Meiji.

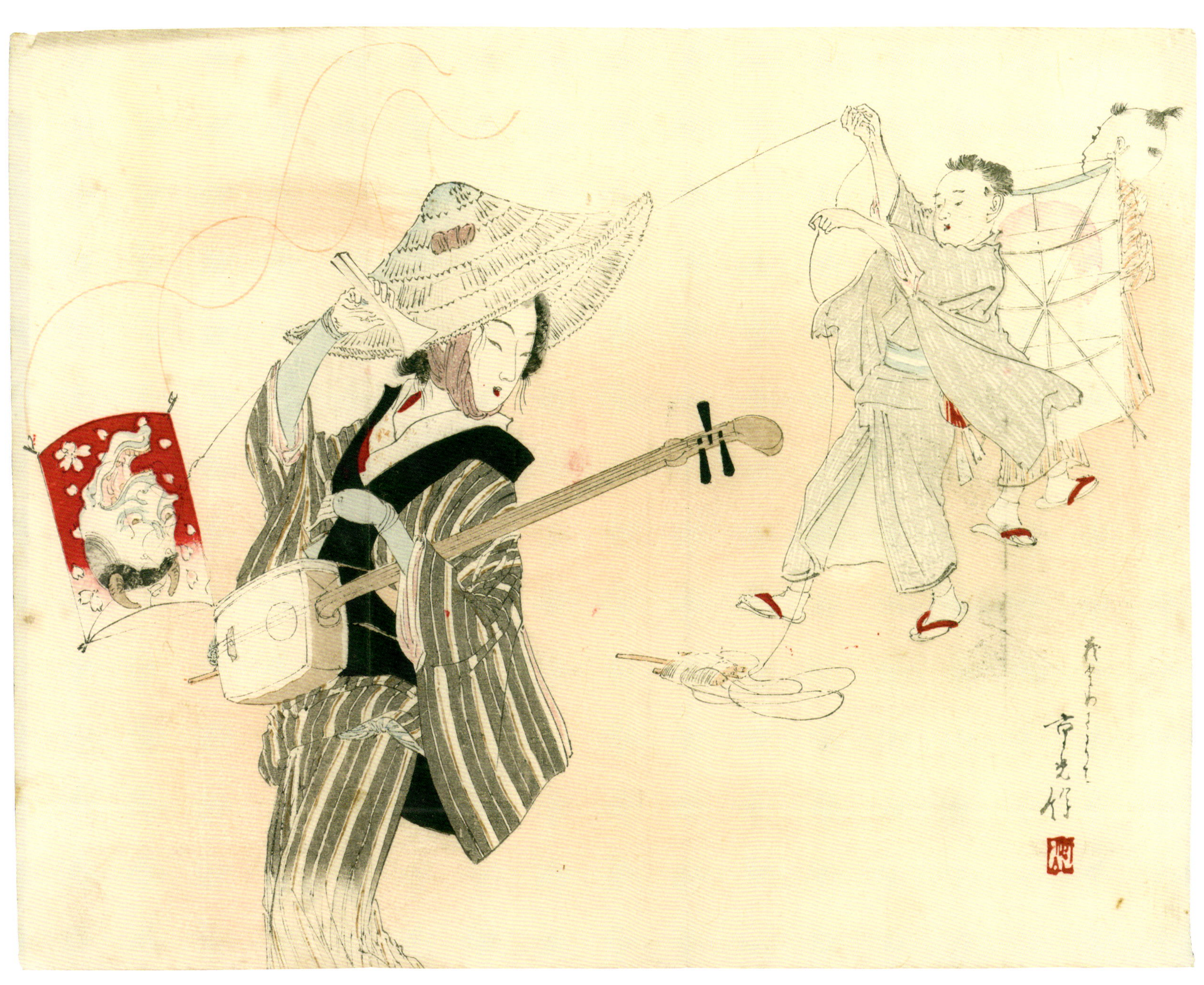

88

Beauty of the Kaei Era
Toyohara Chikanobu (1838–1912)
signed: *Toyohara Chikanobu*
1896 sixth month
ōban (37.6 × 25.2 cm)

In his series *Jidai kagami* (Reflections of the Ages), Chikanobu uses this *bijin* to represent the Kaei era, 1848 to 1854. She is dressed in the fashion of the period, including her elaborate *tsubushi shimada* coiffure with its comb and hair ornaments. In the upper vignette is a New Year scene: a fallen *yakko* kite has caught in a *kadomatsu* decoration. A man identified as a seller of board games accompanies a buyer of secondhand New Year presentation fans, who represents the season; we have seen him four times already in this book. Though the theme of the upper vignette is New Year, this is not a New Year print but part of an exploration of different historical fashions of feminine beauty. The series is a look backward into Japan's history rather than the celebration of novelty and contemporary fashion that till well into Meiji was a hallmark of *ukiyo-e*.

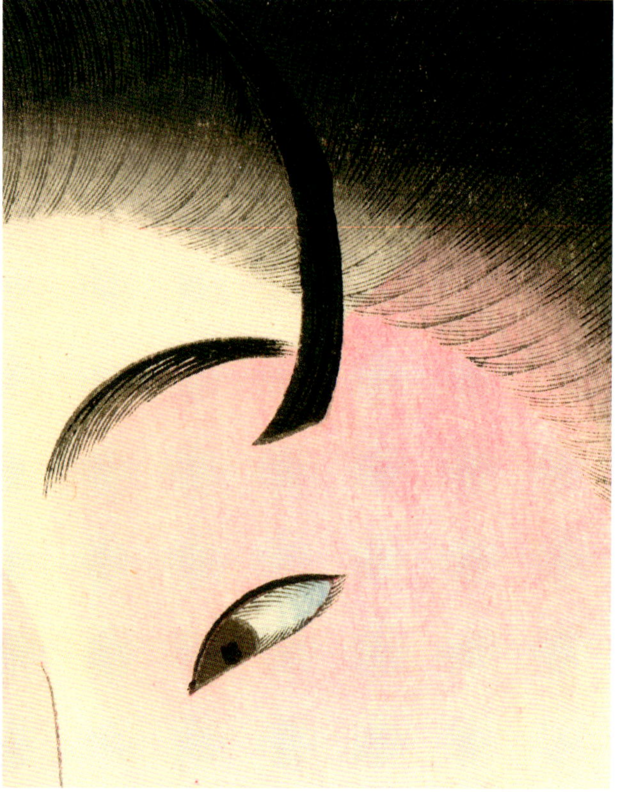

The print is very fresh and colorful. The engraving of the girl's hair is extremely fine. The black lines of her face have been softened by carefully registered pink lines, and the pink flush around her eyes, achieved by color grading, is masterly. After a century of European scientific advances in the manufacture of dyestuffs, artists had all the colors of the rainbow at their disposal.[1] Faced with competition from imported forms of mass communication such as lithography and photography, Japanese woodblock prints were in serious decline by the end of Meiji, but the craftsmen who produced them had never been more skillful. An article in the Tokyo newspaper *Asahi Shimbun* of February 25, 1908, deplored the decline of the market for woodblock prints. Production costs had become uneconomically high compared to other printing processes, said the article, and only foreigners were interested in purchasing recently made woodblock prints. The situation was contrasted with that of twenty years before; Yoshitoshi's *Tsuki hyakushi* (One Hundred Aspects of the Moon) was mentioned as being the product of a time when many skilled engravers and printers were available for hire; now these craftsmen were seeking other forms of employment.

1. Delamare and Guineau 2000 is fascinating on the subject of color and the chemistry of dyes.

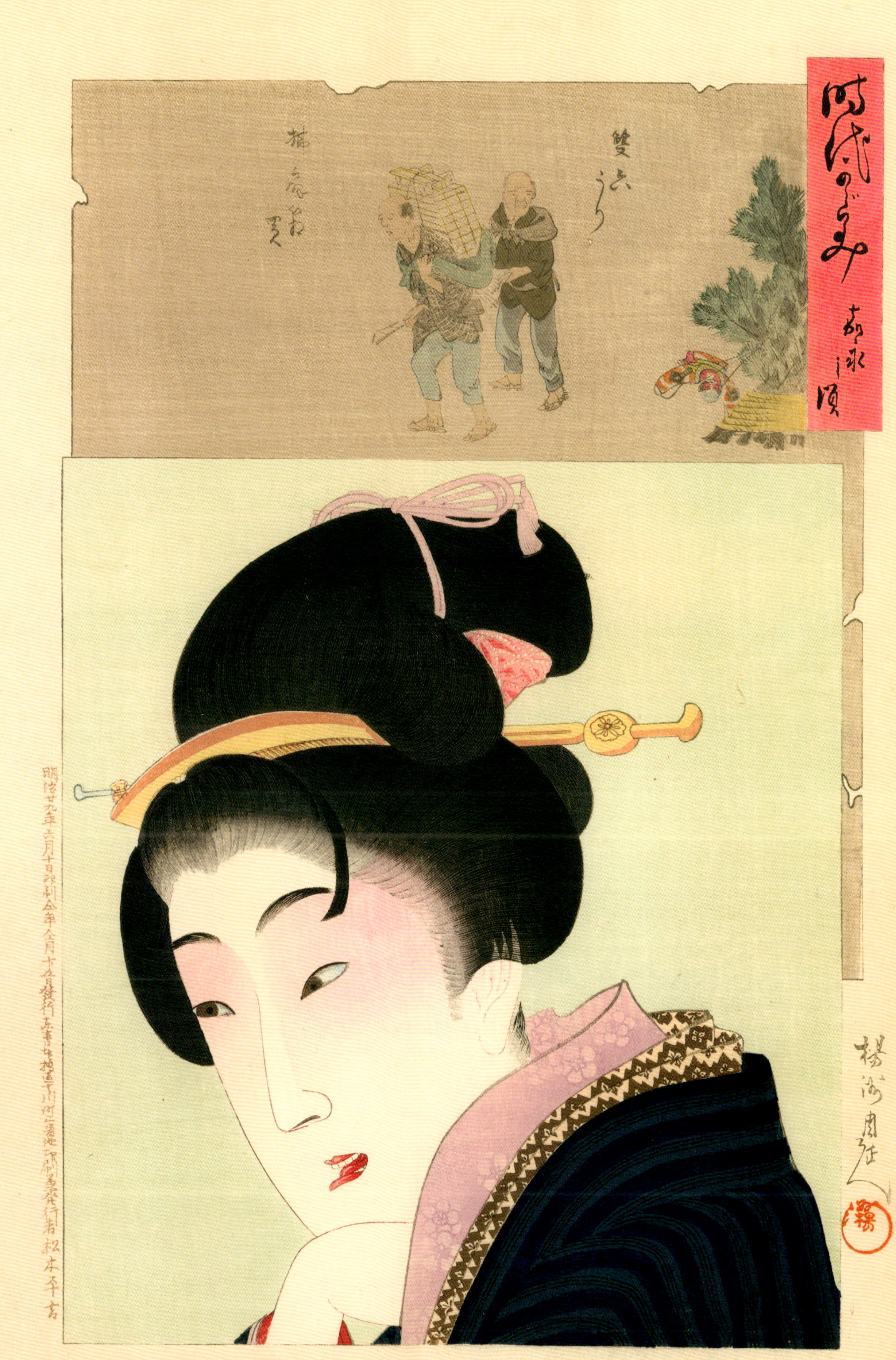

時代かゞみ
安永之頃
雙六うり
楊洲周延

89

Japanese Officer and Chinese Mandarin
Miyagawa Shuntei (1873–1914)
sealed: *Miyagawa Shuntei*
publisher: Akiyama Buemon
1897 second month
ōban (35.2 × 22.9 cm)

The uninvited intrusion of Commodore Perry's fleet in 1853 shocked the shogun's government and increased the instability that ultimately swept it away. After the Meiji Restoration of 1868, Japan deliberately set out to westernize its institutions, hoping to make itself strong enough to resist the colonization by western powers that it saw sweeping through Asia. Soon Japan came to want colonies of its own. Japan owed great cultural debts to China, but China's military and technical weakness lost it Japan's respect and made it prey for Japanese expansionism. In 1895 Japan went to war with China, where the modernized Japanese army won quick victories and annexed Taiwan.

The two boys with their western haircuts have been raised in this social and political climate. They are preparing a kite that shows a heroic Japanese officer with a sword slashing at a Chinese mandarin with a spear. The officer has a military moustache and smart western-style uniform; the Chinese wears traditional, that is, old-fashioned, Qing-dynasty clothes. The design treats the enemy less contemptuously than do many woodblock prints of the Sino-Japanese War, most designed by artists who never visited the front but used their imagination to satisfy the public's curiosity about the war.

This piece of social commentary was designed by Shuntei, known more for his gentle studies of children and young women than for war prints. The design is from his series *Kodomo fūzoku* (Children's Customs) and is titled *takoage* (kite-flying); besides the kite with the military design, two more kites fly in the background. The print is dated to the second month; the series depicts children's games and activities of all sorts, and this print is part of a study of traditions that were beginning to fade, rather than a New Year print. The craftsmen still existed to produce objects such as a painted kite or a woodblock print—the delicate printing here and in Shuntei's next design is as skillful as any in this book—but the rationale for producing prints was becoming increasingly self-conscious and removed from the vigorous commercialism of *ukiyo-e.*

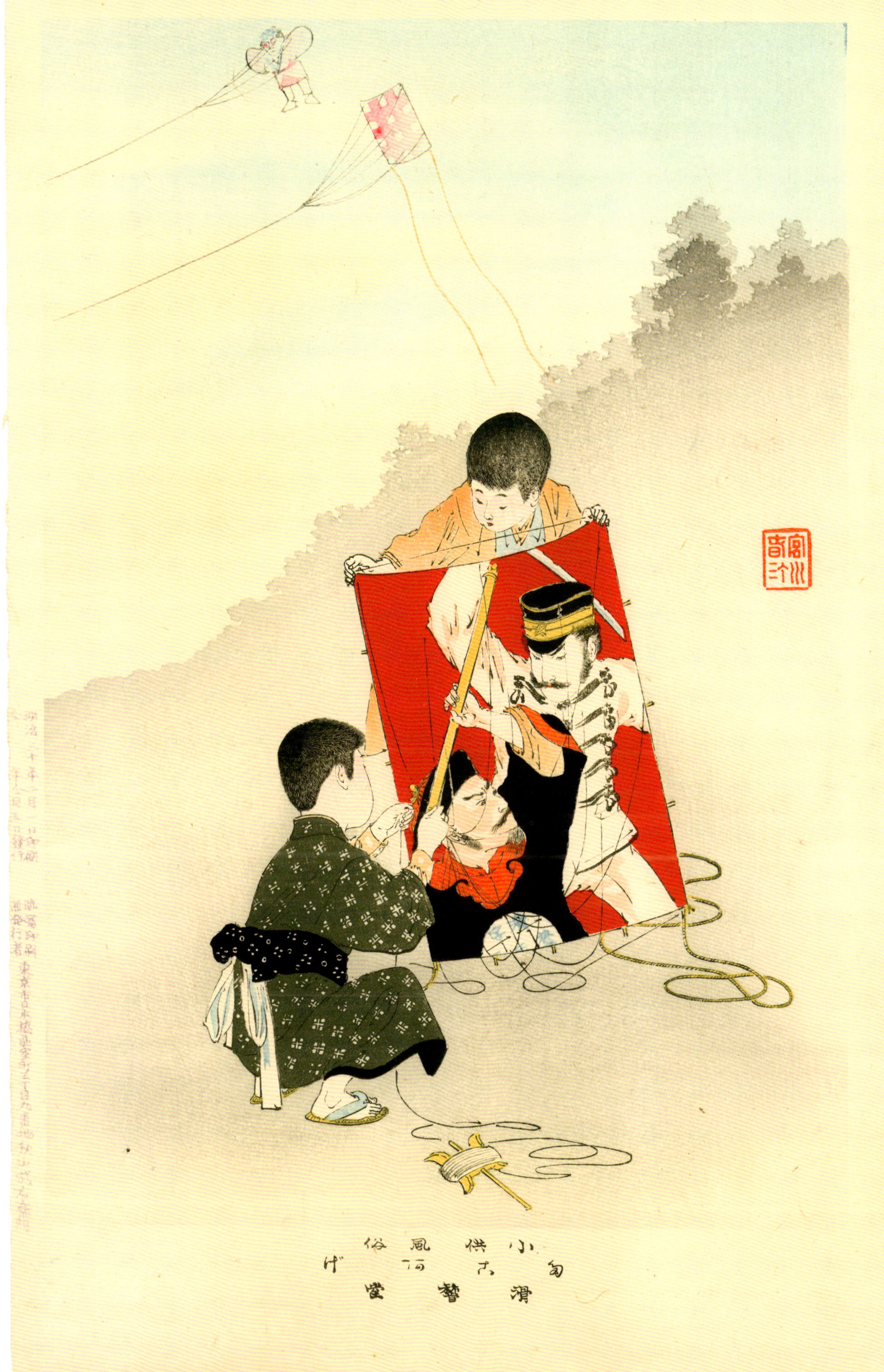
小供風俗
滑稽堂

Here is a nonpolitical New Year print by Shuntei, one that reflects the unselfconscious spontaneity and love of ordinary life that characterize *ukiyo-e.* Girls dressed in their holiday best are playing *hanetsuki,* shuttlecock and battledore, in a garden. A shuttlecock lies on the ground and a girl chases her friend with a writing brush in hand as their companions cover their mouths with their hands in amusement. The aim of the game was to bat the shuttlecock back and forth without letting it fall to the ground. A player who dropped it either paid a forfeit or received a dab of ink on the face (like Kintarō in plate 2). A *yakko* kite is caught in a barely budding plum tree.

The design is from a series titled *Bijin jūnika getsu* (Beauties of the Twelve Months)—this is identified as *Sonoichi oihago* (First Month, Running after the Shuttlecock). Each girl wears fashionable platform *geta.* Their kimonos have the very long sleeves worn by young girls; the fabric is luxurious, with imaginative floral designs and daringly juxtaposed colors. The printing is magnificent, with crisp lines and smooth bright colors, beautifully graded. Details are highlighted with an expensive metallic pigment.

The yellow pyramids in the garden are straw coats for plants, perhaps peonies. These coats protected the plants against both cold and insects; insects would hibernate in them rather than in the plant and would be destroyed when the straw was burned at the end of winter.

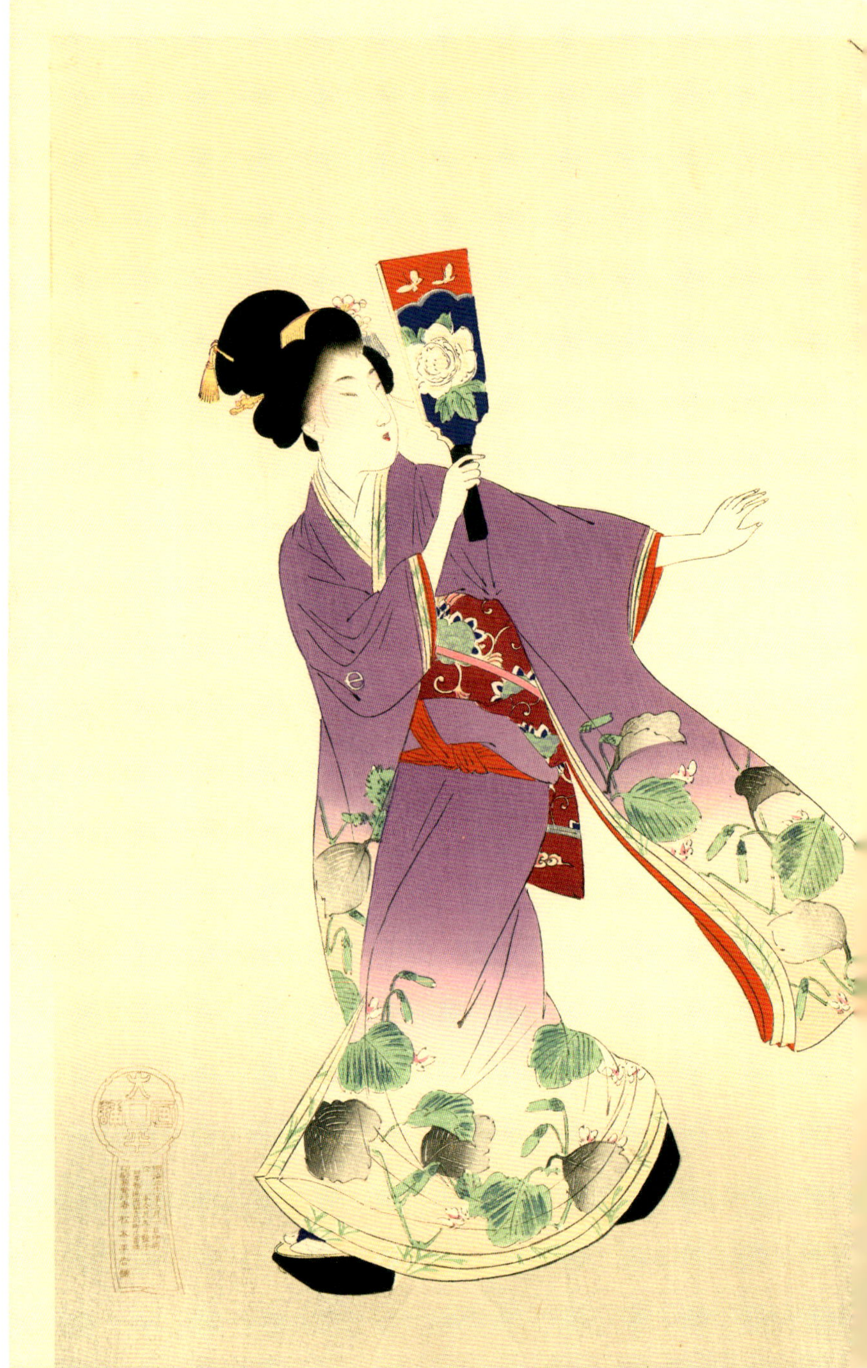

90

Running after the Shuttlecock
Miyagawa Shuntei (1873–1914)
signed: *Miyagawa Shuntei*
publisher: Matsumoto Heikichi
1898 second month
ōban triptych (each sheet approximately 36.9 × 25.3 cm)

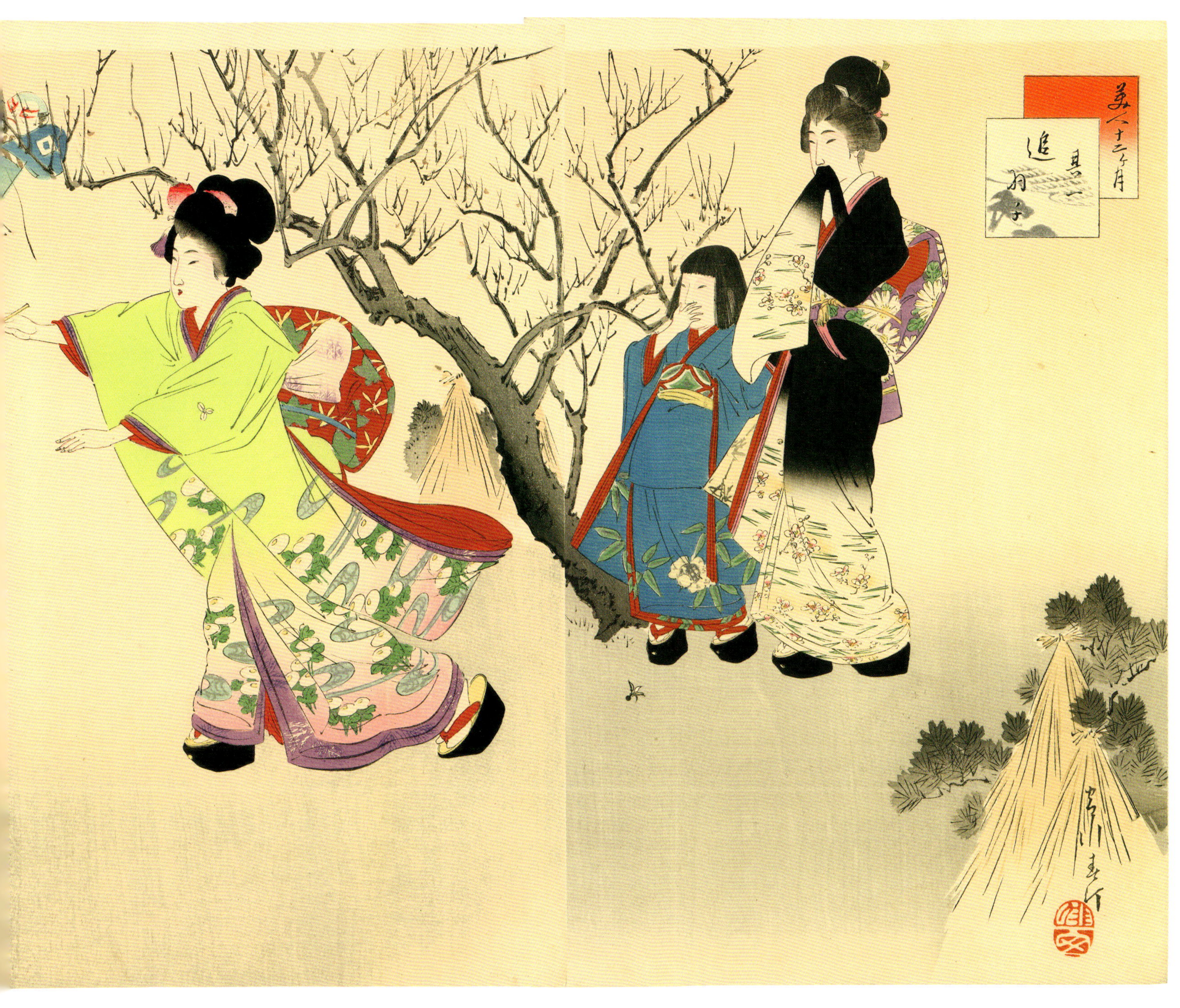
美人十二ヶ月
追羽子

91

Watchtower, Fuji, and Kites
Ogata Gekkō (1859–1920)
signed: *Gekkō ga*
publisher: Matsuki Heikichi
c. 1900
25 × 36.5 cm

Kites surround a watchtower in downtown Tokyo; a bell hangs under the upper eaves ready to rouse neighbors in case of a fire or other emergency. The colors are muted and the edges of the lines are soft, with interesting textures achieved by the application of diluted ink to the woodblocks before printing. There is no title-cartouche, but Mount Fuji appears faintly in the background and this design is part of Gekkō's undated series One Hundred Views of Mount Fuji.

This is a charming, well-executed picture, but it appears to be generic rather than a depiction of a recognizable location, and therefore untied to the real world. The format with its wide margins is not traditional. By the beginning of the twentieth century, prints were becoming art for art's sake, not intertwined with the flow of daily life. The specificity of Hiroshige's views of the capital, for example, which were easily identified by their audience, had given them a validity that this print does not have. Who would have bought this print and why? How would it have been displayed? There is no wit at play here, none of the direct relation between the audience and a seasonal celebration, or a souvenir of a particular Kabuki performance, or a visit to a particular place, that gave meaning to most of the designs in this book. Losing their specificity, woodblock prints had lost their roots.

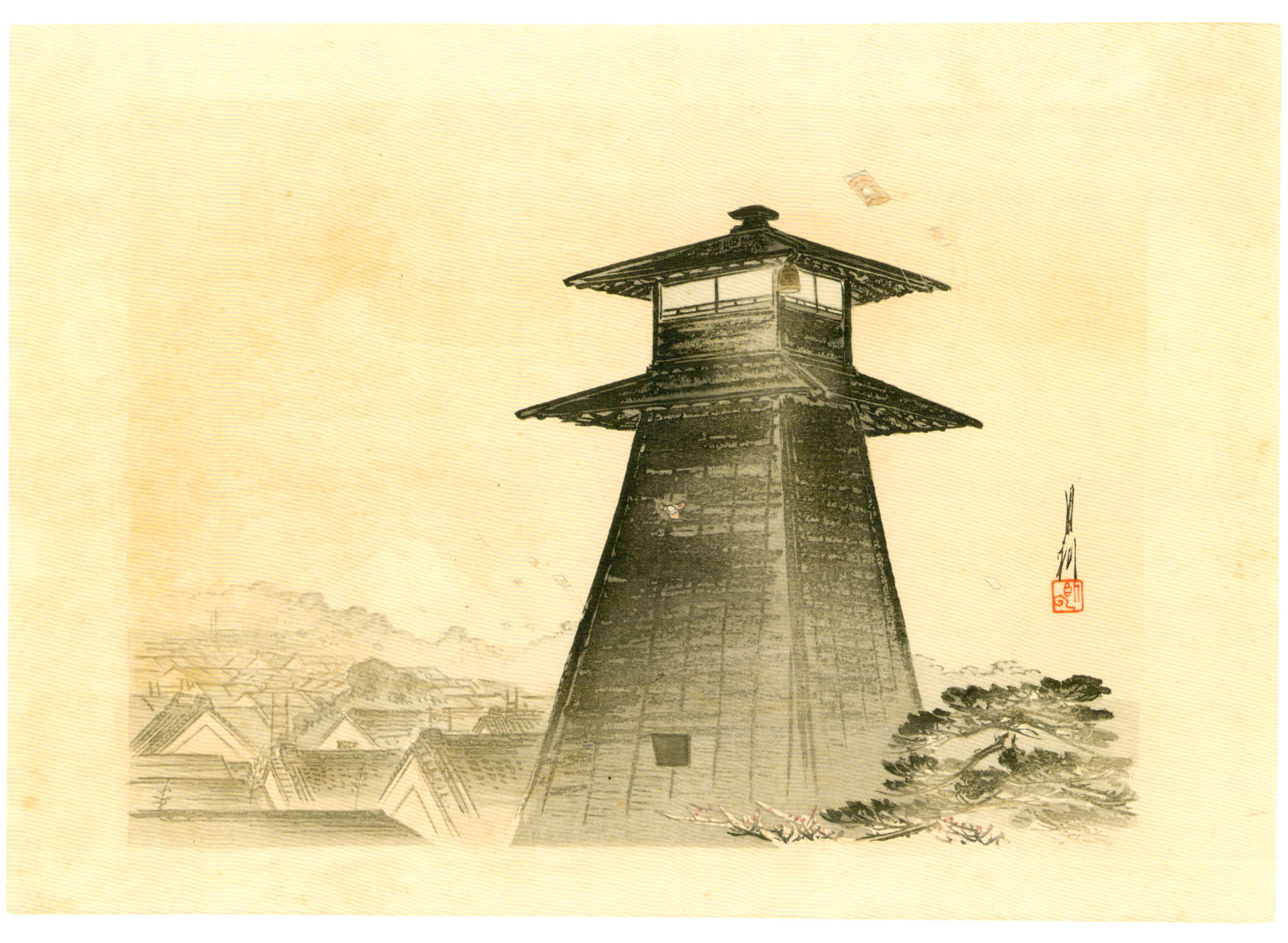

92

Kite Miscellany
author: Shimizu Seifu
publisher: Yamada Naosaburō
1911
two book pages (each 25.1 × 17.5 cm)

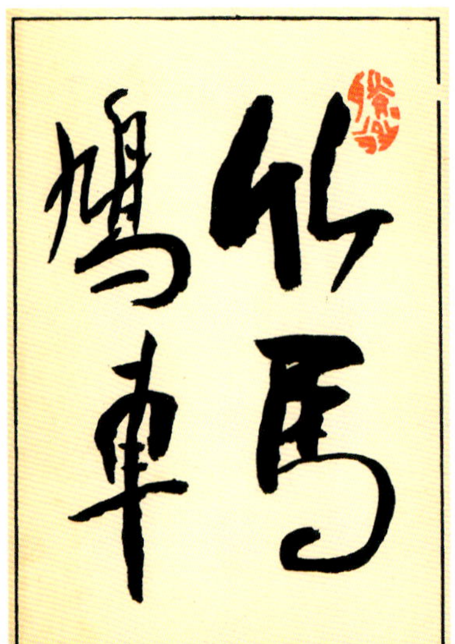

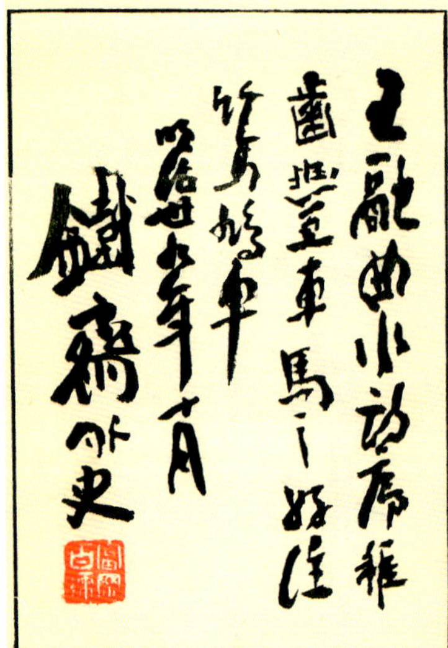

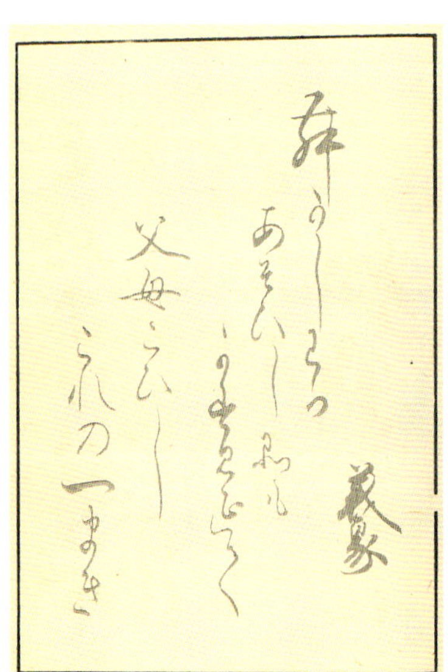

This two-page spread of kites is taken from the third volume of a woodblock-printed book titled *Unai no tomo* (Collection of Folk Toys). It shows a large Hamamatsu kite with a chrysanthemum pattern and five smaller kites: one in the shape of a fan, three birds (crane, crow, and owl), and a *yakko.* From the third to the fifth day of the fifth month, a quarter of a million people still gather to celebrate Boy's Day at the kite festival held on the mile-long beach at Hamamatsu, located on the Pacific coast a hundred miles southwest of Tokyo; in 1928 the emperor attended the festival. Hamamatsu kites can be very large but much lighter than their counterparts from Shirone, Hoshubana, and elsewhere (page 12). Around 1850, chrysanthemums, along with clouds and cranes, were typical of the richly painted decoration of Hamamatsu kites; fifty years later, single characters were the most popular designs. A Hamamatsu kite with a rising-sun design is illustrated in plate 53.

In his introduction to the book, the author, Shimizu Seifu, explains how he became interested in folk art in 1880 and started collecting toys of all kinds. Some were new; some dated from the Edo period that was already fast receding into the past. This was long before Yanagi Soetsu established the *mingei* movement that recognized folk objects as an art form.

The book, published in Kyoto, is beautifully printed, with fine engraving and deep, saturated colors (see figure 7 in the Introduction for another example). The front page shows four large characters in an idiosyncratic calligraphy that reads *takeuma hatoguruma,* meaning bamboo horse (that is, stilts) and pigeon vehicle (a papier-maché bird with wheels). The two following pages contain poetry about the toys from two other contributors to the book. One continues the bold, stylish Chinese characters of the first page in deep-black ink; the other uses a more consciously Japanese cursive script printed in a silver pigment.

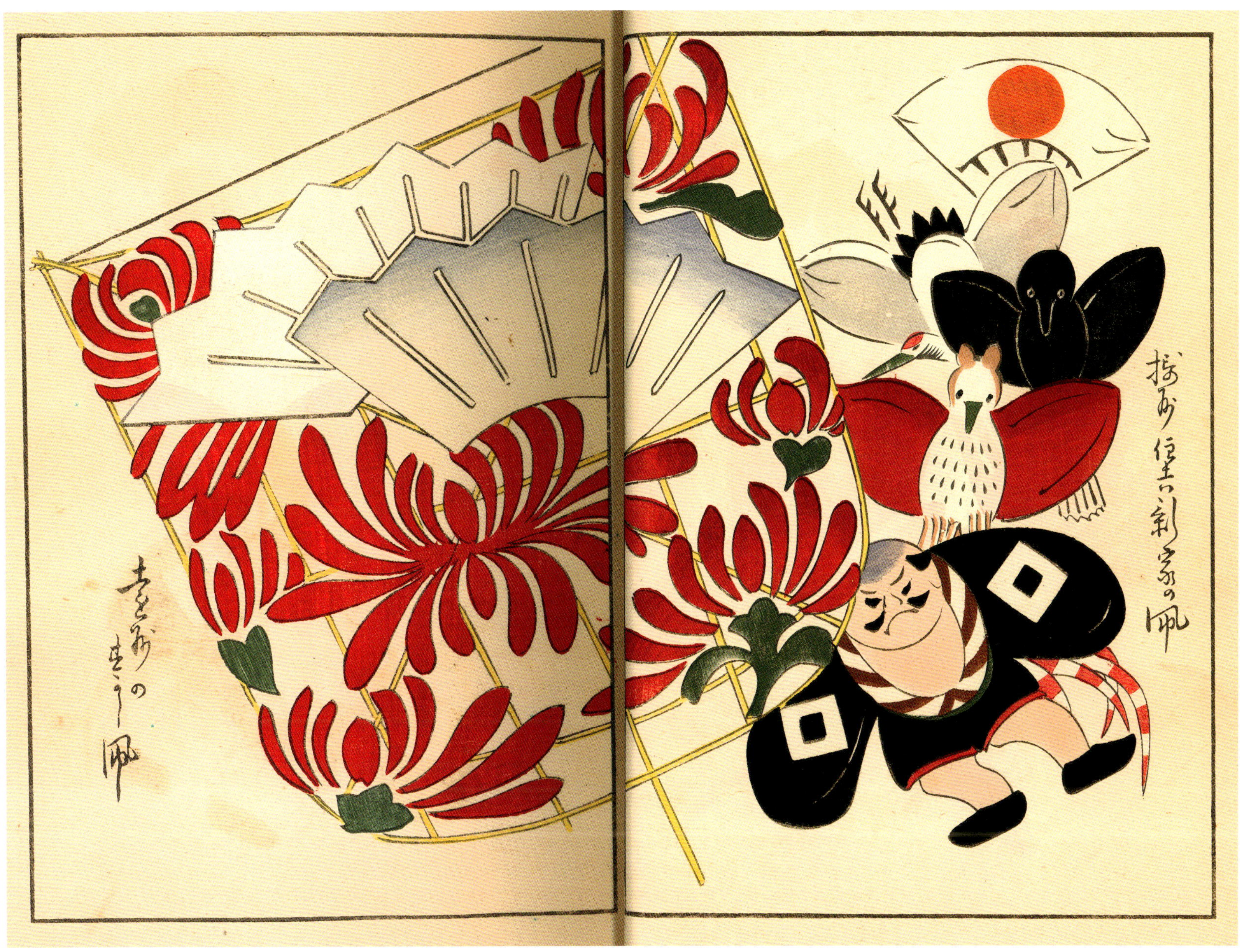

93

Girls Flying Kites
Bertha Lum (1869–1954)
signed in pencil: *copyright 1913 by Bertha Lum no. 152*
1912
20.3 × 36.2 cm

Bertha Lum was an American who made several extended visits to Japan and was captivated by the richness of Japan's culture. Using traditional woodblock techniques, she produced consciously exotic prints for a foreign audience. Here, inspired by children flying kites, which she must have seen in the city and countryside, she depicts a group of chubby girls and two young boys, set in a romantic landscape and flying an imaginary form of sail-kite. One, folded, lies on the ground in the bottom right corner. The scene is highly idealized and there is little attempt at realism. Visual props include a twisted pine and a bridge to nowhere, and there is a hint of Fuji in the sloping mountain to the left, seen across an open bay.

Bertha Lum's sentimental designs have an orientalist charm and were well received by foreign residents and visitors to Japan. This image of girls at play fits the perceptions of early western visitors that the Japanese were in a real sense infantile, absorbed with play, sensual and happily immoral, with a childlike innocence.[1] The design was published in the magazine *International Studio* in December 1912, the same year that Lum was invited as the only foreigner to participate in the Tenth Annual Art Exhibition in Ueno Park, Tokyo.

The number 152 appears in the bottom right corner, following the western practice of numbering the individual prints of a series. Before the twentieth century, Japanese artists and publishers never bothered to number an edition; prints were produced in batches and sold until there was no more stock, whereupon another batch was made. Some of Hiroshige's extremely popular landscapes, for example, were issued in dozens of informal editions (see the wear on the blocks of the two different impressions of plate 25), but none were numbered; identifying early or late editions from small changes in color or idiosyncracies in the carved blocks is a minor industry in the minutiae of *ukiyo-e* scholarship. Estimating how many impressions formed a batch is controversial; an "edition" may have been around two hundred, which was about as many sheets as a printer could pull from a particular color-block in one day. These two hundred sheets were hung up to dry overnight and another color added to them from another block the next day. The print was built up block by block, color by color, until the two hundred sheets of the design were complete.

Some early-twentieth-century woodblock masters such as Goyō and Kotondō considered their *bijin-e* to be high art and numbered their prints; the accomplished landscape prints of Yoshida Hiroshi, however, were not numbered. By the Taishō era, 1912–26, woodblock prints had changed their market, their raison d'être, and their fundamental character. Artists were self-consciously producing art for connoisseurs rather than products with the novelty and vitality demanded by a large-scale commercial audience.

1. Japanese commentators protested against such views in vain: Okakura Tenshin (1862–1913) believed that a demonstration of military strength would dispel this patronizing view of his country, but he was mistaken. Even after Japan had humiliated China and Russia in victorious wars, articles in the western press, such as "Japan: Child of the World's Old Age" (*National Geographic* 1914/6), continued to reinforce the perception; thanks to Christine Guth for this reference.

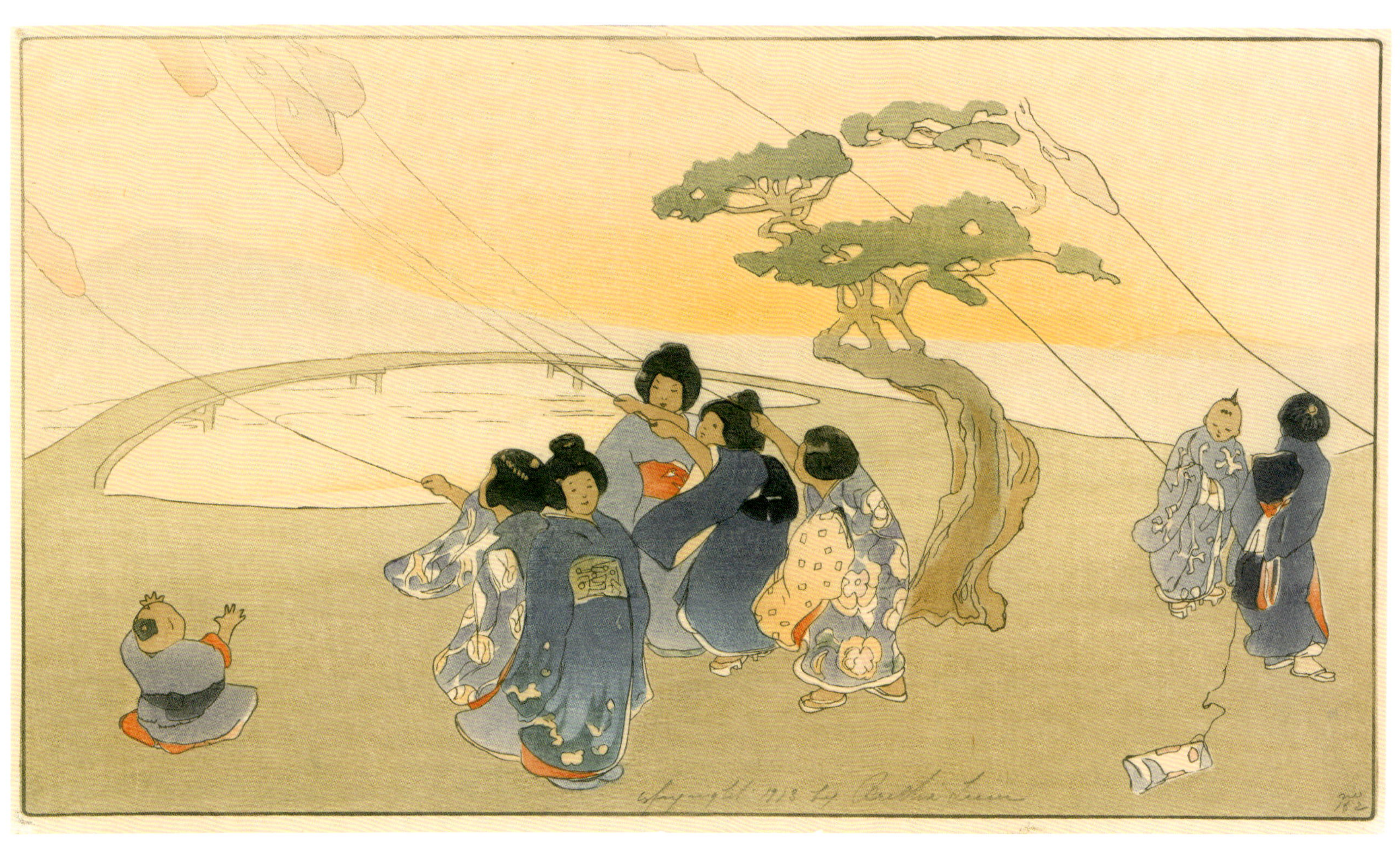
Copyright 1913 by Bertha Lum

94

Yakko and Butterfly Kites
Yamamoto Chikuun (1820–88)
signed: *Chikuun rōjin Shōunsei*
1884
hanging scroll, ink and color on silk satin
(130.7 × 34.4 cm not including mount)

The Skinner Collection includes three paintings related by subject matter to the prints.

The first is by the painter Chikuun, who was born and is buried in Kyoto and lived part of his life in Osaka. Most of his paintings are in the Chinese literati style called *nanga.*[1] Japanese kites are an unusual subject for a *nanga* artist, and this painting of *yakko* and butterfly kites, with their auspicious and happy associations, is probably a commission. The painting bears a forty-character poem and an inscription that translates, "On a spring day in 1884, painted while at the Stone Mountain guest-hall at the request of Master Kamiya, presented at this point in the operations of heaven by Old Man Chikuun, called Shōunsei." Kites are strongly associated with boys, and perhaps Master Kamiya had a new son.

The three seals on the painting suggest Chikuun's satisfaction with his cultured old age; when he made this painting he was already four years beyond his achievement of five complete zodiacal year-cycles. The seals read, *Shunseki Dōjin* (Spring Stone Recluse); *Rinraku* (Happiness in a Grove of Trees); and *Kaisei Robi* (Reborn Beautifully Old). The soft surface of silk satin is not an easy medium on which to paint, and its use is a mark of an accomplished artist.

1. *Nanga* means literally southern paintings, after Dong Qi Chang's seventeenth-century categorization of Chinese paintings. Two of Chikuun's Chinese-literati-style landscapes are illustrated in Rogers 1999, 295.

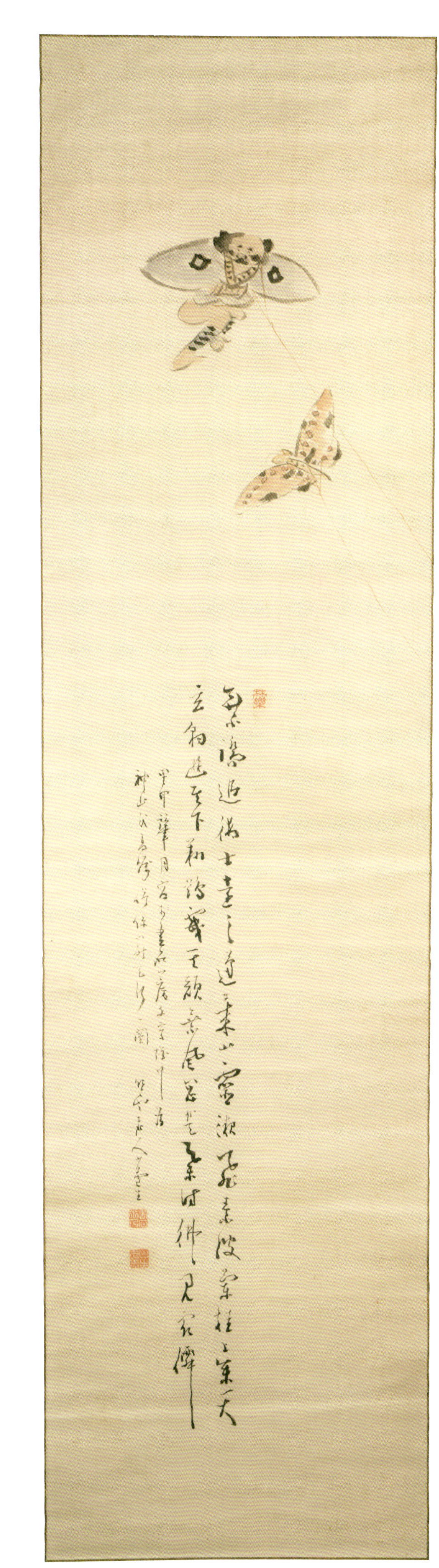

95

Boy with Owl Kite
Yukino
signed: *Yukino*
c. 1930
hanging scroll, color on silk
(painting 111.2 × 26.9 cm,
including mount 191.9 × 32.3 cm)

This delightful painting shows a little boy in a red kimono and traditional hairstyle running hard to keep his kite aloft. The kite is shaped like an owl and looks rather like a pre–World War II airplane. The painting is in the *nihonga* style. *Nihonga* is a disputed term, used first in the early years of Taishō (1912–26) and meaning literally no more than Japanese painting. It covers so many artists and styles that it may best be used as a general term to distinguish paintings using Japanese themes and materials from western-style paintings that used western formats and materials introduced during Meiji.

The scroll has a striking diagonal mounting that slants in parallel with the kite line, adding to the liveliness and movement of the painting. The rollers, *jikusaki,* on the projecting ends of the scroll are made of an appropriate but highly unusual striped ceramic. The painting's original *tomobako,* its individually constructed box, contains the label of a famous Osaka mounter.[1] This suggests both that Yukino may have been an Osaka artist and that the original owner of this painting regarded it highly, considering it worthy of an unusual and expensive mounting.

1. Thanks to Paul Berry for this observation. Morioka and Berry 1999, 296–301, is very useful regarding boxes and box inscriptions. Much more care has traditionally been lavished on the presentation of Japanese paintings than on, for example, Chinese paintings. The often very carefully considered mounting of a Japanese painting, its seals and signatures, colophons on the painting and its mount, and inscriptions on the *tomobako* become integral parts of a painting, and there is increasing awareness among westerners of how much can be learned by treating them all as a whole.

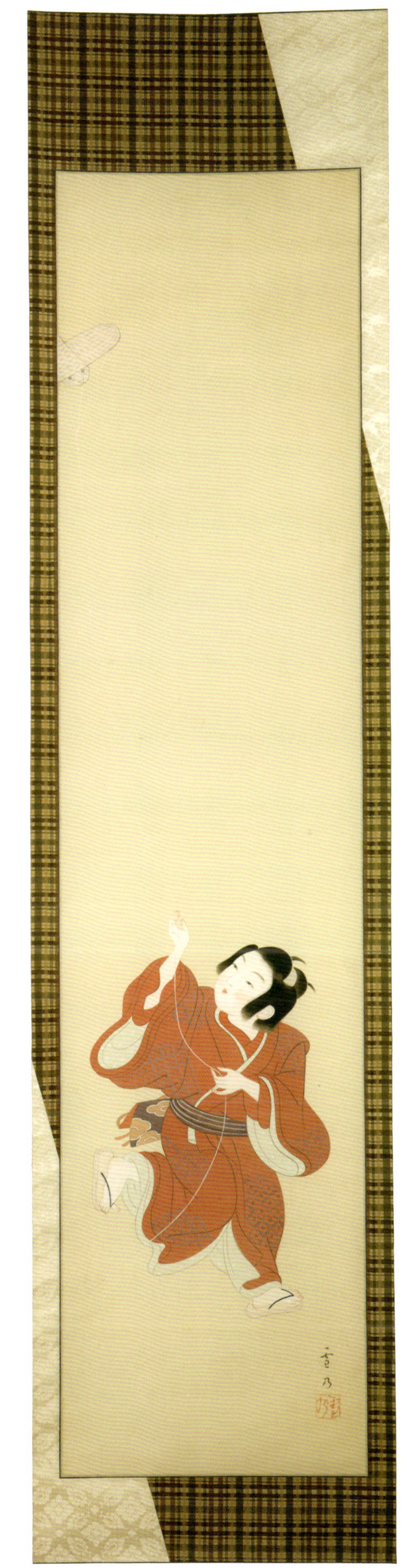

96

Oiran with Kite
Masami Teraoka (1936–)
c. 1988
watercolor (56.2 × 37.8 cm)

Masami Teraoka was born in Japan, trained in Japan and California, and works in Hawaii. In many of his paintings he uses watercolor to simulate Edo woodblock prints, especially the prints of Kunisada, juxtaposing *ukiyo-e's* rich imagery and conventions with modern artifacts to comment on contemporary issues, especially environmental degradation and AIDS. This painting is a study of *Oiran* and Kite from Teraoka's AIDS Series. Many of his later paintings have combined the horrors of AIDS with the message that the disease can be combated through education, including the use of condoms. He wishes to dispel any lingering embarrassment about a sometimes taboo subject.

Here a girl with elaborate robes and hairstyle holds a pack of condoms in one hand and a kite in the other. She is an *oiran,* the highest class of courtesan, epitomizing sexual desirability. Teraoka says that he chose a kite here because "a kite could be a good educational tool, nonthreatening but a lightweight method to communicate about AIDS and educate people about condoms. . . . Flying a kite is such a traditional entertainment toy in Japan and also a local pastime entertainment here in Hawaii."[1]

The calligraphy is written in the flamboyant style used on posters outside a Kabuki theater, which the artist identifies here as the Masami Theater. The design uses a composition similar to a well-known series of beauties set against backgrounds of *jōruri* scripts, designed by Kunisada in 1832.[2] The kite bears an *ensō,* a circle often used in Zen paintings to indicate the unity of the universe; here it also suggests the shape of an unused condom. "Condom, extra large," is written in *hiragana* on each package. The mushroom motif used to decorate the girl's kimono and the calligraphic background is appropriately and intentionally phallic in the Japanese tradition (see plate 69). The artist's signature appears in two small cartouches similar to those on Kunisada's later work. There is even a painted facsimile of a censor's *kiwame,* approved, seal. With its playfulness, wit, and relevance to contemporary issues, this painting embodies several of *ukiyo-e's* most attractive traditions.

1. Email of April 2003.

2. Examples from the series are illustrated in Suzuki 1969, figure 25, and Izzard 1993, figures 62/1–4.

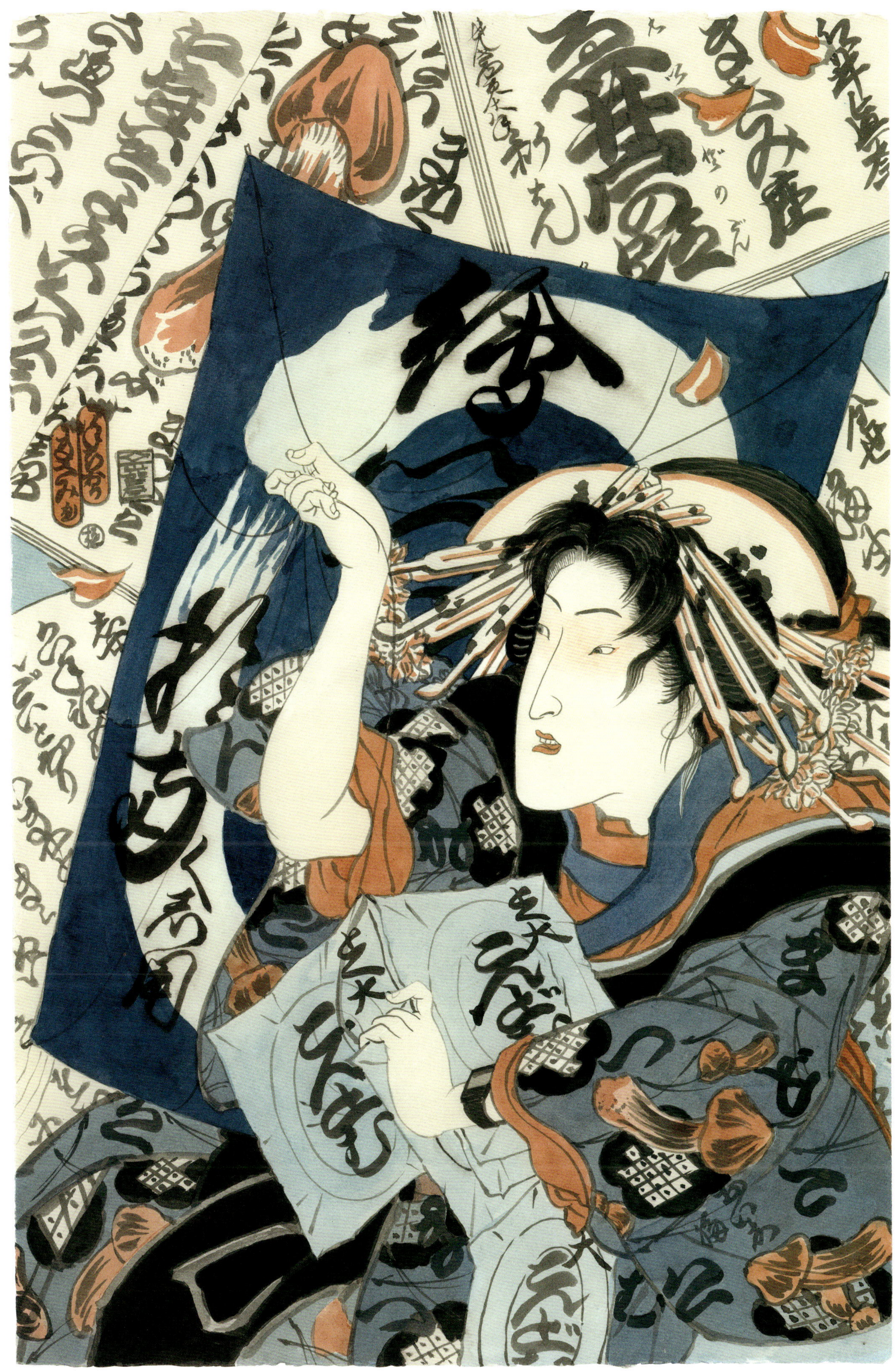

ANATOMY OF A WOODBLOCK PRINT

Here are two prints, one late Edo (1859), one Meiji (1884), showing how the artist's name, publisher, and other details were typically arranged. See also the analysis of the fan print in plate 50.

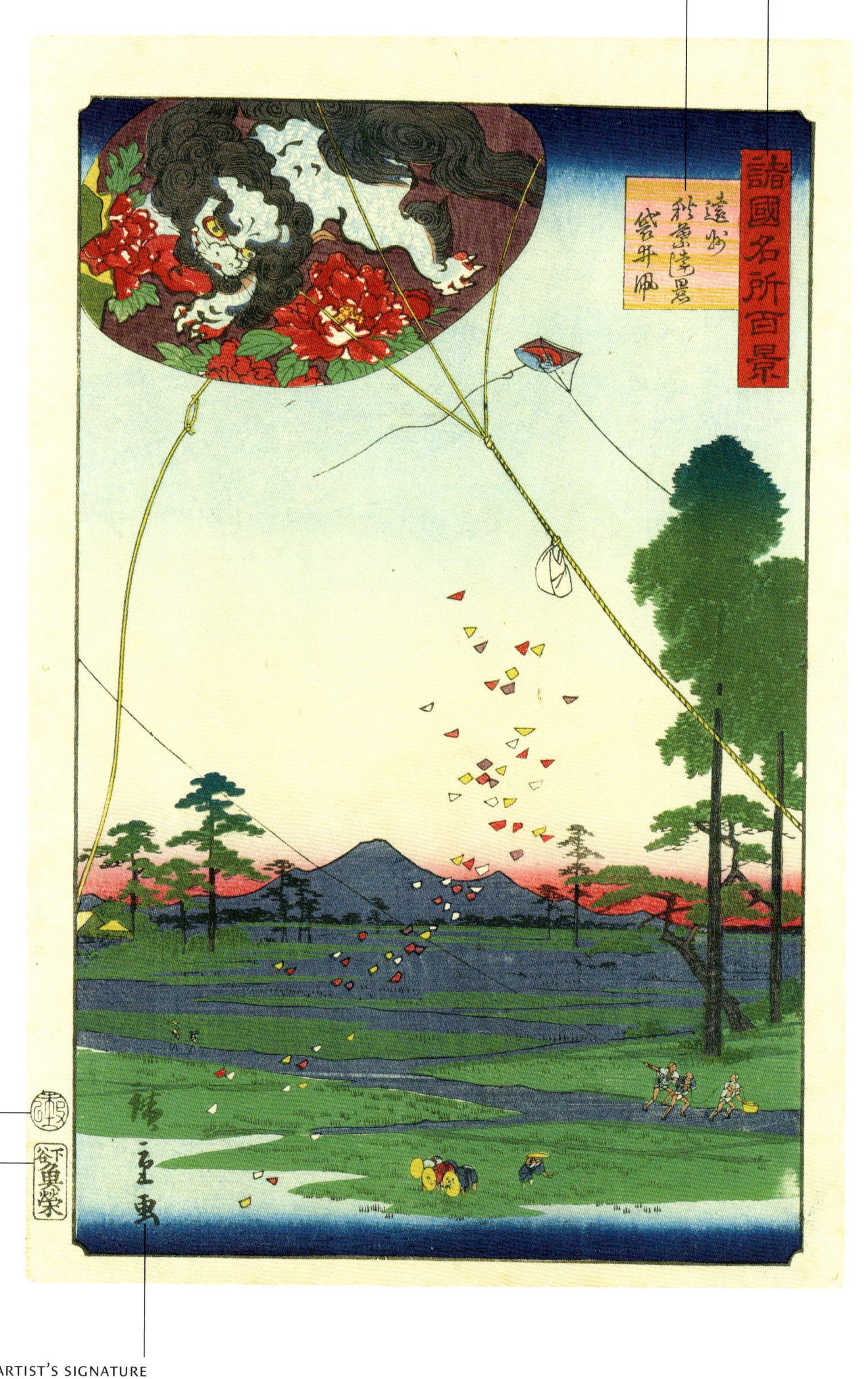

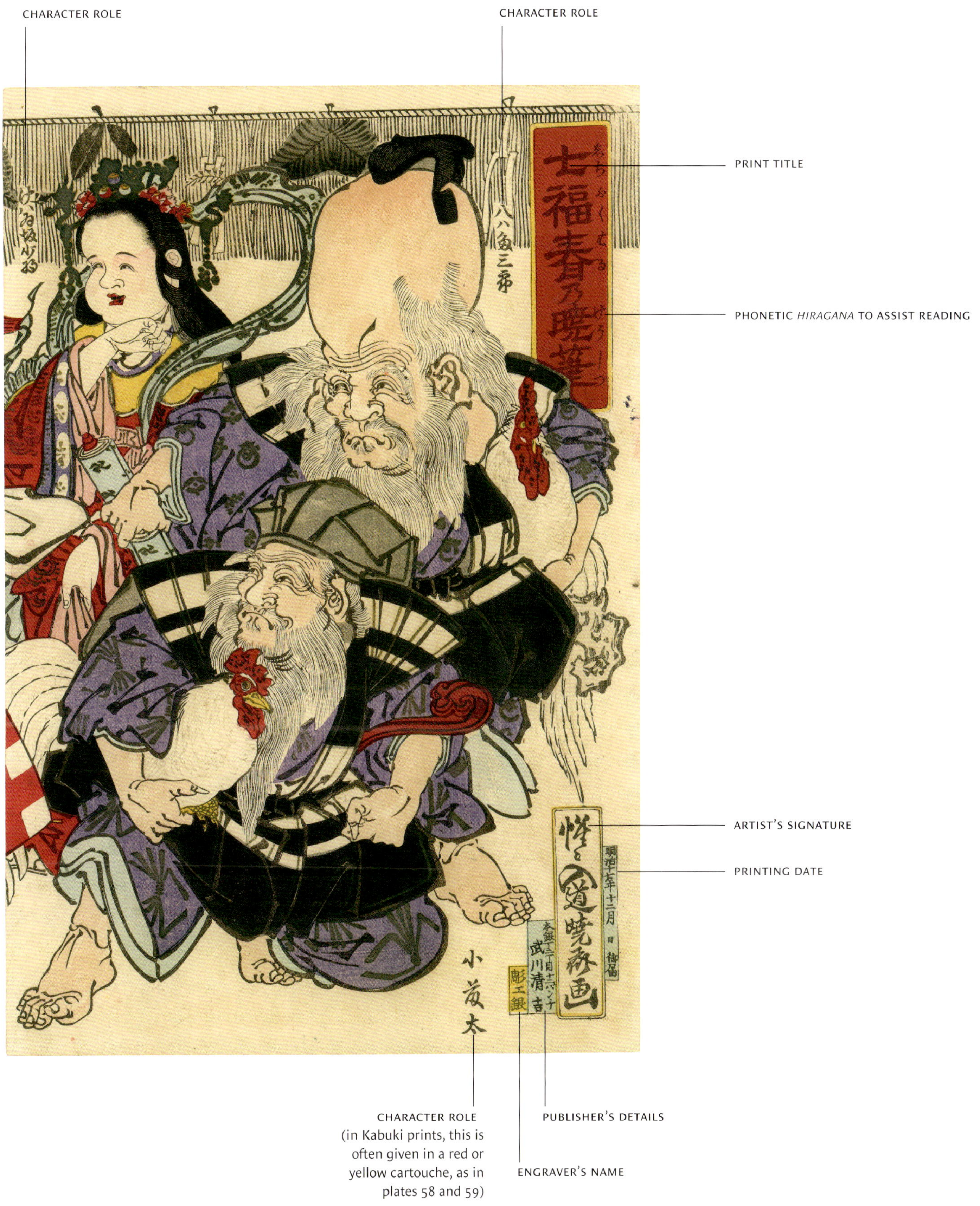
CHARACTER ROLE
CHARACTER ROLE
PRINT TITLE
PHONETIC *HIRAGANA* TO ASSIST READING
ARTIST'S SIGNATURE
PRINTING DATE
CHARACTER ROLE
(in Kabuki prints, this is often given in a red or yellow cartouche, as in plates 58 and 59)
PUBLISHER'S DETAILS
ENGRAVER'S NAME

DATING JAPANESE PRINTS

In the ninth month of 1790 the shogun's government began requiring a seal of approval for prints and books before they were issued. Publishers submitted a final drawing to government censors, who applied one or more seals of approval, carved in archaic, stylized seal script. These were engraved into the wooden key-block of the print and appear as part of the design. Such seals often enable a print to be precisely dated, especially after 1842.

1790–1842
kiwame (meaning approved); here are two of many variations

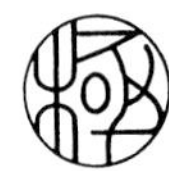

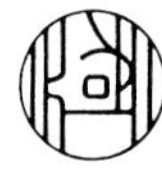

1806–11
kiwame plus a seal with the character of the year's zodiacal animal (the month is sometimes shown in the space below the animal):

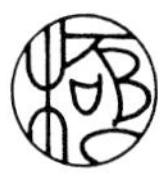

1806
Tiger, *tora;* this seal shows *tora* combined with the numeral eleven, for eleventh month

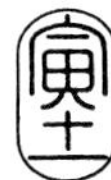

1807
Hare, *u*

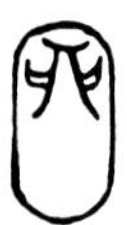

1808
Dragon, *tatsu*

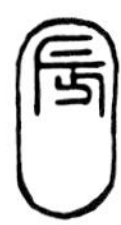

1809
Snake, *mi*

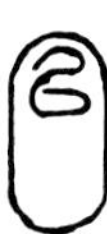

1810
Horse, *uma*

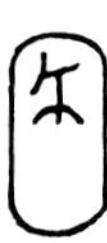

1811
Goat, *hitsuji*

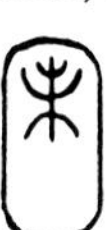

1842

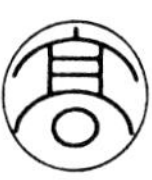 or 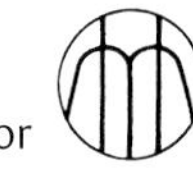

1843–45
any one of these five seals

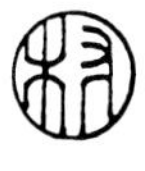
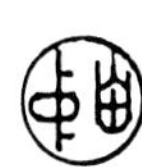
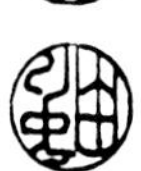
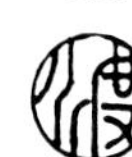
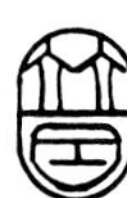

1843–46
The personal seal of censor Muramatsu Genroku

1843–46
the personal seal of censor Hama Yahei

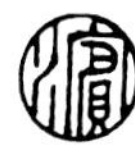

1843–46
the personal seal of censor Yoshimura Gentarō

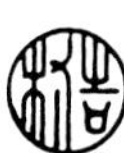

1843–46
the personal seal of censor Kinugasa Fusajirō

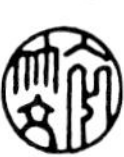

1846
the personal seal of censor Murata Heiemon

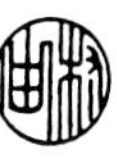

1847–53
combinations of the above censors' seals and others:

1847–48

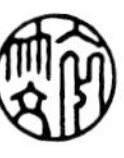

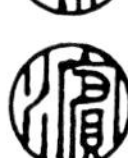

1847–48

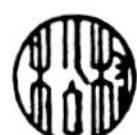

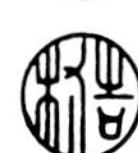

1847–50

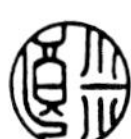

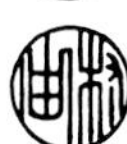

1849

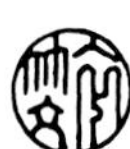

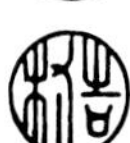

1849–50

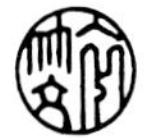

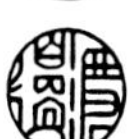

1849–53

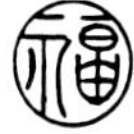

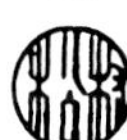

1849–53

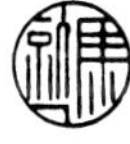

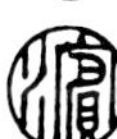

1851–53

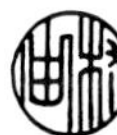

1851–53

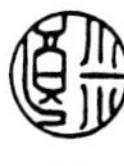

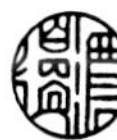

1854–57

aratame (meaning examined) in combination with a seal with a stylized character of a zodiacal animal:

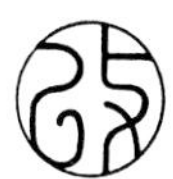

1854

Tiger

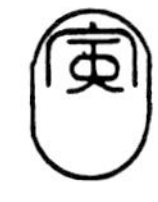

1855

Hare; the second example shows *u* combined with the numeral seven, for seventh month

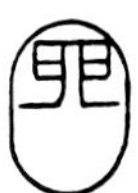 or 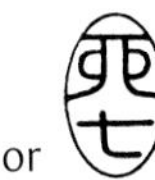

1856

Dragon

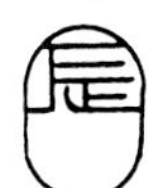

1857

Snake

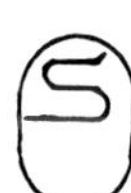

1858

Horse (without *aratame* seal)

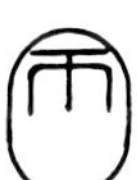

1859–72

a single seal in which the character *aratame* is combined with a zodiacal animal:

1859

Goat

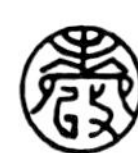

1860

Monkey, *saru;* the second example shows *aratame, saru,* and the numeral four, for fourth month

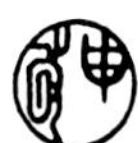 or 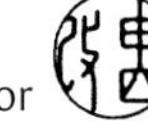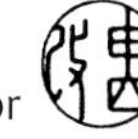

1861

Cock, *tori;* the second example shows *aratame, tori,* and the numeral ten, for tenth month

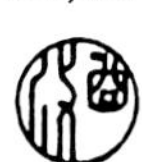 or 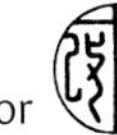

1862

Dog, *inu;* this example includes a stylized numeral one for first month

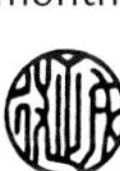

1863

Boar, *i;* this example includes a stylized numeral four for fourth month

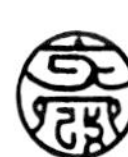

1864

Rat, *ne*

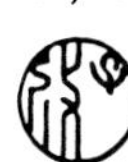

1865

Ox, *ushi*

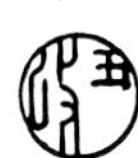

1866

Tiger; the second example shows *aratame, tora,* and the numeral three, for third month

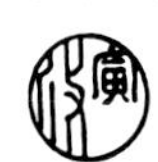 or 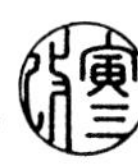

1867

Hare

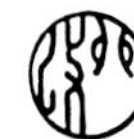

1868

Dragon

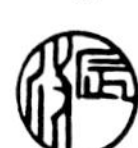

1869

Snake

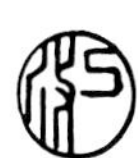

1870

Horse

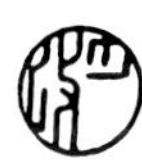

1871

Goat

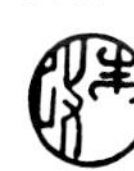

1872

Monkey

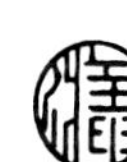

1873

Cock

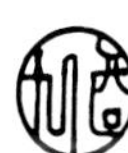 or 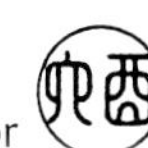

1874

Dog

1875

Boar

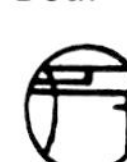

Formal censorship ended in 1875 but publishers were expected to include their names and addresses on a print plus the date according to the emperor's reign year. The first year of the Meiji emperor's reign, 1868, counted as year one, so the tenth year of Meiji corresponds to 1877, Meiji fifteen to 1882, and so on.

1868–1912

Meiji

明
治

1912–26

Taishō

大
正

1926–89

Shōwa

昭
和

BIBLIOGRAPHY

Baten, Lea. *Playthings and Pastimes in Japanese Prints.* New York: Weatherhill, 1995.

de Becker, J. E. *The Nightless City, or the History of the Yoshiwara Yūkwaku.* Tokyo: Charles E. Tuttle, 1971 (originally published 1899).

Bogel, Cynthea J. *Hiroshige: Birds and Flowers.* New York: George Braziller, 1988.

Bowie, Theodore, et al. *Art of the Surimono.* Bloomington: Indiana University Art Museum, 1979.

Brandon, Reiko Mochinaga, and Barbara B. Stephan. *Spirit and Symbol: The Japanese New Year.* Honolulu: Honolulu Academy of Arts, 1994.

Clark, Timothy. *Ukiyo-e Paintings in the British Museum.* Washington, D.C.: Smithsonian Institution, 1992.

Clark, Timothy. *Demon of Painting, the Art of Kawanabe Kyōsai.* London: British Museum Press, 1993.

Clark, Timothy. "*Mitate-e:* Some Thoughts and a Summary of Recent Writings." *Impressions,* Number 19, 6–27. New York: Ukiyoe Society of America, 1997.

Clark, Timothy. *100 Views of Mount Fuji.* London: British Museum Press, 2001.

Clark, Timothy, et al. *The Dawn of the Floating World, 1650–1765: Early Ukiyo-e Treasures from the Museum of Fine Arts, Boston.* London: Royal Academy of Arts, 2001.

Dalby, Liza Crihfield. *Geisha.* Berkeley: University of California Press, 1983.

Dalby, Liza Crihfield. *Kimono: Fashioning Culture.* Seattle: University of Washington Press, 2001.

Delamare, Francois, and Bernard Guineau. *Colors, the Story of Dyes and Pigments.* New York: Harry Abrams, 2000.

Edmunds, Will. H. *Pointers and Clues to the Subjects of Chinese and Japanese Art.* London: Sampson Low Marston, c. 1934.

Finn, Dallas. *Meiji Revisited: The Sites of Victorian Japan.* New York: Weatherhill, 1995.

Forrer, Matthi, ed. *Essays on Japanese Art Presented to Jack Hillier.* London: Robert G. Sawyers, 1982.

Guth, Christine. *Art of Edo Japan: The Artist and the City 1615–1868.* New York: Harry Abrams, 1996.

Guth, Christine. *Longfellow's Tattoos.* Seattle: University of Washington Press, 2004.

Hillier, Jack. *Utamaro, Colour Prints and Paintings.* Oxford: Phaidon Press, 1961.

Hillier, Jack. *The Art of Hokusai in Book Illustration.* London: Sotheby's, 1980.

Hillier, Jack. *The Art of the Japanese Book.* 2 vols. London: Sotheby's, 1987.

Hillier, Jack, and Lawrence Smith. *Japanese Prints: 300 years of albums and books.* London: British Museum Publications, 1980.

Hiroi Chikara. *Tako* (Kites). Tokyo: Mainichi Shinbunsha, 1973.

Hockley, Allen. *Inside the Floating World: Japanese Prints from the Lenoir C. Wright Collection.* Greensboro, NC: Weatherspoon Art Museum, University of North Carolina, 2002.

Hockley, Allen. *The Prints of Isoda Koryusai: Floating World Culture and its Consumers in Eighteenth-Century Japan.* Seattle: University of Washington Press, 2003.

Illing, Richard. *The Art of Japanese Prints.* London: Octopus, 1980.

Inagaki Shinichi and Isao Toshihiko. *Kuniyoshi kyōga* (Kuniyoshi's Crazy Pictures). Tokyo: Tōkyo Shoseki, 1991.

Izzard, Sebastian. *Hiroshige: An exhibition of selected prints and illustrated books.* New York: Ukiyo-e Society of America, 1983.

Izzard, Sebastian. *Kunisada's World.* New York: Japan Society, 1993.

Izzard, Sebastian. *Masterpieces of Ukiyo-e: Paintings from the Manno Art Museum.* New York: Sebastian Izzard LLC, 2003.

Jansen, Marius B., and Gilbert Rozman, eds. *Japan in Transition: from Tokugawa to Meiji.* Princeton: Princeton University Press, 1986.

Jenkins, Donald, et al. *The Floating World Revisited.* Portland: Portland Art Museum, and Honolulu: University of Hawai'i Press, 1993.

Kawanabe Kusumi. *Kawanabe Kyōsai: Selected Works from the Israel Goldman Collection.* Tokyo: Ōta Memorial Museum of Art, 2002.

Keyes, Roger S. *Courage and Silence: A Study of the Life and Color Woodblock Prints of Tsukioka Yoshitoshi, 1839–1892.* Ann Arbor: University Microfilms International, 1983.

Keyes, Roger S. *The Art of Surimono: Privately published Japanese woodblock prints and books in the Chester Beatty Library, Dublin.* 2 vols. London: Sotheby's, 1985.

Keyes, Roger S. *The Male Journey in Japanese Prints.* Berkeley: University of California Press, 1989.

Keyes, Roger S. "Tani Seikō and his circle." *Andon* 72, 73. Leiden: Society for Japanese Arts, 2002.

Keyes, Roger S., and Keiko Mizushima. *The Theatrical World of Osaka Prints.* Philadelphia: Philadelphia Museum of Art, 1973.

Keyes, Roger S., and George Kuwayama. *The Bizarre Imagery of Yoshitoshi.* Los Angeles: Los Angeles County Museum of Art, 1980.

Kita, Sandy, et al. *A Hidden Treasure: Japanese Prints from the Carnegie Museum of Art.* Pittsburgh: The Carnegie Museum of Art, 1996.

Leiter, Samuel L. *Kabuki Encyclopedia: An English-Language Adaptation of* Kabuki Jiten. Westport, CT: Greenwood Press, 1979.

Link, Howard A. *Hiroshige: The James A. Michener Collection.* Honolulu: Honolulu Academy of Arts, 1991.

Machida City Museum. *Shōsai Ikkei Meiji shoki Tōkyo o egaku* (Shōsai Ikkei, Illustrating Scenes from Early Meiji). Tokyo: Machida City Museum, 1993.

Meech-Pekarik, Julia. *The World of the Meiji Print.* Tokyo: Weatherhill, 1986.

Michener, James A. *The Hokusai Sketch-books.* Tokyo: Tuttle, 1958.

Mirviss, Joan. *The Frank Lloyd Wright Collection of Surimono.* Tokyo: Weatherhill, 1995.

Mirviss, Joan, and John Carpenter. *Jewels of Japanese Printmaking: Surimono of the Bunka–Bunsei Era 1804–1830.* Tokyo: Ōta Memorial Museum of Art, 2000.

Modeki Masaaki, ed. *Edodako daizenshū* (Large and Complete Collection of Edo Kites). Tokyo: Sankai-dō, 1988.

Morioka Michiyo and Paul Berry. *Modern Masters of Kyoto:* Nihonga *from the Griffith and Patricia Way Collection.* Seattle: Seattle Art Museum and University of Washington Press, 1999.

Nagasaki meishō zue (Pictures of Scenic Spots in Nagasaki). Nagasakishidankai, ed., Nagasaki: Fujiki Hakueisha, 1930 (originally published c. 1820).

Nagata Seiji et al. *Dai Hokusai ten* (The Great Hokusai Exhibition). Tokyo: Asahi Shimbun, 1993.

Nakane Chie, Shinzaburō Oishi, et al. *Tokugawa Japan: The Social and Economic Antecedents of Modern Japan.* Tokyo: University of Tokyo Press, 1991.

Newland, Amy, and Chris Uhlenbeck, eds. *Ukiyo-e to Shin Hanga.* New York: Mallard Press, 1990.

Ostier, Janette. *Les objets tranquilles: natures mortes japonaises XVIIIe–XIXe siècles.* Paris: Galerie Janette Ostier, 1978.

Oyokawa Shigeru and Yamaguchi Seiichi. *Kyōsai no giga* (Playful Pictures of Kyōsai). Tokyo: Tōkyo Shoseki, 1992.

van Rappard-Boon, Charlotte, et al. *Surimono: Poetry and image in Japanese prints.* Leiden: Hotei Publishing, 2000.

Robinson, Basil W. *Kuniyoshi.* London: Her Majesty's Stationery Office, 1961.

Rogers, Howard, et al. *Kaikodo Journal XII.* New York: Kaikodo, 1999.

Rotondo-McCord, Lisa. *An Enduring Vision: 17th- to 20th-Century Japanese Painting from the Gitter-Yelen Collection.* New Orleans: New Orleans Museum of Art, and Seattle: University of Washington Press, 2002.

Rousmaniere, Nicole Coolidge, ed. *Kazari: Decoration and Display in Japan, 15th–19th Centuries.* New York: Japan Society, and London: The British Museum Press, 2002.

Saito Tadao. *Edodako e-shi* (Pictorial History of Edo Kites). Tokyo: Graphic-sha, 1980.

Saito Tadao et al. *Nihon no tako daizenshū irodori to katachi no mingei* (Large and Complete Collection of Japanese Kites: Folk Art of Color and Shape). Tokyo: Tokuma Shoten, 1976.

Schwab, Dean J. *Osaka Prints.* New York: Rizzoli, 1989.

Screech, Timon. *Sex and the Floating World.* Honolulu: University of Hawai'i Press, 1999.

Screech, Timon. *The Shogun's Painted Culture.* London: Reaktion, 2000.

Seigle, Cecilia Segawa. *Yoshiwara: The Glittering World of the Japanese Courtesan.* Honolulu: University of Hawai'i Press, 1993.

Shimizu Seifu. *Unai no tomo* (Collection of Folk Toys). Kyoto: Yamada Naosaburō, 1911.

Shindo Shigeru. *Kunisada yakusha-e no sekai* (Kunisada: The Kabuki Actor Portraits). Tokyo: Graphic-sha, 1993.

Shinsaka Kazuo. *Edo no giho tezukuri dako no gihou to tanoshimi kata* (Techniques of Picture Kites: How to Create and Enjoy Handmade Kites). Tokyo: Bijutsu Shuppan Sha, 1987.

Singer, Robert T., et al. *Edo: Art in Japan 1615–1868.* Washington, D.C.: National Gallery of Art, 1998.

Skinner, Scott, and Ali Fujino, eds. *Kites: Paper Wings Over Japan.* New York: Thames and Hudson, 1997.

Smith, Henry D. II. *Hiroshige: One Hundred Famous Views of Edo.* New York: Braziller, 1986.

Smith, Henry D. II. "'He Frames a Shot!': Cinematic Vision in Hiroshige's *One Hundred Famous Views of Edo.*" *Orientations,* vol. 31, no. 3 (March 2000), 90–96.

Spate, Virginia, et al. *Monet and Japan.* Canberra: National Gallery of Australia, 2001.

Stevenson, John. *Masami Teraoka: From Tradition to Technology, the Floating World Comes of Age.* Seattle: University of Washington Press, 1997.

Streeter, Tal. *The Art of the Japanese Kite.* Tokyo: Weatherhill, 1974.

Suzuki Jūzō and Oka Isaburō. *The Decadents.* Tokyo: Kodansha International, 1969.

Thomson, Sarah E., and H. D. Harootunian. *Undercurrents in the Floating World: Censorship and Japanese Prints.* New York: Asia Society Galleries, 1991.

Tobu Museum of Art et al. *Katsushika Hokusai.* Tokyo: Tobu Museum of Art, 1993.

Waterhouse, David. "Some Confucian, Buddhist, and Taoist *Mitate-e* by Harunobu." *Impressions,* Number 19, 6–27. New York: Ukiyoe Society of America, 1997.

White, Julia M., et al. *Hokusai and Hiroshige: Great Japanese Prints from the James A. Michener Collection, Honolulu Academy of Arts.* San Francisco: Asian Art Museum, 1998.

Yonemura, Ann, et al. *Masterful Illusions: Japanese Prints in the Anne van Biema Collection.* Washington, D.C.: Arthur M. Sackler Gallery, and Seattle: University of Washington Press, 2002.

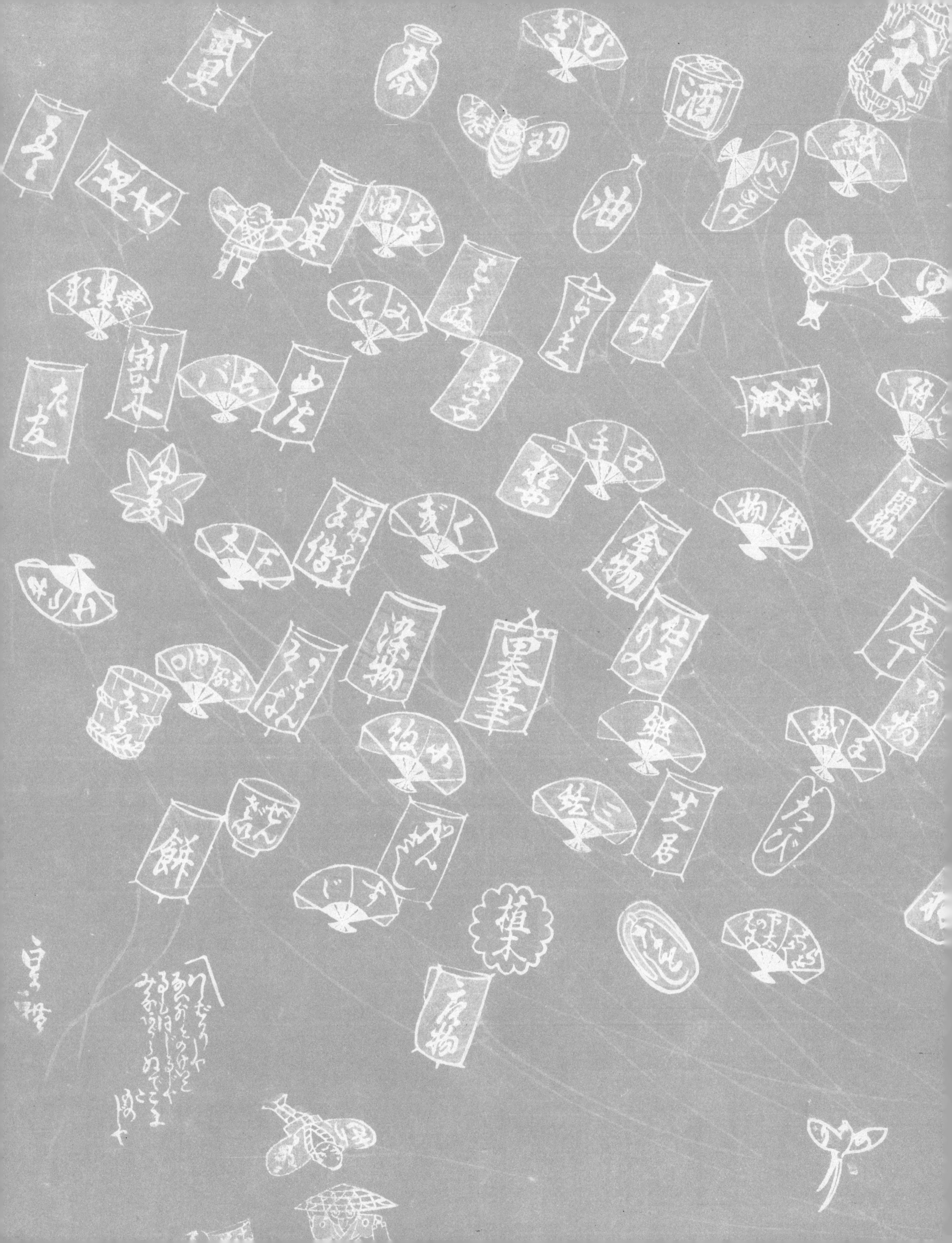